'Innovation is driving economic and societal change, but it is still a myth or a black box. Professor Jay Mitra's new book dissects the myth and sheds light into the black box. *The Business of Innovation* is a brilliant, comprehensive tool to understand the critical factor dominating the knowledge economy in the 21st century.'

Sergio Arzeni
President, International Network for SMEs (INSME)
Former Director, OECD Centre for Entrepreneurship
Rome, Italy

'Edith Penrose memorably remarked that entrepreneurship was a slippery concept, in part because it reflected the diverse temperament and personal qualities of individuals. In *The Business of Innovation*, Jay Mitra successfully overcomes that slippery challenge by documenting how entrepreneurs bring about the conversion of innovative ideas into marketable products. His target audiences are high-end students and policy-makers. Both groups will appreciate this careful review of the evidence on how entrepreneurship "works".'

Professor David Storey, OBE
Professor of Enterprise (Business and Management)
University of Sussex, UK

'No doubt innovation is decisive to make our future world a worthwhile place to live in. *The Business of Innovation* is outstanding in focusing on the macro and micro aspects of innovation as well as on the not less crucial view on innovation as a process. It does not only deal with innovative organizations and environments, but also with innovative people – mostly neglected in compilations on innovation research. Particular attention deserves the emphasis on innovative women. Once again, Jay Mitra provides a deeply-delving study which presents an overall picture just as much as an in-depth analysis. Jay Mitra argues with acute perception – precise, prudent, critical and with foresight. This book is rounded off by vivid illustrations and cases from different areas in the world. It will be a must read at the library of our new MCI Innovation Lab and I recommend this book to every reader interested in innovation research and practice.'

Dr Silke Tegtmeier
President-elect, European Council for Small Business
Associate Professor of Entrepreneurship
University of Southern Denmark, Denmark
and Leuphana University, Germany

'In a world characterized by accelerated dynamism, innovation is a sine qua non for everyone irrespective of their life and work conditions. While this is the overall message conveyed by Jay Mitra's new book, *The Business of Innovation*, he goes much beyond to provide a comprehensive analysis of the phenomenon highlighting its macro, micro and processual level features, operations and impact. Though the book is positioned primarily for graduate and research students, it is indeed a must-read for all who struggle to manage their lives in a VUCA world.'

Professor Mathew J. Manimala
Director, Xavier Institute of Management &
Entrepreneurship, Bangalore, India
Editor, *South Asian Journal of Management*
Former Professor, Indian Institute of Management
Bangalore, India

'This book offers a fresh look on the different facets of innovation processes. Jay Mitra says what it takes to be innovative. In combining the key economic and social theories with the empirical evidence he provides animating advice for global innovation practice as well as important guidance for politicians! *The Business of Innovation* is an excellent guidebook for students, practitioners and all other who are interested in the issue.'

Professor Dr Michael Fritsch
Professor of Economics and Chair of Business Dynamics,
Innovation, and Economic Change
Friedrich Schiller Universität, Jena, Germany

THE BUSINESS
of INNOVATION

JAY MITRA

Los Angeles | London | New Delhi
Singapore | Washington DC | Melbourne

Los Angeles | London | New Delhi
Singapore | Washington DC | Melbourne

SAGE Publications Ltd
1 Oliver's Yard
55 City Road
London EC1Y 1SP

SAGE Publications Inc.
2455 Teller Road
Thousand Oaks, California 91320

SAGE Publications India Pvt Ltd
B 1/I 1 Mohan Cooperative Industrial Area
Mathura Road
New Delhi 110 044

SAGE Publications Asia-Pacific Pte Ltd
3 Church Street
#10-04 Samsung Hub
Singapore 049483

Editor: Matthew Waters
Assistant editor: Lyndsay Aitken
Production editor: Imogen Roome
Proofreader: Leigh C. Timmins
Marketing manager: Alison Borg
Cover design: Francis Kenney
Typeset by: C&M Digitals (P) Ltd, Chennai, India
Printed by CPI Group (UK) Ltd, Croydon CR0 4YY

© Jay Mitra 2017
Foreword © Zoltan Acs 2017

First published 2017

Library of Congress Control Number: 2016954330

British Library Cataloguing in Publication data

A catalogue record for this book is available from
the British Library

ISBN 978-1-4462-1080-2
ISBN 978-1-4462-1081-9 (pbk)

To my parents for their love
To Gill and Daniel for showing what love is
To my students for their love of innovation

'When he cut it, the star inside
held seeds of other stars, the way within
a life are all the lives you might live,
each unnamed, until you name it.'

From 'That New' by Susan Rothbard[1]

CONTENTS

ABOUT THE AUTHOR

Jay Mitra is Professor of Business Enterprise and Innovation and Director of The Venture Academy at Essex Business School, University of Essex, UK. He has acted as a Scientific Adviser to the OECD (Organisation for Economic Co-operation and Development) and is a visiting Professor at University Externado in Colombia. He has held similar positions at the Institute of Management Technology in India School of Management, Fudan and Jilin Universities in China, and at Bologna University, Italy. He is a Fellow of the Royal Society of Arts in the UK. Jay Mitra also leads the International Entrepreneurship Forum (IEF) a unique network and forum for researchers, policy makers and business practitioners working on entrepreneurship, innovation and regional development. The IEF's fifteen conferences around the world to date has provided a unique platform for academic researchers, innovative practitioners and reflective policy makers to pursue and highlight critical issues of and a range of perspectives on regional entrepreneurship, innovation and economic development.

He trained in the private sector in the UK, worked as a Principal Officer for local government also in the UK, specialising in economic and business development, and taught at 3 other universities before joining the University of Essex. At Essex he established the first and highly successful School of Entrepreneurship and Business (SEB) in 2005 which preceded his contribution to the creation of Essex Business School in 2008. He also created the first International Centre for Entrepreneurship Research (ICER) leading it since its inception in 2006. In 2014-15 he re-established the MBA programme into a successful and viable project, increasing the student intake 6 times, and revised and reaccredited the course. His work at the Venture Academy supports graduate students to develop entrepreneurial mind sets, create new ventures, and become pro-active players in the entrepreneurial ecosystem. These achievements follow the setting up of pioneering Centres for Entrepreneurship at two other universities and the creation of two new businesses in the UK.

He has written widely on the subjects of entrepreneurship, innovation and economic development in refereed journals worldwide and won several best research paper awards at major academic conferences in the UK and the USA. The *'Business of Innovation'* follows his recent books on *'Entrepreneurship and Knowledge Exchange', (2015) and 'Entrepreneurship, Innovation and Economic Development'* (2012), both published by Routledge. He has represented his institution as a keynote speaker in distinguished international policy, practitioner and research forums, and has worked with leading agencies such as the OECD, the United Nations Conference on Trade and Development (UNCTAD), the United Nations Industrial Development Organisation

(UNIDO), the European Union (EU), the Association of South East Asian Nations (ASEAN), the International Network of Small and Medium Sized Enterprises (INSME), and several government agencies and industry federations worldwide. He acts as an adviser to the board of tech start-ups and a fast growing global logistics firm, and is also a member of the board of the Impact Investment committee of the European Business Angel Network.

He is the editor of the *'Journal of Entrepreneurship and Innovation in Emerging Economies'*, published by Sage, and he is a member of the editorial board of various referred international journals. His main research interests are in opportunity development, entrepreneurship and innovation policy, regional development, social, female and international entrepreneurship, and migration and entrepreneurship.

FOREWORD

The *Business of Innovation* must be about business. But what kind of business is this? What does it do? How does it do it? This is the subject of this new book by Jay Mitra. Years ago I was a student of innovation. In an influential book on innovation in large and small firms I discovered an anomaly. Those innovations were not exclusively coming from large firms in the economy as a host of scholars had predicted.

For most of the twentieth century innovation was the purview of large firms: General Motors, General Electric and ATT. These firms had social capital (organizations), financial capital (money) and human capital (educated employees). All three of these were available in most large firms and they enabled the firm to innovate and introduce new products into the market driving productivity and economic growth.

These large firms invested in research and development that created knowledge and then knowledge was turned back into money through innovation. The innovation led to a product that was sold to the public. The business of innovation was in the company but the company was housed in a system of innovation. National systems of innovation looked at the whole set of institutions that supported the business of innovation including government, laws, education and the military. While the system varied from country to country, the business of innovation was more or less the same. Large organizations engaged in the business of innovation.

What I discovered close to half a century ago was that innovation still came from industries with large firms, but that the innovations were coming from the smaller firms in the industry. This was an anomaly because small firms did not have human capital, financial capital or social capital. Over the years we learned that indeed they had human capital because these were being done by the best and the brightest, they had financial capital from venture capital and angel investors, and they had social capital because these were all started in a regional ecosystem like Silicon Valley. What we learned from this discovery was that the business of innovation had changed, but how it changed remained a work in progress.

Fast forward 30 years and the biggest and most valuable companies are a new collection of firms that do not really resemble the innovative firms of the past like General Motors, Telefonica or Siemens. The new businesses are household names and are more a part of our lives than the companies of the past. They are Alibaba, Apple, Facebook, Google, Microsoft, News Corp, Rakuten, Tencent and Visa. What are these firms? How do they innovate? What is their business model?

In order to understand this it is useful to have a simple picture of the global ecosystem. Three forces have come together in the twenty-first century: the digital ecosystem, the entrepreneurial ecosystem along with globalization. The figure below shows a two by two picture that depicts the digital and the entrepreneurial ecosystem. The digital ecosystem is made up of digital infrastructure and digital users. The entrepreneurial ecosystem is made of up institutions and entrepreneurs. The digital infrastructure is driven by technology. Six turbocharging technologies have come together in the twenty-first century to drive this ecosystem: more powerful chips; the internet; the World Wide Web; broadband communications; programming languages and operating systems; the Cloud.

The entrepreneurial ecosystem is driven by institutions or the rules of the game. In the area of institutions the world has moved rapidly to develop institutions that support entrepreneurship, including better property rights, the rule of law, economic freedom, ease of contracting, intellectual property protection, market economies and free trade. The institutional changes have led to better governance in almost all countries in the world. The other two pieces of this puzzle are agents that have become entrepreneurs in increasing numbers in all parts of the world to bring new products to market and users that have embraced digital technologies in social and economic activities.

This leads to four new concepts to help us understand innovation today: digital user citizenship; digital infrastructure governance; digital entrepreneurship and the digital marketplace. Better governance means that the rules of the game are fair and create the right incentives. Better digital citizenship means that users find it easy to participate in the share economy. Better digital entrepreneurship means that it is easier for individuals to become entrepreneurs and try to create better products through innovation. The users and the agents come together in the digital marketplace.

The Global Business of Innovation

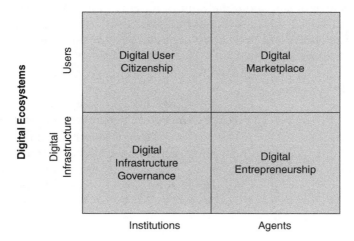

But where is business in this global business of innovation? The answer lies in the digital marketplace. The digital marketplace includes all those business that use multisided platforms: Alibaba, Apple, Facebook, Google, Microsoft, News Corp. What is new about business today is that they are different from businesses in the past.

Traditional businesses bought inputs, transformed them and sold the product, often innovating in the process. Their main focus was on attracting customers and selling to them on profitable terms. In today's digital business ecosystem, businesses are multisided platforms. Multisided platforms are technologies that reduce transaction costs or market frictions for users. Multisided platforms need to attract two or more types of customers by enabling them to interact with each other on attractive terms. In this business model, the most important inputs are generally their users. Millions of users are needed for each platform to have a multisided platform.

Matchmaker businesses are called multisided platforms because they usually operate in a virtual place that helps the different types of users get together. A digital platform includes all the different customers. Think of Uber. It brings together users wanting a ride with users wishing to offer a ride. A multisided platform brings together millions of users in a business model of innovation. The same is true of Airbnb. It is the digital technologies that make this possible both at a location and globally at all locations.

The role of digital entrepreneurs is to identify opportunities for multisided business models. However, a multisided platform is one of the toughest business models to get right. The entrepreneur has to solve a tough puzzle and use counter intuitive strategies to make a go of it. It is much easier to write an app that becomes a part of a business platform like for the Apple or the Microsoft platform.

The multisided, multi-complex world of innovation needs careful, calibrated and critical study. Jay Mitra's book captures the evolution of the multiplex phenomenon of innovation – its range, its usefulness and its influences across the globe – and offers its readers an in-depth, scholarly text. The key building blocks of the book – innovative people, innovative organisations and innovative environments – provide us with an opportunity to revisit what we know but sometimes from different perspectives, explore new territory, and urge us to consider what we do not know, creatively, cogently and comprehensively.

Zoltan J. Acs
University Professor, School of Public Policy
Director, Center for Entrepreneurship and Public Policy
George Mason School of Public Policy
Co-founder of the Global Entrepreneurship and
Development Index (GEDI)
Co-editor and Founder of *Small Business Economics*
Washington DC

PREFACE

On 7 September 2016, a BBC *Newsnight* programme clip heralded the arrival of the new iPhone 7 with a note of caution. Referring to the heady days of Steve Jobs and his vision of the iPhone and the uses of the Internet, the commentator raised questions about the apparent dearth of innovation in our current climate of economic stasis. The fizz appears to have left the spirit of innovation that marked the later decades of the twentieth century. We may have come nearer to the nirvana of Maslow's self-actualisation (witness the rise of the selfie and Facebook or Twitter and their ability to energise self-promotion) but equally we may have accelerated greater inequality. The comments were augmented by additional references to Robert Gordon, the American economist whose 2012 insights into the US economy and whose latest tome (2016) demonstrates the relative low-growth outcomes of the Internet era compared with previous periods of major technological advances.

Gordon questions whether innovation today has outlived its usefulness and whether we may have to wait many more years before we can see another innovation spark. Gordon's work echoes the thoughts of Tyler Cowen (2011), who argues that 'we have been living off low-hanging fruit for at least three hundred years', and that we are on a technological plateau with more bare tress than we can imagine despite the Internet revolution, the rise of the World Wide Web, the smart people with even smarter mobile phones, the nano depths of the world of manufacturing and health-care, the ubiquitous apps of desire and despair, and our prospective robotic futures. The rapid spread of steam and electric power did not simply increase the amount of power available, but altered completely the mode of travel, transportation and the art of communicating across distance, while lighting up homes, factories and offices, and then enabling air conditioning to make scorching environments habitable (Brynjolfsson and McAffee, 2014). In the Internet era we may be having a lot of fun, and cheap fun at that as Cowen observes, but we do not appear to be delivering on the revenue side and, therefore, in our capacity to reduce both household and business debt.

Could we really make any further progress on a book on innovation if we faltered in the wake of such trenchant observations from some of our best economic analysts and researchers? Fortunately, Gordon and Cowen restrict their critical arguments to the US economy, and as we know and as we will argue further in this book, innovation should not live by the USA alone or even the grand, radically new technological innovations, many of which find their gestation and growth in that country. The destructive power of new innovations does call into question industry structures, business models, employment security and even the way we live, and this can add fuel to any negative thoughts about innovation.

Fortunately we can also rely on other empirics that may allay our concerns about the fading power of innovation today. For instance, we have in the spirited growth (albeit faltering a bit in recent months, due to the more or less moribund global economy) of the emerging economies multiple forms of innovation that are shaping the destiny of tomorrow's mobile phone users in remote locations, and moulding organisations to generate social and economic values to help drive innovations and organisational success in both developed and developing economies. Also, in open access and open source modes of ideas generation, technological inventions and economic activity, there are possibilities for crowdsourcing ideas, crowdfunding projects, engaging the citizen as a consumer, a user, a producer and even as a conscious capitalist, perhaps, to look at new ways of creating goods and services which did not exist before. There is too the story of overcoming the big historical disconnection between our romantic idea of contemplating and thinking and our oversimplified or over-complex idea of making, which lies at the heart of design-based innovative practice. What makes it possible to attain any synthesis is the passion, ingenuity, intuition and inspiration of collaborative people. Thomas Heatherwick, the UK's Olympic design hero, is such an innovative synthesiser, who finds that it is possible to innovate and delight and reassert the beauty of glass structures based on craftwork, as in the Bombay Sapphire gin-distillery project in Hampshire, UK. Innovation emanates also from thinking about an industry such as aerospace in terms of harnessing the opposite of products that hurt, maim or kill people (Heatherwick, 2013).

There are realistic visions in the creation of well-made, well-priced casual clothing, such as in the making of a down coat thick enough to combat chilly temperatures but thin enough to be squeezed into a small bag. Much of this is made possible by Uniqlo, a global clothing phenomenon, the first Japanese brand to make it big in the international market. It does so both by weaving technology into clothing and by challenging assumptions about what to wear in a rather staid market for clothing and, more importantly, the need to question traditional consensus-based decision making and social niceties that drain Japanese initiative and creative thinking (Schuman, 2013). Tadashi Yanai, the visionary head of Uniqlo, is one of a few creative CEOs making change possible in Japan, along with other players such as Rakuten, the online retailer, and Mediwell, which helps patients collect information about doctors online.

Then there is 3-D printing, making it possible to custom-make most products in small factories in ordinary neighbourhoods, close enough for people to pick the products up or for them to be dropped off at home, perhaps by a drone or a human alternative. This is expected to usher in distributed manufacturing, which in turn will aim to address questions about local jobs, the environment and even geo-politics (Maney, 2016). Then there is blockchain too, 'a cryptographically, secure, distributed data base consisting of linked, time stamped blocks of data ... based on decentralized, peer-peer consensus and an incentive-driven model of security'. Beyond day-to-day conversation and easy comprehension perhaps, it supposedly would help to reduce the need for businesses to organise as firms or companies and, therefore, the command and control style of working much loved in even some of our most 'progressive' businesses. Collaborators, rather than just employees, will be able to work as free agents instead of as hierarchical employees, thus upending the very definition of organisations as the necessary vehicle for commerce mediating between individuals and markets (Coyle and Kharif, 2016). Time will tell!

By growing trees, shrubs and other perennial plants in the midst of crops, African farmers are able to revitalise very badly depleted soils and at the same time increase food yields. When you cannot afford fertilisers, and when you see your maize crop yield falling dramatically, it is good to learn about 'fertiliser trees' that capture nitrogen from the atmosphere and to realise that by planting seedlings between the rows of maize it is possible to harvest 10 times as much food than before, feed your family and then sell the surplus. This is what Mariko Majoni, a small-scale farmer, found in Malawi. More than many other stories, the ones which tell us, teach us, inspire us – these narratives of innovation in developing economies – are those that help to crystallise thoughts about innovation in places where it is sometimes believed impossible to achieve. Because it carves out possibilities from scarcity rather than building on abundance, we can find a greater sense of value creation in economic terms. Since it marries the need for personal fulfilment with market opportunities, it generates the kind of social value that is increasingly attracting interest across the world. Innovation can be the catalyst for both economic and social value creation.

There are emerging tales of 'platform technology innovation' which are a kind of marketplace where people and businesses trade under a set of rules laid down by the hub of the network or the lead operator. Emporiums in ancient Greece are a good example, as is the operating system Android for smart phones or Windows for personal computers, e-commerce sites and social networks. Here more than one group of consumers attract each other in swarm-style networks demonstrating strong network effects (*The Economist*, 2016). There are great world-changing ideas of water being purified with oil and new and early treatment for Alzheimer's, of robotic needles offering the prospect of curing blindness, and of accelerators and incubators such as Rocket in Berlin changing the spatial landscape of innovation.

Many of these innovations will need nurturing and commercial exploitation. Many will fail. What they will continue to do is to showcase the wealth of innovative people, innovative organisations and innovative environments that make productive change possible. This then is what the book is about. It sets out to track, trace and provide the necessary testimonies of the varieties of innovation among diverse groups of people in numerous organisational environments and across geographical divides. It is this focus on people, organisations and environments that enables us to grasp better the business of innovation.

WHY THE 'BUSINESS OF INNOVATION'?

In selecting a title in the huge forest of books on the subject of innovation there is an inevitable trade-off between something compelling, at least to the immediate eye and the mind, and the motivation for drawing up something meaningful. In the end the title should reflect easily the contents of the book and its purpose, and therefore it is sensible to desist from selecting something which needs further explanation. In this context, the 'Business of Innovation' is perhaps a cryptic choice. The book focuses on what innovation means for businesses and what businesses, small, medium or large, can do to explore, drive, manage and play with innovation. Since innovation occurs all around us wherever we may be, it is incumbent upon any writer to reflect on the spread and flow of innovation in different contexts. Innovation matters, but it matters differently in different places, and what businesses do with varied forms and types of innovation also needs attention. That is all that needs stating here, and hopefully the reader will judge whether the pages enable him or her as a scholar, a researcher, an innovator, an entrepreneur, a business person, or even as a neutral enthusiast, to value the arguments that are made about innovative people, organisations and the environment.

In the business of innovation I utilise the concept of 'fertilisers' of entrepreneurship. Regarding innovation as the creation of new goods, new services and new forms of organisational practice lays the foundations for entrepreneurship which I see as the identification and realisation of opportunities, the mobilisation of resources and the formation of organisations. A touch or more Schumpeterian perhaps, but I would argue that there is both method and value in this symbiosis for all enterprises looking at new and exciting ways to change the dynamics of doing business.

WHO IS THIS BOOK FOR?

This book is written as a text, in the main, for postgraduate and doctoral students who have a solid background in business management, economics, sociology and related fields. However, as both business practice and evidence from the teaching of innovation and entrepreneurship show, students of the subjects mentioned above do not necessarily hold sway over others entering the domain of innovation and entrepreneurship. So, welcome, all creative and artistic students of anthropology, bioscience, information communications technology, physics, mathematics, fine arts, history, geography, new media, the university of life and the wider universe of emerging thought leaders and practitioners! You may well contribute to a better appreciation of the subject than many others.

Students can identify specific building blocks in the three parts of the book (see below) or, preferably, cover the breadth and depth that it offers. The contents should help prepare them to make sense of innovation as an idea, a social construct, a process, an organisational process, an outcome of other actions and even as a trope. It should also offer critical insights into how innovation works, where it works, who makes it work, in common or differently, so that there is sufficient grounding for more focused research on topics that interest readers. Doctoral students sometimes tend to oversimplify conceptual issues, and I hope this book together with others will help to provide texts which help them navigate conceptual issues and empirical lessons.

The contents should not be seen as out of bounds for undergraduate students. However, here I would urge the reading of some broad primers on the subject first to obtain a reasonable grasp of the main aspects of business management and business economics.

I hope it is read as widely as possible.

SCOPE OF THE BOOK

The business of innovation is more than what businesses alone can offer in terms of prospects and realities of innovation. If we are to believe that businesses play a vital role in not just wealth creation but also social cohesion through the making and organising of products and services of value, then we need to accept that they are embedded in society and the structures of value creation that evolve in different societies. This also means that we locate innovation in all its forms in disparate organisations and environments, ones where businesses take centre stage, and others where non-business agents, institutions and organisations are also seen as innovative change makers. For this reason we draw on insights from a large variety of organisational practices and constructs to explore what innovation means in general and what those practices and constructs could do to influence innovative activity in business.

To allow for this wider scope of innovation for business, the book takes a route which should help the reader to navigate the macro, micro and processual aspects of innovation. There are three parts as shown in the figure here.

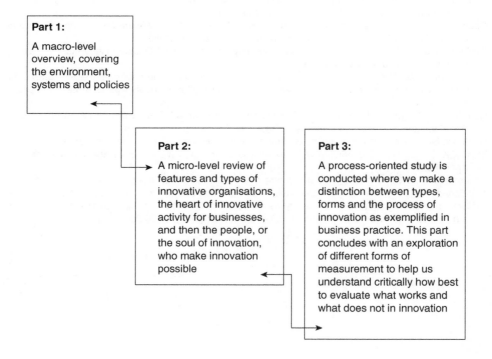

Part 1:

A macro-level overview, covering the environment, systems and policies

Part 2:

A micro-level review of features and types of innovative organisations, the heart of innovative activity for businesses, and then the people, or the soul of innovation, who make innovation possible

Part 3:

A process-oriented study is conducted where we make a distinction between types, forms and the process of innovation as exemplified in business practice. This part concludes with an exploration of different forms of measurement to help us understand critically how best to evaluate what works and what does not in innovation

Neither the size of the boxes nor the ladder effect produced by the arrows in the figure are supposed to represent any order of importance; they are simply the work of a very amateur doodler!

We start with a review of the macro aspects of innovation in a journey across time to search for the meaning of technical change, its force in generating innovations, and its limitations. Chapter 1 deals with these macro-level issues. Chapters 2, 3 and 4 continue on this macro-level journey with attention to the environment and the systems of innovation (Chapters 2 and 3), finishing with a review of policies for innovation and the role of governments and institutions. The switch to the micro aspects of innovation at the organisational and individual or team level is made in two different chapters on innovative organisations (Chapters 5 and 6), distinguishing between their types on the one hand and their features on the other. Chapter 7 then concentrates on people and the essential human factor in the business of innovation. The final part then takes the reader on to the processual elements of innovation. We distinguish between the types of innovation that are given and forms of innovation that emerge or are adopted and customised by firms, tuning eventually to the critical question of measuring the economic and social value of innovation.

This then is the offering – *The Business of Innovation*.

 REFERENCES

Brynjolfsson, E. and A. McAffee (2014) *The Second Machine Age: Work Progress, and Prosperity in a Time of Brilliant Technologies*. New York: W.W. Norton.

Cowen, T. (2011) *The Great Stagnation: How America Ate All the Low-Hanging Fruit of Modern History, Got Sick, and Will (Eventually) Feel Better*. New York: Penguin/ Dutton.

Coyle, P. and O. Kharif (2016) 'This is your Company On Blockchain', Opening Remarks, *Bloomberg Businessweek*, 29 August–4 September.

Gordon, R.J. (2012) 'Is US economic growth over? Faltering innovation confronts the six headwinds', NBER Working Paper No. 18315. Available at: www.nber.org/papers/w18315 (last accessed 20 August 2016).

Gordon, R.J. (2016) *The Rise and Fall of American Growth: The US Standard of Living since the Civil War*. Princeton, NJ: Princeton University Press.

Heatherwick, T. (2013) 'The makers: as chosen by Thomas Heatherwick', *Wired*, October: 100–7.

Maney, K. (2016) 'How 3-D printing will make manufacturing in America great again', *Newsweek*, 15 April, I66 (14).

Schuman, M. (2013) 'What they'll wear to the revolution', *Time*, 13 May: 40–4.

The Economist (2016) 'The emporium strikes back: Platforms are for the future – but not for everyone', Schumpeter, May 21, available from http://www.economist.com/news/business/21699103-platforms-are-futurebut-not-everyone-emporium-strikes-back (last accessed 20 July 2016).

ACKNOWLEDGEMENTS

When I took the decision to write this book, I realised that the only way I could do so was to be eclectic in my approach. A hypothetical sub-title for the *Business of Innovation* could well read: 'An eclectic approach to the study of innovative people, organisations and the environment'. Being eclectic suggests an avowed dependence on a variety of styles, theories, sources of ideas, evidence, intuition and serendipitous insight. The dependence suggests the avoidance of randomness more associated with chaos than eclecticism, and a sense of discipline over the process by which one travels varied and multiple routes to garner an appreciation of innovation. From what I have read, observed, questioned, learnt and speculated upon about innovation, I could not see any other way of expressing my understanding of the subject(s). Being a contrary disciplinarian I have attempted to jump across subject boundaries, academic disciplines, institutional silos and multiple organisation practice, to comprehend the richness of innovation in business. It follows that I could not have written this book without buying into or borrowing from the wealth of knowledge and experience of many others.

You always start with people, and in this case innovative people. Amongst those who have motivated me to find out more about them have been many creative souls in music, the arts, in engineering, either directly or second hand by means of studied discourse. The entrepreneurs who have implemented creative ideas, mobilised the technologies and resources, and diffused them in the markets, remind me continually about the need to watch and learn from them. Who these people are is predicated by the reality of what they do, and I have been fortunate enough to watch and learn a lot from them.

In the heartlands of the industrial districts of northern Italy during a visiting stint at the University of Bologna, I picked up what cooperation and competition meant in both the private arenas of small, medium and large firms and the public spheres of government and support agencies. In Italy, Piero Formica – the most outstanding maverick that I have come across in that country – and Mario Rinaldi – the then head of the School of Engineering in Bologna University – were my benefactors for a long period of time and continue be so in many ways. In India, across that most eclectic country in the world, I learnt clearly that Einstein was right about space and time curving and, therefore, generating different outcomes across geographies. Innovation occurs unequally across countries and regions for different reasons, defying every myopic attempt to reduce it to some limited, grand, liberating concept. These differences generate creative tensions and asymmetries which entrepreneurs utilise to create productive wealth and sometimes unproductive matter or destructive chicanery. Mathew Manimala, former professor at the Institute of Management in Bangalore and Ganesh Natarajan, the CEO of Zensar, a major software firm and the innovation champion at NASSCOM, one of the few local business federations with a truly global presence, have been massive supporters, co-workers and motivators for the quest of local knowledge. No amount of thanks would be enough to acknowledge the time, effort and friendship over a long period of time that YK Bhushan, the pioneering head first at Narsee Monjee Institute and then at the Indian Business School at Mumbai, offered me to learn and enquire further. The Institute of Management Technology at Ghaziabad where I spent a few years as a Visiting Faculty and its enthusiastic staff, my colleagues there, opened up many opportunities to confer and discover innovation at work with the students and the institution's highly entrepreneurial alumni. I have found more recently the same excitement across both business and social enterprise in the considerably talented group of students at the Tata Institute of Social Sciences in Mumbai, and with whose academic staff I have been developing an innovative curriculum on social entrepreneurship for corporates. They have been co-curators of creative thinking about innovation and entrepreneurship.

If China has flourished through imitation, it has done so because it has been better at demonstrating the art of imitation than any other country which has also depended upon imitation for innovation over many centuries. Crucially, China's capability for finding new sources and instruments for innovation surpasses many others across the globe. To witness it first hand both among students at Fudan University, where I was fortunate enough to spend some time, and among the numerous high tech and artisan entrepreneurs, in and out of the clutches of the state, has been a salutary lesson for me. If the state is innovative, it can better inspire its people and organisations to be innovative too. Chunlin Si at the School of Management at Fudan helped me learn about the real value of Shanzhai and so much more about organizational innovation. My Chinese students have always been enormously supportive of my work and have enabled me to discover China in ways that I would not have known. Most notable of them has been Wu Peng, who persuaded me to seek new ideas across China and then to generate a project with one of the leading medical device firms in Weihai City in Shandong province, Shandong Wego Medical Devices Group. I am grateful to all in that highly industrious business for the 5-year partnership, the many case studies that we produced with my colleagues and students, and for their friendship.

Pausing in Europe, my creative engagement in Germany at Leuphana University over the past few years has been possible because of a very good friend, academic co-thinker and writer, Silke Tegtmeier (now at the University of Southern Denmark). Silke has made it possible for me to understand the gender-based nuances of innovation and entrepreneurial opportunity better than most writing on the subject. Each year for the past 6 years Silke and her colleagues at Leuphana have offered me that space to indulge in thought experimentation and empirical validation at their annual entrepreneurship conference, which I value immensely. My understanding of gender and innovation would not be complete without the involvement of my ex-student Asma Rauf and her doctoral and post-doctoral work on first and second generation Pakistani women in the UK. Similarly, the cultivated insights of my other PhD and Masters students into social capital, high low agglomerations. knowledge intensive business services, diaspora entrepreneurs, agile firms, tribal communities and numerous other topics traversing the domain of innovation, laid the foundations of many an intellectual enterprise over the years. Elena Koshcheeva one of my unique group of Russian students pursuing a double Masters in Entrepreneurship and Innovation in at my university the UK with their own degree in Russia, has been a massively creative contributor to the organization of my innovative dissemination platform forum, the International Entrepreneurship Forum, in recent times. Gunnar Prause from Wismar University and the Tallinn University of Technology in Estonia has been a long-term collaborator of ideas dissemination at conferences. In supporting the creation of truly innovative firms by my students I have found much by way of enlightenment. Recently, it has been a pleasure to develop, debate and experiment with ideas with students such as Aaron Jones, who continues to build on his early success with a sustainable, eco-fashion business in London and receive royal acclaim for his work, and Pawel De Sternberg Stojalowski for his breakthrough, high tech, medical instrument company which is being established in Scotland...

Fly me to South America and I will show you how over the past 5 years, my Visiting Professorship at Externado University in Colombia and my interactions with students and staff, in particular Sonia Clara Novoa Vargas and Carlos Restrepo, have opened doors for a better understanding of the different trajectories of innovation. Back in one of the friendliest places in the world, Nigeria, Murtala Sagagi of Bayero University has taught me much about the joy and pleasure of making change work. My former students, Yazid Abubakar and Busayo Ajayi (now colleagues), have paved the ground for my learning there. Esa Tikkanen from the Finnish Ministry of Employment was instrumental in discovering novel ways in approaching the subject of innovation through the use of big data and convergent technologies.

So many organisations, so many people, multiple networks across other countries – Malaysia, Thailand, Brazil, France, Latvia, Lithuania, South Africa where I have co-hosted some of my annual International Entrepreneurship Forum (IEF) Conferences – have all been wellsprings of knowledge creation and development. Fifteen years of these compact, close-knit IEF dissemination events bringing academic researchers, reflective practitioners and decision makers have helped to establish a platform for the exchange of diversity of thought, experimentation and networking, all essentials in my book of innovation.

Then there are those individuals who have directed my thinking and deepened my understanding of innovation, entrepreneurship, small firms and economic development. David Storey at Sussex University and his clinical story-telling (no pun intended) will remain one of the permanent sources of real intelligence beyond data and regressions about small firms. Those times and discussions in and out of conferences and at our respective universities have been invaluable. Another architect of my thoughts and elaboration of ideas, especially on policy matters, has been David Smallbone at Kingston University, one of those rare pro-active knowledge creators in the world of entrepreneurship and innovation. In Michael Fritsch's carefully calibrated work I have found real nuggets of analytical insight into the regional dimensions of entrepreneurship and innovation.

If you ask the question why does it (innovation) matter anyway, and if you sometimes despair, then you simply need to rely on the most inimitable people who have shaped your journey so far. Zoltan Acs (George Mason University and London School of Economics) has by far been the exceptional intellectual catalytic converter of my faith in innovation and small firms. Sergio Arzeni (recently of the Organization for Economic Co-operation and Development (OECD) in Paris and now Director of the International Network for SMEs in Rome), continues to teach me what really lies at the heart of innovation policy at work as he did when I worked with him and his colleagues on various OECD projects. Roger Jinkinson, who innovates with fishermen in Greek islands, never fails to support my work, not least because he started me off once many years ago. To them, their wisdom and their friendship do I extend my hand in trust and for my belief in innovation in theory and in practice.

Very special thanks are due to Matthew Waters, Lyndsay Aitken and Imogen Roome for their incredible patience, guidance and editing to enable *The Business of Innovation* to be implemented through its publication. They spent several months and moments coping with my delays, correcting errors, and re-invigorating ideas and chapters. Therein lies my better understanding of completion.

And to Gill, my wife, for all that is possible and for all that matters! To Daniel, my son, for his constant questioning of what I have achieved in writing so far, and of course its value!

The best of all in this book flows from the sources of inspiration mentioned above. All errors and inadequacies of explanation are mine. In being eclectic there is room for both, I think! How else do we make sense about innovation in a 'post-truth' world?

Jay Mitra, Essex, 2017

NOTE

1. Source: 'That New', from *The Cortland Review* (No. 58,2012). https://www.poetryfoun dation.org/poems-and-poets/poems/detail/91629 (last accessed 30 December 2016).

AN INTRODUCTION TO TECHNOLOGICAL CHANGE AND INNOVATION

1

SCOPE AND OBJECTIVES

- An introduction to the meaning and significance of technological change for innovation, growth, economic and social development.
- A focus on developed economies where technological change has been most pronounced in the last two centuries.
- Critical appreciation of underpinning economic theories that help to explain the relationship among technological change, the knowledge production function, exogenous and endogenous growth, spillover effects, innovation and economic growth.
- An understanding of the contexts of technological change and the significance of organisational and social change generated by advances in technology and innovation.

INTRODUCTION

The connection between innovation, entrepreneurship and technical change is predicated upon the idea that their mutual interdependence leads to improved economic performance at the level of the firm, the industry, the region and the nation. Changes in technology and their use enable the creation of new products and services. The mobilisation of resources through the formation or growth of firms characterises the entrepreneurial process which brings these new products and services to the market. With the gradual diffusion of these innovations, incumbent technologies and businesses give way to new and more productive counterparts. Firms enjoy higher levels of productivity, consumers take advantage of either cheaper or better value products and services for which they may be willing to pay more, new jobs are created, we obtain a better quality of goods and services, and the gross domestic productivity of the nation increases over time. Technical advance prompts the creation of new products and services, the formation of new firms, and economic growth.

Economies grow because of numerous factors that enable growth to occur. Increases in market size enable increases in gains from trade, resulting from the division of labour and competitive resource pools. Investment in physical and human capital causes economic growth. Another key source is technological change (Lipsey et al., 2005). Understanding how the growth process is linked to technical change, innovation and entrepreneurship is vital for any business and policy makers. Understanding the drivers and effects of innovation and entrepreneurship is critically important because we are all conscious of the fact that technical change is related to improvements in performance at the level of the individual business, the industrial sector in which the firms are located, and at the regional and national levels (Link and Siegel, 2007).

An ambitious start-up needs to identify and use key new technologies which give them an advantageous position compared with an incumbent. An existing business has to weigh up options of using its current portfolio of technological assets against possible new improvements, based on the relative returns that can be generated from either option, the opportunity cost forgone for not using the new offering and the strategies adopted by competitors. At the regional level, and across both developed countries and fast-growing emerging economies, it has become commonplace now to see substantial investments in technology-based economic development activity. The consideration of research and development and its commercialisation at universities, together with knowledge transfer, licensing agreements and academic spin-offs, are just some of the activities that are placed on regional economic development agendas. At the national level, even if economic, industrial, fiscal and monetary policies are not determined directly by innovation and entrepreneurship, they are perceived as being crucial for all of these policies.

Incorporating innovation and entrepreneurship within these policy frameworks is given more than lip service by governments. Witness the European Union's agenda for innovation and the Framework Programmes now being given a further uplift with the Horizon 2020 project, India's Knowledge Commission reports and proposals, and China's R&D investment in lithium batteries, solar and wind energy, fintech and cross-border co-operative innovation ('One Belt, One Road') to appreciate how and why technological change and its corollary, innovation, now permeate policy-level discussions and programmes.

Our project on the organisation of innovation requires us to examine the meaning and impact of technical change at level of the firm. In other words, we are concerned with the organisational component of innovation, the uses of technology for innovation and the necessary mobilisation of resources with which to harness those technologies for new products. The organisational component is to be found in new firms that are created to manage the innovation process and in existing firms that search for strategies to compete against the odds with new products, services and structural organisational change (i.e. changes in modes of practice, approaches to management, organisational structure and forms of interaction with the outside world).

What firms do in aggregate has direct implications for economic growth. How they engage in the innovation process through R&D and other means has a bearing not only on firms and their growth, but also on governments because the latter are keen to foster business activity that can spur economic growth. Where such innovation occurs, and where it does not, also have implications for firms, governments and support services. As we will see later, location matters: proximity to other innovative firms can have beneficial effects for firms seeking a new location, while it makes it strategically important for governments to concentrate scarce resources where there is a greater likelihood of their optimisation. The significance of the organisational component is, therefore, embedded in the geography of the firms and in the networks of interaction with private and public agencies, competitors, suppliers, distributors and other players.

But first we need to obtain an understanding of technological change and how that process relates to innovation.

UNDERSTANDING TECHNOLOGICAL CHANGE

Technology can be defined as the physical representation of knowledge (Link and Siegel, 2007). The creation of any useful product provides evidence of the assumptions about knowledge or information that contributed to its creation. While science helps us to understand knowledge, technology is concerned with its application in various contexts. In this sense technology can be considered to be an output that emerges from a formal, rational or specifically undertaken process with a particular purpose. Different technologies are characterised by the varied amounts of information that are embedded in them and their production is dependent on knowledge (which is produced by research and experience). Invention can be regarded as the creation and development of a new technology; its first or new application in a specific context is then the first application of the invention.

At the heart of innovation brought about by technical change is the production of knowledge, referred to in the economics literature as the *knowledge production function* (KPF). This function best explains why innovation is important. Understanding the underpinning theories that have evolved especially since the 1950s can be a useful starting point for a critical discussion. KPF is central to economic arguments about innovation and entrepreneurship. It has a close link with prevalent theories of opportunity recognition, exploitation and realisation which form the hallmark of the literature on entrepreneurship. New knowledge creates new opportunities which, when exploited, can be realised in the form of new products, services and organisations. As we will discuss below, this link is not as obvious as it perhaps sounds. It has taken some time for economists to make the connection and accept the symbiotic relationship, even though Schumpeter had articulated the relationship back in 1934! In trying to make sense of the value of technological change and its relationship with innovation, entrepreneurship and business performance, we need to navigate complementary and overlapping spaces of firms, geography, institutions and policy. This calls for a basic level of understanding of the development of theories of economic growth. We do so first by taking a short journey in the theoretical space of modern economic growth.

TECHNOLOGICAL CHANGE AND OLD GROWTH THEORIES

Economic growth was of considerable interest to Adam Smith and other classical economists, but the orthodoxies of general equilibrium theory and the reality of the

Great Depression of the 1930s obscured its significance. Unemployment rather than economic growth per se was the main macroeconomic obsession until the Second World War, when there was a new interest among public policy makers who were keen to find ways in which to rebuild their ravaged economies. The availability of national economic and product statistics, pioneered by Simon Kuznets, spawned new research activity.

In a specific chapter, 'Economic of growth', in his 1952 publication *A Survey of Contemporary Economics*, Moses Abramovitz noted that a certain level of output was a function of the quantity of land, labour and capital, and factors such as the social and economic conditions, including the industrial and financial organisation, and the legal infrastructure. What lay behind these determinants of growth was of particular significance. Increases in output and economic efficiency were dependent on the ratio of capital to other factors, and, quite crucially, this valorisation effect could be attributed to technical improvements. As part of his examination of US economic activity in the period following the Civil War, from 1869–78 to 1944–53, Abramovitz (1956) argued that the growth in output per unit of labour was dependent on the growth in the stock of knowledge, and not increased revenues per head. The new knowledge that was created was made up of education and research (Link and Siegel, 2007). In doing so Abramovitz was not only referring to the benefits of technical advance, but also anticipating the productive role of human capital. He developed his argument further to include the role of enterprise and entrepreneurial decision making. Referring to Schumpeter, he argued that the marginal productivity of capital depends on enterprise. His reference points, like of those of Schumpeter in 1942, were the large corporations and their industrial research departments, not with smaller firms, but he was equally convinced of the importance of the broader context of culture and institutional factors (Nelson, 2005). Almost all neo-classical models of economic growth have advocated the importance of technical change for economic growth (Nelson, 2005). These models owe their genesis to the work developed in the mid-1950s by researchers such as Solow (1956) and Swan (1956), who drew heavily on the previous work of Harrod (1946) and Domar (1947) and the coinage of the now much vaunted theory of the 'residual'. Technical advance was considered exogenous to economic growth; in other words, it was the mysterious 'given' or, in Solow's term, the 'residual', in the formulation of economic growth.

Examining overall effects in the wider economy, Solow (1957) was the first economist to develop the concept of an aggregate production function model and how the rate of technological change could be assessed. He developed a simple mathematical model for the production function as follows:

$$Q = A(t) \, F(K, L)$$

where K is capital, L is labour and $A(t)$ is an unaccountable variable, or, as Link and Siegel (2007) call it, a 'disembodied shift factor' (p. 76). Increases in K and L can be expected to cause changes along the production function, but the unaccountable or unexplained movements result in an upward shift of the production function curve. Solow showed that more than 87.5% of economic growth (gross output per person) in the period 1909–49 could be attributable to technical change and not to the growth in capital or labour. The remaining 12.5% was due to increased use of capital. Much of the work carried out in the wake of Solow's ideas was being done with due deference to the prevalence of equilibrium conditions, single and steady factors markets and constant returns to scale, in other words the perfect market conditions that are dear to all neo-classical economists. According to them, perfect markets apply to both input and output markets; firms have no market power in either output or input factor markets; they charge a price that is always equal to the marginal cost; and they always pay the market wage for labour. A bunch of leading economists, including Schmookler (1952), Mills (1952) and Schultz (1953), all carried out estimates of the average annual rate of technological change over time periods varying between 1869 and 1953, by weighting inputs of capital and labour by their respective prices.

What Solow could not explain was the cause of the nearly 90% of variation in economic output – what he termed the 'residual'. Solow's contemporary Abramovitz (1956) referred to the 'residual' as a 'measure of our ignorance'. In other words, and at that time, there were things that economists could identify but could not really explain. Although the production function had constant returns to scale, there were diminishing returns with regard to labour and capital.

Getting lost in the notions of perfect competition meant that oversimplification of the market and the development of technologies was another prerequisite of these economists. So just as much as they expected perfect market conditions, these economists also assumed the introduction of a single technology, a single factor in the market system, a given and single market for inputs, a single cost of capital and a single wage. The fact that there could be a variety of effects of technological change, especially when there is a variety of regional factors markets or their evolution over time, was largely ignored (Antonelli, 2003). But much of the neo-classical literature was actually hinting at the reality of differences in the behaviour of various actors, the natural state of disequilibrium in the economy and, crucially, the idea of Knightian uncertainty, all of which characterise economic growth fuelled by technological change.

Crucially, what was forgotten was that, in perfect competition markets, there is very little incentive for firms to invest in R&D or knowledge, not least because there are huge outlay costs. If these costs are to be incurred then the returns on such investment have to be more than adequate and the prices of outputs have to be considerably higher than the marginal cost of production. How else could new knowledge be utilised? How else could the initial new investment costs be recovered? Furthermore, as Nelson and Winter (1977) has shown, the original ideas stemming from Solow's work regarded technological change as an exogenous event, without any serious explanation of its causation. If that was the case, then how could one account for the simple fact that R&D activity was a consciously designed exercise and that innovative outcomes resulted from such purposeful endeavour? Of similar importance was the question about the role of specific actors or the different types of businesses in the investment, the R&D development and the innovation process. As we will see soon, the assumption that larger firms were the main contributors to R&D investment has been found to be a more than tenuous belief.

TECHNOLOGICAL CHANGE AND NEW GROWTH THEORIES

Revisiting Solow's growth model, Paul Romer allowed for increasing returns to scale in the aggregate production function and externalities generated by private capital investment and from a general accumulation of knowledge, human capital and physical capital (Romer, 1986). In other words, instead of assuming constant or diminishing returns on capital investment as Solow did, Romer argued that the addition of human capital and technology produced increasing returns to scale and that this was how economic growth could be explained. This was different from the idea of constant returns to scale and the absence of spillover factors resulting from private investment. Quite importantly, Romer regarded technological change as endogenous to growth because he argued that firms and agents investing in R&D do so in order to optimise their investments. This idea was developed further by Aghion and Howitt (1990), who suggested that technological change was a form of Schumpeterian creative destruction. Grossman and Helpman (1991) advanced the view that each new product innovation was a function of a new firm that replaced the firm selling older products, as part of a 'quality ladder theory', and Klette and Griliches (2000) and Klette et al. (1997) built upon Grossman and Helpman's work with ideas of discrete choice models of product differentiation. These writers were the flag bearers of the new growth theory. New growth theory also considered topics that had been either repressed or not understood before. For example, new insights into the role of the infrastructure and government were formulated by researchers such as DeLong and Summers (1991). Institutional and organisational factors that have an impact on growth were also highlighted by Barro and Sala-i-Martin (1998).

THE KNOWLEDGE SPILLOVER EFFECT

An important part of new growth theory is the idea of knowledge spillovers. Such spillovers occur when businesses invest in making innovative products and services. How does this occur? Romer (1986) argued that whenever a firm invests in new knowledge production through R&D it adds to the existing body of knowledge that is generally available to all firms. Spillover effects from new technology development are created by employees engaged in research activity who move to other firms if they cannot commercialise their research in the previous organisation. University research can also lead to spillovers and spin-off activities by academic researchers, while small firms are often best equipped to make personal contacts with university staff to exploit their research for commercial purposes. The add-on effect takes place because of the following:

(a) The new knowledge from the new R&D activity and the technology that is developed from it can be leaky due to inadequate protection of intellectual property. Sometimes it is difficult to secure protection because obtaining a patent can be a costly affair. It is also possible that the technology develops so quickly (as in software) that it is virtually impossible or meaningless to try and protect it in the first place.

(b) International trading activities between firms, especially where R&D is involved (Grossman and Helpman, 1991; Coe and Helpman, 1995).

(c) Investment in equipment, creating inter-industry spillovers (DeLong and Summers, 1991; De Long et al., 1992).

(d) Active networking among firms, and especially the creator of the new technology, which find that partner firms and other users can derive considerable benefit from the new development. This is particularly common today because of globalisation and the distribution of production activity among a variety of network players.

(e) Learning by doing and the benefits of experience, generating higher levels of productivity (Arrow, 1962).

(f) Labour mobility where an individual moves to another job, perhaps in a rival firm, and takes his or her expertise to that new position, especially after receiving training on a new project with the old firm.

(g) What is referred to as 'imperfect appropriability' unless the firm can discriminate on price to competitive and downstream firms through licensing (Link and Siegel, 2007).

The different forms of spillover, but not necessarily all of them, create what are called thick markets, or 'agglomeration externalities' in the jargon of economics. This, in simple terms, means the concentrations of many firms (suppliers, distributors, customers and even competitors) in one geographical environment where they share and pass on knowledge as a consequence of the spillover effects.

The knowledge spillover concept acknowledges that the KPF has implications beyond the producer of the knowledge. Implicit also is the further enhancement of such knowledge by other players and of the role that geography can play in advancing such knowledge. But we do not really know what the firms themselves do to create new knowledge. The presence of different types of firms in the knowledge production process raises issues about the sources of the various knowledge inputs. The third-party role of universities, research organisations and technology transfer agencies allows for knowledge to spill over. The effect of the spillover is only realised when entrepreneurs create firms to harness that knowledge. But how far does that spillover effect reach? What is its spatial range?

KNOWLEDGE SPILLOVER AND THE SPATIAL ASPECT

In acknowledging the significance of spillovers, Krugman (1991) suggested that there is in effect no geographical boundary. The externalities that flow from technological development traverse organisational, regional and national boundaries. Witness the case of innovative firms such as P&G, GE and Apple and their ability to draw on multiple sources of ideas, technologies, talent and funds to drive competitive advantage for their businesses through innovation. We will discuss open innovation later (Chapter 10), but this process of engagement of people and technologies from both within and without firms also suggests that spatial limitations are perhaps a thing of the past.

As we delve further into research on the subject we find several empirical studies indicating that not only do R&D and other sources of knowledge generate externalities, but also these spillover effects are geographically bounded within the region where they were created in the first place (Jaffe, 1989; Audretsch and Feldman, 1996; Anselin et al., 2000).

In giving prominence to the spatial dimension of knowledge production, Jaffe modified the KPF as follows:

$$I_{si} = IRD^{\beta i} UR_{si}^{\beta 2} \left(UR_{si} GC_{si}^{\beta 3} \right) \varepsilon_{si}$$

where I as the innovative output is the function of IRD which stands for corporate (private) R&D expenditures, UR represents research expenditure at universities, and GC is the measure for geographic coincidence of corporate and university research. For estimation purposes the units of observation are at the spatial level s for state and i for industry. Through the use of this equation we now have an opportunity to examine the knowledge production function at the spatial or geographic level. The unit of analysis is the specific geographic unit, not the firm (Acs and Audretsch, 2005). Jaffe's (1989) argument was that the proximity of university research to corporate laboratories enables the increase of potency of spillovers from the universities.

What enables knowledge production at the spatial level (e.g. the region) to generate economic growth, however, is not addressed by the spillover researchers mentioned above. Not all spillovers have the same effect across all regions. There are different efficiencies in the spillover process, and this can be attributed to variations in entrepreneurial activity across those regions (Acs and Armington, 1999; Acs and Storey, 2004).

GENERAL PURPOSE TECHNOLOGIES

Major advances in technology can also cause important spillover effects. Such technological advances are an outcome of enabling technologies or general purpose technologies (GPTs). A GPT can be defined as a 'generic product, or process, or organizational form that [is] … recognisable as one generic thing throughout … although modern PCs differ from their early ancestors, they and intervening ancestors are recognizable as examples of one generic technology'. The same definition applies to the steam engine, the electric dynamo, lasers, the domestication of animals and of course the Internet. A GPT is, therefore, an enabling technology which on adoption leads to changes in production, consumption and behaviour. In this sense a GPT has an overwhelming impact at the level of the production process, the market and consumer behaviour, and also the wider society. Bresnahan and Trajtenberg (1995) have suggested three distinctive characteristics of GPTs: pervasiveness, an inherent capacity for technology improvements, and innovation complexities that result in increasing returns to scale. A GPT enables major economic changes by fostering new applications in a range of downstream sectors or 'innovation complementarities', generating new industries and revamping old ones. To take the obvious example of the Internet, we find that it has created Internet service providers (ISPs), network communications equipment providers, and software and consulting services for Internet and Web applications.

A GPT tends to be introduced to the market as an unfinished product which then gets refined over time, quite often by the economic concerns with price, competition, opportunity cost, returns on investment and even government policy. This movement from a stage of technological underdevelopment to the emergence of an economically viable product over time can be described as a transition from exogenous (to the economy) to endogenous development. However, sometimes the economic signals may not be the only driver for the development of such technologies in the early stages. The development of electricity, for example, was made possible by means of a research programme with antecedents from the early sixteenth century. Similarly, research on magnetism arose from practical problems of navigation during the early days of seafaring pioneers of Europe, when their compasses played strange tricks with their directions and journeys. Needless to say, in both cases, and in examples of several other technologies, we find the awareness of economic potential attracting entrepreneurial activity with which to diffuse such technologies.

The various origins of GPTs, historic, scientific and economic, suggest that they all followed an evolutionary pathway, sometimes exogenous (especially in the early stages) and sometimes endogenous (especially through the diffusion of those technologies). In the process they may acquire the status of Schumpeterian 'creative destruction' technologies, but this does not mean that they are necessarily technologically radical. As Lipsey et al. (2005) point out, steam engines powering iron ships had a long evolutionary gestation going back two centuries before they could be used in large ships. In this sense GPTs are perhaps more 'use-radical', evolving more through the use of related technologies over time rather than emerging out of the blue to shock and disrupt both our knowledge and our economic systems in which we produce, consume and grow. The disruption of 'use-radical' technologies tends to occur more at the organisational level when changes in technologies are not complemented by effective management and organisational activities with which to harness these technologies. The rapid development of open innovation processes and network technologies demands an understanding of both the benefits of web-based applications and large volumes of data, arising out of advances in Internet technology.

All GPTs that are eventually used widely in society go through a process of improvement and selection. The development of the technology affects the costs of operation. The introduction of computer-aided design is an example of cost reduction and value addition to cars. The value of the original invention is improved through supporting technologies, as in the case of car tyres or ancillary products such as the global positioning system (GPS). The introduction of organisational technologies such as mass production and just-in-time supply systems results from improvements in technologies.

As we have noted earlier, GPTs are characterised by spillover effects. Technological change induced by GPTs stretches way beyond the originators of such change, as they start to impact on incumbent technologies, creating opportunity for both rookie agents and incumbents to alter and enhance what is currently available on the market. This generates possibilities for profitable investments, which in turn enhances opportunity.

Lipsey et al. (2005) refer to computers which enabled the development of precisely controlled robots, one outcome of which was the reorganisation of factories along strictly automated lines.

GPTs do not emerge continuously in any economy. They tend to cluster together following a long evolutionary process. When they do emerge as a cluster of technologies they can be seen as the major drivers of economic and social change. Schumpeter's explanation of the creative destruction process helps us to understand how this occurs.

SCHUMPETER AND THE CREATIVE DESTRUCTION PROCESS OF TECHNOLOGICAL CHANGE

The creative destruction process is the beginning of an evolutionary process. As new products emerge successfully in the market they stimulate and encourage both initiation and competition. This is made possible by entrepreneurs. The outcome, which is one of increased flow of goods and services, and the growth in the demand for property and capital equipment, help to achieve an economic boom.

However, the duration of booms is not necessarily long because of increasing competition which reduces the value of profits as well as profit levels, discouraging additional investment. Continuing flows of goods and services dampen prices, and rising costs and interest rates choke profit margins, leading eventually to the economy falling into a recession (Schumpeter, 1939).

The cyclical fluctuations that occur in an economy are best explained by Schumpeter's theory of business cycles, which was predicated on the idea that discontinuity through innovation and the associated technological, organisational and resource changes is the main cause of cyclical fluctuations. While the cycle may be interrupted by way of recessions or depressions, the latter are part of a normal process of adaptation! As economies are depressed the contractions from depression compel organisations to change their production processes. Greater efficiency can be the outcome of lower costs and the removal of inefficient business practice. At the same time new products, services, processes and methods replace the old. This evolutionary process of change is what Schumpeter described as a 'perennial gale of creative destruction' (1939: 85).

Three types of business cycles – short, medium and long – were identified by Schumpeter. The short cycle of 3–4 years was referred to as the 'Kitchen Cycle', the medium one of 9–10 years was called the 'Jugular Cycle', and the longer fluctuation of 54–60 years was identified as the 'Kondratieff Cycle'. The Kondratieff Cycle consists of three waves: the first from the 1780s to 1842 (associated with the Industrial Revolution); the second from 1842 to 1897 (linked with the development of the railways); and the third from 1898 to the 1930s (connected with innovations in the chemical, electric power and automobile industries). The cyclical movement was characterised by a clustering of innovations rather than any movement in outputs, suggesting that specific innovations appear and are absorbed over half-century cycles (Mitra, 2012).

Dahmen (1950; 1970), who came up with the idea of 'development blocks', promoted Schumpeter's idea of 'clusters of technologies'. These 'blocks' described an integrated industrial system within a country where different institutions and businesses support each other because of their dependence on the same or related raw materials, or production processes. This dependency or complementarity was generated by new innovations, for example in railways and electrification, and the 'blocks' have enabled old firms to consider new locations while letting new firms be formed as part of the change process.

EVOLUTIONARY CONCEPTS OF INNOVATION

Arguing that both the exogenous (old growth theory) and endogenous (new growth theory) production functions were not necessarily the best instruments to use to understand technical change, Nelson and Winter (1982; 2002) developed the evolutionary theory of production and economic growth. Instead of agents who are representative of the economy, Nelson and Winter (1974) proposed that all firms are different because their ability to innovate is dependent on their varied internal routines and competencies. The differences between the firms formed the basis of both co-evolution and competitive selection for the survival and growth of firms. The selection process does not necessarily lead to the survival of the fittest due mainly to the concept of 'increasing returns' on technological investments, which is a dynamic concept based on ideas of path dependency and learning by doing. The focus here is on the individual firm, and what happens with innovation and technical change is firm-specific. With Nelson and Winter, we note a significant departure from ideas of aggregate value, 'diminishing returns' and the 'average firm' in the economy.

As Nelson (2005) notes, almost all evolutionary theories of economic growth draw their inspiration from Schumpeter and his *Capitalism, Socialism and Democracy* (1942), where the latter developed a theory of endogenous technological change improvement emanating from investments made by firms to outcompete or operate on a par with their rivals. In developing their own evolutionary models, Nelson and Winter (1974) argued that firms, rather than individual people, were the main actors. What makes them profitable and act as carriers of technologies and productive practices are 'routines'.[1] Routines are habits or customs or behaviours that are appropriate only in the specific settings in which they are raised or found, and which involve profit-oriented learning and selection. There are probably three different kinds of routines:

- standard operating procedures (what and how much a firm produces in different situations given what it has in stock and its constraints);
- investment behaviour (measurements of growth or fall as a function of its profits and possible other factors); and
- deliberative processes (investigating better alternatives for doing things).

An overriding feature of all these routines is the need to find or 'search' for new or improved techniques for production. This search is variously referred to as R&D or learning. In general there is also a large degree of variation in how firms search for and use technologies and how they improve their productivity or profitability. Firms which use more profitable technologies grow; they are then imitated by other firms, leading to the diffusion of new technologies (Soete and Turner, 1984; Metcalfe, 1995).

IMPROVEMENTS AND LEARNING

The diffusion of new technologies is marked by the improvement of individual technologies and the enhancement of more productive technologies, resulting in increased productivity in an industry or an economy as a whole. Therefore, growth at the aggregate level is the outcome of two different factors. As opposed to the idea of a search from a basket of technologies, writers such as Silverberg et al. (1988) argued that there were only two technologies – one better than the other.

However, the potential for using the better technology can only be achieved if prevailing practice is improved. So search is replaced by improving prevailing practice, which involves learning by doing or learning that is connected directly to the operation of the technology. In the process some of the learning 'spills over', allowing others who did not invest in that technology to use it to improve their productivity. A firm developing such a technology can gain or lose competitive advantage depending on how well it can protect the spillover effect. The payback on a technology that is initially less productive can be higher if effort is put into its use and improvement through learning by doing. The petrol-fuelled internal combustion engine may not have been a technology superior to the steam engine or the battery-powered ones, but it was its use, and the cumulative learning generated by such use, that led to its dominance. Once a choice is made for a specific technology, and once its use is repeated, the learning process that flows from it can make competing technologies redundant because of the need for firms to close gaps in performance.

NETWORKING EXTERNALITIES AND SOCIALISATION

Linked to the idea of cumulative learning is the notion of network externalities and complementarity. The more the users of a technology buy similar or compatible products, the more likely a specific variant of that technology is to succeed. The case of telephone networks in which users have a particular interest in others possessing compatible products is a good example of compatible product development. Compatible software usage for computers is a typical example of complementarity (Nelson, 2005). Inherent in these examples and the idea of cumulative technologies and learning are the theories of path dependency and dynamic increasing returns developed by Arthur (1988) and David (1985; 1992).

As technologies become dominant and as industries become more established, we find not only the emergence of technical and quality standards, but also pronounced levels of interaction among firms, suppliers, distributors, customers, both within the same and across different industries, and even between firms and the government. Economic activity becomes embedded in social exchange among all the actors, with weak or strong ties among them (Granovetter, 1985). The socialisation process involves the industry moulding its peculiar selection environment by establishing the rules of the game, codes of behaviour and modes of interaction through the creation of industry bodies or spatial concentrations of firms in clusters. Other stakeholders, such as universities and publishers of technical journals, become entangled in this process through the supply of knowledge and trained people.

The involvement of external stakeholders can have a varied effect on both knowledge production and the derivation of advantage from such knowledge. Knowledge as a public good can dilute the process by which a firm gains advantage over new entrants, not least because of the availability of different technological alternatives that flow from university research. As different institutions and organisations become involved, other imperatives surface. There are pressures on new legislation, such as those of patents and intellectual property, infrastructure and skills development, which requires governments to intervene with adequate policies that are conducive to technological, industry and firm development.

THE IDEA OF A SYSTEMIC VIEW

What emerges is a 'systemic' view that considers the evolution and embedding of firms and industries together with support organisations at the sectoral, regional and national levels. What matters here is not necessarily the amount of R&D or technical advance, but the distribution of the R&D and the technological harvest that can be obtained. Here the role of governments and the creation of regional and national innovation systems is worth noting (Lundvall, 1992; Freeman, 1995; Mazzucato, 2013).

So far we have examined evolutionary ideas from an economic perspective. Now let us look at technical change and innovation from a technological perspective and see whether the patterns of change and the momentous technological changes of recent times offer insights into the future.

AN INFORMATION-BASED EVOLUTIONARY TECHNOLOGY PERSPECTIVE

One way of understanding evolution is to see it as a process of 'creating patterns of increasing order' (Kurzweil, 2005), and especially the order in which information is processed over time. A biological approach to technological evolution and change enables us to understand that every stage of our evolution as human beings, working with and developing new technologies, uses information processing methods of the previous stage or epoch in order to create the next one. Kurzweil refers to six epochs, the consideration of which suggests that evolution works through indirection with each epoch building on the advances of the previous one. The six epochs are depicted in Figure 1.1.

Kurzweil's interpretation of the evolution of technology is measured in terms of units of information. Such an interpretation is in part inherent in the various other economic explanations discussed above. Other interpretations of evolutionary change also rely on the creation of specific capabilities at a certain time and place,

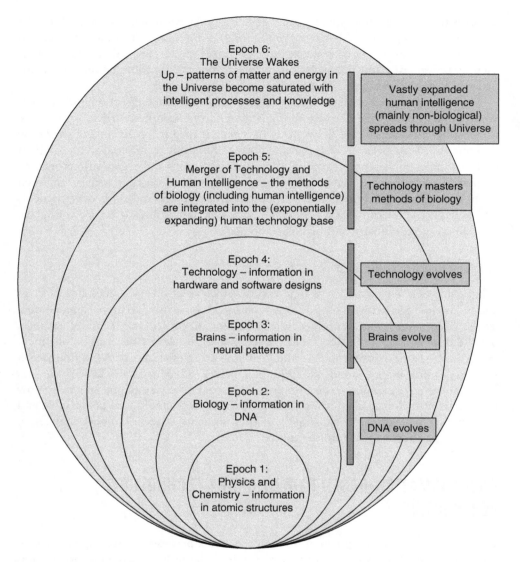

FIGURE 1.1   **The six epochs of evolution**

Source: Adapted from Kurzweil (2005)

and then their evolution to the next stage or epoch. However, rarely do we find a critical discourse on innovation management that provides a basis for understanding evolution and technical change through the lens of information. The discourse leads us right to the heart of innovation today, and the specific significance of information technology in the innovation process and in the making and use of products and services. Kurzweil also offers us an insight into the correspondence between biological evolution and information-driven technological evolution in a way that is not easily available in other work:

The rules of our universe and the balance of the physical constants that govern the interaction of basic forces are so exquisitely, delicately and exactly appropriate for the codification and evolution of information (resulting in increasing complexity) that one wonders how such an extraordinary unlikely situation came about. Where some see a divine hand, others see our own hands – namely the anthropic principle which holds that only in a universe that allowed our own evolution would we be here to ask such questions. (2005: 15)

This is why we will stay with Kurzweil to obtain a different perspective on innovation evolving over the six epochs sketched above.

Epoch 1 represents the origins of life and information in terms of patterns of matter and energy. Time and space can, according to modern theories of physics, be broken down into fragments of information. Atoms formed several thousand years after the Big Bang as electrons were caught in orbits around nuclei made up of protons and neutrons. Their electrical structure made them what Kurzweil describes as 'sticky', and their structures began to store and represent discrete information. Many millions of years later the atoms unified to become molecules which had more stable structures. While most elements could bond in one to three directions, carbon was probably the most flexible, multifaceted and adaptable of the elements, being versatile enough to form bonds in four directions. The consequence was the availability of complex, information-heavy, 3-D structures.

Epoch 2, which is estimated to have started many billions of years ago, saw the increasing complexity in carbon-based compounds which led to the emergence of self-replicating mechanisms formed from the aggregations of molecules, leading to the origin of life. Eventually, DNA was the result of the evolution of biological systems enabling the storage of information which described a larger social agglomeration of molecules. Kurzweil describes DNA as a precise digital system. The supporting structure of codons and ribosomes helped to maintain a record of the evolutionary experiments of this stage. This epoch's mechanisms included the epigenetic information of proteins and RNA fragments that manage gene expression in a way that defined the information processing system of the brain and the nervous system.

Epoch 3 witnessed a paradigm shift to a new level of 'indirection' when DNA-directed evolution produced organisms that could find information with the help of their own sensory organs and processes, storing such information in their own nervous systems and brains. Early animals began to recognise patterns that account for the major part of the activity of our brains. Our own species subsequently developed the competency to create abstract mental models of our experiences and to imagine, consider and evaluate the rational implications of these models.

Epoch 4 saw the evolution of human-generated technology, starting with simple mechanisms developing into complex automated mechanical machines. This was possible because of the mix of the abilities for rational and abstract thought in conjunction with what Kurzweil (2005) describes as 'our opposable thumb'. Elaborate and sophisticated computational and communication devices now allow for sensing, storing, retrieving and evaluating complex patterns of information. What is worth noting is the relative speed of the biological and technological evolutions. Again as Kurzweil (2005) notes, while the most advanced mammals added one cubic inch of brain matter every thousand years, the computational capacity of computers more than doubled each year. It took 2 billion years from the origin of life to cells, while the time that has passed from the making of the first PC to the Web is only 14 years. This may not be a like-for-like comparison, and the actual size of the brain or indeed the computer may not be an indicator of intelligence, but they do help to determine such intelligence and also to point to the difference in time frames of biological and technological evolution respectively – 100,000 years for the former and only a decade for the movement from inception to the mass adoption of the Web.

The first four epochs account for biological and technological evolutions to date. The above summary attempts to demonstrate how, by adopting an information perspective on the evolutionary process, we are able to see a kind of natural fusion between the biological and technological trajectories of evolution. What we can also note is the continual acceleration of the evolutionary process, with biological evolution leading directly to human-directed technological development. Critical events have generated landmarks by various writers, from Carl Sagan (1989) to Theodore Modis (2003), the latter identifying 28 clusters of events or 'canonical milestones' based on the events drawn from lists of other researchers.

Epoch 5 is what we can describe as the 'harbinger' state where we could (or as Kurzweil does) merge human technology with human intelligence, epitomised in the Kurzweilian notion of 'singularity'. Singularity will be evinced in the bringing together of the speed, capacity, connectivity and knowledge-sharing features of our technologies with the vast amount of knowledge located in our brains. The so-called 'human–machine' civilisation will work towards transcending the limitations of only 100 trillion slow connections of our brains (Kurzweil, 2005).

Epoch 6 will ride on the crest of the Epoch 5 wave, and, according to Kurzweil, the singularity will reorganise matter and energy to optimal levels of computing capability.

These two latter epochs may allow people, organisations, societies and economies to overcome typical human problems and unleash higher levels of creativity, or provide succour for the destructive inclinations of those who may acquire the ability to do so. In summary, singularity is dependent, inter alia, on the following principles:

- The accelerating rate of technological innovation (doubling every decade).
- Acceleration combined with exponential growth in price performance, speed, capacity and bandwidth.
- The deployment of additional resources for further development as technology becomes more cost effective, thus increasing the rate of exponential growth.
- The availability of hardware (supercomputers and personal digital devices) to copy human intelligence, with computers combining the traditional strengths of human intelligence (pattern recognition, new knowledge acquisition, creation of mental models to carry out 'what-if?' sensitivity experiments) with the power of machine intelligence.
- The sharing of machine knowledge at very high speed, processing and switching signals close to the speed of light (approximately 300 million metres per second compared with 100 metres per second for the electrochemical signals used by the brains of biological mammals).

- Access to all the knowledge of human–machine civilisation through the Internet, and the freedom of design and architecture together with consistent performance. (Kurzweil, 2005)

Abstraction and predictions of the future will never be out of the range of controversy. We can only grapple with such abstractions when we can find answers to down-to-earth questions about the nature and type of innovation that might emerge from this exponential growth of information and computational capability. We could ask, for example, where are we likely to see the innovations occurring while the law of accelerating returns helps to achieve a Kurzweilian singularity?

We can see already in the very first two decades of the twenty-first century the overlapping revolutions of genetics, nanotechnology and robotics, fired by, among other technologies, artificial intelligence. Discussions on the ever-expanding realm of each of these spaces of innovation, covering cell therapies, gene chips, the reversal of degenerative disease and the ageing process, overcoming cancer and heart disease, the use of nanotechnology to rebuild the physical world and improve the environment, and the widespread adoption of non-biological intelligence represented by robots, are beyond the scope of this volume.

It is possible for us to predict a frightening future of new machines replacing all our jobs, extending inequality and upending society because of the implications of artificial intelligence (AI). But our concern now is with the discussion about technical change and its impact on innovation for the economy, the interests of business and the implications for wider society. In this regard, it is appropriate to mention how far we have travelled down the road when we are considering the possible handover of human tasks to machines, which is what the fast-moving AI technology offers. *The Economist* refers to the McKinsey Global Institute's understanding of the significance of AI which is contributing to a 'transformation of society happening ten times faster and at 300 times the scale, or roughly 3,000 times the impact, of the Industrial Revolution' (2016: 3). Of particular importance is the anticipated impact on jobs that are non-routine, the possible amoral independence of the deep learning machine which might not share human goals and instead turn on us, and the threat of use of AI by a modern-day Caligula rather than Marcus Aurelius, as Elon Musk warns us (*The Economist*, 2016). In his highly analytical thesis presented in the book *Rise of the Robots*, Martin Ford (2015) assesses the particular power and range of a new GPT, information technology, as the latter is assimilated into new business models and business scenarios of less labour-intensive work across the board. Firms such as Facebook, Uber, Tencent, Grab, D and even Google achieve sensational market valuations while employing relatively (to their size) few people. What Ford fears is:

Beyond the potentially devastating impact of long-term unemployment and underemployment on individual lives and the fabric of society, there will also be a significant economic price. The virtuous feedback loop between productivity, rising wages and increasing consumer spending will collapse. (2015: xvii)

We are witnessing this in an extended period of sluggish economic growth, lower levels of spending despite interest rates just short of zero (as I write, here in the UK), and accelerating inequality with on average the top 5% of households being responsible for approximately 40% of spending (Ford, 2015). Is such a negative outcome the price of technological change and innovation? Is AI generating the same economic and social trepidations that mechanisation unleashed in the nineteenth century? Or is it a question of redefining jobs, restructuring industries, transforming education and adopting new regulatory measures? If innovation through AI, robots, nanotechnology and genetics could, however, transform our urban environment with reduced pollution enabled by driverless cars and, therefore, reduced car ownership, then perhaps we could see prospects of a better quality of life by allocating breathing space to more parks, housing, bicycles and pedestrian zones. If it helps people to chat and interact with 'things' such as cars and homes, in the same way that they do with computers through the use of the web browser and touch screens, we could enter a new world of 'augmented reality' overlays aided by graphics. If real-time translation between people using different languages could be developed further, it could help to integrate and offer new opportunities for the millions of displaced refugees, as numerous initiatives are attempting to do in Germany today. If AI could sift through large volumes of data, posit new hypotheses and identify new correlations for possible investigation, as IBM's Watson AI technology does, then it might push the frontiers of cancer, genome and climate change research (*The Economist*, 2016). These then are the positive signs of future innovation.

We will await the future. For now, let us reflect on a story about technological change in two parts of the sceptered isle of Great Britain.

VIGNETTE 1.1   THE EVOLUTION OF TECHNOLOGICAL CHANGE IN ENGLAND AND WALES

This is a story about England and Wales. It is a story of technology and social factors that have evolved and changed the industrial landscape over the last 170 years and of how people work and what they do. It provides us with insights into what new knowledge has been created over the years at the behest of technology, human capital, organisational change and the responses to these changes during that period. A sweep of the 170 years shows us that, by 2011, fewer than 1 in 100 people worked in agriculture, while services formed the dominant industries in England and Wales.

Our starting point is the early nineteenth century (Figure 1.2). Between 1801 and 1837 the steam locomotive (1801) brought about the invention of the high-pressure steam engine and the electric telegraph (1837). These were the GPTs of the time. Railway engines, ships and roadworthy vehicles were being driven by the steam engine, while electricity began to be used to build the railway networks. Its social effect was to change the distribution of both goods and workers at the same time as helping to power machinery for use by the manufacturing industry. The telegraph enabled better communication about train delays and locations and eventually about other forms of connectivity among people and industry. The manufacturing industry emerged as the world leader, and thus began the story of the Industrial Revolution.

Steam locomotive		
	1801	Electric telegraph
Bessemer process	1837	
	1856	Patent for liquefying gas
	1876	
Steam turbine	1884	
	1902	1902 Education Act
Penicillin discovery	1928	Nuclear power
	1956	
First microprocessor	1971	World Wide Web
	1989	

FIGURE 1.2 Developments that have changed industries in England and Wales

Source: Adapted from *Economic and Labour Market Review* (2013)

As cities and towns became better connected because of the two new technologies, the length of the railway more than tripled in about 50 years from 5,000 miles to well over 18,000 miles (8,000 to 29,000 km). Those who had moved from their rural, agricultural homes to build the railways did not return to their previous lifestyles, which led to a drop in the number of people involved in agricultural work. By 1875 steam-powered railways and ships were being used in other parts of the world. The USA used these technologies to export surplus cereal. Most interestingly, the technologies impacted on the development of other new technologies such as refrigeration, enabling meat and other agricultural products to be imported by the UK from Australia, New Zealand and South America. Liquefying gas was part of a basic refrigeration technology, and its invention in the mid-nineteenth century allowed food to be stored and transported for longer periods. The higher the level of these exports, the lower the dependency on agricultural activity in the UK.

Fertilisers, herbicides and pesticides were developed and used to ensure lower levels of crop failure.

Improvements in and increased usage of machinery, such as tractors, mechanical threshers and combine harvesters, throughout the twentieth century dispensed with the need to use as many workers as were used in the past. Scale economies were surfacing rapidly. While in 1900 one agricultural worker fed approximately 25 people, the same agricultural worker could feed 200 people in 2010. Add to this the globalisation phenomenon and the dependence on imports for the UK to feed itself. Back in 1841, 22% of workers were part of the agriculture and fishing industries. Steady decline over the last 170 years has resulted in less than one in a hundred employed people (1% or 0.2 million people) being engaged in the same industry.

(Continued)

(Continued)

England and Wales were moving up the 'S' curve of development, from an agrarian economy to a more efficiency-driven economy led by manufacturing. The growing infrastructure created by the railways and the telegraph in the first place allowed for goods and fuel to be moved around at cheaper rates. More people could be employed in factories because of new production machinery. By 1856, the Bessemer process for mass producing steel from molten pig-iron increased the speed and scale of production. The consequent advances in the iron and steel industry augmented the value of the steam engine and the telegraph in economic development. By 1884 the first model of a steam engine connected to a dynamo generated electricity, helped with the diffusion of electricity as it became cheaper to use and plentiful in supply.

Advances in steel and machinery spawned developments in the textile manufacturing industry, which became a world leader in the 1800s. The repressive colonial adventures and the suppression of textile industries in outposts such as India notwithstanding, we can observe the nature of the spillover effects of GPTs and the emergence of clusters of industrial activity in England and Wales. At the same time, towns and cities grew in density, with people forging a new way of living there that was different from what they were used to in the rural areas.

The new forms of social organisation of their lives was a key feature in the enhancement of both the manufacturing industry and city life. Science was at the service of improving social lives when the antibiotic penicillin was discovered in the late 1920s. Urban living coupled with the growth of manufacturing in cities subjected people to many diseases, and here was this amazing discovery that provided for safe and effective treatment and better health care. A little earlier, in 1902, the Education Act had created the first local authorities to allow for better civic governance at a local level.

Alongside this development there was recognition of the importance of education, resulting in the expansion of the stock of school buildings. By the mid-1950s and the dawning of the modern era in the twentieth century, nuclear power was used to produce electricity at Calder Hall.

Advances in technology have their own way of impugning the capabilities of people to keep up with such developments. The progressive mechanisation of process lines and incremental innovation has made mass manufacturing and the production of low-value goods, such as steelmaking, more efficient at the expense of labour. Many of these heavy industries have changed in shape and size, with smaller firms being able to produce more high-value goods. Many of the components of manufacturing such as industrial design have moved over to services as they find greater economies of scope in working across a range of industries, such as aerospace and electronics. The first microprocessor developed in the 1970s which provided the heartbeat for ordinary computers has helped to develop low-cost computers, facilitating digital control over a range of industrial processes and devices, such as mobile phones.

Software development and the introduction of the World Wide Web in the 1980s have connected businesses globally, again changing the way people communicate and do business across the world.

Globalisation and the rate of change in economies around the world have inevitably had an effect on British industry. They have helped to reduce the labour component of routine manufacturing while creating greater levels of interdependency (see Chapter 10 for a discussion on the changing modes of innovation in the world today) in trade and manufacturing. These interdependencies are created by spillovers of technology, especially in the form of multiple levels of application of new technologies.

A major shift has occurred in the nature and scope of industrial activity in England and Wales. New business creation based on new technologies has seen a rise in the service industries, including hotels and restaurants, distribution, transport and communication, banking, finance and insurance, public administration, education, health, the media, arts, entertainment and recreation. These then are the new 'knowledge'-based industries of our times, so called because of their ostensible reliance on brain power as opposed to brawn power. By 2011, four out of five workers (approximately 81%) were employed in the service industries. This compares with only a third of workers in the service industries in 1841. However, there has been a dramatic change in the nature and scope of the service industries over time. Back in 1841, services constituted domestic work and personal services. Then these services engaged about 18% of the workforce. By 2011, the major service industry players included the wholesale and retail trade and motor repairs. About 4.2 million people, or roughly 16% of the labour force, are employed in these industries. Heath care and social work activities is another big service industry with 13% of working people operating in this, the second biggest industry in England and Wales.

With a population of 56.1 million (2011 figures), and with 41.1 million of them in the 16–74 age bracket, England and Wales have a working population of 26.5 million. The services dominate the industrial landscape now, with 92% of women and 71% of men being employed in these industries. All the others – manufacturing (13% and 5% for men and women), energy and water (2% and 1%), construction (13% and 2%), agriculture and fishing (1% and 1%) – are way below in terms of opportunities for work or new business creation leading to new jobs. Probably the biggest message in this shift is the increasing importance of women in the new industrial landscape, a point which raises key issues about how we live and work in our societies today.

CONCLUDING OBSERVATIONS

Our exploration of the value and meaning of technological change and its relevance for innovation has taken us through a number of linked pathways. Firms, regions and countries all benefit from productive economic growth, the causes of which are various. Technological change is one reason for economic growth, and over the years various studies have nailed the mast of economic growth to the technological change pole. At the heart of technological change and growth in the economy is the importance of the knowledge production function, which has been understood in terms of exogenous, endogenous and evolutionary growth models, each with their own explanations of the different factors that underpin those models. Much of this is being questioned by the transformation that is occurring on the digital and new information technology landscape. We do not know whether machine learning will aid or make redundant humans and their capacity for knowledge production and use.

The production of knowledge is dependent not only on technological inputs and investments in technology, but also on human capital, government policy and institutional factors. They combine differently at the level of the firm, the region and the country. Each of these levels are used as appropriate units of analysis for the purpose of investigating technological change and how such change facilitates the production of new goods and services, and, crucially, the type of organisations necessary to mobilise the resources to make those changes. Knowledge spills over for a number of reasons, creating more opportunities for the development of new products and services in different contexts. These then are the building blocks of technological change and its corollary, innovation. But the very combination of multiple factors enabling technological change suggests that technology alone is not the driver of innovation. What happens with innovation at the level of the firm, the region or the country requires us to observe and analyse critically how organisations manage technological change and innovation, how different forms of socialisation and human intervention adopt and use different technologies, and how geography affects the scope of innovation in different regions. These are the issues that we go on to examine in the following chapters. We will examine later how the trajectory of technological change today is disrupting long-held views and organisational structures, thereby adding higher levels of uncertainty to the innovation process while producing multiple opportunities for generating new ideas, new products, new services and unusual recombinations of organisational structures.

 —— SELF-ASSESSMENT AND RESEARCH QUESTIONS ——

1. What constitutes the knowledge production function and what is its significance for innovation and economic growth?

2. Explain the differences between exogenous, endogenous and evolutionary theories of economic growth.

3. How does knowledge spill over and in what way do spillovers affect the innovation process?

4. What are general purpose technologies and why do we need to understand their importance for innovation?

5. How can we measure technological change and why does it matter?

NOTE

1. The concept of routines is analytically similar to the genes in biological theory or the memes or culture in sociobiology (Nelson, 2005: 95).

 —— REFERENCES ——

Abramovitz, M. (1952) 'Economics of growth', in B. Haley (ed.), *A Survey of Contemporary Economics*, Vol. 2. Homewood, IL: Richard D. Irwin. pp 132–178.

Abramovitz, M. (1956) 'Resource and output trends in the United States since 1870', in *Resource and Output Trends in the United States since 1870*. Cambridge, MA: National Bureau of Economic Research (NBER). pp. 1–23.

Acs, Z.J. and Armington, C. (1999) 'Job flow dynamics in the service sector', Discussion Paper, Centre for Economic Studies, Bureau of the Census, Washington, DC, pp. 99–14.

Acs, Z.J and Audretsch, D.B. (2005) *Entrepreneurship, Innovation and Technological Change.* Boston, MA: now publishers.

Acs, Z.J. and Storey, D.J. (2004) 'Introduction: entrepreneurship and economic development', *Regional Studies*, 38(8): 871–7.

Aghion, P. and Howitt, P. (1990) *A Model of Growth through Creative Destruction* (No. w3223). Cambridge, MA: National Bureau of Economic Research.

Anselin, L., A. Varga and Z.J. Acs (2000) 'Geographic and sectoral characteristics of academic knowledge externalities', *Papers in Regional Science*, 79(4): 435–43.

Antonelli, C. (2003) *The Economics of Innovations, New Technologies and Structural Change*, Routledge Studies in Global Competition Series. Abingdon: Routledge.

Arthur, W.B. (1988a) 'Self-reinforcing mechanisms in economics', in P. Anderson, K.J. Arrow and D. Pines (eds), *The Economy as an Evolving Complex System*. Reading, MA: Addison-Wesley. pp. 9–31.

Arthur, W.B. (1988b) 'Urban system and historical path dependence', in J.H. Ausubel and R. Herman (eds), *Cities and Their Vital Systems*. Washington, D.C.: National Academy Press. pp. 85–97.

Audretsch, D.B. and Feldman, M.P. (1996) 'R&D spillovers and the geography of innovation and reproduction', *American Economic Review*, 86(3): 630–40.

Barro, R.J. and Sala-i-Martin, X. (1998) *Wirtschaftswachstum*. Munich: R. Oldenbourg Verlag.

Bound, J., C. Cummins, Z. Griliches, B.H. Hall and A. Jaffe (1984) 'Who does R&D and who patents?', in Z. Griliches (ed.), *R&D Patents and Productivity*. Chicago, IL: University of Chicago Press. pp. 21–54.

Bresnahan, T.E. and M. Trajtenberg (1995) 'General purpose technologies', *Journal of Econometrics*, 65: 83–108.

Coe, D.T. and Helpman, E. (1995) 'International R&D spillovers', *European Economic Review*, 39(5): 859–87.

Dahmén, E. (1950) *Svensk industriell företagarverksamhet: kausalanalys av den industriella utvecklingen 1919–1939* [Entrepreneurial activity in Swedish industry in the period 1919–1939; with an English summary; Vol. 3]. Industriens utrednings-institut.

Dahmén, E. (1970) *Entrepreneurial Activity and the Development of Swedish Industry: 1919–1939.* Homewood, IL: Published for the American Economic Association by RD Irwin.

David, P.A. (1992) 'Knowledge, property, and the system dynamics of technological change', *The World Bank Economic Review*, 6(1): 215–48.

DeLong, J.B. and Summers, L.H. (1991) 'Equipment investment and economic growth', *Quarterly Journal of Economics*, 106: 445–502.

De Long, J.B., Summers, L.H. and Abel, A.B. (1992) 'Equipment investment and economic growth: how strong is the nexus?', *Brookings Papers on Economic Activity*, (2): 157–211.

Domar, E.D. (1947) 'Expansion and employment', *The American Economic Review*, 37(1): 34–55.

Ford, M. (2015) *Rise of the Robots: Technology and the Threat of a Jobless Future.* New York: Basic Books.

Freeman, C. (1995) 'The "National System of Innovation" in historical perspective', *Cambridge Journal of Economics*, 19(1): 5–24.

Granovetter, M. (1985) 'Economic action and social structure: The problem of embeddedness', *American Journal of Sociology*, 91(3): 481–510.

Grossman, G.M. and Helpman, E. (1991) 'Quality ladders in the theory of growth', *The Review of Economic Studies*, 58(1): 43–61.

Harrod, R. (1946a) 'Price flexibility and employment by Oscar Lange', *The Economic Journal,* 56(221): 102–7.

Harrod, R.F. (1946b). 'A new view of the economics of international readjustment: a comment', *The Review of Economic Studies*, 14(2): 95–7.

Jaffe, A.B. (1989) 'Real effects of academic research', *American Economic Review*, 79(5): 957–70.

Klette, T.J. and Griliches, Z. (2000) 'Empirical patterns of firm growth and R&D investment: a quality ladder model interpretation', *The Economic Journal*, 110(463): 363–87.

Klette, T.J., Møen, J. and Griliches, Z. (2000) 'Do subsidies to commercial R&D reduce market failures? Microeconometric evaluation studies', *Research Policy*, 29(4): 471–95.

Krugman, P. (1991) *Geography and Trade*. Cambridge, MA: MIT Press.

Kurzweil, R. (2005) *The Singularity is Near.* New York: Penguin Books.

Link, A.N. and Siegel, D.S. (2007) *Innovation, Entrepreneurship and Technological Change.* Oxford: Oxford University Press.

Lipsey, R.G., Carlaw, K.I. and Bekar, C.T. (2005) *Economic Transformations: General Purpose Technologies and Long-term Economic Growth*. Oxford: Oxford University Press.

Lundvall, B.A. (1992) *National Systems of Innovation: An Analytical Framework*. London: Pinter.

Mazzucato, M. (2013) *The Entrepreneurial State: Debunking Private vs. Public Sector Myths*. London: Anthem Press

Metcalfe, J.S. (1995) 'Technology systems and technology policy in an evolutionary framework', *Cambridge Journal of Economics*, 19(1): 25–46.

Mills, F.C. (1952) *Productivity and Economic Progress*, Occasional Paper 38. New York: NBER.

Mitra, J. (2012) *Entrepreneurship, Innovation and Regional Development: An Introduction*. Abingdon: Routledge.

Nelson, R.R. (2005) *Technology Institutions and Economic Growth.* Cambridge, MA: Harvard University Press.

Nelson, R.R. and Winter, S. (1974) 'Neo-classical vs evolutionary theories of economic growth: critique and prospectus', *Economic Journal*, 84 (December): 886–905.

Nelson, R.R. and Winter, S.G. (1977) 'In search of useful theory of innovation', *Research Policy*, 6(1): 36–76.

Nelson, R.R. and Sidney, G. (1982) *An Evolutionary Theory of Economic Change*. Cambridge, MA: Harvard University Press.

Nelson, R.R. and Winter, S.G. (2002) 'Evolutionary theorizing in economics', *The Journal of Economic Perspectives*, 16(2): 23–46.

Romer, P.M. (1986) 'Increasing returns and long-run growth', *The Journal of Political Economy*, 94(5): 1002–37.

Sagan, C. (1989) 'Why we need to understand science', *Parade Magazine*, 10.

Schmookler, J. (1952) 'The changing efficiency of the American economy, 1869–1938', *The Review of Economics and Statistics*, 34: 214–31.

Schultz, T.W. (1953) *The Economic Organization of Agriculture*. New York: McGraw-Hill.

Schumpeter, J.A. (1939) *Business Cycles: A Theoretical, Historical and Statistical Analysis of the Capitalist Process*. New York: McGraw-Hill.

Schumpeter, J.A. (1942). *Capitalism, Socialism and Democracy*. New York: Harper and Brothers.

Silverberg, G., Dosi, G. and Orsenigo, L. (1988) 'Innovation, diversity and diffusion: a self-organisation model', *The Economic Journal*, 98(393): 1032–54.

Soete, L. and Turner, R. (1984) 'Technology diffusion and the rate of technical change', *The Economic Journal*, 94(375): 612–23.

Solow, R.M. (1956) 'A contribution to the theory of economic growth', *The Quarterly Journal of Economics*, 70(1): 65–94.

Solow, R.M. (1957) 'Technical change and the aggregate production function', *The Review of Economics and Statistics*, 39(3): 312–20.

Swan, T.W. (1956) 'Economic growth and capital accumulation', *Economic Record*, 32(2): 334–61.

The Economist (2016) 'Artificial intelligence: the return of the machinery question', Special Report, *The Economist*, 419(8995): 1–16.

THE INNOVATIVE ENVIRONMENT   2

```
                                      SCOPE AND OBJECTIVES
    •   The meaning and importance of an external innovative environment and the
        spaces of innovation.
    •   A critical appreciation of the key components of the innovative environment, and
        underpinning contextual, situational and embeddedness issues.
    •   Varied examples, common factors and the richness of differences.
    •   How economic value is derived from the social dimensions of an innovative
        environment.
```

INTRODUCTION

Discussions on the topic of an innovative environment help us to connect innovative people and innovative organisations to the contexts in which they demonstrate their innovativeness. We will argue in this chapter that the innovativeness of individuals and organisations is dependent on the circumstances, location, local connections, networks and value creation in and of a particular environment. In taking this argument forward we will aim to triangulate a model of innovation which proposes that:

(a) *innovative people* can be best found in innovative organisations (either their creation or those of others) in environments which support them both;

(b) *innovative organisations* are shaped and formed by innovative people in environments that are conducive to innovative outcomes; and

(c) *innovative environments* foster innovative people and innovative organisations, and ordinary environments are made innovative by people and organisations.

We explore the subjects of innovative organisations and innovative people in Chapters 5 and 7 respectively. In focusing on the third dimension – the innovative environment – in this chapter, we will draw on the literature covering the social and spatial dimensions of innovation, including regional studies and entrepreneurship. Any discussion on connections between different units of observation suggests that there are both social and economic forces at play in both spatial and temporal contexts. Innovation occurs uniquely in certain spaces and often in particular times depending upon the connections to which they refer. There are connections between social factors that support the innovation process and the institutional environment, the idea of double or mixed embeddedness as proposed by Martinelli (2002; 2004) and Kloosterman et al. (1999).

Environments for innovation are both internal to a firm and external to it and to others with which they compete and cooperate. The chapter on innovative organisations covers the arguments about environments specific to different firms, so we give attention in this chapter to the external environment and how that impacts on firms and their innovative activities.

NO ONE SPECIAL INNOVATIVE ENVIRONMENT: FROM NECESSITY TO OPPORTUNITY AND BACK AGAIN

Situations and circumstances shape innovators and entrepreneurs in different economic and social environments. In poor economies where there are limited opportunities for economic activity people can be pushed towards self-employment or setting up small-scale business operations. Jobs are scarce, and so the only alternative mode of survival and income generation is self-employment or small (often micro-level) business activity. In richer economies the offer of a range of opportunities between paid employment and business creation allows people to make decisions based on utility functions or sometimes out of a notion of continuous improvement (Mitra, 2012).

According to the Global Entrepreneurship Monitor (GEM) Reports, specific conditions create 'necessity'- or 'opportunity'-driven entrepreneurs. While the former are essentially a product of push factors in situations lacking choice, the latter are generally found in environments where there are numerous opportunities for innovation and entrepreneurship to flourish and provide many economic benefits. These are simplistic but powerful observations based on the idea of economic progression down one established pathway. It is questionable whether constant and universal circumstances of poverty prevail in some countries while the obverse is true in other nations. Regional variations within countries indicate that there are considerable differences in economic conditions between those regions. California or Boston cannot really be compared with Detroit in the USA; Gujarat in India is rich and prosperous while Bihar is not. Wuxi or Tianjin tell different stories from those of Tibet or Guizhou in China; Lagos offers a distinctive, vibrant business environment from Maiduguri in Nigeria.

It is easier to follow the tried and tested formula of measuring the capacity and capabilities of different environments according to weighted indices of achievement. Attempts to do so follow the arguments about benchmarking one environment with another (a country and/or a region), and the necessary adoption of particular policies and instruments to reach higher levels of innovation, realised by opportunities instead of necessities. There is no gainsaying that people and organisations seek better quality environments, or that governments and institutions are judged by their efforts in attaining better conditions for their citizens. It is, however, highly dubious to suggest that regions and countries can gradually move up the economic growth or social development ladders by pursuing directions adopted in other locales. It may not even be necessary to demonstrate social, economic and human progress by one definition or a single set of measures obtained in one specific environment. Arguing along these lines breaks down the 'necessity–opportunity' trade-offs (Mitra, 2012).

What generates opportunity in a particular situation may well be born out of necessity (take the example of the solar refrigerator in a tropical climate such as in India). What creates opportunities may not be necessary in specific circumstances (consider the numerous 'apps' that often add to our work burden rather than solving problems!). What emerges as an innovative outcome may have little to do with necessity, but may have something to do with changing lives in poor economic climates (take mobile telephony in various African countries). What is created as necessary for helping the disadvantaged and poor often provides for opportunities for well-developed enclaves (take the notebook computer created initially to help the poor in developing countries, but which actually makes money among the highly mobile community of young workers in Europe and North America). Innovation occurs widely; it offers different solutions to many problems in regions and societies. Consequently, new knowledge is created and disseminated across regions and countries disparately for different purposes.

DIFFERENT ENVIRONMENT AND DIFFERENT GEOGRAPHIES: HOW AND WHY INNOVATION OCCURS ACROSS VARIED SPACES

The fact that different circumstances give rise to innovative outcomes mean that innovation, however measured, does not occur systematically or uniformly across all regions. The evidence that researchers have picked up over the ages indicates that there are variations in the levels and rates of different types of innovation and that there are often concentrations or clusters of innovation. Special conditions prevail and influence innovation processes in varied environments. If so, we could argue that there may well be a geography of innovation. This raises the question of not simply the type or scale of innovation, but where innovation is done and how knowledge and skills for innovation are acquired and diffused or transferred from one place to another.

Interestingly, while a vast body of research on innovations in different countries or regions examines funding allocations, patents, R&D inputs and various unidimensional measures, it tends to miss out on the location, as in a city or a rural place where the measure of innovation can be tested. Understanding where innovation occurs, together with an insight into the wide dispersion of places of innovation, helps us to understand how innovation is created, acquired or shared (Polenske, 2007). Geography is indeed fundamental, not incidental to the innovation process itself: that one cannot understand innovation properly if one does not appreciate the central role of spatial proximity and concentration.

If one considers the production and circulation of new knowledge to be at the core of innovation then it is important to have a sound understanding of the nature of the different types of knowledge involved and their geographical tendencies. (Asheim and Gertler, 2006)

History provides us with rich examples of the geography of innovation, of the special quality of certain cities, regions and other agglomerations where different types of innovation made these places outstanding hubs of new knowledge creation. These innovations are made possible because of the interplay of various factors, including the identification of relevant technologies, social, cultural and behavioural issues, the critical use of data and information, and the absorptive capacity of people, their networks and institutions.

VIGNETTE 2.1   THE UNIQUE HISTORIC VALUE OF DATA, TECHNOLOGY AND INGENUITY IN AN ENVIRONMENT FOR INNOVATION

Let us go back to the dawn of early civilisation. In fact, innovation can be directly associated with the development of civilisation. Much of this development was connected with technological innovations. But progress is also linked to the acquisition of complex cognitive processes, and especially the abstract manipulation of data. Data manipulation, a much vaunted skill of our times (see the endless references to Big Data in academic research, public policy measures and advertisements by consulting organisations), has been instrumental in the development of urban society and the creation of objects, particularly for counting and accounting. These artefacts were associated with the emergence of the very first civilisation around 3300–3100 BC in Sumer, Mesopotamia. Clay tokens and writing on clay tablets document the importance for an administration to process large amounts of information in ever-greater abstraction (Schmandt-Besserat, 1992).

At that time, power in the form of accumulated capital lay in the hands of the priests. They could use the tokens and the clay tablets to levy taxes and organise forced labour as part of what could be described as a 'temple economy'. This economy generated long-distance trade and fostered key industries such as metallurgy (Moorey, 1985), which in turn engendered innovations in crafts through the use of metal tools such as metal saws that could cut circular shapes out of wooden planks, leading to the invention of the wheel (Littauer and Crauwel, 1979). Technology and innovation have long had a working relationship with war. While 'metal value added' meant more metal weapons which changed the course of fighting and conquest, the clay tokens and tablets could be used for the administration of war nearby and in faraway places (Algaze, 1993). At another level the temple economy enabled the development of new cognitive skills, changing the way people thought about life, products, services and work (Schmandt-Besserat, 1996), while securing institutional control for the priesthood over labour and the production of real goods; in other words, the means, processes and outcomes of innovation.

The early ecosystem of innovation left a rich legacy as clay tokens of various shapes were used as part of a system for storing/communicating information since about 8000 BC and the beginning of agriculture. A single token represented one unit of merchandise, such as a cone and a sphere, each representing a small and a large measure of grain, and an ovoid for a jar of oil. Big Data is an abstract concept and it is this abstraction that gives it value today as much as it did in BC times. It meant that day-to-day commodities could be valued across the community. By 'translating daily-life commodities into miniature, mostly geometric counters, [they removed] the data from its context and the knowledge from the knower' (Schmandt-Besserat, 1999).

The rise and splendour of most Near Eastern civilisations were to a great extent predicated upon these artefacts for counting and writing. The Sumerians were followed by the Indus Valley civilisations at around 2500 BC, when the latter devised a script that had no links with the Mesopotamian-like tokens recovered in pre-Harappan sites (Possehl, 1996). In the Greek civilisation, researchers found Minoan clay counters shaped in the form of miniature vessels. In North Africa, Egypt imitated the Sumerians by producing a complete system of writing based on the rebus principle (Ray, 1986). 'These examples imply that the multiple cognitive steps from concrete to abstract data manipulation occurred only once in the Near East' (Schmandt-Besserat, 1999).

Source: Adapted from Schmandt-Besserat (1999)

SITUATIONS, PLACES AND THEIR UNIQUE FEATURES

There are two vital points to consider over and above many others in the case presented in the vignette above. The first point refers to the last quote and is about the uniqueness of a form of new knowledge creation and a process of harnessing technology through the use of numerous cognitive steps of data manipulation, from the concrete to the level of abstraction. The idea of this process occurring at a certain time might indicate that this could happen only once. The uniqueness of that time and place in the special environment gives meaning to the argument about specific innovations occurring at certain times in particular habitus.

However, the universality of the innovation process can be found in the second central point made in the first quote, namely that of removing knowledge from the knower. The great value of innovation lies not so much in the creation of new knowledge, but in its dissemination and fundamentally in its application in artefacts, products, services and organisations, for the use of many and not simply the holder of the original knowledge, whether that be a person or a place. This is an important consideration because we may find innovations occurring due to certain special factors in a region at a particular point in time, but their significance often stretches across time and place, albeit in different forms.

The Sumerian and other Near Eastern historical lessons also highlight the powerful case of multiple connections or intersections of people (priests, artisans, general labour, abstract thought, generic) and computational technologies (metals, metallurgy, clay tokens and tablets) and institutions (the priesthood, taxation, war) in special circumstances in unique places.

What may have been achieved through imposition could also be regarded as a reflection of the prevailing modes and practices of the time. It is doubtful whether imposition alone could have enabled creative outcomes; the capacity to absorb different ideas and then to implement their new incarnations is more likely to have been prompted by a process of sharing knowledge and practice among people.

We can see differences in various environments and identify the mores and practices as they evolve in those environments. Let us look at another example, namely Florence in Europe in the fifteenth century. A banking family, the Medicis, had a different notion of banking and innovation than those that we know of in the first decade of this century. The Medicis relied less on complex algorithms and more on funding creative people from a wide variety of backgrounds and disciplines, which included sculptors, scientists, poets, philosophers, painters, architects, and not forgetting that other source of creative talent – financiers. When this disparate talent group converged in Florence they learnt from each other and created a unique, creatively explosive environment of new ideas that spawned the Italian Renaissance. They created what Johansson (2004) refers to as the Medici effect: that is, the effect of an explosion of remarkable innovations occurring as a result of the convergence or intersection of different cultures, domains, disciplines and insights in emergent ecosystems.

The great sociologist Emile Durkheim had another expression – 'collective effervescence' – resulting from social interaction and the power of new institutions and new values in society. The effervescent spirit enables a new dynamic to take root in society, causing radical social, political and economic change. Revolutions, such as the French, American and the Industrial ones, are examples of such change, as are, perhaps, the less tumultuous but highly fraught happenings of our times: the Arab Spring movements in Egypt and Tunisia, and the activities of the Occupy movement. The outcome of such change movements is characterised by the connection between considerations of social change in and out of institutions and the idea of social movement, which helps to create social, moral and political entrepreneurs (Becker, 1963; Jenkins, 1983, cited in Swedberg, 2000).

What then are the forces or factors that make intersections and unique competitive capabilities possible? People and places produce knowledge, they learn and create spaces for learning, and they form institutions and systems so that their environments form crucibles of innovation. Let us start with knowledge and learning with particular reference to geography, or, more precisely, the different spaces of knowledge creation and learning.

SPACES OF KNOWLEDGE AND LEARNING

What allows spaces and regions around the world to connect is the availability of what is referred to as explicit or codified knowledge – the form of knowledge that can be shared or traded easily through manuals, published research, free exchanges of know-how at conferences, technology transfer and observation. Commonality and tradable knowledge are good for universal development, but their ubiquity is not conducive to demonstrating uniqueness driving competition. So if space and geography are important considerations then they need to accommodate unique value through unique forms of knowledge creation that are not easily codifiable. According to some writers, such uniqueness for innovation and value creation is provided by tacit knowledge (Maskell and Malmberg, 1999; Pavitt, 2002).

Tacit knowledge is what Polanyi (1958; 1967) describes as 'that which we know but cannot tell'. Attributable to Polanyi, the concept of 'tacit knowledge' probably has earlier antecedents in a fifth-century Indian, Bharthari: 'the expert's knowledge of the genuineness of precious stones and coins, incommunicable to others, is born of practice and not of reasoning' (Ayer, 1965: 46). Referred to as knowledge which cannot be coded or exchanged, especially over any distance, tacit knowledge is also associated with procedural knowledge or what the Greeks referred to as 'techne' or practical knowledge, as opposed to 'episteme' or the knowledge about things (Noteboom, 2000).

Tacit knowledge provides much of the basis for the way we interact with people and situations. It is embodied in people and in social and institutional contexts from where it derives its meaning, rather than in any codified form or in tangible objects. In most cases it is difficult to transfer such knowledge between people or places, and it is its context-oriented nature that makes it 'sticky' in spatial terms (Gertler, 2003).

Nonaka and Takeuchi (1995) offer some suggestions for developing mechanisms for transferring tacit learning and knowledge to general situations. They refer to the idea of shared space (or *ba* in Japanese) as being central to the relationships of knowledge creation. In this space, knowledge is generated through a spiralling process of exchange and interactions between tacit and codified or explicit knowledge, including:

- 'socialisation';
- 'externalisation';
- 'combination'; and
- 'internalisation'.

'Socialisation' between people helps to make the sharing of such knowledge possible, and this form of interaction can take place within the firm or outside with those not directly connected to the firm. 'Externalisation' occurs when tacit knowledge is expressed for transmission to others, and 'combination' takes place when either tacit knowledge is transformed through sharing into explicit knowledge, or explicit knowledge is converted to even more complex knowledge through a mix of tacit and explicit forms. Finally, 'internalisation' is a manifestation of the conversion of newly created knowledge into the organisation's collectively understood and accepted tacit knowledge base (Mitra, 2012).

How is such interaction and knowledge creation achieved? It is made possible through the availability of shared space, or more precisely four types of shared space – 'face-to-face', 'peer-to-peer', 'group-to-group' and 'on-site' – with each space making possible the conversion of an individual's knowledge to a shared platform of knowledge for a group or organisation, and the conversion of the latter to a form understood by the former (Nonaka and Takeuchi, 1995).

Knowledge requires functional usage in order for it to generate any value as measured in terms of new products and services. Both tacit and explicit knowledge contribute to such value creation and one of the key instruments that make this possible is learning.

LEARNING AND PATH DEPENDENCY TO CREATE NEW KNOWLEDGE AND TO INNOVATE IN ANY GIVEN SPACE

Learning is not just concerned with specific activities. It is also connected to or embedded in social communities. This means that learning implies becoming a social partner in innovative activities. Learning from this perspective suggests being able to be involved in new activities, to perform new tasks and functions, to master new understandings as part of and within a socially constructed environment (Lave and Wenger, 1991). These activities can be seen as part of broader systems of relations in which they have meaning (Lave and Wenger, 1991). Both learning and knowledge are, therefore, not decontextualised, abstract or general (Tennant, 1997), but are situated in a specific context and are at the heart of the creation of a new organisation or the development of a new product or a service. What happens in these communities of practice is 'situated learning'.

A social activity suggests the involvement of and connectivity of various social actors or economic entities,[1] all involved in a form of situated learning. They include firms of customers, suppliers and distributors, public agencies (policy makers and support services) that include development agencies, science and technology parks, universities and research centres. There is an expectation of the flow of knowledge, of spillovers from one source to another, and of interactions between these actors who, as a consequence, create a 'learning economy' (Lundvall and Johnson, 1994). The consequence of these flows is the production of new knowledge necessary for innovation. These interactions and flows can, therefore, be understood in terms of the knowledge production function (KPF) as formalised by Griliches (1979) and the knowledge spillover theory. Chapter 1 provides a detailed account of the knowledge production function and knowledge spillover theories. Readers are therefore urged to recapitulate these ideas by referring to that chapter.

The corollary of 'stickiness' and social interactions is learning which helps to acquire what Kenneth Arrow referred to as economic knowledge (1962). The capacity of an economy to accumulate economic knowledge is dependent on its ability to innovate and also to absorb knowledge from elsewhere through socialisation, externalisation, combination and internalisation at both the national level in terms of how technology is diffused in a country (Grossman and Helpman, 1990; Coe and Helpman, 1995; Keller, 2004) and at the regional level as found in the regional science literature (Jaffe et al., 1993; Audretsch and Feldman, 1996; Anselin et al., 1997; 2000).

PROXIMITY FACTORS

SPATIAL PROXIMITY

A large body of literature (see Chapter 1) suggests that the process of exchange, interactions and combinations occurs best under conditions of geographical proximity, where firms, institutions, talented people and support services are set up close to each other. This is because knowledge spillover appears to have geographical boundaries (Jaffe, 1989; Audretsch and Stephan, 1996; Anselin et al., 2000). The benefits from technological activity and knowledge transfer arise from firms and other organisations being located close to each other. Knowledge is traded and deemed pecuniary because an economic value is attached to it, or externalities are at work allowing knowledge to spill over from universities to firms, from firm to firm and across different services.

Proponents of learning environments and learning regions (Lundvall and Johnson, 1994; Florida, 1995; Lundvall and Maskell, 2000) have argued that knowledge, and especially tacit knowledge, does not travel easily. The process of transmission is underpinned by cognitive and social codes of communication, shared practices made possible because of personal knowledge, and a common institutional environment. Learning by doing and learning by interacting are made possible by user–producer interactions, where users provide 'tacit and proprietary, codifiable knowledge to producers in order to enable the latter to devise innovative solutions to users' practical problems', and indirectly with customers (Asheim and Gertler, 2006).

Together these actions generate social assets which tend to evolve gradually over time because of path-dependent development (Adyalot, 1986; Camagni, 1991; David, 1994) and the emergence of 'routines' (Nelson, 1994).

INNOVATIVE MILIEUS

The evolutionary notions have led to the creation of innovative milieus, 'a set of territorial relationships encompassing in a coherent way a production system, different economic and social actors, a specific culture and a representation system, and generating a collective learning process' (Camagni, 1991: 130). The Groupe de Recherche Européen sur les Milieux Innovateurs (the GREMI group), used the notion of path dependency to explain why vertically disintegrated, generally smaller firms in Europe (referred to as Third Italy) and in the USA were good at specialising in certain technological and industrial fields, often clustering together as part of a collective learning environment. Their coming together as a coherent group of firms in a particular space helped to foster newness (products and processes). Collective learning could help to lower transaction costs and enable better coordination among firms. In dense networks of firms it is easier to transfer information about specialist functions and practices and develop a common culture of trust and routines. They make possible the creative use and accumulation of intangible and uncodified knowledge, and the resulting knowledge spillover plus the involvement of supporting local authorities, research and development facilities, and industry networks, provide for local comparative advantage. This advantage manifests itself through a process of agglomeration of firms in particular regions enjoying the benefits of the spillover effects and what Arthur (1994) refers to as 'increasing returns' or the continuing higher marginal value derived from every additional unit of production.

The real benefits of proximity and spillover effects lie in the way different organisations derive value from them. Chapter 15 provides insights into and explanations of how large, medium and small firms appropriate resources to innovate, and there is not much point in repeating the ideas here. Suffice it to say that there are different ways in which knowledge is understood, appropriate and produced in different organisations. Knowledge as a factor of production differs from the traditional ones of labour and physical capital, and not just in terms of how it is valued and how it is traded, or indeed how it spills over.

We appreciate that path dependency is an historical outcome as learning, networking, interactions, and fundamentally trust and local tacit knowledge evolve over time. Often, the benefits of such dependency, as outlined above, have become major barriers over time too. Writers such as Grabher (1993) have pointed out that path dependency can cause problems with adaptability to new technologies and ideas, the 'not invented here' syndrome which prevents new ways of doing things being absorbed because of path-dependent learning capabilities. Markets for specialist products can become saturated, while diminishing returns on investment in technologies can limit productivity gains. Cost sensitivity becomes the norm for doing business as opposed to innovation, and if larger firms are in operation their progressive inclination for vertical integration leads to oligopolistic structures which tend to hamper innovation. This can result in lock-in or inertia, or what Olson (1982) referred to as 'institutional sclerosis'. Old industrial regions such as those in the West Midlands in the UK, the Ruhr area in Germany and the textile industries of Lyon in France fell into the 'trap of rigid specialisation' (Boschma and Lambooy, 1999).

NON-SPATIAL PROXIMITY

Other writers have argued that non-local factors may be equally important for producing innovations. Krugman (1991) has argued that since knowledge flows are in reality invisible, it is difficult to find the necessary paper trails. Boschma (2005) has emphasised that other factors, such as cross-regional or cross-border institutional, social and technological links, can overcome the limitations of spatial boundaries and offer non-spatial benefits. Here cognitive, relational and cooperative ties come into play and act as the main drivers of knowledge production and diffusion (Carrincazeaux and Coris, 2011).

What we obtain from the arguments above is that proximity matters, but such proximity may not necessarily be spatial in scope and character. Other a-spatial forms could also allow for knowledge transmission and innovation through institutional and technological connectivity, networking and socialisation. Moreover, proximity factors can generate negative externalities and a form of socialised dysfunctionalism leading to 'lock-in'. Pure geography may not provide answers to either the questions about the economic value of innovation or the social and cognitive dimensions of the innovation process (Corrado and Fingleton, 2012; Mitra, 2012). In other words, proximity and the benefits of spillover effects (or indeed their negative outcomes) need to be understood in geographical, technological, social and organisational terms.

The nexus of spatial, technological, social, cultural and organisational aspects of innovation in an environment reveals special features of regions. Making these connections possible are entrepreneurs who capitalise on opportunities that are created through this nexus.

VIGNETTE 2.2   THE INNOVATION NEXUS AND ENTREPRENEURIAL OPPORTUNITY

Take Wenzhou on China's south-eastern coast. It is surrounded by mountains and has relied on trade for many centuries, not least because it has little arable land. Wenzhou started flourishing from the 1970s and has emerged as a model of small low-cost manufacturing and private enterprise. It is known for making electrical switches, water valves, shoes, buttons and the vast majority of the world's cigarette lighters.

In tracing the origin of the Wenzhou model of private enterprise we find that the concept of the 'household contract responsibility' was well established in China in the 1980s. An organisational innovation of an operation form, 'guahu' enabled various kinds of household, industrial and commercial activities to be legitimised from their previous underground status. Parris (1993) described such firms as being connected to established collectives or state units, paying a fee for the use of their name, stationery, letters of introduction, bank account numbers and the payment of taxes. This alternative form of enterprise building was also to be found in 'red hat' (*hongmaozi*) enterprises, which were registered as collectives with administrative offices of the neighbourhood committee or the local village. These small enterprises which were widespread in Wenzhou in the 1980s sold a range of goods from handicrafts to low-technology-based small commodities.

The small commodity-based enterprises learned to innovate through imitation, while the local government supported family industry through innovative economic models such as the 'guahu' operational system. The local economy was protected, but the household entrepreneurs also learnt to reduce the cost of trading and generate higher levels of income (Mau and Furan, 2005).

However, at the beginning of this decade the economic environment took a battering. Weak demand for manufactured goods in overseas markets, especially in the USA and Europe, as well as rising wage and material costs had a telling and disastrous effect on the cluster of firms in the city. Such a downturn is common in many other regions, especially across developing economies dependent on their manufactured goods being sold in North American and European markets during the recession.

There is, however, a specific local factor that has probably had a much bigger adverse impact on Wenzhou than the global whirlwind of the recession. This unique Wenzhou factor is that of private lending. The local tradition of private lending backs private enterprise and this connection has flourished over the years, mainly because formal, institutional loans are generally made by Chinese banks and preferably to larger state-owned enterprises which are backed by the central government. Private lending, including peer-to-peer lending with Chinese characteristics, has acted as

(Continued)

(Continued)

the acceptable and most useful resource for private enterprises looking for non-bureaucratic and more informal forms of credit and financial support. It is reported that local investors, which include a good proportion of the businesses in the city, have been the beneficiaries of high-interest loans, giving them returns of up to 60%! However, legitimate forms of private lending have come under considerable strain because of the Chinese government's drive to control inflation in recent times. This has restricted bank credit but has also had the opposite effect of pushing up demand for underground loans. Underground loan supply generated an annualised return of 34.5% on loans attracting a 2.5% monthly rate of return. This turnaround has threatened the local economy, but has also affected enterprises across China as many of these Wenzhou investors have penetrated investment right across the country. As reported by Zachmann in *Time* in 2011, the *Shanghai Daily* referred to the Wenzhou financial malaise meltdown as 'China's sub prime crisis'.

The sub-prime crisis analogy was befitting of a situation where high-interest loans were sustaining real estate projects, almost in the same way that that the real estate market in the west was affected by the same infamous network of private lending and real estate development. The Chinese government estimated that almost 90% of Wenzhou households had borrowed money from private lenders (and 60% of all Wenzhou businesses). It is not difficult to understand why problems were compounded when borrowers stopped repaying or could not do so. Innovators like Hu Fulin, President of the eyeglass manufacturer Xintai Group, fled to the USA with debts of over $300 million! In the meantime lenders started hoarding as much money as they could as the Wenzhou bubble burst.

Wenzhou remains heavily in debt, and although the city streets are jammed with traffic, the city is at risk of defaulting on its loans, according to Nomura Holdings.

Nomura has found 30 provincial authorities and 265 cities, especially third- and fourth-tier cities, to have high credit risks, and Mizuho Securities Asia has calculated that China's regional liabilities are somewhere in the region of 25 trillion yuan ($4 trillion), which is larger than Germany's economy (Curran, 2015). It remains to be seen whether China's Wenzhou is able to avoid the Detroit syndrome and save its innovative governmental and private enterprise from defaulting on all fronts.

Sources: Adapted from Zachmann (2011); Mau and Furan (2005); Curran (2015)

What can we take away from the Wenzhou story? Perhaps the two most important aspects are that of the unique culture of private lending and the mushrooming of household enterprises in the 1980s. Much of this was supported by the state with its unique organisational or economic innovations. This public sector innovation was leveraged and capitalised by the ingenuity of these household and other entrepreneurs. Private lending weaved its way into this milieu when banks concentrated their lending to the state-owned enterprises backed by central government. Despite the meltdown story of recent times which resonates with those of Detroit, and regions in Spain, Italy and Iceland, the developmental story is rendered unique by those special features of government-led innovation, private lending and household enterprise. They provide evidence of the social processes underpinning the varied forms of regional innovation. These stories are difficult to capture through economic models comparing regions using homogenised statistical models, thus preventing us from understanding those nuances that shape the particular components of innovation in different regions.

What we also understand is that social processes underlie many economic outcomes. These processes do not necessarily follow linear paths because chance and disruption can play their own part in obtaining particular advantages for regions at certain times. Chance events could occur as a result of triggers that are available in an environment, due to previous developmental patterns, or they could be accidental because it is uncertain where and how new industries may emerge in different spaces. It is also difficult to explain which set of triggers (e.g. seeking solutions to technical problems or labour shortages) results in specific innovations. Advocates of chaos theory would probably reflect on the 'butterfly effect' to account for random, ungeneralisable events (Boschma and Lambooy, 1999). Yet another dose of complexity can be added if we reflect without too much effort on how globalisation has added to both the uncertainty and consolidation of specialisation in different environments.

The spatially directed theoretical explanations behind the formation or decline of innovative environments emphasise the critical significance of agglomerations of industries and support service organisations in particular regions. External or exogenous factors or their internal and endogenous counterparts have caught the imagination of researchers. Research conducted in particular environments where the idea of the 'region' is defined in terms of path dependent and evolving historical institutions tends to emphasise endogenous factors. These appear to coalesce sometimes and take the form of clusters in specific spatial environments.

CLUSTERED SPACES OF INNOVATION

That spaces and environments acquire different shapes and build their own configurations for innovation is now well established. One such popular configuration is that of clusters which tend to have a presence in specific geographical regions. Clusters represent the advantages of the agglomeration process in particular regions, and the numerous explanations of the features, characteristics and values of clusters have attempted to elucidate the benefits for business in regions where firms and institutions cluster. Clusters constitute a critical mass of interconnected firms and institutions in a specific field where proximity to customers and suppliers offers shared advantages through the aggregation of expertise, specialised resources, networking, and intellectual and technology spillovers, as characterised by Porter (1990), Glaeser et al. (1992), Enright (1999), Audretsch and Stephan (2002), Arzaghi and Henderson (2008), Ellison et al. (2010) and various others.

Many of the ingredients of innovation in geographical space referred to earlier, such as knowledge spillovers, inter-firm relationships, interdependencies between forms and people and use of functional resources, together with tacit and explicit forms of knowledge exchange, are typical features of regional clusters. These features generate social connectivity and much heralded social capital for the region.

Together they are all supposed to contribute to innovation. But Porter's concept of clustering does not necessarily explain the particular and continuous forms of emergence of high-growth firms and their innovations. Gaining competitive advantage through specialisation and benefiting from knowledge spillovers as a result of proximity is one thing (as in the collocation of metal-based industries of jewellery, guns and ammunition, coins and motor cars and car components in the West Midlands from the nineteenth and early twentieth centuries), but sustaining a constant flow of commercialisation of new technologies, and regular entry into and the creation of new global markets is another issue (Mitra, 2012). Where this set of new opportunities and new commercial gains obtains, as if in a constant flow, is what Engel (2015) defines as clusters of innovation (COIs).

COIs may be similar to the Porterian cluster in that they refer to the agglomeration of similar or related businesses, but they are conceptually and qualitatively different because the concentration of talent and the spillover effects lead to more than just specialised competitive advantage. In these COIs we find both convergence of technologies and the divergence of firms from within (as in a move away from the original business concentration) and in disparate (not similar or related) sectors.

Engel (2015) refers to the emergence of high-growth biotech firms in the midst of semiconductor and computer firms in Silicon Valley rather than in the pharmaceutical business cluster of Philadelphia in the USA. The various mutations and cross-fertilisation of actors in the cluster suggest that it is not so much the specialisation advantages gained by individual firms that can explain why innovation occurs so rapidly and systematically, but rather the stages of development of the constituent parts of the cluster, their behaviour and the relationships between them (Engel and del-Palacio, 2009).

So we can examine COIs in terms of:

(a) the various local ingredients or component parts of the cluster;
(b) the behaviour of the component parts; and
(c) the nature and scope of the relationships between the component parts.

INGREDIENTS AND COMPONENT PARTS OF A COI

One way of understanding a COI is to identify and examine the component parts of an archetypal COI. Engel (2015) refers to Silicon Valley, building on previous work by Porter, while others suggests a three-tiered structure starting with three critical parts made up of three key stakeholders, followed by a set of four major institutions, and then by two sets of important support services, as shown in Table 2.1.

In understanding the roles of each of these tiers of stakeholders, recognition needs to be made of the often overlapping functions and ties between what appear as discrete agents of cluster development. One could argue that there is nothing distinctive here when reflecting on previous insights into clusters. These older insights have indicated that the consequence of innovative evolution has resulted in clusters attracting public and private finance; chambers of commerce and trade associations generating commercial market research; regional government providing industry-specific infrastructure; and local educational institutions undertaking industry-specific training

TABLE 2.1

Tiers	Components of clusters of innovation			
1	Entrepreneurs	Venture capital investors	Major corporations, strategic investors, R&D centres, potential acquires	
2	Universities	Management	Professions	Government
3	Large pools of private capital		Public stock markets	

Sources: Adapted from Engel (2014; 2015)

and research. This combination of integrated and leveraged activity is often at the heart of innovation and collective learning, as the literature on innovation highlights (Malecki, 1997; Rosenberg, 1982). It is only when we start looking at the behaviour of and the relationships between the component parts that we begin to notice the differences in the descriptions of and arguments about business clusters and COIs.

THE BEHAVIOUR OF AND RELATIONSHIPS BETWEEN THE COMPONENT PARTS OF COIS

Engel (2015) refers in particular to the kind of behaviour that supports and encourages the development of high-impact potential entrepreneurial ventures, ones that continually seek new opportunities and create new ventures or change their organisational make-up to work with new technologies, products and services, sometimes without regard to resource limitations. These firms manage to sustain turnover and employment growth together with new product development. The resource constraints are overcome quickly as venture capital is attracted to these high-risk firms that prospect for high returns on their investment. Certain other complementary behavioural characteristics include a 'heightened mobility' of finance, human capital, intellectual property and information, and an affinity for collaborative behaviour and a sharing of common values, often reinforced by recursive entrepreneurial activity by the same set of serial entrepreneurs setting up different ventures or financing them in their new guise as business angels or venture capitalists. These behavioural patterns define the nature of the relationships that are forged over time.

The gradual establishment of relationships suggests that successful clusters evolve organically. Organic evolution is not simply a natural process enshrined in luck or good fortune. It entails considerable endeavour on the part of entrepreneurs and the nexus of clustered stakeholders. They have to persuade, socialise, bargain and reciprocate with others to create and maintain relationships. So alongside the spillover effect from new technologies and R&D, the attitudes and behaviour of these stakeholders coupled with their perception of clustering benefits are key considerations.

The constant entrepreneurial motion provides for a regular flow of small, innovative firms. But most small firms suffer from resource constraints while demonstrating an ability to generate a disproportionate share of innovations, especially in regional contexts where there is a presence of larger firms (Acs and Audretsch, 1990). Contrary to received wisdom, small firms, especially high-technology firms in conventional industries, in, for example, the UK, have a greater R&D intensity than their counterparts in the high-technology industries (Hughes and Wood, 1999), which is complemented by a greater reliance on flows of information through collaboration and networking among firms, including R&D and information systems at the local level. Different forms of networked alliances and entrepreneurial endeavour help to create a diverse industry base and this diverse base allows for greater collaboration, new firm creation and innovations (Feldman and Audretsch, 1999; Audretsch and Stephan, 2002).

But when and how do these relationships of innovation occur?

STAGES OF DEVELOPMENT OF COIS

Understanding cluster-based specialisation helps us to locate the proximity of the different players, but it does not explain how firms establish close relationships in that environment. We can assume that these relationships are in place, though all relationships are formed over time and in response to a set of needs and incentives. If these relationships are established over a period of time then we could also assume that there are stages to such development, stages which are particularly conducive to innovation occurring in those spaces. In each of these stages different relationships are forged, with many of them linked to forms of tacit or explicit learning as firms move from one form of organisational practice to another to create new portfolios of products and services.

In their study of Italian industrial districts (IDs), Carbonara and Mitra (2001) found that the evolutionary process of most IDs manifests itself in three stages:

1. the start-up stage of 'formation';
2. the 'development' stage; and
3. the growth stage of 'maturity'.

'Craft-like' manufacturing systems localised in a specific geographical area characterise early-stage cluster formation, which is then followed by networking processes among firms that help to implement an integrated system of production activities in accordance with the 'flexible specialisation' model (Piore and Sabel, 1984). The ensuing relationships among the networked actors foster technical–operative, tacit and informal knowledge which grows rapidly in the local area.

Capello (1999) argues that the growth of technical–operative knowledge, supported by processes of learning by doing and learning by using, all as part of a form of 'dynamic socialisation', results in 'widespread innovative capacity' (WIC) (Bellandi, 1989; 2000). Some care has to be taken when describing such possibilities in clusters. The description offered above is most likely to prevail in static economic conditions. Recessionary conditions can play havoc with these complex and dense relationships when markets dry out and when there is an over-reliance on 'locked-in' skill sets or forms of knowledge associated with traditional production processes.

COIs offer a way out of the 'lock-in' problem for two vital reasons: their entrepreneurial capability and their affinity for global collaborations based on a strong, globally cultural perspective (Engel, 2014; 2015). The entrepreneurial capability provides for the necessary social and economic surplus generated by the mobilisation of resources to create new firms as vehicles for the pursuit of innovative opportunity. So for innovation to have an effective economic outcome, there is this critical necessity for the constant supply of new firms. This development explains why the prospect of venture capital firms and business angels is more likely to take root in Silicon Valley in the USA, in Cambridge and London in the UK, and now increasingly in Bangalore in India and Shanghai in China. These financial power-houses supporting innovation do not feature so prominently in typical Italian IDs.

INTERNATIONALISATION AND GLOBAL CONNECTIVITY OF COIS

The second special COI feature is the cultural disposition and economic practice of internationalisation and global connectivity. Engel and del-Palacio (2009; 2011), in their examination of global COIs, have referred to international linkages in terms of 'weak ties, durable bonds and covalent bonds'. The most successful groups of entrepreneurs in Silicon Valley are those from the Indian, Chinese and Israeli immigrant communities. These communities have established their own professional associations and linked up with networks in their own countries of origin, partly through family connections and partly through alumni associations. They create opportunities for entrepreneurial activity in their 'home' countries alongside their adopted home in the USA, emerging as a new band of transnational entrepreneurs situated in their dual habitus (see the section 'Transnational Innovators and Entrepreneurs' in Chapter 5). They have helped to create a new concept of brain circulation (Saxenian, 1994; 1996; 2005) that accounts for their roving economic presence in their dual habitus.

Weak tie-based relationships enhance the mobility of asset transfers between countries, contractual relationships and the reduction of transaction costs. These outcomes in turn create 'durable bonds' which, together with the typical advantages that accrue from aggregation (economies of scale and scope, access to suppliers and customers), also establish platforms for creating and sharing adaptive knowledge. They enable these bonds to connect COIs across geographies. When individuals and organisations create and maintain a presence in both clusters they act as 'covalent bonds'. Businesses in one cluster become embedded in the functions and processes of businesses in the other cluster, enabling new relationships based on trust, reciprocity and relatively easy information exchange (Engel, 2015). Examples of such connected COIs include Silicon Valley and the Israeli high-tech sector, and the Silicon Valley and Bangalore software clusters.

Clusters are not without problems. Their growth leads to serious traffic and other physical congestion problems (lack of space, power supply) as any visitor to Bangalore, Shanghai or even the Valley will confirm, an over-concentration of skills and expertise in a narrow range of areas, the 'lock-in' factor which impedes new knowledge flows and absorption and accelerates the decline in relative expertise and competitive advantage (Mitra, 2012). Of equal importance is the fact that not all clusters evolve in the same way and in the equivalent period of time. Contexts matter and so do the challenges that face each of these contexts.

CONTEXTUAL DIFFERENTIATION AND UNIQUENESS OF COIS

One can create an index of clusters and regions and even establish a hierarchy of COIs. Such an exercise will not yield any value beyond a sense of superiority for

TABLE 2.2 Varied environments for clusters of innovation

Country	Particular region	Context	Challenges	Interventions
Europe:				
Germany	Munich	Historical entrepreneurial boom in the 1800s and after the Second World War; emergence of global firms such as BMW, Siemens and Allianz	Despite Germany's continuing economic prosperity, Munich has not been able to sustain high-growth start-ups	Government-financed initiative at Techinsche Universität Munchen (TUM) plus donor-supported but self-financing entrepreneurship centre (UnternehmerTUM) provide spin-out support, entrepreneurship education, seed financing, industry and global linkages Four Munich universities formed a consortium (4Entrepreneurship) sharing best practice and offering training and incubation programmes to 100,000 university students in Munich
Middle East:				
Israel	Overall	Strongest high-tech cluster outside USA exhibiting entrepreneurial culture; skilled immigrant population; government defence and civilian R&D funding; and local venture capital industry	Highly susceptible to global economic downturns because of reliance on exports and foreign capital. Retention problem as best start-ups migrate overseas or are bought out early. Lack of 'bridge' capital prevents creation of larger domestic firms plus recent drop in government R&D expenditure	Expectations of government intervention to expand higher education budget, diversification of high-tech sector, reduction of risks for growth of larger firms

Country	Particular region	Context	Challenges	Interventions
Asia:				
Japan	Overall	Like Germany's post-war birth and growth of large organisations, such as Panasonic, Toyota, Canon, Sony and Honda	Two lost decades of last 20 years with minimal economic growth, continuous recessions and absence of new innovative firms partly attributed to local culture and educational, legal and financial factors	National government identifies entrepreneurship as vehicle to restart economy and universities as drivers for innovation in the 2000s; universities given intellectual property rights and made financially independent (à la Bah-Doyle Act in the USA) University of Tokyo has developed the Innovation and Entrepreneurship Office to facilitate entrepreneurship education, technology transfer and seed funding partners with private donors to create incubation facility
Latin America:				
Colombia and Mexico	Medellin and Monterey	Overexploitation of resources with low-value return, high levels of corruption and poor legal infrastructure, lack of trust, unthinking transfer of development models from elsewhere; indifference to social welfare and environmental safeguards	Two leading cities of industrial and commercial importance in the twentieth century destroyed by drug cartel warfare (1980s and mid-2000s, respectively), exodus of talent and capital, and high levels of corruption	In Medellin, the Colombian military disbanded drug militias in 2002-5; new partnerships of city government, universities and private industry to create industrial district with research technology park; public investment in public transport and services. Citigroup chose Medellin as 'most innovative city in the world' In Monterrey, government investment in public safety, infrastructure and job development; new initiative with the private sector to link and align stakeholders with needs to knowledge-based economy

Source: Adapted from Engel (2009; 2015)

those who set the standard for such an index. What may, however, be revealing and useful for local policy mediation is local organisational activity, such as networks, and identification of international ties of relevance to the region. Table 2.2 is an extract from an exercise carried out in the USA by 20 entrepreneurship educators, researchers, industry practitioners and policy makers from all over the world, and who considered how the Silicon Valley ecosystem applied to their own regions. The table does not provide for any ranking as measured against the success of Silicon Valley; rather it explains the specific contexts, challenges and interventions for each of the selected environments.

These snippets from Engel's more comprehensive analysis of COI-type environments show how difficult it is to adapt one model of innovation-based growth (in this case, clusters of innovation drawn from the Silicon Valley example). Different environments need to build on local strengths and address local problems directly, including political, economic and social issues. A direct initiative for high-tech start-ups or the attraction of R&D institutions may not be appropriate in some places, but creating an infrastructure for stakeholder involvement and alignment with new knowledge creation could be seen to be more relevant in the first instance. The table makes no reference to African countries or regions in that vast continent. However, there are very robust signs of novel forms of innovative activity that have both historical roots evinced in the way people in communities overcome economic odds and changing patterns through the unique adaption of new mobile technology, as found in the unique story of local cash remittances supported by the M-Pesa mobile technology and the M-Kopa solar technology stories.

In essence, in regions that accommodate COIs, we find a combination of innovation and entrepreneurial activities that emerges out of a complex set of social and economic relationships. Part of the emergence is that of the cluster itself, as a unit of analysis of a form of organisational innovation. The necessary structures, processes, talent and institutions that come together in different ways may not be replicated in other areas. This is because people's means of earning their livelihoods, improving their habitat and obtaining social respect is made possible through collective endeavour and learning processes situated in the problems and issues affecting their lives in their environment. Regionally-based organisational innovation is then a function of the region, its people and institutions, including that of government policy.

THE ROLE OF GOVERNMENT AND PUBLIC POLICY

Only meagre reference has been made so far to the role and functions of government in building or enhancing the innovative environment. It would, however, be entirely wrong to assume that government's role is that of a 'back seat driver' or at best a purely arm's-length facilitator creating broad-based infrastructure or benign policy instruments to support innovation. There is plenty of evidence – stretching from the heartland of private entrepreneurial activity in the USA to new, smart, urban environments in Europe and to small and distant regions – of the importance of direct and indirect government intervention. Examples include the direct action of the government in the redesign of an entire new urban district in Barcelona through the 22@project, the 100 Smart Cities Mission in India, the financing of advanced new technology development by Apple by the US government, and direct intervention in the attempts to eradicate and replace drug cartels with triple-helix-like innovation infrastructure in Colombia. We will discuss the role of government in promoting and driving innovation in Chapter 4.

SPACE, INNOVATION AND GLOBALLY NETWORKED ENVIRONMENTS

Dramatic changes in the wake of the global economy have turned the dynamics of countries and regions on their head, setting up different relationships between organisations in different countries. Much of this interest in the new regional dynamics and transnational business activity stems from enquiries into the activities of multinational firms. Massey (1979; 1984), for example, refers to the spatial division of labour that occurred as a consequence of the dynamic relationship among foreign direct investment by large firms, the organisation of their production through transnational firms and multi-plant operations, and social relations between regions. The analysis of the role of multinationals in regions is seen primarily in terms of corporate control of business activities and the unevenness of different power relations between the core metropolitan regions in the west and the periphery in the developing countries. The ability of local firms to mediate and in some situations to develop their entrepreneurial agenda is ignored.

While regional studies have focused on regional learning, innovation, networks and associations (Braczyk et al., 1997; Cooke et al., 2007; Morgan, 2007; Amin and Roberts, 2008; Fritsch, 2008), they appear to have missed out on linkages between global and local firms. A concentrated focus on the region is attributable to some degree of historical and topical myopia about the influence of both these factors on the interrelationships enjoyed by globally connected regions. Bialasiewicz (2006) refers to Veneto, a region much praised for its unique regional clusters:

> the fortunes [of Veneto] could not have been made without the global market and its hypermodern thirst for innovation, a thirst that Veneto entrepreneurs have been masterful in exploiting. (2006: 46)

Bialasiewicz impugns the narrowness of thinking about the regionally exclusive Veneto model and its self-organising system based on hard work and local creativity. The markets for excellent products and services are often global and the interplay with suppliers, distributors, component makers, subcontractors and end users should suggest that other parts of a country or the rest of the world are not passive consumers.

A 'relational' view of regional development (Amin, 2004; Allen and Cochrane, 2007; Massey, 2007; Sunley, 2008) points to regions as self-sustaining territories. However, these regions are not closed systems and their networked environment is open to global exposure. Newer studies in regional development (Harrison, 2007;

Pike, 2007; Pike et al., 2007: Coe et al., 2008, 2010) have articulated the intricate relationship between regional change and globalisation and the particular arrangements fostered by global production networks (GPNs).

Developments in East Asia and rapid economic growth there provide insights into the structural, institutional and organisational change in the context of globalisation, nation states and regions. As Yeung (2010) argues, developments engender a need to study the 'strategic coupling' of various economic actors, including small, medium and large firms together with their lead firms which 'orchestrate trans-regional networks on a global scale'. These players (both regional and lead firms) and the institutions are part of the GPNs and they both play major roles. Firms not only produce new goods and provide new services, but also actively influence the formation and reshaping of the regional economic landscape, enabling cluster formation, promoting inter-regional competition for investment and technologies, and the creation of 'economic space' (McKendrick et al., 2000).

VIGNETTE 2.3   THE EAST ASIAN CANVAS OF GLOBAL AND LOCAL SPACES OF INNOVATION

The recent history of local contexts provides insights into the varied forms of strategic coupling in East Asia. Yang (2010), contrasting Taiwan and China, argues that the nature of the strategically 'coupled' relationship mutates over time and space. He shows how the difference between strategic coupling of regional development in China and other East Asian regions can be understood by the fact that China is short of large local business firms, and how in other parts of East Asia such local firms actively cooperate with lead firms both from the region and outside, including multi-nationals. The state also plays a big role in China through the development of local initiatives supporting such collaboration.

Various tiers of Taiwanese computer firms drive the strategic coupling of regional development in the Pearl River and Yangtze River deltas. Yang (2010) notes that while the *desktop cluster* in Dongguan has been driven by bottom-up dynamics of Taiwanese three-tier firms without the need for local initiatives, the *notebook cluster* in Suzhou has to a great extent been supported by top-down local government actions. In both cases we can find the evolution of an innovative region based on multiple forms of strategic coupling between global lead firms, regional large firms, local firms and institutions. Businesses are the main engines for production, but it is in the interplay between different types of firms and institutions, and their constant readjustments and responses to different market situations and technological changes, together with the smart use of relational assets with institutions, that we find the creation of critical regional innovation mass leading to growth and development.

Speed and flexibility also play important roles, while the cost dimension in East Asia is often overplayed. It is almost a truism to state that there is always someone who produces something cheaper. Therefore, reliance on cost for competitive advantage does not help to explain the dynamics of the regional environment. Mathews (2005; 2006) and Kenney and Florida (2004) have shown that flexibility and speed are probably more important considerations. Reorganising production in the past would have required the relocation of plants and production somewhere else. Innovations currently in vogue and which help firms to improve the flexibility of their operations include outsourcing, Original Equipment Manufacturing (OEM), Original Design Manufacturing (ODM), Customer Management (CM) and Enterprise Service Management (EMS) arrangements. These arrangements help to foster various forms of Global Production Networks (GPNs) and the global orientation of manufacturing.

What we obtain from this model are two forms of innovation – technological and organisational – shaping spatial arrangements and the regional contours of production. This form of strategic coupling is a response to market disequilibrium which opens up opportunities for Kirznerian arbitrage between different firms and institutions. This development may also be regarded as a form of Schumpeterian 'new combination' among different types of organisations, skills and technologies, creating a form of permanent disequilibrium in a climate of constant change of coupling partners across time and space.

Strategic coupling reflects the positive role of institutions, especially governments in East Asia, and their active involvement in developing fiscal, industrial strategies. These strategies have followed different trajectories. Taiwan and South Korea rely mainly on domestic firms collaborating with high-technology firms from the USA and Japan for their role in GPNs, through for example direct investment in infrastructure, such as the Hscinchu Science-based Industry Park and the Industrial Technology Research Institute in Taiwan, and the development of the Korea Institute of Science and Technology (KIST), the Korea Institute of Electronics Technology and the business conglomerates or 'chaebols' of Hyundai, Samsung and LG. Industrial districts and selected growth regions have also been part of institutional involvement in development strategies. Taken together we can observe a remarkable outcome for regional development with, for example, chip design work moving from Silicon Valley to Asian clusters (Yeung, 2010).

The key technological ingredients enabling and supplementing innovation and usage capabilities include electronic data interchange (EDI) with customers and suppliers, Internet-based integration of manufacturing and service sectors, end-user platforms bringing users of products and services upstream with producers, enterprise resource planning systems, third-party logistics, global tracking and information systems. These are the instruments of cooperation and innovation. They promote increasing specialisation of production and manufacturing together with connections to different parts of the value chain across different regions in the automobile, clothing, electronics, logistics and retailing sectors. They are accompanied by new business models that accommodate such specialisation and connectivity, with global lead firms engaged in R&D (upstream) and marketing, distribution and post-sale services (downstream), and international strategic and supply chain partners in charge of the rest of the value chain:

> Knowledge is diffused both as a result of the interactions of different agents and also because of the complementary capabilities exchanged between firms and the regions. It is not always the case that there is an equal quantum of expertise in connected regions; what do we have is a complementary resource capability which is capable of being developed through those connections. In some cases the connectivity is made possible only between institutions in one region and firms in another, and in other cases it is simply a process of transferring knowhow from partner firms of lead organisations through OEMs sand ODMS, coupled with local firms in the region. (Mitra, 2012)

Source: Mitra (2012)

MEASURING ECONOMIC GAIN IN SPACES OF INNOVATION

It is in the dynamics of innovation activities and the players that we find the main proponents of these activities. It is in the actions and performances of these players too that we find a sense of purpose in innovation, a way of measuring the outcomes that benefit a region. Job creation as an outcome is often regarded as a measure of the success of innovation processes, and among the key players in enabling job creation are the numerous small and medium-sized enterprises (SMEs) located across regions with a high or low capacity for innovation.

THE CONCENTRATION OF SMALL, INNOVATIVE FIRMS AND THEIR CONTRIBUTION TO REGIONS: CREATING JOBS AND IMPROVING PRODUCTIVITY

The relationship between SME innovation activities and employment is one of the fields of interest in the innovation literature due to its importance for the economic growth of countries, and as such draws particular attention from policy makers. In spite of a growing literature on entrepreneurship, innovation and employment growth (Acs and Armington, 2004; Audretsch and Lehman, 2005; 2007; Audretsch and Dohse, 2007), surprisingly little attention has been given to investigating the influence of different types of innovation (product, process and management innovations) on employment growth at the regional level (Abubakar and Mitra, 2013).

In recent years, differences between rates of employment growth between firms have been linked to differences in rates of innovation (Geroski and Machin, 2013). Certainly, the idea that such activities spur employment growth performance of firms has had significant influence on government policy and academic fashion (Acs et al., 2008). Innovating firms grow faster than non-innovators (Geroski and Machin, 1992). Roper (1997) examined 2,721 small firms in the UK, Ireland and Germany to show that innovation has a positive impact on growth. Freel (2000) studied 228 small firms in the UK manufacturing sector and found that innovators have a higher tendency to grow. Fesser and Willard (1990), Neifert (2006) and Coad and Rao (2008) corroborate this relationship between innovation and higher growth rates. It follows that the stock of innovative firms in particular regions has a positive impact on business and employment growth.

A recent paper (Love and Roper, 2015) benchmarking local innovation in the UK identifies the geography of innovation, states that 'more localized policy design in England has created a renewed interest in local economic indicators', and points to the importance of innovation to the productivity of different types of product and service innovation in specific regions in the UK. Other studies have examined sectoral variations in innovation (Evangelista and Savona, 2003; Peters, 2004; Bogliacino and Pianta, 2010). However, few studies have attempted to triangulate the innovation and growth question with both spatial and temporal considerations.

WHAT HAPPENS WHEN?

We assume that there are not just spatial factors which need attention, but that the spread of or limitations on innovation are affected by conditions that obtain in specific periods of time. Recessionary economic environments and related institutional constraints are often regarded as fertile ground for innovative capabilities, as conscious customers and truly entrepreneurial ventures seek a new economic equilibrium through the provision of goods and services that meet the exacting demands of higher levels of uncertainty in inclement times. Furthermore, how these considerations vary across different sectoral categories, as in the knowledge-intensive and creative sectors and non-knowledge-intensive industries, has not been given sufficient attention. Yet how policies could be shaped in certain times, across different and related sectors and in particular regions, is essential to a nuanced approach to decision making for both businesses and governments.

The literature has attempted theoretically and empirically to address and measure this effect. However, there are still issues that need clarification, not least because of contradictory findings and conclusions. For example, studies that investigate the relative influence of firms' ability to develop product, process and management innovations and their ability to generate high rates of employment at the 'regional level', particularly pre- and post-recessionary periods, are scarce. Thus, the relative influence of different types of innovation and regional employment growth remains unclear, partly because time effects are not taken into consideration (particularly recessionary periods) and partly because studies on innovation and employment growth often focus on one 'type' of innovation. Therefore, some studies found a positive relationship between innovation and employment growth while focusing on one type of innovation only (Piva and Vivarelli, 2005). For example, empirical analyses of product innovation employment effects in the main report a positive relationship (Brouwer et al., 1993; Antonucci and Pianta, 2002; Jaumandreu, 2003; Pianta, 2005; Antonucci, 2007; Hall and Lotti, 2008; Harrison et al., 2008; Bogliacino and Pianta, 2010) but with some exceptions (Evangelista and Savona, 2003). Effects of process innovations are mixed (Jaumandreu, 2003; Peters, 2004) or negative (Antonucci and Pianta, 2002; Pianta, 2005; Antonucci, 2007; Harrison et al., 2008; Bogliacino and Pianta, 2010).

Apart from product and process innovation, management or organisational innovation is generally considered complementary to new product development and indispensable as a contributor to employment (Pianta, 2005).

Studies introducing panel data analysis show that both product and process innovations act differently in different time lags (Lachenmaier and Rottmann, 2011) or that they are sector specific (Evangelista and Savona, 2003; Peters, 2004; Bogliacino and Pianta, 2010). These effects in turn impact on employment growth and regional development unequally. We can hypothesise that variations in time lags and differences in sectoral outputs of product and process innovation have variegated impact on employment growth.

Empirical studies use different measures of both employment and innovation variables. Employment is measured as employment growth in a region (Jaumandreu, 2003; Hall and Lotti, 2008), or as firm-level employment (Piva and Vivarelli, 2005; Lachenmaier and Rottmann, 2011), annual rate of change of employment (Antonucci and Pianta, 2002) and other measures. There is even more variation in attempts to measure innovation, from the number of firm innovations (Acs and Audretsch, 1988; Van Reenen, 1997) to innovation output in terms of sales growth from innovative products (Peters, 2004) and innovative investments or expenditure (Antonucci and Pianta, 2002; Piva and Vivarelli, 2005). The variations occur as a result of studies using different country- or region-based secondary data sources, which do not employ comparable survey-based data gathering techniques (Van Reenen, 1997; Antonucci and

Pianta, 2002; Lachenmaier and Rottmann, 2011). Measurement variations based on regional differences and data lead us to consider the possibility of the quality and quantity of data sources impacting on how innovation is measured at firm or regional levels.

NETWORKS OF COOPERATION AND THEIR SPATIAL SIGNIFICANCE

Understanding the spatial dimension of firms' cooperative activities that matter for innovation and employment growth, particularly in recessionary periods, can help provide empirically informed direction for government officials to design better policies for encouraging innovation, spurring employment growth through inter-firm cooperation at differentiated spatial levels. Previous research focuses mainly on the non-spatial benefits of cooperative activities on firms' innovation capacity. For example, researchers argue that cooperation agreements with different actors (government, consumers, suppliers, competitors, research institutions) have beneficial effects on firm innovation (Freel, 2003; Rycroft and Kash, 2004; Belderbos et al., 2004; De Man, 2005; Nieto and Santamaría, 2007; Zeng et al., 2010; Mention, 2011), the mechanism of which is knowledge spillovers (Fritsch and Franke, 2004), while others suggest the relationship to be ambiguous or insignificant (Fritsch and Franke, 2004; Zeng et al., 2010). It is argued that 'partner type' is critical for cooperative innovations (Belderbos et al., 2004; Nieto and Santamaría, 2007). Studies have also found cooperation with research institutions to be of significance (Belderbos et al., 2004; Zeng et al., 2010), especially in the case of university spillovers and spin-offs (Audretsch and Lehmann, 2005; Löfsten and Lindelöf, 2005).

Some studies focus on different forms of networking and argue that different innovations require different volumes and varied forms of networks. Typically, complex innovations involve more knowledge acquired from different network sources and more strong ties (Belderbos et al., 2004; Freel and De Jong, 2009). Studies also argue that innovation outcomes are sector specific, service firms for example benefiting highly from science partners (Mention, 2011), and small firms being more innovative in sectors where there is a strong presence of larger counterparts (Acs and Audrestsch, 1994). Networks of both direct and indirect ties are self-organising and global, with each generating substantial benefits for firms across the networks (Rycroft and Kash, 2004). Mutuality of benefits raises issues about firm-specific determinants (such as firm absorptive capacity, management openness to cooperation, control considerations) which are important for network-driven opportunities (Boschma, 2005). We could, therefore, argue that the nature, scope and type of networking influences cooperative behaviour for innovation outcomes and employment growth prospects.

Finally, our understanding of the impact of innovation on the structure of markets in different regions, and therefore on regional employment, appears to be limited. It is argued that innovation has a positive effect on industry concentration, but that substantial innovation output (especially of small firms) is less likely in highly concentrated industries (Koeller, 1995). However, these findings do not address questions of how or where specific innovations could be best exploited in order to contribute to regional development. The literature that comes close to that relationship can be found in international business, where it is argued that firms need to operate in international markets (Kafouros et al., 2008) to be able to benefit from innovation. Therefore, the proposition that innovative firms' operations in different markets may bring different employment effects seems plausible.

THE URBAN METAMORPHOSIS

Urban spaces constitute important places in the lives of a vast majority of people around the world. This is where many live, work, innovate, fail or succeed in making a significant impact on our social, economic, environmental and democratic wellbeing. The majority of people inhabit the world's cities, and by 2016 close to 4 billion people were living in them. Seventy million more people were expected to move by the end of 2016 to the urban hives of cities (Acuto.and Parnell, 2016) b In 20th century cities grew more than ten fold, from 250m to 2.8bn and by 2050 six billion of the world population of nine billion will form part of the urban population. The very fact of their importance can often mean that the spread of interests of people can be crowded out by powerful voices representing vested interests in metropolitan and rural settings. The conversation can be directed towards 'saving' and 'conserving' rather, the very antithesis of innovation which depends on 're-thinking', ' re-energising' and making progress based on new ideas, new products and new ways of managing resources and organisations. Interestingly, the sense of conservatism may lie in the smaller urban town rather than the city.

Cities have been at the forefront of economic growth, innovation and opportunity for centuries. While technological progress may promise greater proximity of people divided by geography, the reality of our creative lives has drawn people to concentrate in cities. People do so in large or medium –sized urban agglomerations, notwithstanding the congestion and pollution that result from such (Glaeser, 2011).

Large concentrations of people, homes, businesses, places of entertainment and the movement of goods, services and people in cities have helped to create multiple complex systems accommodating the food chain, housing, transportation, energy and a range of sociocultural models of practice. They can create tension but most importantly they coevolve as they are managed by a diverse set of public and private institutions. Cohen, et al (2016) write about cities becoming living laboratories for rapid prototyping and testing innovations to address a range of local challenges to a better quality of life. These living laboratories open up possibilities for vibrant innovation practice. Entrepreneurs create new products and services. They can help to solve business and social problems, and they do so by means of exchange of ideas and of resources sometimes even over a drink in a bar. The plethora of bars, cafes and restaurants in urban agglomerations facilitate easy networking. Urban environments mutate from poverty to prosperity through interchange of ideas among people in high urban density. Average income reaches a level 5 times in countries that are mostly urbanized, relative to countries where most people live in countryside, while individual earnings can increase by 20% as density doubles (Glaser 2011). Cities as hubs of global commerce provide opportunities for selling goods & services, as we see in London, New York, Shanghai, Tokyo, Mumbai and Lagos.

Cities face deeply rooted sustainability challenges too: they produce a high level of pollution, consume large amounts of energy and, given their high concentration of

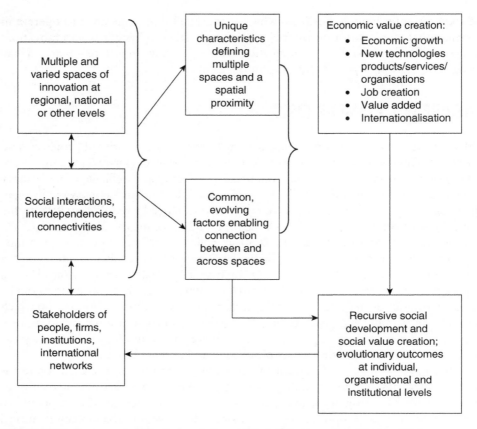

FIGURE 2.1   A conceptual framework for understanding spaces of innovation

people, they are vulnerable to the human, social and economic loss caused by climate change and natural disasters. The challenges of living in crowded, congested and highly polluted places fester alongside deep-seated wealth and income inequalities. While cities offer networking and social space for the "haves", loneliness and the lack of a community characterize the experience of many others. In many parts of the developing world, despite the palpable presence of wealth, the absence of access to basic services and livelihoods in urban environments leads to a life of accentuated scarcity in slum settlements which are set to treble between now and 2050 (UNDESA, 2013).

Innovation is forged in this smithy of complexity and paradox. Cities do this by attracting and retaining creative talent to engender higher levels of start-up innovative activity as opposed to innovations by established R&D type organisations. This is because the urban 'high tech' industry is less absorbed by hardware which demand extended, larger factory space. In cities it is the pool of app producers, people working with social media and in the multimedia world of news and entertainment, music and games, for example who define innovation practice. All of this is enabled by dense networks, university-business relationships and a social structure of innovation underlined by openness and diversity, and critically the talent of content writers, designers, scenarists, marketeers, copywriters and linguists. The constant attraction of talent together with the social structures help with the deep embedding of innovation in cities (Florida and Mellander, 2016). Of growing significance is the evolution of socially-oriented urban entrepreneurship and innovation which thrives on collaboration between local institutions and local residents or citizens (see Chapter6 for an overview on' Citizenship Innovation'). Here collaborative effort aims to resolve local issues of health, housing, environmental decay, mediated in the non-market space and driven by a moral intensity of purpose (Munoz and Dimov, 2017).

The city as a space of innovation is regarded today as the 'Smart City' A smart city is not a reality but an urban development strategy, and generally a technology driven future vision. But it is also about how citizens are shaping the city and how they are empowered to contribute to urban development. This empowerment is possible when there is a community of citizens, business enterprises, knowledge-based institutions, social organisations and local government agencies collaborate, often using the key new open sourced data and technologies. A Smart City can be regarded as an urban laboratory providing for an urban "innovation ecology" and acting as an accelerator and agent of change.

Barcelona's Smart Districts(22@Barcelona) involve triple helix type collaborations, Living Lab initiatives(22@Urban Lab, Live, Bdigital, i2Cat, Fablab, Cornella), new infrastructure building: alongside improvements to traditional architecture, the integration of ICT, from fibre optic to Wi-Fi, open data: sensors, open standard, and city platforms providing new services to citizens. In launching its IoT program, the city capitalized on 500 kilometers of fiber optic cable within the city, a network that was developed 30 years ago when two municipal buildings were connected by early fiber technology. The new fiber network is the backbone for integrated city systems providing for 90% 'fiber-to-the-home' coverage and a direct link to the Internet for Barcelona's residents and visitors. Barcelona's Smart City architecture is based on the three pillars of: a) ubiquitous infrastructures; b)information from sensors, open data, and citizens; and c)human capital, actors, communities. We find similar but locally shaped developments in, inter-alia, Thessolonaki in Greece, Helsinki in Finland, Manchester and Bristol in the UK, Aarhus in Denmark, Singapore, the Smart City initiative in India and in Abu Dhabi. In London.

URBAN IN THE RURAL?

Increasing innovation environments change and emerge in unusual places. Often it is not just technology which is the driver of 'smart' outcomes. Often it is not just the big city but the small town in a rural setting which attempts to wriggle out of deprivation. They depend on the nurturing of a sense of local place, and identifying social connections.

Tupelo in Mississippi was once one of the poorest parts of the poorest state in the US, of which William Faulkner wrote: 'The past isn't over; it isn't even past'. Its fame rested then on Elvis Presley surviving the 1936 tornado which killed or injured nearly 1,000 people. Back In 1940, the average family income was a quarter of the national average, and high levels of functional illiteracy accompanied the dominant presence in employment terms (80%) of a declining cotton industry. Neither natural beauty nor natural resources offered the salvation of tourism on which it could build an alternate future. Yet today Lee County is among the most prosperous in a local economy that has remained relatively stable over time. . It now has a large furniture manufacturing and Tupelo is regarded as the upholstery capital of the world. It is also home to a large healthcare sector, a fabric industry, a Toyota manufacturing plant, the largest non-metropolitan medical centre in the US, university satellite campuses and the head-quarters of two substantial banks. Elvis Presley's birthplace has also 're-surfaced' as a tourist attraction. The aftermath of the tornado galvanized minds. Business leaders and the community of farmers formed rural councils and a Community Development Foundation and helped to change the crop farmers to become dairy and poultry farm-ers. An early form of crowd sourcing saw the community pool resources to introduce artificial insemination long before it became popular in the industry (Carnegie Trust).

Innovative environments provide a magnet for collaboration and convergence to change minds and to change lives through economic and social innovations.

CONCLUDING OBSERVATIONS

As we have seen, understanding the geography of innovation can help us to discern the different ways in which innovation occurs across regions and countries. So what we can observe from a review of the literature from the short case studies or vignettes above is that:

- spaces of innovation vary greatly in their capacity and capabilities for generating innovation as evinced in knowledge creation, diffusion, dissemination and commercialisation, enabling the creation of a geography of innovation;
- identifying the unique characteristics of different innovation spaces provides us with a better understanding of what actions can be taken where and when;
- underpinning the uniqueness capacities and capabilities of different innovative spaces are common factors of interconnectedness between firms, institutions, people and social values which can change over time as part of an evolutionary path of development or decline;
- paradoxically, it is both the uniqueness of specific spaces and the variations in common factors that enable connectivity in global networks of production and innovation;
- the economic value of spatial innovation is often measured in terms of new products made and services provided in specific spaces, together with job creation and other added-value considerations; and
- economic value creation is possible only through the effective engagement of social actions of people, networks and institutions.

Each of these observations can be used to construct an overarching conceptual map for understanding and analysing the basic components of the idea of spaces of inno-vation, as shown in Figure 2.1.

We are left with one important question, and that is about how the interactions and the networks and capacities for innovation are formed or shaped in different spaces. Inherent in much of the discussion above is the role of institutions and the evolution of systems of practice that foster, guide and sometimes even hinder innovation. These include national and regional systems of innovation, institutions and mechanisms such as clusters. Their value and substance have informed numerous studies across the world and encouraged policy development across the world. It is these systems, institutions and mechanisms that we turn our attention to in the next chapter to examine whether they help us to make sense of spaces of innovation and their constituent elements.

 SELF-ASSESSMENT AND RESEARCH QUESTIONS

1. What we do we mean when we refer to the spatial aspect of innovation?
2. How is new knowledge and its commercialisation made possible in different spaces?
3. Why does proximity matter and what are the different types of proximity that we could consider?
4. How is economic value derived from a socialisation process?
5. Why and how are spaces of innovation globally connected?

NOTE

1. Since the argument here is that all economic activities are socially embedded, it follows that economic entities are social actors.

 REFERENCES

Abubakar, Y.A. and Mitra, J. (2013) 'The venturesome poor and entrepreneurial activity in Nigeria: The role of consumption, technology and human capital', *The International Journal of Entrepreneurship and Innovation*, 14(4): 235–54.

Acs, Z.J. and Armington, C. (2004) 'The impact of geographic differences in human capital on service firm formation rates', *Journal of Urban Economics*, 56(2): 244–78.

Acs, Z.J. and Audretsch, D.B. (1988) 'Innovation in large and small firms: an empirical analysis', *The American EconomicReview*, 78(4): 678–90.

Acs, Z.J. and Audretsch, D.B. (1990) *Innovation and Small Firms*. Cambridge, MA: MIT Press.

Acuto, M. and S. Parnell (2016)'Leave No City Behind'; editorial in Special Section on 'Urban Planet' *Science* ; Vol. 352: Issue 6288; p. 873. 20 May, (http://www.sciencemagazinedigital.org/...n?article Title=&articlePrintMode=false&start=1&end=178&prettyPrint=false&lm=1463686413000[5/24/2016 9:23:30 PM: last accessed 10 January, 2017)]

Adler, L. (2016). How Smart City Barcelona Brought the Internet of Things to Life'; Data Smart City Solutions. (from: http://datasmart.ash.harvard.edu/news/article/how-smart-city-barcelona-brought-the-internet-of-things-to-life-789 - last accessed February, 2017)

Adyalot, P. (1986) *Milieus Innovateurs en Europe*. Paris: GREMI I.

Algaze, G. (1993) *The Uruk World System*. Chicago, IL: University of Chicago Press.

Allen, J. and Cochrane, A. (2007) 'Beyond the territorial fix: regional assemblages, politics and power', *Regional Studies,* 41(9): 1161–75.

Amin, A. (2004) 'Regions unbound: towards a new politics of place', *Geografiska Annaler: Series B, Human Geography*, 86(1): 33–44.

Anselin, L., Varga, A. and Acs, Z. (1997) 'Local geographic spillovers between university research and high technology innovations', *Journal of Urban Economics*, 42(3): 422–48.

Anselin, L., Varga, A. and Acs, Z.J. (2000) 'Geographic and sectoral characteristics of academic knowledge externalities', *Papers in Regional Science*, 9(6): 435–43.

Antonucci, T. (2007) 'Innovation and employment in Europe: A sectoral perspective', in U. Cantner and F. Malerba (eds), *Innovation, Industrial Dynamics and Structural Transformation*. Berlin: Springer.

Antonucci, T. and M. Pianta (2002) 'Employment effects of product and process innovation in Europe', *International Review of Applied Economics*, 16(3): 295–307.

Arrow, K. (1962) 'Economic welfare and the allocation of resources for invention', in R.R. Nelson (ed.), *The Rate and Direction of Inventive Activity*. Princeton, NJ: Princeton University Press. pp. 609–26.

Arthur, B. (1994) *Increasing Returns and Path Dependency in the Economy*. Ann Arbor, MI: University of Michigan Press.

Arzhagi, M. and J.V. Henderson (2008) 'Networking off Madison Avenue', *Review of Economic Studies*, 75(4): 1011–38.

Asheim, B. and Gertler, M.S. (2006) 'The geography of innovation: regional innovation systems', in J. Fagerberg, D.C. Mowery and R.R. Nelson (eds), *The Oxford Handbook of Innovation.* Oxford: Oxford University Press. pp. 291–317.

Audretsch, D.B. and Dohse, D. (2007) 'Location: A neglected determinant of firm growth', *Review of World Economics*, 143(1): 79–107.

Audretsch, D.B. and Feldman, M.P. (1996) 'R&D spillovers and the geography of innovation and production', *The American Economic Review*, 86(3): 630–40.

Audretsch, D.B. and Lehmann, E.E. (2005) 'Does the knowledge spillover theory of entrepreneurship hold for regions?', *Research Policy*, 34(8): 1191–202.

Audretsch, D.B. and Stephan, P.E. (1996) 'Company-scientist locational links: the case of biotechnology', *American Economic Review*, 86(3): 641–52.

Audretsch, D.B. and Stephan, P.E. (2002) 'Knowledge spillovers in biotechnology: sources and incentives', in U. Cantner, H. Hanusch and S. Klepper (eds), *Economic Evolution, Learning, and Complexity*. Heidelberg: Physica-Verlag. pp. 127–38.

Ayer, A.J. (1965) 'Chance', *Scientific American*, 213(4): 44–54.

Becker, H.S. (1963) *Outsiders: Studies in the Sociology of Deviance*. New York: The Free Press.

Belderbos, R., Carree, M. and Lokshin, B. (2004) 'Cooperative R&D and firm performance', *Research Policy,* 33(10): 1477–92.

Bellandi, M. (1989) 'Capacita iinovativa diffusa e sistemi locali di imprese', in G. Beccatini (ed.), *Modelli locali di sviluppo.* Bologna: Il Mulino. pp. 149–72.

Bellandi, M. (2002) 'Italian industrial districts: An industrial economics interpretation', *European Planning Studies,* 10(4): 425–37.

Bialasiewicz, L. (2006) 'Geographies of production and the contexts of politics: dis-location and new ecologies of fear in the Veneto città diffusa', *Environment and Planning D: Society and Space*, 24(1): 41–67.

Bogliacino, F. and Pianta, M. (2010) 'Innovation and employment: a reinvestigation using revised Pavitt classes', *Research Policy*, 39(6): 799–809.

Boschma, R. (2005) 'Proximity and innovation: a critical assessment', *Regional Studies*, 39: 61–74.

Boschma, R.A. (1997) 'New industries and windows of locational opportunity: a long-term analysis of Belgium', *Edkunde*, 51(1): 1–19.

Boschma, R.A. and Lambooy, J.G. (1999) 'Evolutionary economics and economic geography', *Journal of EvolutionaryEeconomics*, 9(4): 411–29.

Bosma, N.E., Acs, Z.J., Autio, E., Coduras, A. and Levie, J. (2008) 'The global entrepreneurship monitor', Babson College, Universidad Del Desarrollo, London Business School.

Braczyk, H., Cooke, P. and Heidenreich, M. (eds) (1997) *Regional Innovation Systems*. London: UCL Press.

Brockhaus, R.H. (1980) 'Risk taking propensity of entrepreneurs', *Academy of Management Journal*, 23: 509–20.

Brouwer, E., Kleinknecht, A. and Reijnen, J.O. (1993) 'Employment growth and innovation at the firm level', *Journal of Evolutionary Economics*, 3(2): 153–9.

Camagni, R. (ed.) (1991a) *Innovation Networks: Spatial Perspectives*. London: Belhaven Press.

Camagni, R.P. (1991b) 'Technological change, uncertainty and innovation networks: towards a dynamic theory of economic space', in D. Boyce, P. Nijkamp and D. Shefer (eds), *Regional Science*. Heidelberg: Springer. pp. 211–49.

Capello, R. (1999) 'Spatial transfer of knowledge in high technology milieux: learning versus collective learning processes', *Regional Studies,* 33(4): 353–65.

Carbonara, N. and Mitra, J. (2001) 'New actors for the competitiveness of local clusters and industrial districts: a cognitive approach', in *Proceedings of the 46th International Council for Small Business World Conference*, Taipei. pp. 17–20.

Carnegie Trust (2016). *'Changing Minds, Changing Lives'*; Carnegie United Kingdom Trust. November

Carrincazeaux, C. and Coris, M. (2011) 'Proximity and innovation', in P. Cooke, B.T. Asheim and R. Boschma (eds), *Handbook of Regional Innovation and Growth*. Cheltenham: Edward Elgar. pp. 269–81.

Coad, A. and Rao, R. (2008) 'Innovation and firm growth in high-tech sectors: A quantile regression approach', *Research Policy*, 37(4): 633–48.

Coe, D.T. and Helpman, E. (1995) 'International R&D spillovers', *European Economic Review,* 39(5): 859–87.

Coe, N.M., Dicken, P. and Hess, M. (2008) 'Global production networks: realizing the potential', *Journal of Economic Geography,* 8: 271–95.

Coe, N.M., Dicken, P., Hess, M. and Yeung, H.W.C. (2010) 'Making connections: global production networks and world city networks', *Global Networks*, 10(1): 138–49.

Cohen, D. E. Almiral and H. Chesbrough (2016). 'The City as a Lab: Open Innovation Meets the Collaborative Economy'; Special Issue on City Innovation, *California Management Review*, Fall; Vol, 59, No. 1: pp. 5-13

Cooke, P., De Laurentis, C., Tödtling, F. and Trippl, M. (2007) *Regional Knowledge Economies: Markets, Clusters and Innovation.* Cheltenham: Edward Elgar.

Corrado, L. and Fingleton, B. (2012) 'Where is the economics in spatial econometrics?', *Journal of Regional Science*, 52: 210–39.

Curran, E. (2015) 'Is the next Detroit in China?', *Bloomberg Business week*, 11 June. Available at: www.bloomberg.com/news/articles/2015-06-11/could-wenzhou-be-china-s-detroit- (last accessed 20 August 2015).

David, P.A. (1994) 'Why are institutions the "carriers of history"'? Path dependence and the evolution of conventions, organizations and institutions', *Structural Change and Economic Dynamics*, 5(2): 205–20.

Desai, M., Gompers, P. and Lerner, J. (2003) 'Institutions, capital constraints and entrepreneurial firm dynamics: evidence from Europe', NBER Working Paper No. 10165.

Easterly, W. and Levine, R (2003) 'Tropics, germs and crops: how endowments influence economic development', *Journal of Monetary Economics*, 50: 3–39.

Ellison, G., Glaeser, E.L. and Kerr, W.R. (2010) 'What causes industry agglomeration? Evidence from coagglomeration patterns', *The American Economic Review*, 100(3): 1195–213.

El-Namaki, M.S.S. (1988) 'Encouraging entrepreneurship in developing countries', *Long Range Planning*, 21(4), 98–106.

Engel, J.S (2014) *Global Clusters of Innovation: Entrepreneurial Engines of Economic Growth Around the World*. Northampton, MA; Edward Elgar.

Engel, J.S. (2015) 'Global clusters of innovation: lessons from Silicon Valley', *California Management Review*, 57(2): 36–65.

Engel, J.S. and del-Palacio, I. (2009) 'Global networks of clusters of innovation: accelerating the innovation', *Business Horizons*, 52(5): 493–503.

Engel, J.S. and del-Palacio, I. (2011) 'Global clusters of innovation: the case of Israel and Silicon Valley', *California Management Review*, 53(2): 27–49.

Enright, M.J. (1999) 'Regional clusters and firm strategy', in A. Chandler, O. Solvell and P. Hagstrom (eds.), *The Dynamic Firm*. Oxford: Oxford University Press. pp. 315–42.

Evangelista, R. and Savona, M. (2003) 'Innovation, employment and skills in services: firm and sectoral evidence', *Structural Change and Economic Dynamics*, 14(4): 449–74.

Feldman, M.P. and Audretsch, D.B. (1999) 'Innovation in cities: Science-based diversity, specialization and localized competition', *European Economic Review,* 43(2): 409–29.

Fesser, H.R. and Willard, G.E. (1990) 'Founding strategy and performance: a comparison of high and low growth high tech forms', *Strategic Management Journal*, 11(2): 87–98.

Florida, R. (1995) 'Toward the learning region', *Futures*, 27(5): 527–36.

Florida, R. and C. Mellander (2016). Rise of the Start-Up City: The Changing Geography of the Venture Capital Financed Innovation'; Special Issue on City Innovation, *California Management Review,* Fall; Vol, 59, No. 1: pp. 5-13

Freel, M.S. (2000) 'Barriers to product innovation in small manufacturing firms', *International Small Business Journal*, 18(2): 60–80.

Freel, M.S. (2003) 'Sectoral patterns of small firm innovation, networking and proximity', *Research Policy*, 32(5): 751–70.

Freel, M. and De Jong, J.P. (2009) 'Market novelty, competence-seeking and innovation networking', *Technovation*, 29(12): 873–84.

Fritsch, M. (2008) 'How does new business formation affect regional development? Introduction to the special issue', *Small Business Economics*, 30(1): 1–14.

Fritsch, M. and Franke, G. (2004) 'Innovation, regional knowledge spillovers and R&D cooperation', *Research Policy*, 33(2): 245–55.

Geroski, P. and Machin, S. (2013) 'Think again: Do innovating firms outperform non-innovators?', *Business Strategy Review*, 24(2): 82–6.

Gertler, M. (2003) 'Tacit knowledge and the economic geography of context, or the undefinable tacitness of being (there)', *Journal of Economic Geography*, 3(1): 75–99.

Glaeser, E. (2011) *Triumph of the City: How Our Greatest Invention Makes Us Richer, Smarter, Greener, Healthier, and Happier*. London: Macmillan.

Glaeser, E., Kallal, H., Scheinkman, J. and Shleifer, A. (1992) 'Growth of cities', *Journal of Political Economy*, 100: 1126–52.

Grabher, G. (1993) 'The weakness of strong ties: the lock-in of regional development in the Ruhr area', in G. Grabher (ed.), *The Embedded Firm: On the Socio Economics of Industrial Networks*. London: Routledge.

Griliches, Z. (1979) 'Issues in assessing the contribution of research and development to productivity growth', *The Bell Journal of Economics*, 10(1): 92–116.

Grossman, G.M. and Helpman, E. (1990) 'Trade, knowledge spillovers, and growth', *National Bureau of Economic Research*: w3485.

Hall, B.H. and Lotti, F. (2008) 'Employment, innovation, and productivity: evidence from Italian micro-data', *Industrial and Corporate Change*, 17(4): 813–39.

Harrison, J. (2007) From competitive regions to competitive city-regions: a new orthodoxy, but some old mistakes. *Journal of Economic Geography*: 7(3): 311–32.

Harrison, R., Jaumandreu, J., Mairesse, J.J. and Peters, B. (2008) 'Does innovation stimulate employment? A firm-level analysis using comparable micro data from four European countries', NBER Working Paper No. 14216.

Hughes, A. and Wood, E. (1999) 'Rethiking innovation comparisons between manufacturing and services: the experience of the CBR SME surveys in the UK', Working Paper, no. 140; ESRC Centre for Business Research, Cambridge: University of Cambridge.

Jaffe, A.B. (1989) 'Characterizing the "technological position" of firms, with application to quantifying technological opportunity and research spillovers', *Research Policy*, 18(2): 87–97.

Jaffe, A.B., Trajtenberg, M. and Henderson, R. (1993) 'Geographic localization of knowledge spillovers as evidenced by patent citations', *The Quarterly Journal of Economics*, 108 (3): 577–98.

Jaumandreu, J. (2003) 'Does innovation spur employment? A firm-level analysis using Spanish CIS data', Paper prepared for discussion as part of the European project 'Innovation and Employment in European Firms: Microeconometric Evidence'. Available at: www.eco.uc3m.es/temp/jaumandreu.pdf (last accessed 20 November 2011).

Johansson, F. (2004) *The Medici Effect: Breakthroughs, Insights at the Intersection of Ideas, Concepts & Cultures*. Boston, MA: Harvard Business School Press.

Johnson, S., Kaufmann, D., McMillan, J. and Woodruff, C. (2000) 'Why do firms hide? Bribes and unofficial activity after communism', *Journal of Public Economics*, 76: 495–520.

Kafouros, M.I., Buckley, P.J., Sharp, J.A. and Wang, C. (2008) 'The role of internationalization in explaining innovation performance', *Technovation*, 28(1): 63–74.

Keller, W. (2004) 'International technology diffusion', *Journal of Economic Literature*, 42(3): 752–82.

Kenney, M. and Florida, R. (eds) (2004) *Locating Global Advantage: Industry Dynamics in the International Economy*. Stanford, CA: Stanford University Press.

Kloosterman, R., Van der Leun, J.P. and Rath, J. (1999) 'Mixed embeddedness, migrant entrepreneurs and informal economic activities', *International Journal of Urban and Regional Research*', 14(5): 659–76.

Koeller, C.T. (1995) 'Innovation, market structure and firm size: a simultaneous equations model', *Managerial and Decision Economics*, 16(3): 259–69.

Krugman, P.R. (1991) *Geography and Trade*. Cambridge, MA: MIT Press.

Lachenmaier, S. and Rottmann, H.(2011) 'Effects of innovation on employment: A dynamic panel analysis', *International Journal of Industrial Organization*, 29(2): 210–20.

Lave, J. and Wenger, E. (1991) *Situated Learning: Legitimate Peripheral Participation*. Cambridge: Cambridge University Press.

Littauer, M.A. and Crauwel, J.H. (1979) 'Wheeled vehicles and ridden animals in the ancient Near East', in *Handbuch der Orientalistik*, Vol. 7. Leiden: E. J. Brill.

Löfsten, H. and Lindelöf, P. (2005) 'R&D networks and product innovation patterns – academic and non-academic new technology-based firms on Science Parks', *Technovation*, 25(9): 1025–37.

Love, J.H. and Roper, S. (2015) 'SME innovation, exporting and growth: A review of existing evidence', *International Small Business Journal*, 33(1): 28–48.

Lundvall, B.Å. and Johnson, B. (1994) 'The learning economy', *Journal of Industry Studies*, 1(2): 23–42.

Lundvall, B.Å. and Maskell, P. (2000) *Nation States and Economic Development.* Oxford: Oxford University Press.

Malecki, E.J. (1997) 'Technology and economic development: the dynamics of local, regional, and national change'. University of Illinois at Urbana-Champaign's Academy for Entrepreneurial Leadership. Historical Research Reference in Entrepreneurship.

Martinelli, A. (2002) 'Il modello Comunità e impresa: stakeholder e responsabilità sociale', in L.Hinna (ed.), *Il bilancio sociale*. Milan: Il Sole/24 ore.

Martinelli, A. (2004) 'The social and institutional context of entrepreneurship', in G. Corbetta, M. Huse and D. Ravasi (eds), *Crossroads of Entrepreneurship*. New York: Springer. pp. 53–73.

Maskell, P. and Malmberg, A. (1999) 'Localised learning and industrial competitiveness', *Cambridge Journal of Eeconomics*, 23(2): 167–85.

Massey, D. (1979) 'In what sense a regional problem?', *Regional Studies*, 13(2): 233–43.

Massey, D. (1984) *Spatial Division of Labour: Social Structures and the Geography of Production.* London: Macmillan.

Massey, D. (2007) *World Cities.* Cambridge: Polity.

Mathews, J.A. (2005) 'Strategy and the crystal cycle', *California Management Review*, 47(2): 6–32.

Mathews, J.A. (2006) 'Catch-up strategies and the latecomer effect in industrial development', *New Political Economy*, 11(3): 313–35.

Mau, Y. and Furan, T. (2005) 'Institutional innovation and functional transition of local government and development of private sector in Wenzhou and Yiwu', Centre for East and South-East Asian Studies, Masters Programme in Asian Studies (last accessed 20 August 2015).

McKendrick, D.G., Doner, R.F. and Haggard, S. (2000) *From Silicon Valley to Singapore: Location and Competitive Advantage in the Hard Disk Drive Industry.* Stanford, CA: Stanford University Press.

Mention, A.L. (2011) 'Co-operation and co-opetition as open innovation practices in the service sector: Which influence on innovation novelty?', *Technovation*, 31(1): 44–53.

Mitra, J. (2012) *Entrepreneurship, Innovation and Regional Development: An Introduction.* Abingdon: Routledge.

Moorey, P.R.S. (1985) *Materials and Manufacture in Ancient Mesopotamia.* Oxford: BAR International Series.

Morgan, K. (2007) 'The learning region: institutions, innovation and regional renewal', *Regional Studies*, 41(S1): S147–59.

Munoz, P.and D. Dimov (2017). 'Moral Intensity as Catalyst for Opportunities for Sustainable Development' in *Sustainability, Society, Business Ethics and Entrepreneurship'*; ed. By A.J. Guerber, G.D. Markman and S. Chih-Yi Su (The World Scientific Reference on Entrepreneurship, World Scientific Publishing, February

Nelson, R.R. (1994) 'The co-evolution of technology, industrial structure, and supporting institutions', *Industrial and Corporate Change*, 3(1): 47–63.

Nieto, M.J. and Santamaría, L. (2007) 'The importance of diverse collaborative networks for the novelty of product innovation', *Technovation*, 27(6): 367–77.

Nonaka, I. and Takeuchi, H. (1995) *The Knowledge-Creating Company: How Japanese Companies Create the Dynamics of Innovation.* Oxford: Oxford University Press.

Noteboom, B. (2000) *Learning and Innovation in Organisations and Economies.* Oxford: Oxford University Press.

Olson, M. (1982) *The Rise and Decline of Nations.* New Haven, CT: Yale University Press.

Parris, K. (1993) 'Local initiative and national reform: the Wenzhou model of development', *The China Quarterly*, 134: 242–63.

Pavitt, K. (2002) 'Knowledge about knowledge since Nelson & Winter: a mixed record', *SPRU-Science and Technology Policy Research*, Electronic Working Papers 83.

Peters, B. (2004) 'Employment effects of different innovation activities: micro econometric evidence', ZEW – Centre for European Economic Research Discussion Paper No. 04073. Available at: http://ssrn.com abstract=604481 (last accessed 19 October 2011).

Pianta, M. (2005) 'Innovation and employment', in J. Fagerberg, D. Mowery and R. Nelson (eds), *The Oxford Handbook of Innovation*. Oxford: Oxford University Press. pp. 568–98.

Pike, A. (2007) 'Editorial: Whither regional studies?', *Regional Studies*, 41: 1143–8.

Pike, A., Rodríguez-Pose, A. and Tomaney, J. (2007) 'What kind of local and regional development and for whom?', *Regional Studies*, 41(9): 1253–69.

Piore, M.J. and Sabel, C.F. (1984) *The Second Industrial Divide: Possibilities for Prosperity*. New York: Basic Books.

Piva, M. and Vivarelli, M. (2005) 'Innovation and employment: evidence from Italian microdata', *Journal of Economics*, 86(1): 65–83.

Polanyi, M. (1958) *The Study of Man*. Chicago, IL: University of Chicago Press.

Polanyi, M. (1967) *The Tacit Dimension*. Garden City, NY: Doubleday.

Polenske, K. (ed.) (2007) *The Economic Geography of Innovation*. Cambridge: Cambridge University Press.

Porter, M.E. (1990) 'The competitive advantage of notions', *Harvard Business Review*, 68(2): 73–93.

Possehl, G.L. (1996) *Indus Age: The Writing System*. Philadelphia, PA: University of Pennsylvania Press.

Ray, J.D. (1986) 'The emergence of writing in Egypt', *World Archaeology*, 17(3): 307–15.

Rodrik, D., Subramanian, A. and Trebbi, F. (2002) 'Institutions rule: the primacy of institutions over geography and integration in economic development', NBER Working Paper No. 9305.

Roper, S. (1997) 'Product innovation and small business growth: a comparison of the strategies of German, UK and Irish companies', *Small Business Economics*, 9(6): 523–37.

Rosenberg, N. (1982) *Inside the Black Box: Technology and Economics*. Cambridge: Cambridge University Press.

Rycroft, R.W. and Kash, D.E. (2004) 'Self-organizing innovation networks: implications for globalization', *Technovation*, 24(3): 187–97.

Saxenian, A. (1994) *Regional Advantage: Culture and Competition in Silcion Valley and Route 128*. Cambrige, MA: Harvard University Press.

Saxenian, A. (1996) 'Regional networks: industrial adaptation in Silicon Valley and route 128', *Cityscape: A Journal of Policy Development and Research,* 2(2): 41–60.

Saxenian, A. (2005) 'From brain drain to brain circulation: transnational communities and regional upgrading in India and China', *Studies in Comparative International Development,* 40(2): 35–61.

Schmandt-Besserat, D. (1992) *Before Writing*, 2 vols. Austin, TX: University of Texas Press.

Schmandt-Besserat, D. (1996) *How Writing Came About*. Austin, TX: University of Texas Press.

Schmandt-Besserat, D. (1999) *The History of Counting*. Glasgow: Harper Collins.

Schmandt-Besserat, D., Wilson, R.A. and Keil, F.C. (1999) *Artifacts and Civilisation*. Chicago, IL: Chicago University Press.

Simon, H.A. (1959) *Administrative Behaviour*, 2nd edn. New York: Macmillan.

Simon, H.A. (1976) 'From substantive to procedural rationality', in S.J. Latsis (ed.), *Method and Appraisal in Economics*. Cambridge: Cambridge University Press.

Simon, H.A. (1979) 'Rational decision making in business organisations', *American Economic Review*, 69: 493–513.

Specht, P.H. (1993) 'Munificence and carrying capacity of the environment and organisation formation', *Entrepreneurship Theory and Practice*, 17(2): 77–86.

Sunley, P. (2008) 'Relational economic geography: a partial understanding or a new paradigm?', *Economic Geography*, 84(1): 1–26.

Swedberg, R. (2000) *Entrepreneurship: The Social Science View*. Oxford: Oxford University Press.

Tennant, N. (1997) *The Taming of the True*. Oxford: Oxford University Press.

Totdling, F. and Kaufmann, A. (1999) 'Innovation systems in regions of Europe: a comparative perspective', *European Planning Studies*, 7(6): 699–771.

UNDESA (UN Department of Economics and Social Affairs) (2013) *World Economic and Social Survey: Sustainable development challenges.* New York: UNDESA.

Van Reenen, J. (1997) 'Employment and technological innovation: evidence from UK manufacturing firms', *Journal of Labor Economics*, 15(2): 255–84.

Yang, C. (2009) 'Strategic coupling of regional development in global production networks: redistribution of Taiwanese personal computer investment from the Pearl River Delta to the Yangtze River Delta, China', *Regional Studies*, 43(3): 385–407.

Yeung, H.W.-C. (2005) 'Rethinking relational economic geography', *Transactions of the Institute of British Geographers*, 30: 37–51.

Yeung, H.W.-C. (2010) *Globalising Regional Development in East Asia: Production Networks, Clusters and Entrepreneurship*. Abingdon: Routledge.

Zachmann, P. (2011) 'When Wenzhou sneezes', *Time*, 178(21): 34–7.

Zeng, S.X., Xie, X.M. and Tam, C.M. (2010) 'Relationship between cooperation networks and innovation performance of SMEs', *Technovation*, 30(3): 181–94.

SYSTEMS AND INSTITUTIONS OF INNOVATION

3

SCOPE AND OBJECTIVES

- How interactions, interdependencies and connectivities help to create systems of innovation.
- How systems accommodate different types of institutions, the meaning, value, scope and type of institutions, institutional constraints, and mechanisms for developing institutions such as clustering for effective innovation in specific environments.

INTRODUCTION

The previous chapter outlined an understanding of the importance of spaces of innovation. Inherent in the discussion and analysis of such spaces was the idea that firms, including manufacturers, service providers, suppliers, distributors and customers, are interdependent and often connected with other types of organisations including government and universities. Taken together (the organisations and their interdependencies), they can be described as constituting a system. Where they are connected to create, develop and commercialise knowledge, thus making innovation possible, they could be described as 'systems of innovation' (SIs).

In accordance with general systems theory, 'systems such as SIs are made up of components and the relations between these components' (Edquist, 2006). They have a function aimed at achieving certain outputs and outcomes, and they have boundaries which separate them from anything outside their functions (Inglestam, 2002).

Using the theory of social systems, notably the work of the German social scientist Niklas Luhmann (1984; 1986; 2000), we find that systems can be different from the environment in which they are located and that they are sometimes able to reproduce this difference. An examination from a social system perspective indicates that SIs are systems that collect information from their (external) environment and process, retrieve and interpret this information before generating actions and operations from them. Social systems are organised to provide symbolic meanings which enable the ordering of the system by way of identifying and defining roles, priorities and routines. The boundary is drawn once a shared set of interpretations and values emerges between the various interactions among different actors in the system. Furthermore, the specific actions of production, innovation and institutions encourage positive feedback loops strengthening the conditions for self-reproduction. The behaviour of these interdependent players and the system itself are shaped, modified and governed by institutions, including laws, rules, norms, routines, incentives and constraints (North, 1990a; Edquist, 2005; Nelson and Nelson, 2002).

How best can we understand SIs? We find that there are possibly three perspectives to the idea of SIs. These include national, sectoral and regional perspectives which, as Edquist (2005) suggests, can be brought together under the term of generic SIs. These perspectives have been developed by the pioneers of the study of innovation systems, namely Chris Freeman, Richard Nelson ad Bengt Lundvall, and then questioned and reshaped by others to give meaning to systems occurring in different spaces of innovation – the region, the sector, the local environment.

NATIONAL SYSTEMS OF INNOVATION

ORIGINS

It was Freeman (1987) who first used the idea of a national SI, which he explained in terms of networks of institutions, firms and their range of interactions in initiating, importing and diffusing new technologies. The idea presupposes the existence of nation states, a political process underlying economic development from around the eighteenth century. Technology-based development did occur before that time: Smith and Nicholson (1887), Fukyama (2012), Ashraf and Galor (2011), Frank (1998), Acemoglou and Robinson (2012) and Frankopan (2015) have discussed the wealth of nations, cities and towns since the decline of the Roman Empire and have explored how these developments in the Chinese, Indian, Persian and Islamic Empires nurtured or hindered technological change and innovation. Earlier, in 1841, Friedrich List's concept of national systems of production and learning considered both institutions (including education and training providers) and infrastructure (transportation networks), ignored scarce resource allocation, but emphasised the development of productive forces.

The motivation for most of these writers was to examine the gaps in economic performance and living standards of people in different political units. There was also a recognition of the movement from a dependence on trade, shipping and finance to manufacturing and the use of technology from around the eighteenth century, marking the advent of what Freeman describes as the 'capitalist industry' (2002) which influenced the enquiry of Adam Smith and others.

EVOLUTION

Lundvall (1992) developed the idea of the national system of innovation (NSI) as an alternative to the neo-classical tradition by emphasising the significance of interactions – learning, between user and producer – and consequent innovation. These interactions are at the centre of the 'structure of production' and the necessary 'institutional set-up' – two key dimensions defining a system of innovation (Edquist, 2005). Lundvall distinguishes between 'narrow' and 'broad' SIs (see Table 3.1). The distinction lies in the first system concentrating on the promotion, acquisition and dissemination of knowledge as the primary sources of innovation ('narrow'), and the second system's ('broad' system) espousal of the so-called 'narrow' institutions and embedding them in a wider socio-economic ecosystem. In the latter system political and cultural influences mix with and shape economic policies to determine the type, purpose and measurement of innovative activities. Table 3.1 shows the features of each of these two systems, with reference to developments in Great Britain only.

Nelson (1993), on the other hand, is mainly concerned with empirical studies, with many of them focusing attention particularly on R&D systems and inputs. Following similar lines of argument about structural and institutional aspects, Nelson and Rosenberg (in Nelson, 1993) focus on organisations that created and disseminated knowledge. In effect both Nelson and Lundvall point to specific determinants that influence innovation processes, and which in turn define NSIs. Where they differ is in the identification of and importance given to different factors. So while we could include all important economic, social, political, organisational, institutional and other related factors influencing the development, promotion, diffusion and application of innovation (Edquist, 1997), identifying which ones were more important than others is what differentiates one author from another.

FACILITATION AND OVERCOMING SYSTEM FAILURES

A major factor that led to the conception of the idea of NSIs was the recognition that innovation was more than simply a linear process, that both long-term and close relationships between the various actors were important, as was the nature of the relationships. Close and long-term relationships needed to be more than transactional and therefore non-price based. Interactive learning helped to transmit qualitative information which both markets and organisational hierarchies fail to offer. Crucially, understanding why there could be different SIs resulting in varied economic performances meant that some care had to be taken with the varieties of innovation in different places and at different times (Freeman et al., 2002). Studies on long-term relationships in Korean chaebols and Japanese keiretsus, together with those on trust and reciprocity and the norms, habits and routines in societies (often referred to as institutions), also helped to recognise some of the key factors that make innovation possible. They contributed to the idea of NSIs, emphasising the relationships and not just the presence of different actors.

We could interpret the interactions between various actors in NIS and the resulting outcomes as a new form of Schumpeterian combination, bringing together similar

TABLE 3.1 Features of national systems of innovation in Great Britain

Narrow systems of innovation	Broad systems of innovation
17th century: Academies of Science, Royal Society 1662, 'proceedings' and journals, internationalism of science, science education	*18th and 19th centuries*
	Strong links between scientists and entrepreneurs
18th century: 'Industrial Revolution' (factories), technical education, nationalism of technology, consulting engineers	Science has become a national institution, encouraged by the state and popularised by local clubs. Strong local investment by landlords in transport infrastructure (canals and roads, later railways)
19th century: Growth of universities, PhD and science faculties, institutes of technology, government laboratories, industrial R&D in-house, standards institutes	Partnership form of organisation enables inventors to raise capital and collaborate with entrepreneurs (e.g. Arkwright/Strutt or Watt/Boulton)
20th century: Industrial in-house R&D in all industries, 'Big Science and Technology', research councils, etc., Ministries of Science and Technology, service industries, R&D, networks, science and technology parks, incubators, industry-research collaboration	Profits from trade and services available through national and local capital markets to invest in factory production and in infrastructure. Economic policy strongly influenced by classical economics and in the interests of industrialisation. Strong efforts to protect national technology and delay catching up by competitors. British productivity per person was already about twice as high as European average by 1850
21st century: Accelerators, industry-research extensions, development of concepts of appropriate technologies, frugal innovation	Consulting engineers develop and diffuse best practice technology in waterwheels, canals, machine-making and railways. Part-time training, night school and apprenticeship training for new factory technicians and engineers
	Gradual extension of primary, secondary and tertiary education
	20th and 21st centuries
	Growth of intermediary institutions, globalization, information, communication and convergent technologies, global networks supported by governments
	Advances in the knowledge economy, questions about the death of distance and uneven global development, recognition of differences in spaces of innovation

Source: Adapted from Freeman (2002). The references to the 20th and 21st century are this author's adaptations.

and contradictory aspects and processes of organisations, including existing elements and radically new ones, for innovation. From a purely theoretical perspective, Lundvall et al. have suggested that the NIS, or the Aalborg version of it,

> may be seen as a combination of four elements: the neo-Schumpeterian reinterpretation of national production systems, empirical work based on the home-market theory of international trade, the microeconomic approach to innovation as an interactive process inspired by research at Science Policy and Research Unit at Sussex University (SPRU) and, finally, insights in the role of institutions in shaping innovative activities. This combination reflects that the concept was developed to get a better understanding of economic growth and trade specialisation in a small open economy characterised by high income per capita but with a weak representation of science-based firms. It also reflects an emphasis on the economic and technological history of countries with a gradual change in the intra- and inter-national division of productive and innovative labour. (2002: 217)

The establishment of an NIS in any country presupposes the need to go one step further than addressing market failures when trying to optimise innovation performance. Why talk in terms of an NIS if the system does not deliver positive results? Adopting an NIS would, therefore, mean avoiding system failures which impede the interactions between different innovation stakeholders, the flow of knowledge creation and the commercialisation of such knowledge. These system failures could include the following:

(a) Network failures – lock-in of capabilities and knowledge (lock-in/path dependency failures (Smith, 1999) being the inability of complete (social) systems to adapt to new technological paradigms; note that Edquist et al. (1998) address the same failure (but do not distinguish so strictly between transition and lock-in failure), inadequate capacity for social capital supporting human capital, and too many structural holes not utilised to take advantage of weak ties.

(b) Capability and competency failures – lack of range, depth and variety of skills base, poor vehicles of knowledge creation and managerial incompetencies.

(c) Infrastructural failures (Edquist et al., 1998; Smith, 1999) – the physical infrastructure that actors need to function (such as IT, telecoms and roads) and the science and technology infrastructure.

(d) Transition failures (Smith, 1999) – the inability of firms to adapt to new technological developments.

(e) Hard and soft institutional failures – hard institutional failures being failures in the framework of regulation and the general legal system (Smith, 1999). These institutions are specifically created or designed (Edquist et al., 1998), for which reason Johnson and Gregersen (1994) refer to them as formal institutions. Soft institutional failures are failures in social institutions such as political culture and social values.

Some care has to be taken in ensuring that the above categories are not confused and that distinctions can be made between the different practices, the outcomes and the actors contributing to the different types of failure. To this end Woolthuis et al. (2005) have argued for an approach that would enable us to analyse, justify and evaluate the different types of systemic failures. Thus actors could be seen as demand-side players such as consumers and large buyers; producers could be seen as firms; intermediaries could include research institutions and universities; third-party and supply-side actors could be found among banks, venture capitalists and government institutions. Each of them would use different rules of the game that may or may not result in failures.

LIMITATIONS AND CHALLENGES TO THE CONCEPT OF NATIONAL INNOVATION SYSTEMS

The Aalborg version of the NIS also points to some of the challenges to and problems of NISs. Used as a benchmarking tool and as a contributing factor to the development of indices, NISs run into the same neo-classical economics problem that spurred on structural economists such as Hirschman (1958), Perroux (1969) and Dahmen (1970). Driven by their interest in combining Leontief's input–output model and Schumpeterian theories of entrepreneurship and innovation, they often misjudged what works in different countries and economic climates. In placing countries in a typical hierarchical system, they assumed that because different sectors affected growth variously, the most dynamic elements were located 'upstream', such as in machine tools. Therefore, the USA and Germany had a stronger economy than France because the former duo had production systems capable of specialising in machine tools (an upstream production function). So if countries wanted to move up the innovation value chain or even be considered to be innovative then they had to follow the same path. Before they could do that they would be considered as inferior innovation economies wallowing in 'factor-driven' or mass production economies. Worse, leading economists and policy makers advising developing countries would recommend the development of sectors producing such machinery (Lundvall et al., 2002). These ideas about benchmarking or indexing are often led by short-term criteria.

It is possible that a system of innovation in any given country could develop a specific model that reflects the cultural and social dynamics as strongly as the economic and political ones. Lundvall et al. (2002) point to Denmark as a highly egalitarian society in terms of high income generation (in terms of income level) and income distribution, as well as a well-functioning democracy with an enviable degree of gender equality – all of which characteristics impact on the Danish innovation system. What is possible in high-income countries may not work in lower-income counterparts where we need to work with alternative conceptualisations of both innovation systems and growth. Here innovation may not be associated with R&D-based activities but rather with the necessities of everyday life and the competencies of people, the capacity of the institutions, and economic turnaround needs. Ironically, where concepts of frugal innovation have found shelter, we find outcomes and the development of innovation processes that have led to their adoption in developed economies through a process of reverse innovation (Winter and Govindarajan, 2015) thus suggesting how different countries at different stages in a hierarchical system can learn from each other.

FROM THE NATIONAL TO THE MESO AND THE REGIONAL LEVEL

Wide variations within nation states have added fuel to the argument about interactions between a variety of stakeholders, but not necessarily at the national level. At the same time, those variations have led a group of researchers to question the value of NSIs. We expect large countries to accommodate varieties of economic and social configurations in their different regions. However, significant differences occur between regions in smaller countries too. The UK is a good example. Economic differences between, for example, London and the south east and north east (measured in terms of employment, GDP, stock of business, new product development, financial investment) all point to the complex ways in which networks of actors operate in these environments (Ferreti and Parmentola, 2015).

The local region is also seen as a smaller entity than the nation state, but has its own governance capacity and an alternative sense of cohesion that is unique to these territories in terms of both character and functionality. This uniqueness offers opportunities for analysis at the regional level (Tötdling and Kaufmann, 1999) but also makes it difficult to measure and compare across other regions. However, Iammarino's (2005) idea of an 'evolutionary integrated' view of regional innovation systems makes it possible to investigate the mid-ground between the macro level of NISs and the micro level of local and individual actors. Referred to as the 'meso perspective', this idea based in evolutionary economics has spawned various concepts such as the learning regions, industrial districts, regional innovation systems and local innovation systems (Ferreti and Parmentola, 2015).

REGIONAL INNOVATION SYSTEMS

Asheim and Isaken (2002) and Doloreux (2002) define regional innovation systems (RISs) as social systems made up of interactive and systematic relationships between firms, institutions in both private and public sectors, in almost a carbon copy of the definition of NISs as adopted by the various scholars referred to earlier. The critical distinction is the regional factor. The idea of a region invites considerations of political, economic and social governance at a level that lies somewhere between the nation state and the level of a concentration of individual firms. Governance is organised among public agencies such as local municipal authorities and local enterprise agencies, and through private organisations such as local chambers of commerce. The scope of these organisations and the realm of their governance extend to the boundaries of the region. By 'region' we refer typically to subnational geo-political boundaries where governance is equated with the administrative aspect of a region and its institutions. A region such as the Eastern Region in the UK is an administrative region with its constituent administrative institutions including local authorities covering several counties and districts within it. Different countries have used the term as the formal name for a type of entity at the level of a sub-national administrative unit, as for example the Administrative Region of Quebec in Canada or the Autonomous Community of Murcia (*Región de Murcia*) in Spain. The Brazilians group their *estados* as the primary administrative divisions into *grandes regiões* or greater regions for statistical purposes (Mitra, 2012).

Where a region has a defined core then the special characteristics derived from that core diminish with distance from it. In these circumstances it is often referred to as a nodal or a functional region. The node is linked functionally to its surrounding areas by various types of tangible economic activity, transportation and communication systems. Travel to work distances, commuting habits and patterns, the flow of goods and services, and personal consumption behaviour as expressed in the use of shopping malls between these nodes are often regarded as typical measures of their nodal value. Sometimes these regions are difficult to define in terms of size, and are confused with smaller 'districts' or 'quarters' such as the cultural quarter of London's Silicon Roundabout in Hoxton or the creative heartland of Soho, the creative district of Xu-hui or Tianzifang in Shanghai, so called because of the natural or engineered concentration of specific creative industries in those sub-regions. What is important to note is that the

> typology of regions offers insights into their different economic and social compositions, the involvement of different stakeholders, and the creation and availability of different sets of opportunities mediated by entrepreneurs and by institutions. (Mitra, 2012: 269–70)

Now that we have an idea about what a region might mean, what precisely are RISs? Asheim and Cooke (1999) refer to it as the institutional infrastructure that enables and supports innovation within a given production structure of a region. Regional networks, including business clusters and research institutions, help to make this possible (Lundvall and Borrás, 1999). But to grasp the nettle of RISs one must pay close attention to the interrelationships that we discussed in the previous chapter. Their governance creates a system. More than interrelationships there is the question of interdependence, and if this interdependence works effectively it fosters region-specific and regionally specialised knowledge, technology and supplier bases supported by particular routines and norms of behaviour.[1] The specialisation is maintained because of trust, close face-to-face interactions and the externalities of knowledge creation evinced in spillover effects (see Chapters 1 and 2). So the critical issue is that of process rather than the static and exclusive presence of silo entities. Operations are often located in clusters of firms which cooperate with each other, while their specialisation engenders global connections with both subcontractors and customers.

TYPES OF RISs

Asheim (1998), Asheim and Isaken (2002) and Cooke and colleagues (1998) have identified three different type of RISs:

(a) Territorially embedded RISs – where firms rely on localised learning processes enabled by spatial, cultural and social proximity, but not necessarily on interactions with knowledge-producing organisations, such as universities. Examples include Emilia Romagna in Italy, one of the most prosperous regions in Europe, where innovation networks, technology centres and sector- or operationally-oriented regional development agencies prevail.

(b) Regionally networked RISs – the planned and intentional organisation of institutional infrastructure in the region through publicly funded universities or R&D institutions and training organisations. Good examples are found in Germany, Austria and the Nordic countries where the notion of the public good and the welfare model of economic development are strong and successful. Baden-Württemberg's RIS is a good example.

(c) Regionalised NISs – a functionally integrated institutional infrastructure along national policy lines. Here innovative activity is generally a function of cooperation with external actors from outside the region. Consequently writers such as Bunnell and Coe (2001) have called for the inclusion of extra-regional relationships to influence innovative activity in a particular region. Cooke (1998) refers to this model as the 'dirigiste RIS', which features institutional dominance and a linear model of innovation (from R& D to factory) dependent on scientific know-how enjoyed by particular scientific or sectoral communities of practice (Amin and Cohendet, 2004; Wenger, 2009). Planned entities such as science and technology parks accommodating well-resourced firms are often the principal custodians of such RISs.

The marked diversity of different RISs suggests that we should be cautious in the use of the term. Some writers have argued that regions are too large a concept (Rantisi, 2002) and that the specific functionalities and relationships that prevail in particular districts or sub-regional levels are important reasons for disaggregating levels, types or rates of innovation in any one region. In other words, the region is too big or too varied an entity.

SECTORAL INNOVATION SYSTEMS

One way of overcoming this problem of regional disaggregates and boundaries is to consider a sectoral approach as developed by Breschi and Malerba (1997). They focus their attention on groups of manufacturing firms in specific sectors. The firms create technological opportunities and derive specific advantage from that sector. As Malerba writes, a 'comparison of actors, sources, institutions and policies for innovation in different sectors shows striking differences' (2006: 380–1). Industry sectors demonstrate a unification of a set of activities meeting a particular demand, enabled by linking product groups with a common or shared knowledge platform. The unification affords a system characterised by three linked but distinctive domains of knowledge and technology, namely, actors and networks and institutions. Note that the range of actors could be the same as those found in RISs, but they are all located in the same sector or related sectors (as in pharmaceuticals and biotechnology). However, such a system is not necessarily localised in that sectors may be connected locally (as in small industrial units in the famous Italian IDs or an RIS), nationally (as part of an NIS) or globally (as between corporates and associates or subsidiaries). Various economies, such as those of Japan in the 1970s and 1980s, the USA in the 1990s and Italy, through their IDs, have claimed economic growth driven by particular sectors (Malerba, 2006).

FROM REGIONAL TO SECTORAL TO PLAIN INNOVATION SYSTEMS

An extra level of sophistication is provided by Oinas and Malecki (2002), who have come up with the idea of a spatial innovation system that examines the over-laps and interlinkages among national, regional and sectoral systems. They argue that all of these different systems emerge and evolve as different configurations in space, changing shape and structure as part of this evolutionary process. So what do we finally get from all these different systems? We find that there are common components to all them, including:

(a) interdependencies between firms based on networking through markets and strong and weak ties;
(b) the active involvement of institutions such as universities, R&D laboratories, incubator science parks, all creating and exchanging knowledge;
(c) the development of new markets and an emphasis on quality requirements based on technical sophistication and commercial and marketing know-how among producers and users;
(d) the formation of new organisations, and entrepreneurship with firms at high levels of specialisation marking their entrepreneurial growth;
(e) the emergence and development of support and ancillary services;
(f) local connectivities supplemented by global connectivities; and
(g) collective learning.

These features are born out of the strengths of such systems which encourage inter-disciplinarity, the accommodation of an evolutionary perspective centred round the effective functioning of institutions, non-linear development and the full range of innovations, from product to service and organisational forms (Edqusit, 2011; Martin and Simmie, 2008). We also note that hidden in these explanations of different systems are concepts of industrial districts, learning regions, innovative milieus and business or economic clusters. The place or the spatial factor is a function of social embeddedness (Granovetter, 1985) that stresses the importance of personal relationships above eco-nomic or transactional ones, based on trust and reciprocity and the discouragement of opportunistic behaviour. Then again, the personal relationships do not simply foster social activities; they engender economic transactional activities too.

Abubakar and Mitra (2013) identify this anomaly in their study of two sub-regions in the east of England – Cambridgeshire and Essex – analysing the different strategies for knowledge production as a function of a mix of pecuniary and spillover effects. Not all firms follow the same modes or patterns of new product or service development. Even where relationships are strong, firms make behavioural decisions based not on reductionist formulae but on a mix of gut feeling, heuristics, a scan of the evidence, cost–benefit analysis, and perhaps even a sense of feeling lucky. Moreover, with respect to territorial innovation systems, we should also be in a position to understand how one particular system is defined in terms of its knowledge base and how it is related or connected to other systems.

SOCIAL EMBEDDEDNESS

Ferrenti and Parmentola (2015) link the idea of social embeddedness to the particular character of the knowledge base using Asheim and Gertler's (2004) dichotomous classification of the synthetic or analytic knowledge base of regions. The synthetic knowledge base can be found in environments where existing knowledge is recombined, recalibrated or reapplied through informal and experiential processes of 'learning by doing, using or interacting'. Incremental innovations are generally the outcome of such processes where training and the use and sharing of experience enjoy an edge over R&D. Social embeddedness can be either low in these knowledge bases as in a cluster (concentration of similar or related firms and institutions) or high as in an industrial district (concentration of firms in specific industries where social and business communities are closely intertwined; Becattini, 1989).

Analytic knowledge is drawn mainly from scientific research relying more on cognitive processes and formal models of enquiry, methods and evaluation. Accessing formal or codified knowledge from research institutions and commercialising such knowledge create a science push environment generating radical or strategic innovations. Social embeddedness is high in local innovation systems as discussed earlier, but low in supply-side interventionist environments provided by technopoles or science and technology parks which tend to house proprietary high-technology firms in physical and service-oriented infrastructures, but with relatively limited or only highly formalised relationships with external actors in the region.

REVIEWING CRITICALLY AND CONNECTING CONCEPTUALLY DIFFERENT SYSTEMS OF INNOVATION

What is apparent in all this complexity is, first, the extensive overlap of concepts, from interactions to interdependencies and networks, through to spatial proximity, learning environments, embedding and the production and use of synthetic or analytic knowledge. Scholars have used these concepts to distinguish different types of NISs and RISs. Cooke (2001), for example, separates entrepreneurial, analytic knowledge-based RISs (ERISs) of the UK and USA from traditional, synthetic knowledge-based institutional RISs (IRISs) of Baden-Württemberg in Germany or the Nordic countries.

Ferreti and Parmentola (2015) distinguish between territorial and regional systems and local innovation systems. These are useful classifications and distinctions which enable one to estimate whether lock-ins are more likely, or where experimentation is a more common occurrence. We are entering analytical territory where cultural factors appear to distinguish how innovation occurs in different regions. There is a danger here of presenting static snapshots of environments based on clinical observation at a particular time. In some cases such an analysis might work, but even in fairly monocultural spaces as in China or Japan, we find exposure to non-local factors having a profound effect on the ways in which a country or region promotes innovation. As we have argued in the previous chapter, differences between countries and regions are attributable less perhaps to fixed notions of cultural orientation than to an evolution of such a perspective which allows for the nature of mutation in the culture, its people and institutions to be particularly important for analysis.

Soskice (1991) and Hall and Soskice (2001) have argued that different institutional forms of activity in the guise of varieties of capitalism evolve over time to support different types of economic activity. Diversified forms of production based on quality relying more on a synthetic knowledge base are generally available in coordinated market economies, such as in Switzerland, Germany or the Nordic countries. Non-market forms of collaboration and cooperation between public and private stakeholders drive such economies. Here complex production systems and the development of complex products in well-established industries as in machine tools industries, such as in machine tools, tend to benefit from such collaboration. Liberal economies, such as those in the UK and USA, also produce complex products, but these are complex *systemic* products, such as those of IT and defence technologies, where analytic knowledge is dominant.

What then about emerging economies (countries or regions)? What then of varieties of regions in one variety of capitalism (as in Detroit or California in the USA)? How can we create environments where we do not have access to organised resource exploitation or institutional activity? Let us look at two vignettes of local development based on key technologies and the planned intervention of regional government.

VIGNETTE 3.1   ACCELERATING GAZA, PALESTINIAN START-UPS AND FILMING SARAJEVO

EYEFUL IN GAZA

The Gaza Strip engages everyone's mind with images of inextricable conflict, grinding poverty and the power of recalcitrant ideologies. It is no wonder that utilities such as electricity or property, as in office space, are not easy to find when one is contemplating setting up a new, technology-based venture. But Ilana Montauk, Head of Gaza Sky Geek (GSG), a start-up accelerator in Gaza city, has other ideas. She has faith in youth, smart phones and apps, and believes the young coders in Gaza are as talented as the ones she has met at Harvard and in Silicon Valley. Montauk's faith stems from her previous experience as a Harvard graduate and as a member of staff of Google, who have backed her venture and which is operated by the US charity Mercy Corps for whom Montauk works. GSG intends to develop business ideas and make the necessary connections between investors and entrepreneurs. This attention to creating viable businesses is a change from the original focus of GSG, which was to educate young people about technology. GSG was formed in 2011 and Google provided $900,000 of the initial costs.

Operational costs have been met via crowdfunding, raising $250,000 from more than 800 people, which has been used by Mercy Corps and GSG to cover rent, salaries and access to the Internet.

Israel has blockaded Gaza for over 8 years now, and this action prevents or restricts imports of chemicals, concrete and other materials that have both civilian and militaristic use. Ironically, the other instruments of positive civic engagement or negative forms of networking, smart phones, computers and the English language are used widely. Perhaps this paradoxical situation offers opportunities as well as challenges for the aspiring entrepreneurs, 40 of whom turned up recently for a 5-day boot camp.

Montauk worked with her team to build partnerships with seed investors, follow-on investors, corporate partners (mobile operators, large banks, etc.), US accelerators, local incubators, mentors (from MENA, the USA, Europe, Africa, etc.) and the Israeli Army (to allow start-ups to exit Gaza for market expansion opportunities).

The early results are also promising. An Arabic language driving game has been launched by mobile gaming company Baskalet, founded recently by 27-year-old Mohammed Ezzdeen. Nawal Abusultan, a 32-year-old attendee, whose site MENAship aims to connect Arab students with university scholarships abroad, first heard about GSG from a Facebook post, and has created a team of four people despite not knowing anything about start-ups before she developed her project. Four GSG firms have secured investment from Arab-centric venture funds, and another four might well be on their way to attracting such funding within a year. In more general terms GSG has prioritised the plan to keep running operations elsewhere in case war rears its ugly head again. However, the 'shuttered' airport of Gaza does not help, and neither does the routine permission that locals need from Israel or Egypt to leave the strip. War has intervened in a major way. A year ago in the summer when Montauk was away, the fighting killed 2,000 people. When Montauk returned she found 60 people waiting to discuss their start-up plans.

So how can the entrepreneurs of Gaza, Montauk, GSG, Mercy Corps and Google secure the 'hope dividend'? Well, some observers, notably Shikhar Ghosh from Harvard who has studied Arabic businesses, suggest that since costs and valuations are lower, there are real opportunities for creating a technology-based ecosystem which is directed towards the production of goods and services aimed at the Arab communities' rising middle-class population. Then there is this belief among the young to rise above the ravages of conflict to create a new world view based on entrepreneurship, technology and the discovery of opportunities for innovation. It sounds like a mission that stretches beyond constraints, an innovation of the community presence combining with innovation in new products and services. For it is the power of innovation and entrepreneurship which prevails over all else.

(Continued)

(Continued)

PALESTINE START-UPS

Start-ups from the USA, Europe or other developed countries often complain about the lack of investment, tough tax regime, or a culture that does not really favour entrepreneurship. These are real problems, of course, but they pale in comparison with those their Palestinian colleagues have to face on a daily basis. Frequent electricity shortages, lack of 3G connectivity, border restrictions, difficulties in moving in and out of the country, not to mention the ongoing tension with neighbouring Israel, are all factors that could demoralise even the most well-intentioned business people. In spite of this – or perhaps partly due to it – the Palestinian start-up scene is alive and kicking.

Flagship companies include: Yamsafer, a Booking.com-like website, which is focused on the Arab world, active in 18 countries, and recently received $3.5 million series B funding from Global Founders Capital; Souktel, which helps people in developing countries with no broadband but with basic mobile phones to receive alerts, information and multimedia content through an SMS-based platform; WebTeb, which provides health and medical information; and Batuta, an online travel portal with more than 1.5 million unique monthly users that secured in June a $2.5 million investment from the Siraj Fund. Last year, ICT accounted for around 6% of Palestine's GDP.

Most of these companies are based in Ramallah, in the West Bank, where the tech ecosystem is thriving in ways that has led some to define it as 'Tel Aviv, without the track record'.

THE SONGS OF SARAJEVO

The passion of life mission draws a parallel from another part of the world, in Sarajevo, where in 1995, during the siege of Sarajevo and the Bosnian War, the Sarajevo Film Festival was born. It is now in its 21st year, and it brings in 100,000 visitors per year, the majority of them being 'locals' from Vienna to Istanbul. Danis Tanovic, Bosnia's film hero and Oscar winner for his first film *No Man's Land*, tells the story of how, one night at the launch of the festival when the shelling had recommenced, he and his friends ran along the street thinking they were going to die. They did not perish, but huddled in a small cinema full of people and watched the American blockbuster *The Bodyguard*! Crazy as it was, it was a time to push back the feelings about the death of friends and family and find relief in the power of cinema.

Gaza is not Sarajevo, and high-technology business does not compare with the art of cinema. But in both stories there is this sense of achievement based on desire and ingenuity, in finding the opportunity to deliver something unique, to overcome the severity of almost intractable odds in a given space. GSG and SFF (Sarajevo Film Festival) are the extraordinary outcomes possible in certain spaces. It would be difficult to portray both stories as examples of regional or local innovation as explained earlier. They are not the stories of specific products and services born out of the application of synthetic or analytic knowledge or the prevalence of certain institutional virtues. Possibilities do of course emerge from the confluence of ideas, motivation, the interdependencies of people and organisations, and we see the creation of hubs of knowledge that change the environment, even if it is just once a year as in Sarajevo.

In Gaza, local innovation is made possible because of local capability and global technology and financial support. A local environment is, therefore, created in a globally connected setting. Crucially, what we also comprehend is the dramatic break from established and entropic patterns of violence and despair, at least in a small space. This does not follow the gradualist trajectory of evolution but a form of creative destruction of negative values. When Montauk first moved to the Gaza Strip in 2013, what most struck her was the drive and focus of the citizens and not the poverty, the lack of electricity or the rubble from many decades of conflict. What mattered was the quality of the people and their enthusiasm and the ability to develop a diverse network based on an abundance of structural holes which normally would lie unutilised. Coupled with the personal drive and enthusiasm was the buy-in of one of the world's largest private organisations, Google. Gaza is a testimony to the value that can be generated through transnational innovative and entrepreneurial activity.

In a different way, Sarajevo's success is also sourced internationally through the way it attracts a growing global audience each year, supporting local endeavour. An institution, the SFF, has evolved there, providing a kind of meeting place for mainly regional film makers now, as if it were drawing from Sarajevo's past as a convergent point, historically, for different cultures rooted in the Ottoman and Hungarian Empires and later in socialism.

Sources: Campbell, M. and S.A. Ramadan (2015) *Bloomberg Businessweek*; Daniel, C. (2015) *Financial Times*, 25 August; Federico Guerrini, 26 August 2015, www.zdnet.com/article/coding-for-the-challenges-of-the-arab-world-palestines-growing-startup-scene/ (last accessed 27 April 2016)

Much can be learnt about how regions remake their local environments using different raw materials for innovation from these experiences. They do not provide the same reference points that scholarly studies for RISs and NISs do, but they point to possibilities based on region-specific experiences. It is not possible to recreate an RIS in war-torn Gaza and the ravaged city of Sarajevo. But what we can argue about is the necessary seeds that can be sown for a future innovation harvest. The innovation process starts with the sowing of these seeds and not in the copy of a system that exists elsewhere. The conditions of immediacy have to be met to construct Gaza's and Sarajevo's own systems. The learning issue here is about taking each environment where it stands and examining ways in which that particular environment takes innovative shape.

The Gaza and the West Bank illustrations serve to highlight five important issues about different systems of innovation:

(a) The fact that systems evolve uniquely in their particular environments depending upon the type, scope and depth of problems that the particular environment faces at specific times.

(b) That the uniqueness is a condition of both the problems and the necessary local solutions that can be found in a mix of talent, technology, social capital and natural and other resources, coupled where appropriate with global networking and market opportunities.

(c) The resolution of problems does not necessarily lead to a convergence of practice or the development of a common set of tools with which to address or evaluate systems of innovation worldwide.

(d) It is necessary to study common and disparate systems and communities of innovation in order truly to understand the richness and variety of economic opportunities serving people and communities.

(e) How the development of a regional ecosystem of innovation can leapfrog national boundaries to create radical changes in regions otherwise devastated by conflict.

Oftentimes the availability and appropriation of abundant natural resources found in the most unlikely of places (especially those deemed to be poorly endowed with them) raise the profile of a place sufficiently to warrant the development of soft and hard infrastructure, and a systemic approach to the nurturing of skills, capabilities and technologies in that place. These are circumstances when a significant change occurs as in the amelioration, if not eradication, of poverty. Take Rajasthan in India, for example, and the story of a hard bean, guar, in the following vignette.

VIGNETTE 3.2   THE HARD BEAN OF INNOVATION AND LOCAL ECONOMIC DEVELOPMENT

Rajasthan, in north-western India, is one of the most attractive tourist destinations in India. Its Rajput history, the rich forts and palaces of the maharajas and princes of several dynasties (many converted in part to luxury hotels), the romantic desert, the vast and varied landscape suffused with the colour of the land and the clothes of the locals, magical festivals and trade shows, all contribute to the coffers of tourism. Yet many parts of Rajasthan are considered to be the some of the poorest places in the world. Heat and hunger in a relatively parched land have been common characteristics assailing the poor for a very long time.

Farmers in the state have used guar, a hard bean, hard enough to crack teeth, to feed both their cattle and families for centuries. Where the sources of nutrition are limited, animals and humans often share a common resource. But guar also absorbs water 'like a souped-up corn starch', and a grounded, powdered form of the bean helps to keep savoury pastries crisp and thicken ice-cream. Once this discovery was made, the bean began to attract widespread commercial interest. More recently, it was discovered that guar can stiffen water to a degree that allows a mixture to carry sand sideways into wells drilled by horizontal fracturing, a technique otherwise known as fracking.

Just as China dominates the world's supply of rare earth minerals, India produces approximately 85% of the global supply of guar. Fracking experts, such as Michael Economides of the University of Houston, claim that without guar it is not possible to have fracturing fluids. What makes it worse is that there is an absolute paucity of guar supply in the world, according to Economides. Like most natural resources, the growth of guar is dependent on climatic conditions, and especially rain. When in 2012 there were serious worries about that year's delay in the monsoon, trading in guar futures was suspended, not least because inadequate supplies could only overheat speculation in the futures market.

The advent of fracking has unleashed a boom in that market mainly because it has prompted a surge in natural gas production coupled with less reliance on oil imports, and a gradual move away from what some argue as dirty coal-fired plants, especially in the USA. The UK has also followed suit with a growing corporate and governmental interest in fracking. Calling into question this new demand for new energy resources is the genuine concern of environmentalists who have identified the damage fracking can do to rural water supplies and to the land because of the considerable depths to which digging and drilling is required. For poor Rajasthani farmers, however, guar's new-found and proven potential is a source of food and shelter. Instead of a fragile mud hut, the farmers can now build a house of stone by obtaining a better income. An alternative to eating only guar and a few other grains is the availability of regular food for the families of these farmers. This huge asymmetry in expectations, benefits of livelihood and environmental damage sets the scene for a new drama in international development. How best can systems of innovation address this asymmetry that affects different regions of the world united by the availability of a unique resource, yet divided by attitudes towards the environment because of the different levels of economic growth, and between basic livelihoods in a poor environment and concerns for a safer environment in an economically richer part of the world?

Systems often break down when there are opposite forces and tensions. In an interconnected world, knowledge creation is dependent on certain forms of mutuality that are a far cry from the traditional problems of one-sided appropriation by the stronger economic power, common in previous trajectories of trading relationships and arrangements for global production.

Since around 2013, a large-scale international effort has taken place to try and meet the growing demand for guar. Thousands of farmers have been mobilised by an Indian firm, Vikas WSP, that specialises in making powders out of guar beans. Since most farmers sold their seed stock last year, when the delays in the monsoon fuelled speculation, the price of guar has increased dramatically. Vikas WSP's strategy for overcoming this supply-side problem was to hold rallies in small towns and distribute free seeds, which included new hybrids with a high yield, to the farmers. Farmers with irrigated land in Punjab State, north of Rajasthan, were persuaded to plant guar instead of cotton, and the new crop gradually began to enter the market. If the farmers agreed to plant guar the company signed contracts which guaranteed returns of $800 per acre (or $2,000 per hectare) to the former. The vagaries of the monsoon notwithstanding, there is a high expectation of harvesting a heavier crop. Vikas has built two new plants in the historical city of Jodhpur in Rajasthan and doubled its processing capacity, with plans for producing 86,400 tons of guar powder each day.

High prices mean a search for alternative sources of supply of the same bean or even alternatives to guar. The drop in revenues for a major oil-services corporation such as Haliburton will inevitably mean that the latter will attempt to source cheaper supplies. California and parts of Australia and China have been identified as potential places for the supply and production of guar. Some energy analysts anticipating a slowdown in the fracking boom have suggested that guar alternatives could be found in the near future. For the foreseeable future, however, guar prices are expected to remain high because there does not appear to be any let-up in the demand for fracking, together with interest outside the USA. Until another cycle of change occurs, the farmers of Rajasthan and Punjab could satisfy basic quests for economic betterment in their lives. Some have built new homes with stone instead of mud, a few have bought gold and got married, and others have travelled to Europe! The sales figures for tractor companies such as Massey Fergusson have doubled in Jodhpur, and Vikas WSP continues to augment its plans for developing an even more resilient system of hard bean innovation. They all look up to the sky and wonder about the monsoon, come June!

Sources: Harris (2012); emirates.com

The guar story of Rajasthan replicates the same set of issues we found in Gaza and the West Bank, albeit in a completely different environment in terms of its geography, economic conditions and political exigencies. Neither of these vignettes provide compelling evidence of a standard model found in the west, but they offer a different understanding of the possibilities of regional innovation systems. The Palestinian stories reveal the power of human capital and resilience against all odds to create an innovation ecosystem based on technology and talent, while the Rajasthan anecdote provides insights into how natural resources properly harnessed and resourced for production could lead to the establishment of a local innovation system involving the creation of new supply-side institutions for the global energy market. One demonstrates how the instruments and function of innovation can find purchase in spaces of conflict and war, while the other offers a vital source of entrepreneurial opportunity based on the effective utilisation of natural resources that helps to tackle poverty and address in part the global energy crisis. In both examples we find that dependence on national priorities, policies or systems of innovation is necessarily relevant for innovation to find a home in the region. We can see, however, the emergence of a regional model of innovation that could form the basis of a national system of innovation addressing critical priorities of those countries. In both narratives we can also see the unique possibilities of connecting regional innovation constructs to policies and platforms for international development. This could offer pathways for the development of a new approach to foreign policy initiatives in developed economies that are framed in ways which allow for direct support for regional economic development based on innovation in emerging countries.

Throughout our discussion on SIs we have made reference consistently to institutions and institutional factors that underpin the evolution of these systems and practices in regions of innovation. The context in which innovation thrives or perishes is that in which an institutional support system provides for or disengages with all the stakeholders of innovation. The nature and type of institutions in these environments create the context in which innovators can operate. What then are these institutions and what role do they play in supporting entrepreneurship?

INSTITUTIONS AND INNOVATION

In Mitra (2012) I state that a good starting point is Douglass North's idea of institutions and institutional change. North (1990b) refers to institutions as rules of the game in a society, 'or more formally, the humanly devised constraints that shape human interaction' (p. 3) and help to provide a structure for incentives in political, social and economic environments. In a discussion on innovative environments, incentives could refer to legal forms such as patents and licences or other forms of intellectual protection for the innovating organisation, the norms and behavioural practices and sanctions that characterise specific organisations and locations. They enable an understanding of both prevailing currencies of behaviour and norms that have evolved over time. These sets of accepted and normative patterns of behaviour and incentives reduce uncertainty because they provide structures for human interaction in markets, in businesses and in society. However, normative patterns are not universal and institutions operate in different ways with varying degrees of potency in different countries and environments.

INCENTIVES AND CODES OF CONDUCT

The way in which incentives and behaviour obtain in specific environments is through constraints which are both formal (rules and regulations) and informal (conventions and codes of behaviour). These rules and codes of conduct are created by mediation or choice (examples include the Indian and the US Constitutions) or evolve over time (such as the Common Law in the UK). What these constraints mean effectively in practice is that they either permit people to pursue activities (such as starting a new innovative, hybrid organisation that meets both social and economic objectives) or prevent/prohibit certain types of behaviour (e.g. environmental pollution as a result of the development of a new mode of production using diesel engines). The constraints can take the form of either written rules and codes of conduct (formal constraints)[2] or unwritten conventions and codes of practice (informal constraints), with all forms allowing for the monitoring of the behaviour of people and organisations depending upon the prevailing culture and circumstances of particular environments.

INSTITUTIONS AND ORGANISATIONS

Institutions are not the same as organisations, although common usage suggests that they are. For example, we refer to an educational institution which is also an organisation providing specific education services. But there is a critical difference between the two. Organisations depend on strategies, competencies, skills, resources and models with which to operate within a set of rules or conventions of practice. These sets of rules are what we describe as institutions. Innovation practice in any organisation needs to take place within the rules of the game set in specific environments and the incentives offered for participation and for emerging with new solutions to problems. The creation, development, fine tuning, evolution and outcomes of the rules of the game follow a different and independent process from those of organisations (Mitra, 2012).

Let us consider innovation as the making of a new product. This product needs to have the technology, talent, financial resources and organisational capacity to make it work in the market. The market with its 'rules of the game' has to accept this new product, but between the making of the product and its acceptance in the marketplace there are several steps of individual and organisational ingenuity. The learning process, the search for legitimacy, the protection of intellectual property, and the realisation of an innovative outcome coupled with the entrepreneurial arrangements for their presence and success in the market, can be considered to be those steps of ingenuity.

THE RULE OF LAW AND PROPERTY RIGHTS

There is a general and widespread belief in the rule of law and property rights as being the most important institutions in society and in a prosperous economy (Baumol, 1990;

Easterly and Levine, 2003; Rodrik et al., 2004). These institutions help to stop corrupt actions such as bribe taking, pure rent seeking or destructive forms of business practice. They can also help to reduce the uncertainty associated with the development of a new product, service and venture by making transparent what it is possible to do or make. If, for example, bribery and inadequate legal protection take precedence in particular societies, as Johnson et al. (2000) found in five different former Soviet countries, then the incentive to invent and commercialise something new is jeopardised as access to information, resources, skills and technologies can be compromised. The way in which institutions of any one country or region are subsumed by wider imperatives, as in the European accession story of Central and Eastern European countries, can often lead to a dilution or ineffectual redirection of existing routines and norms of behaviour. Arzeni and Mitra (2008) found in their study of youth entrepreneurship in Central and Eastern European countries that the pressures of being part of a linked European economy and globalisation led to the abandonment of old skills favouring youth employment. Paradoxically, since they did not have sufficient work experience to take up employment, younger people did enjoy the option of self-employment and creative endeavour alongside education and emigration.

CULTURAL AND BEHAVIOURAL NORMS AND PRACTICES

Another example of a proper appreciation of the role of institutions helps us to retrace our steps back to the points made about the uniqueness of specific environments in this chapter and the previous one. Key factors of culture, attitudes and behaviour influence different contexts for innovation. Saxenian (1996), in her seminal study of Silicon Valley and Route 128 in the USA, referred to the crucial difference of the former's pioneer entrepreneurial spirit with that of the culture of corporatism and secrecy of the latter. Explaining why this difference could have occurred, Gilson (1999) pointed out that legal rules allowing for the enforceability of an old covenant not to compete in Massachusetts, compared with the way California interprets its employment law banning such covenants, explains why Silicon Valley was able to develop its dynamic culture (cited in Mitra, 2012).

Given the nexus of variables, organisations, institutions and their connections across systems, could we possibly consider the idea of some kind of meta system? We may have some help at hand here when we find that much effort has been made to define ecosystems of innovation. So let us consider what these systems mean.

ECOSYSTEMS OF INNOVATION

Let us imagine an environment which is loosely coupled, clustered round a particular domain or interrelated domains, and where all actors or species are proactive and responsive in their effort to conserve the environment for its own benefit. Such an environment can be described as an ecosystem (Chang and West, 2006). What makes an ecosystem is the interplay of its two key elements: the species and the environment. Borrowing from concepts of networks and networking, we find that

that species or actors need to interact with each other, balancing their needs, and if the environment is conducive to such interaction then the species can sustain themselves from one generation to another. From time to time different actors may play a leading or coordinating role, acting as a catalyst or a role model to facilitate better connectivity among all the actors. But the overall system supports collaboration and communication among the actors.

THE BIOLOGICAL ECOSYSTEM

Much of what we know about ecosystems stems from our knowledge of biology and biosystems. Species can be classified and individuals that tend to resemble one another or are able to have a functional existence together tend to intermingle, cross-fertilise and interbreed. Chang and West (2006) suggest that there are four essential elements of ecosystems:

(a) *Interaction and engagement* – signifying the need for interdisciplinary interaction for social well-being, to share resources and, where appropriate, to unite to defend themselves against pollution, natural disaster or remote species. One does not have to go far to see ants at work. Then there are coral polyps and little animals living in colonies interacting with fish, turtles, sea snakes and molluscs in warm, clear and shallow waters.

(b) *Balance* – the stability, harmony and sustainability within an ecosystem. Each part of a system plays a key role, and if one is disproportionately out of tune with the rest, then the entire ecosystem could collapse. Yet a failure need not mark total disaster; it can contribute to the balance of welfare to the whole ecosystem through its conversion from a living form to a support structure. When coral polyps die, their remains become a stony, branching structure as part of a reef, providing for shelter and support for the reef for a long time into the future.

(c) *Domain clustering and loose coupling* – choice determines one's entry and role in an ecosystem. Species gravitate towards 'loosely coupled, taxonomic groups' where members appear to share the same culture, habits, interests and desires. This loose coupling in turn engenders proactiveness and responsiveness mainly for their own benefit.

(d) *Self-organising* – the loose coupling and the sharing of mutual interests and actions do not detract from the independence and self-empowerment of the species. What connects the species is a form of swarm intelligence which allows information drawn from self-coordination to feed into necessary actions at the ecosystem level. Self-organising obviates the need for dependency on authority at times of critical need.

The typical biological ecosystem sustains the living organisms (biotic factors) alongside its physical environments (abiotic factors) in a state of equilibrium with a relatively stable set of conditions. The functional characteristics of the ecosystem monitor and regulate change to ensure its stability.

Sustainability and stability afforded by the state of equilibrium are dependent on the energy dynamics and described by modelling the energy dynamics of the ecosystem. In a biological ecosystem the dynamics are represented by the predator–prey relationship, the burning of calories in consuming prey and the transfer of energy by plants to the soil for regeneration by other plants. The 'whole' as opposed to the parts defines the ecosystem (Jackson et al., 2009).

THE INNOVATION ECOSYSTEM

The origin of the term 'innovation ecosystem' can be traced back to James Moore and his introduction of the idea of the business ecosystem in 1993. Whether the new term denotes any departure from the old reality of ecosystems is a moot point to consider, especially if we can detect any major shift in the way we think about and live with ecosystems. But as Andersen (2011) states, the new notion of the innovation ecosystem raises two important questions:

1. How should we understand innovation ecosystems in the evolutionary context of global economics and innovation?
2. How should we operate and interact strategically with innovation ecosystems from a company perspective?

Much of what we know about innovation ecosystems is owed to the evolution of systems of innovation which we have discussed above, but also to the numerous examples of geographic, economic or industrial agglomeration across the world. These agglomerations are found in regions, but also, as we will discuss later in successful ICT platforms (iPhone, Android), in new industries such as cloud computing (Andersen, 2011).

We may expect the four critical elements of interaction and engagement, balance, domain clustering and loose coupling and self-organising to obtain in an innovation system as well. But while the former elements can be modelled around the energy dynamics referred to above, innovation ecosystems encapsulate the economic and social dynamics of the layered relationships among actors who are driven by the need to achieve technological development and innovation (Lang, 1998). The actors here are a combination of human capital (people, skills) and tangible resources that help to bring together institutional participants in the innovation ecosystems (universities, venture capitalists, research institutes, centres of excellence, national or local economic development and business assistance organisations, funding agencies, policy makers and other stakeholders).

The other important point to note is that the innovation ecosystem is primarily concerned with economic functions driven, and given its specific identity, by the innovation process and its contribution to economic growth and development. We can find two fairly distinct economies within an innovation ecosystem: the knowledge economy and the commercial economy. These two economies may be considered to be two separate economies, but there is a considerable amount of interdependence when we examine how economies grow and how innovation contributes to such growth. The knowledge economy is defined as one which allocates scarce knowledge resources and grows the knowledge base through fundamental research. The commercial economy is driven by the exigencies of the market. But what is the source of investment in the knowledge economy, the money which enables the creation and development of research laboratories, the education and employment of scientists and technicians, and the pure, blue sky research that opens up possibilities for discoveries and inventions? Tax revenues generated by the profits of the commercial sector go a long way in supporting the functioning of the knowledge economy, including the operations of governmental R&D units.

We could argue that any well-meaning economic strategy for growth and development in any country would accommodate the means by which the knowledge economy is coupled with the commercial economy. Ensuring that the commercial sector operates successfully would be an objective of both industry and government. Attaining this objective is in part also dependent on the innovation ecosystem being developed around a specific set of technologies. This suggests an interventionist approach of the kind we discussed in the chapter on policy. Jackson (2011) refers to two examples of focused ecosystems: the US Department of Energy's Innovation Ecosystem Development Initiative, which is aimed at accelerating the adoption of energy innovations, and the European Innovation Initiative's Digital Ecosystem technologies. Another example referred to by the same author is The Engineering Research Center's (ERC) programme at the National Science Foundation which was established more than a quarter of a century ago. A relatively smaller scale innovation ecosystem, the ERC programme was created to push selected niches in technology and engineering which transform engineering systems. The success of this venture lay in its ability to provide successive regimes which took up the work of various smaller ecosystems when the initial period of government funding had ended after a period of 10 years. The current success rate for graduated ERCs is 82% (Williams and Lewis, 2010).

What is clear from the discussion above is that innovation ecosystems can be organised and structured around most subject matter. What matters is the establishment of unique combinations of key stakeholders, ideas and technologies that consolidate their convergence. But how do we know whether an ecosystem works or not and, crucially, whether it is thriving or not? Jackson (2011) notes that in a successful innovation ecosystem the resources invested in the knowledge economy (through private, government or direct business investment) are eventually replaced by the outcomes and outputs from increased profits in the commercial economy. When the two economies – knowledge and commercial – reach a balanced equilibrium point the innovation ecosystem can be regarded as healthy. This process can be described as a virtuous cycle of R&D resources being replenished by profits from the private sector. An equation explains the functioning relationship (from Jackson, 2011):

$$P = P_0(I_{R\&D}) + \Delta P = P_0(1 - \alpha) + \Delta P$$

Where P_0 is defined as the initial profit before the investments in fundamental research are made, 'P' is defined as profits corrected for investment, $P_0(I_{R\&D}) = P_0(1 - \alpha)$, $I_{R\&D} = \alpha P_0$, is defined as the commercial economy's research investment in the research economy, and ΔP is the innovation induced growth in the economy (Jackson, 2011: 4).

The challenge for any innovation system is to maintain equilibrium and ensure that a growth situation can subsist. This is possible when R&D activity leads to successful product outcomes which generate profits. However, since the knowledge and commercial economies have two rather different reward systems, it is often rather difficult to provide an effective pipeline for fundamental research to lead to innovative and profitable commercial products.

The challenge in creating a growth situation for an ecosystem is to figure out how to turn the breakthroughs of R&D efforts into products that lead to profits. Achieving this goal is complicated by the fact that the two economies operate on different reward systems, thereby making it difficult to link discoveries derived from fundamental research with innovative products that can translate into profits in the marketplace, unless the cycle is internal to a firm. This can create a gap between resources for fundamental research at one end and resources for commercially-oriented innovative products at the other end, a gap often referred to as the 'Valley of Death'. Ecosystem players involved in moving the research and the technology demonstration to its commercialisation can lose themselves in this valley as a result of the gap.

One way of mitigating risk and overcoming possible failures is to focus attention on the various intangibles that govern the complex relationships that subsist in an innovation ecosystem and across the spectrum described above. This can occur through persuasion and incentivisation of the key actors at either end of the spectrum (academic institutions and commercial firms, respectively) to move in either direction and examine ways in which they work towards multiple objectives. Could universities, for example, give equal if not greater recognition to commercially-oriented outputs for their research? Could businesses (larger firms individually, and small firms collectively) be encouraged to top-slice profits for joint research with academia? In the current climate of rarefied peer group-supported publications like academic journals on the one hand and short-term earnings yield on the other, this does not seem likely.

The ecosystem debate poses significant challenges for research on innovation. The unit of analysis shifts from firms or government organisations to the entire system and the relationship between them. Few empirical studies have attempted to introduce variables and their composite alternatives or indeed complex methodologies to produce effective research design to examine ecosystem outcomes, outputs and processes. Qualitative studies have compensated with case studies, if only to emphasise the differences between various ecosystems. The stress on R&D in the innovation process also tends to ignore multiple ecosystems of innovation occurring in environments which are not rich in R&D. In this mix we now find new discourse emerging on digital ecosystems, highlighting the new domain of digital innovation.

DIGITAL ECOSYSTEMS[3]

The term 'digital ecosystem (DE)' is defined as 'a self-organizing, scalable and sustainable system composed of heterogeneous digital entities and their interrelations focusing on interactions among entities to increase system utility, gain benefits, and promote information sharing, inner and inter cooperation and system innovation' (Li et al., 2012: 119). Since the early part of this century when the term emerged, DE has been applied to business, knowledge management, the service industry, health care, manufacturing, social networks and education. Its application to many modes of economic and social activity has also unleashed interesting new possibilities for innovation.

DE is the combination of all relevant digital 'components': the people who interact with them, the economic and social processes that enable such interaction and the technology environment that support both. In general any ecosystem consists of elements, interlinks and functions:

- The elements define the ecosystem.
- The 'interlinks' demonstrate how the elements are connected together, and how information flows within the ecosystem. These include requests for content, contributions of content to social platforms, transactions, and even communications between internal and external audiences.
- The function is what the ecosystem is trying to achieve through specific actions involving the elements and their interactions to help provide for a purpose of the ecosystem. (Department of Business Innovation and Skills, 2015)

These three components of the DE can be identified in terms of actors, instruments, the technical environment, and processes. They include:

(a) Digital touch points (social media, company sites and search engines). Three types of digital touch points are worth noting:
  i. Controlled touch points: People can control their business by using websites and applications.
  ii. Social publishing touch points: Examples include YouTube, Twitter, Facebook and LinkedIn. A business can design the platform and publish content for public consumption.
  iii. Third-party touch points: Social review services and search engines such as Yelp.
(b) People or communities using the system and internal people within the ecosystem who will work on developing the ecosystem.
(c) The digital soft infrastructure (skills, resources, core competencies) – see more later. It also includes business processes for improving the management of the digital ecosystem community, and for receiving and responding to audience feedback.
(d) The technical environment: the Internet, hosts, servers, application infrastructure, cloud services (e.g. for storage), networks (wired and wireless) (bitstrategist, 2011).
(e) Interconnections: information flows which cover communication between social platform transactions and between external and internal audiences.

In many respects the DE provides for the same components of multiple stakeholders, connectivity, intangibles and resource mobilisation that characterise analogue innovation ecosystems. Crucial differences are the speed of connectivity, the global reach among actors and the multiple layering of projects, technologies, organisations and people, all being engaged with numerous innovations made possible by digital technologies. What makes this possible is the decentralisation and creation of a flexible socio-technical approach to the creation and sustenance of both local and global production and innovation networks. We still have the loosely coupled systems and transactions of businesses and other actors who network with each other at both the local and global levels.

As an ecosystem the DE enables innovation in ways that have probably not been possible before. First, it combines living and non-living components, thus allowing for a proxied convergence of biosystems and other business or innovation ecosystems referred to above. The digital technologies (see above) can be viewed as the non-living component, while the people who use these technologies are the living component. The dynamic interactions of these two components result in continuous changes, and it is this dynamic that constitutes the behaviour of an ecosystem. This convergence and the dynamic are themselves innovative. The specific ecosystem is both producer- and user-driven at the same time, with fluid boundaries enabling the change of roles. It is open source oriented (Dini et al., 2011), emphasising the pivotal role that producers and users (including both consumers and citizens) play in the ecosystem. The advancement of digital technologies and also artificial intelligence has led to a more complex system in the form of a digital infrastructure (Tilson et al., 2010), and the growing prospect of deep machine learning acting as a possible substitute for many of the roles that traditional actors play in an innovation system.

This DE space will need to watched over time to see how both the product of emergent innovations and the process by which they are generated upend our understanding of innovation, the economic functioning of producers and users, and the nature of production and consumption.

CONCLUDING OBSERVATIONS

In this chapter we have examined different types of innovation systems and found that there is a variety of critical opinion on these different types and their scale, scope and geography. Common to all systems is, first, the existence of key component parts made up of multiple stakeholders, and their interrelationships. Understanding these relationships helps us to understand better why regions and nations rise and fall and why an innovation differential obtains across countries, regions and organisations. The fact that good systems are susceptible to influences and that they evolve over time underlines the robustness of effective systems. The variety of systems also suggests the significance of different environments and how the culture, institutions and innovation practices shape those systems. They call into question any superior system simply because the state of a nation or a region, its economic, social and cultural contours, demands appropriate innovations for their people. Institutions at both formal and informal levels buttress systems of innovation, and their evolution over time also reflects how people, organisations and environments interact to work out how best to govern both the process and the outcomes of innovation over time.

This brief account of the importance of systems and institutions in the innovation process engenders considerations of organisational structures and arrangements, public policy and the role of government. Government policies for innovation can play a significant part in either the advancement or the drawing back of innovation frontiers in any economy. So we now turn our attention in the next chapter to public policy issues and the role of government in the innovation process.

 ———— SELF-ASSESSMENT AND RESEARCH QUESTIONS ————

1. What constitutes systems of innovation and to what extent do they reflect specific spatial and environmental conditions?

2. What are the different types of innovation and their unique characteristics? Do these types have common elements?

3. Are national and regional systems of innovation necessarily linked?

4. What are 'institutions' and what role do they play in the innovation process?

5. Define innovation ecosystems and explain their importance. Are digital innovation ecosystems any different from analogue innovation ecosystems?

NOTES

1. Care has to be taken to not confuse such norms of local behaviour as being some kind of homogenized monocultural identity. Silicon Valley's legendary innovators and entrepreneurs have different cultural origins, and the same could be said about Hoxton. The more diverse the cultural origin base, the greater the propensity seems for a wealth of ideas, enterprises and productive outcomes.

2. For a fuller discussion on formal and informal constraints see Mitra (2012: chapters 5 and 6).

3. This section draws on recent work for the Digital Exploration Centre (DEC) in Southend, Essex, UK that I have been developing with the support of four of my postgraduate students – Tryphaena Isaac, Jamil Hunedi, Chien-Yu Huang and Elif Mavis – for the Digital Exploration Centre in Essex. I wish to thank these students and the DEC for this work.

 ———— REFERENCES ————

Abubakar, Y.A. and Mitra, J. (2013) 'The venturesome poor and entrepreneurial activity in Nigeria: the role of consumption, technology and human capital', *The International Journal of Entrepreneurship and Innovation*, *14*(4): 235–54.

Acemoglu, D. and Robinson, J.A. (2012) *Why Nations Fail: The Origins, Power, Prosperity and Poverty.* New York: Crown Business.

Amin, A. and Cohendet, P. (2004) *Architectures of Knowledge: Firms, Capabilities, and Communities.* Oxford: Oxford University Press.

Andersen, J.B. (2011) 'What are innovation ecosystems and how to build and use them'. Available at *Innovation Management* http://www.innovationmanagement.se/2011/05/16/what-are-innovation-ecosystems-and-how-to-build-and-use-them/ (last accessed 26 January 2017).

Arzeni, S. and Mitra, J. (2008) 'From unemployment to entrepreneurship: creating conditions for change for young people in Central and Eastern European Countries', in P. Blokker and B. Dallago (eds), *Youth Entrepreneurship and Local Development in Central and Eastern Europe*. Aldershot: Ashgate. pp. 31–60.

Asheim, B. and Gertler, M. (2004) 'Understanding regional innovation systems', in J. Fagerber, D. Mowery and R. Nelson (eds), *Handbook of Innovation*. Oxford: Oxford University Press. pp. 291–317

Asheim, B.T. (1998) 'Territoriality and economics: on the substantial contribution of economic geography', *Economic Geography in Transition*, 74: 98–109.

Asheim, B.T. and Cooke, P. (1999) 'Local learning and interactive innovation networks in a global economy', in E. Malecki and P. Olinas (eds), *Making Connections: Technological Learning and Regional Economic Change*. Aldershot: Ashgate. pp. 145–78.

Asheim, B.T. and Isaksen, A. (2002) 'Regional innovation systems: the integration of local "sticky" and global "ubiquitous" knowledge', *The Journal of Technology Transfer*, 27(1): 77–86.

Ashraf, Q. and Galor, O. (2011) 'Cultural diversity, geographical isolation, and the origin of the wealth of nations', NBER Working Paper No. 17640.

Baumol, W. (1990) 'Entrepreneurship: productive, unproductive and destructive', *Journal of Political Economy*, 98: 893–921.

Becattini, G. (1989) 'Sectors and/or districts: some remarks on the conceptual foundations of industrial economics', in E. Goodman and F. Bamford (eds), *Small Firms and Industrial Districts in Italy*. pp. 123–35.

bitstrategist (2011) 'Digital ecosystems: a framework for online business'. Available at: http://bitstrategist.com/2011/06/digital-ecosystems-a-framework-for-online-business/ (last accessed 30 March 2016).

Breschi, S. and Malerba, F. (1997) 'Sectoral innovation systems: technological regimes, Schumpeterian dynamics, and spatial boundaries', in Edquist, C. (ed.) *Technologies, Institutions and Organizations*. London: Pinter. pp. 130–56.

Bunnell, T.G. and Coe, N.M.(2001) 'Spaces and scales of innovation', *Progress in Human Geography*, 25(4): 569–89.

Chaminade, C. and Edquist, C. (2006) 'From theory to practice: the use of the systems of innovation approach in innovation policy', in J. Hage and M. Meeus (eds), *Innovation, Science and Institiutional Change*. Oxford: Oxford University Press. pp. 141–58.

Chang, E. and West, M. (2006) *Proceedings of iiWAS2006*, Digital Ecosystems and Business Intelligence Institute, Curtin University of Technology, Western Australia.

Cooke, P. (2001) 'Regional innovation systems, clusters, and the knowledge economy', *Industrial and Corporate Change*, 10(4): 945–74.

Cooke, P., Uranga, M.G. and Etxebarria, G. (1998) 'Regional systems of innovation: an evolutionary perspective', *Environment and Planning A*, 30(9): 1563–84.

Dahmen, E. (1970) *Entrepreneurial Activity and the Development of Swedish Industry: 1919–1939*. Homewood, IL: RD Irwin.

Department of Business Innovation and Skills (2015) *Digital Capabilities in SMEs: Evidence Review and Re-survey of 2014 Small Business Survey Respondents*. Available at: www.gov.uk/bis (last accessed 2 May 2016).

Dini, P., Iqani, M. and Mansell. R. (2011) 'The (im)possibility of interdisciplinarity: lessons from constructing a theoretical framework for digital ecosystems', *Culture, Theory and Critique*, 52(1): 3–27.

Doloreux, D. (2002) 'What we should know about regional systems of innovation', *Technology in Society*, 24(3): 243–63.

Easterly, W. and Levine, R. (2003) 'Tropics, germs, and crops: how endowments influence economic development', *Journal of Monetary Economics*, 50(1): 3–39.

Edquist, C. (1997) *Systems of Innovation: Technologies, Institutions, and Organizations*. London: Psychology Press.

Edquist, C. (2011) 'Design of innovation policy through diagnostic analysis: identification of systemic problems (or failures)', *Industrial and Corporate Change*, 20(6): 1725–53.

Edquist, C., Hommen, L., Johnson, B., Lemola, T., Malerba, F., Reiss, T. and Smith, K. (1998) 'The ISE Policy Statement – the Innovation Policy Implications of the *Innovations Systems and European Integration*', Research project, Linköping University.

Edquist, H. (2005) 'The Swedish ICT miracle – myth or reality?' *Information Economics and Policy*, 17(3): 275–301.

Ferretti, M. and Parmentola, A. (2015) *The Creation of Local Innovation Systems in Emerging Countries: The Role of Governments, Firms and Universities*. Springer.

Frank, A.G. (1998) *ReOrient: Global Economy in the Asian Age*. Berkeley, CA: University of California Press.

Frankopan, P. (2015) *The Silk Roads: A New History of the World*. London: Bloomsbury.

Freeman, C. (2002) 'Continental, national and sub-national innovation systems – complementarity and economic growth', *Research Policy*, 31(2): 191–211.

Freeman C. and Soete, L. (1997) *The Economics of Industrial Innovation*, 2nd edn. London: Pinter.

Fukuyama, F. (2012) 'Future of history: can liberal democracy survive the decline of the middle class?', *Foreign Affairs*, 91: 53.

Gilson, R.J. (1999) 'Legal infrastructure of high technology industrial districts: Silicon valley, route 128, and covenants not to compete', *NYU Law Review*, 7: 575.

Granovetter, M. (1985) 'Economic action and social structure: The problem of embeddedness', *American Journal of Sociology*, 91(3): 481–510.

Hall, P.A. and Soskice, D. (eds) (2001) *Varieties of Capitalism: The Institutional Foundations of Comparative Advantage*. Oxford: Oxford University Press.

Harris, G. (2012) *Portfolio*, Issue 81, September: 44–7.

Hirschman, A.O. (1958) *The Strategy of Economic Development* (No. HD82 H49). New Haven, CT: Yale University Press.

Iammarino, S. (2005) 'An evolutionary integrated view of regional systems of innovation: concepts, measures and historical perspectives', *European Planning Studies,* 13(4): 497–519.

Ingelstam, L. (2002) *System: att tanka över samhälle och teknik*. Eskilstuna: The Swedish Energy Agency.

Jackson, D.J. (2011) *What is an Innovation Ecosystem?* Arlington, VA: National Science Foundation.

Jackson, S.T., Betancourt, J.L., Booth, R.K. and Gray, S.T. (2009) 'Ecology and the ratchet of events: climate variability, niche dimensions, and species distributions', *National Academy of Science*, 106: 19685–92.

Johnson, B. and Gregersen, B. (1994) 'System of innovation and economic integration', *Journal of Industry Studies*, 2: 1–18.

Johnson, S., Kaufmann, D., McMillan, J. and Woodruff, C. (2000) 'Why do firms hide? Bribes and unofficial activity after communism', *Journal of Public Economics*, 76(3): 495–520.

Lang, J.T. (1998) 'European Community antitrust law: innovation markets and high technology Industries', *Journal of Reprints for Antitrust Law and Economics*, 28: 631.

Li, W., Badr, Y. and Biennier, F. (2012) Digital ecosystems: challenges and prospects. In *Proceedings of the International Conference on Management of Emergent Digital EcoSystems* (pp. 117–122), October. Association of Computing Machinery (ACM).

Luhmann, N. (1984) *Soziale systeme*. Frankfurt am Main: Suhrkamp.

Luhmann, N. (1986) 'The autopoiesis of social systems', in F. Geyer and J. van der Zouwen (eds) *Sociocybernetic Paradoxes*. London: SAGE. pp. 172–92.

Luhmann, N. (2000) 'Familiarity, confidence, trust: problems and alternatives', in D. Gambetta (ed.), *Trust: Making and Breaking Cooperative Relations*. Oxford: Basil Blackwell. pp. 94–107.

Lundvall, B.Å. (1992) *National Systems of Innovation: An Analytical Framework*. London: Pinter.

Lundvall, B.Å. and Borrás, S. (1999) *The Globalising Learning Economy: Implications for Innovation Policy*. Luxembourg: Office for Official Publications of the European Communities.

Lundvall, B.Å., Johnson, B., Andersen, E.S. and Dalum, B.(2002) 'National systems of production, innovation and competence building', *Research Policy*, 31(2): 213–31.

Malerba, F. (2006) 'Innovation and the evolution of industries', *Journal of Evolutionary Economics*, 16(1–2): 3–23.

Martin, R. and Simmie, J. (2008) 'Path dependence and local innovation systems in city-regions', *Innovation*, 10(2–3): 183–96.

Mitra, J. (2012) *Entrepreneurship, Innovation and Regional Development: An Introduction*. Abingdon: Routledge.

Moore, J.F. (1993) 'Predators and prey: a new ecology of competition', *Harvard Business Review*, 71(3): 75–83.

Nelson, R.R. (ed.) (1993) *National Innovation Systems: A Comparative Analysis*. Oxford: Oxford University Press.

Nelson, R.R. and Nelson, K. (2002) 'Technology, institutions, and innovation systems', *Research Policy*, 31(2): 265–72.

North, D.C. (1990a) 'Institutions and their consequences for economic performance', in K. Cook and M. Levi (eds), *The Limits of Rationality*. Chicago, IL: Chicago University Press. pp. 383–401.

North, D.C. (1990b) *Institutions, Institutional Change and Economic Performance*. Cambridge: Cambridge University Press.

Oinas, P. and Malecki, E.J. (2002) 'The evolution of technologies in time and space: from national and regional to spatial innovation systems', *International Regional Science Review*, 25(1): 102–31.

Perroux, F. (1969) *L'économie du vingtième siècle* (The Economy of the Twentieth Century). Paris: PUG.

Rantisi, N.M. (2002) 'The local innovation system as a source of "variety": openness and adaptability in New York City's garment district', *Regional Studies*, 36(6): 587–602.

Rodrik, D., Subramanian, A. and Trebbi, F. (2004) 'Institutions rule: the primacy of institutions over geography and integration in economic development', *Journal of Economic Growth*, 9(2): 131–65.

Saxenian, A. (1996) *Regional Advantage*. Cambridge, MA: Harvard University Press.

Smith, A. and Nicholson, J.S. (1887) *An Inquiry into the Nature and Causes of the Wealth of Nations*. London: T. Nelson.

Smith, K. (1999) 'Innovation as a systemic phenomenon: rethinking the role of policy', in K. Bryant and A. Wells (eds), *A New Economic Paradigm? Innovation-Based Evolutionary Systems*. Canberra: Department of Industry, Science and Resources, Science and Technology Policy Branch. pp. 10–47.

Soskice, D. (1991) 'The institutional infrastructure for international competitiveness: a comparative analysis of the UK and Germany', in A.B. Atkinson and R. Brunetta (eds), *The Economics of the New Europe*. London: Macmillan. pp. 45–66.

Tilson, D., Lyytinen, K. and Sørensen, C. (2010) 'Research commentary – digital infrastructures: the missing IS research agenda', *Information Systems Research*, 21(4), 748–59.

Tödtling, F. and Kaufmann, A. (1999) 'Innovation systems in regions of Europe: a comparative perspective', *European Planning Studies*, 7(6): 699–771.

Wenger, E. (2009) 'Communities of practice', *Communities*, 22: 57.

Williams, J.E. Jr and Lewis, C.S. (2010) 'Post graduation status of National Science Foundation Engineering Research Centers: Report of a survey of graduated ERCs', prepared for the National Science Foundation by SciTech Communications LLC, January.

Winter, A. and Govindarajan, G. (2015) 'Engineering reverse innovations: principles for creating successful products for emerging markets', *Harvard Business Review*, 93(7/8): 80–9.

Woolthuis, R.K., Lankhuizen, M. and Gilsing, V. (2005) 'A system failure framework for innovation policy design', *Technovation*, 25: 609–19.

INNOVATION POLICY AND THE ROLE OF GOVERNMENT

4

	SCOPE AND OBJECTIVES	

- Innovation policy and activities; demand- and supply-side activities. What makes policy?
- Market and systemic failures as drivers of reactive policy.
- Proactive policy generating innovation; the varied role of the state and context-specific arguments.
- Policies that exclude and inclusive policy making.

INTRODUCTION

Most innovations are generally carried out by economic entities or firms in either the private or public sector. Yet the significance of these innovations is evinced not only in the economic fortunes of these firms, but critically in their wider societal impact. Firms make, produce and sell new products or services in the markets using a range of technological and managerial or organisational processes and they do so in specific contexts. By contexts, reference is made to all the circumstances and situations, the institutions, the state of the economy, cultural and social norms, legislation, and the determinants which influence the process of innovation. In these contexts government policies can lubricate the determinants that facilitate innovation. We can, therefore, argue that innovation policy constitutes actions by public organisations – the government and public agencies which are sponsored by or are arms of the government – that influence innovation processes (Edquist and IFRIS, 2011).

In Chapter 3 we referred to different systems of innovation and the various elements or components of those systems at the national, regional and local levels that have an impact on innovation. These elements include institutions which set, in

North's phrase, the 'rules of the game', and the organisations, and which include the different public and private stakeholders that play this game. But what is it that these organisations and institutions do and what actually takes place within the different systems? What are the activities that occur within these systems? What role does government policy play in these systems?

What we do know is that four specific activities constitute the main determinants of the development and diffusion of innovation, and that they generally tend to include a range as shown in Figure 4.1.

The four activities are the primary catalysts for any specific innovation. The innovation may emanate from any one of these activities or in combination with others. This idea of overlapping activities suggests that there is a multi-causal factor determining the innovation process. Of course it would be misleading to suggest that the factors identified above are all available in any given economic environment, either in terms of place or time. For example, our understanding of the influence of networks or networking and entrepreneurship is relatively new. Several decades ago these activities may not have been given sufficient attention. Neither can it be stated with any certitude that all of the above activities need to be in place for innovation to occur in all environments. However, their use and the relationships between each of them may be of value when determining actions necessary to support innovation in a country or a region.

Many researchers have examined the relative influence of activities and their meaning within systems of innovation (e.g. Edquist, 1997; Galli and Teubal, 1997; Liu and White, 2001; Johnson and Jacobsson, 2003; Edquist, 2005; Bergek et al., 2008; World Bank, 2010). Their discussions highlight the dynamic perspective of innovation and especially the policy imperatives that need to be considered in different environments. All of the activities referred to above can form part of an overall innovation policy developed by any government. It is through the design of effective policies with which to stimulate the activities that governments can influence the innovation process.

Governments need to make strategic choices depending upon the prevailing economic and social conditions, and in certain circumstances they need to work with the private sector to kickstart or promote appropriate actions.

Innovation policy includes elements of fiscal, monetary, R&D, science and technology, infrastructure and education policy, with each of these activities mentioned above falling within the scope of these different policies. In essence, innovation policy is associated with change and economic progress, and therefore governmental support for flexibility, dynamism and the future (Edquist, 1999).

It could be argued that innovation policy can be interventionist rather than being simply facilitative. Actions need to be taken specifically to create and develop prospects for new product and process development, and these actions cannot simply take the form of a benign or hands-off approach to the workings of the market.

One way of understanding how policies work is to examine them in terms of demand and supply, or demand-side policies and activities and supply-side policies and activities. However, as we will see later, many other factors come into play when policies are developed, but a good starting point is the government's role in addressing the basics of demand and supply in the economy.

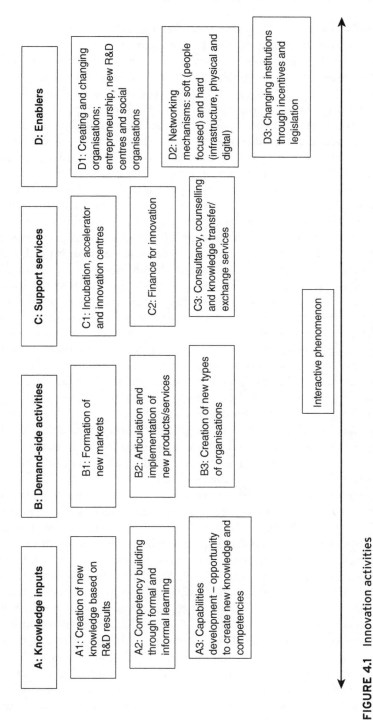

FIGURE 4.1 Innovation activities

Sources: Adapted from Edquist and IFRIS (2011) and Chaminade and Edquist (2006)

DEMAND-SIDE POLICIES AND ACTIVITIES

The idea of public demand for innovation has been gaining ground in recent times, especially with ideas of lead markets for the innovativeness and competitiveness of countries (European Council, 2006). Policy analysts have also informed the new debate with their discourse on the subject (Edler et al., 2005; Edler, 2007; Edler and Georghiou, 2007). Edler (2010) suggests that the main purpose of demand-side policies is to augment demand for innovation in order to generate appropriate incentives for innovation, to enable the higher uptake of innovations through better facilitative conditions, and to accelerate the diffusion of new technologies. Demand-side policies can also support private sector initiatives, especially where there is a dearth of funding or where the markets for new products are in their infancy and consequently inchoate or fragile, as in the case of renewable energy. These forms of activities represent particular rationales that are associated with specific, individual demand-side instruments. Where the demands of society are strong, socially-oriented outcomes, such as improvements in air quality, the health and well-being of a population or an ageing population are vital. Demand-side innovation policies are used to boost innovation performance in those areas and for those causes. In addition it is argued that public spending can become more effective and efficient if innovation is the main driver of public expenditure. In other words, demand-side policies attempt to address market, systemic, capability and institutional failures (see below for a discussion on failures).

Various barriers affect the articulation of demand and the introduction or diffusion of new products and services in the marketplace. For example, information asymmetries occur when producers are ignorant about preferences (of the users) or when users do not know what the producers make which might be useful to them. Another example of a barrier could be the 'lock-in effect' arising from path dependencies in the making and use of technologies over time, creating high entry costs for newcomers or high switching costs for incumbents. Certain products such as ICT ones are often reliant on network effects or high numbers of users for consumer benefits to take hold. At the early stage of a new product the absence of these effects may act as a barrier to their success in the market.

Different situations warrant different types of demand policies or policy instruments, cutting across various policy and departmental domains. Governments can act as the main user of a new technology and enact public procurement to stimulate innovation in businesses. This is especially helpful when a new technology can lead to acceptable changes in social behaviour or in the promotion of niche, technology-based small firms. Procurement processes can help push for the emergence of technologies for which there is an urgent time-bound societal need. Innovation-oriented public procurement can also be implemented to overcome gaps in the supply of risk finance for small early-stage ventures. Consumers could respond to tax incentives or subsidies to acquire new products or services. Public policy geared towards setting up regulations, such as those for health and safety or carbon emission in cars, or by way of standards and certification requirements for different industries, can influence the expression of demand for innovation. The rationale for government action in the area of technical standards corresponds to the public-good characteristics of such standards. Creating standards entails fixed costs, while the gains may not be appropriated by the individual. The development of standards is likely to experience some degree of market failure. By itself, the market may provide too few standards.

Table 4.1 shows how different demand-side policies and policy instruments are connected to different objectives and rationales, together with the various mechanisms that are used to implement them.

Note the different types of failures referred to in the last column. We will discuss these failures later. What government is concerned with here is the stimulation of demand through incentives and constraints, sufficient to generate higher levels of economic activity, consumer participation and tax revenue.

TABLE 4.1 Demand-side public policy instruments – their objectives and rationale

Demand-side policy instruments	Demand-side policy objectives	Supply-side rationale
Public procurement tenders for innovative entrepreneurs	Reduce the barriers for innovative entrepreneurs accessing public procurement	**Institutional failure** (potential biases against SMEs in public procurement)
Proportionate qualification levels and financial requirements	Reduce the barriers for SMEs accessing public procurement	**Institutional failure** (potential biases against SMEs in public procurement)
Cost-reimbursement contracts	Reduce the technological risks associated with the risks of non-completion due to technical features of the procured good or service	**Market failure** due to uncertainty
Guidance, tools and support for innovation-oriented public procurement (including examples of best practice, sample documents)	Stimulate innovation-oriented public procurement within public agencies	**Capability failures**
Creation of incentives to stimulate private demand (e.g. through guaranteed tariffs for innovative products or services)	Develop lead markets to help innovating firms achieve critical mass and competitiveness, bring prices down and encourage further diffusion and adoption of innovations	**Market failure**
Creation of standards	Reduce risks for consumers and foster, thereby, diffusion of innovation	**Market failure**
Consumer policy and education to enhance user-led innovation	Promote innovation in key innovative markets, ensure that confident consumers make informed choices and counter inertia and scepticism towards new goods and services	**Capability failures**

Source: Organization for Economic Co-operation and Development (OECD) (2011)

Public procurement has played a big part in demand-side innovation policy development. In the Netherlands, an action plan by the Dutch public procurement agencies, referred to as the 'Innovation Platform', indicated that at least 2.5% of their total procurement budget would be used for properties or services not yet available on the market from 2006. A Dutch project unit on procurement and tendering (PIA) also organised the proactive diffusion of knowledge of the opportunities afforded by the legal framework created by the 'Innovation Platform' together with arrangements for networking and training. Similarly, in Germany the 'Impulse Circle Innovation Factor State' has been working on promoting innovation by means of procurement strategies and measures in selected technology areas (Edler, 2010). Sweden's programme for the production, improvement and diffusion of energy efficiency technologies aimed at transforming markets through public procurement is a good example of demand-based targeted initiatives. Two agencies, NUTEK and STEM, managed the demand by enabling private demand (or catalytic procurement) via tendering processes. These successful activities have been supplemented by the establishment of user groups who meet regularly to discuss opportunities for technological change, sending appropriate signals to the government and private producers.

SUPPLY-SIDE POLICIES AND ACTIVITIES

The more common approach to public policy for innovation is found in supply-side activities. These activities are generally directed towards offering support to firms undertaking R&D and innovation with a view to enhancing their incentives to invest in innovation by identifying new opportunities or by addressing the more operational question of cost reduction. Most capital markets supplying the finance for investments in innovation tend to function inefficiently, leaving gaps in the market for effective support for the development of new products and services. The result is that firms face liquidity constraints which prevent potential profitable innovations from reaching the market.

Using appropriate policies, governments can decide to work with producers and investors directly both to create possibilities for innovation and for the diffusion of new technologies. R&D funding is offered directly with grants, subsidies, subsidised loans and even equity funding. Quite often governments will typically issue a call and from the response select the best projects for financing. Governments also opt for fiscal measures in the form of favourable tax treatment, tax holidays or tax credits for R&D expenditure, and sometimes accelerated depreciation on R&D equipment, import tariff exemptions on equipment and other research inputs, or exemptions from social taxes for R&D employees. Debt and risk-sharing schemes are also used to reduce the risks faced by investors who wish to finance innovation projects. These schemes favour the provision of financing to viable businesses that would otherwise suffer from credit constraints. Credit guarantee programmes are quite popular in many countries because they help to protect part of the losses caused by any default of the borrower. Yet another supply-side instrument is the technology extension service generally offered to SMEs with the objective of expanding the diffusion and

TABLE 4.2 Supply-side policy instruments – their rationale and objectives

Supply-side policy instruments	Supply-side policy objectives	Supply-side policy rationale
Direct support to innovative firms through grants and subsidies	Facilitate access to finance	Capital market imperfections
Competitive R&D grants	Adopt market-friendly approaches that avoid 'picking winners' and encourage competitive selection of investments that are likely to have the highest social return	Capital market imperfections
Credit guarantees	Increase the incentive for banks to engage in innovative firm lending	Capital market imperfections
Government-subsidised loans	Reduce the cost of debt financing	Capital market imperfections
Support of alternative types of debt finance such as convertible loans and subordinated loans through fiscal incentives to lenders and/or the partial coverage of losses in case of bankruptcy/liquidation	Increase the incentive for lenders to engage in innovative firm lending	Capital market imperfections

Source: Adapted from OECD (2013)

adoption of already existing technology (instead of the development of new technologies) and to help improve the absorptive capacity of targeted firms. Typically an initial assessment of the firm and its operations is followed by a proposal by the firm and then by formal assistance to enable improvements through implementation of the improvement plan. Table 4.2, adapted from the OECD, provides a snapshot of supply-side activities and their rationale.

So far we have described the main types of policies, policy instruments and activities which governments have at their disposal to support innovation from a demand and supply perspective. These perspectives provide a description of government interventions in specific situations, but they do not necessarily explain the rationale referred to in the final columns in Tables 4.1 and 4.2. There are good reasons for governments to support innovation and for being proactive in the promotion of activities that spur innovation. Knowing what those reasons might be can help us to understand and question why governments create innovation policies, the role of governments, and whether they should intervene in the market for goods and services.

WHY DO WE NEED INNOVATION POLICIES AND WHAT IS THE ROLE OF GOVERNMENT?

Government's facilitative role in the economy manifests itself in all the necessary actions it takes to create a climate that is conducive to economic growth and development. It is no less the case with innovation. Creating an innovation climate inevitably involves the work of many departments and the coordination of departmental actions. Facilitating innovation means that government can concentrate on specific generic functions such as providing information, technical and financial support, reducing obstacles to innovation arising from monopolies and from ineffective regulatory frameworks. Facilitation can also be proactive, such as when governments sponsor R&D activities and design education policies to help develop a skilled, creative and innovation-oriented community of people. Leadership, a vision, a wide formulation of the idea of innovation permeating all economic and social programmes, effective and flexible principal–agency relationships, selective approaches to technological and industrial development, are all essential drivers for the implementation of innovation policies. Managing them all, and crucially using specific instruments for particular outcomes, is not an easy task. What may be required in any country is a long-term strategy inspired by what the World Bank (2010) refers to as 'radical gradualism' in keeping with the idea of the 'S curve' of innovation which reflects the different stages of economic development, from agrarian to efficiency-driven to innovative economies, as explained in Chapter 1.

But why play this facilitative role in the first place? The answer to that question lies in acknowledging the importance of innovation and its decisive role in the advancement of economic and social development in most countries and how managing technical change is an imperative for all societies. Chapter 1 discusses in detail the broader issues of economic and social progress brought about by technical change and productivity. Suffice it to say that in today's 'poly-crisis' context with significant disconnects in the environment, in ruptured biodiversity systems in terms of economic inequality, water, food and other resource shortages, demographic imbalances coupled with the accelerated rate of technological enhancement, deregulated markets and globalisation, there is a need for both a solid foundation for innovative evolution and inclusive growth. Energy, matter, life and time – the four coordinates of technological systems – are all affected by these crises, which in turn affect production systems and social forms (World Bank, 2010). Against this we find rapid advances in scientific and technical developments, the development of new materials and new life forms, the emergence of mixed or hybrid organisational arrangements and the acquisition of new skills. Together, the fission of positive developments and negative forces demands policies with which to live productively with the dynamics of such change.

The interplay of positive and negative forces in the environment necessitates different approaches to policy development. Crises occur due to what is often referred to as market failures, or a mismatch between supply and demand resulting in economic disequilibrium and demanding intervention to correct the misalignment. Equally important is the need to anticipate potentially positive developments that could enhance economic and social development. If so, policy makers cannot simply wait to develop corrective measures but must be proactive with strategic interventions to stay ahead of the game, be competitive and achieve growth targets for new technologies, productivity or job creation. The necessary tools for intervention will vary according to specific circumstances both in the local and in the wider global economy. So let us try to understand what we mean by 'market failures' and by 'proactive strategic intervention'.

MARKET FAILURE

The mismatch between supply and demand or between what is produced and what people want or need occurs when there is a gap between private and social benefits and costs linked to transactions in the marketplace. The gap can be identified as a market failure. This interpretation of market failure lies at the centre of any notion of a free competitive market and of that market not being able to reach optimal equilibrium. How and why does such a gap occur? There are numerous explanations ranging from information asymmetries to hold-up problems. We discuss these explanations below.

INFORMATION ASYMMETRIES

Efficient outcomes and allocation of resources are essential to attaining and maintaining equilibrium in the market, but they can be badly affected by information deficiencies. These deficiencies often occur as a result of high levels of uncertainty about the future and when we have to rely on probability forecasts to gauge what may lie ahead. Information may be scarce or, as is often the case, we can rely only on the present and past – that is, what we know already – to predict the future or what we do not know anything about! Since innovation is about the future, inadequate levels of information about how to make new products or offer new services in an uncertain market can create serious problems. It is not surprising, therefore, to find increasing numbers of government agencies engaged in technology forecasting alongside the standard projections about the economy. Even serious but populist publications such as *Scientific American*, *New Scientist*, *Wired* and others are awash with predictions about the next 10 best ideas or the top 50 new devices for the future.

At a more practical and immediate level, a cross-section of people involved in market transactions (within a firm or between buyers, suppliers and distributors, or among shareholders and creditors) hold different information, conferring upon them either an information advantage or disadvantage. The asymmetry problems in information can lead to opportunistic behaviour, erroneous pricing, distrust and the dislocation of markets.

Information asymmetry is considered to be a principal contributor to market failures, not least because it disrupts the process used by individuals to understand the intention of others and the necessary agency functions (Spence, 1976) and to assess the quality of goods and services in the market (Akerlof, 1970). The lack of access to the private information of others can lead to the market not being able to produce acceptable equilibrium prices or to manage the transactions affecting goods or services (Stiglitz, 2000). Two types of information asymmetry can occur: moral hazard and adverse selection. Moral hazard results from the inability of one individual, or principal, to follow or monitor another individual's actions. Adverse selection relates to the inability of the principal to identify and observe the agent's private information (Picard, 1987).

Interestingly, however, and as Barbaroux (2014) notes, economists of the Austrian tradition regard information asymmetry as a condition for market opportunities.

In other words, opportunities emerge precisely because people do not possess or have access to substitutable information sets about the market, the technologies or indeed the conditions in which innovation can succeed (Miller, 2003). Distinctive individual ability, or asymmetrically distributed cognition, is a major source of competition among individuals to identify opportunities, create or enhance capabilities and mobilise resources for innovation. The search for new opportunities is, therefore, predicated upon this imbalance between what people know or do not know and the constant search for or alertness to mutual knowledge of attitudes of demand and supply (Kirzner, 1997).

EXPLOITATIVE OR HOLD-UP PROBLEMS

A good example of an exploitative relationship is when one party to a transaction takes advantage of sunk capital costs from added-value investment made by another for the purpose of making new products. The former may have ongoing or special relationships with the latter as part of a network or as a collaborator and simply free-ride on the initiatives of the latter. This is an example of negative networking externality which can destroy trust among network members and sabotage the network itself. These 'failure externalities' can be realised by third parties when other firms fail. Surviving firms often appropriate the value of the ideas, products and services of failed counterparts. The private investor of the failed firm loses out to the appropriating survivor firm, especially as the value derived from the latter is often intangible. Even where such appropriation is tangible, as in the hiring of talent from the failed firm, there is no gain for the private investor from his or her original investment. Investors are therefore not incentivised to invest because they cannot gain from any returns from these investments and especially from the failure of investee firms (Mitra, 2012).

Large firms may use their muscle and resource strengths to hold up smaller subcontractors through delayed payments, longer than usual credit terms or in terms of contractual constraints which prevent the smaller firm from accessing end users or developing new customers. Employees of firms benefiting from long-term, in-house competency-based training may find themselves not being able to transfer their skills readily elsewhere, unlike their professional football counterparts! Another good example of 'hold-up' can be found in the use and abuses of patents, as Vignette 4.1 explains.

VIGNETTE 4.1   THE TRIALS OF PATENTS AND HOLD-UP THEORY

Patents are an increasingly important element of innovation and business strategy. They have commercial force because of the remedies that are available to patent holders who are able to prove in court that their patents are valid and infringed. Patent holders can be awarded damages based either on the profits they lost due to the infringement or on the 'reasonable royalties' they should have been paid by the infringing party.

Patents are also often the cause of many hold-ups, especially when they are infringed and result in legal action. Typically in a patent infringement case the patent covers a small part of a larger product. The defendant may therefore infringe the patent without meaning to do so since he or she may not know what exactly is covered or because the competitive objective may simply be that of offering another 'equal' product in the market. If an interoperability standard covers the infringing feature, then removing the feature may prevent the bigger product from being operable. In this situation removing a big, competitive product from the market because of a small patent can adversely affect consumers. Furthermore, if as a result a large number of the lawful components are blocked in addition to the infringing one, then this might distort the competition in the market and leave consumers bereft of the opportunity of a potentially better or different product. In a different scenario, if a patent holder threatens an industry by suing a large number of businesses, an injunction would remove many participants from the marketplace and this would have a very negative effect on competition. In all cases the adverse effect on consumers and on competition from an exclusion order created by an injunction is greater than the harm done by the specific infringing component (Chien and Lemley, 2012).

Chien and Lemley refer to the *eBay* v. *MercExchange* case where the US Supreme Court ruled unanimously against the approach taken by the Federal Circuit Court of Appeals, which issued permanent injunctions on 'absent exceptional circumstances'. The Supreme Court's decision was to assert that the District Court has discretion whether to grant or deny injunctive relief based on traditional principles of equity, using a four-factor test. The unanimous opinion was worded by Justice Kennedy, who was joined by Justices Stephens, Souter and Breyer, as follows:

> When the patented invention is but a small component of the product the companies seek to produce and the threat of an injunction is employed simply for undue leverage in negotiations, legal damages may well be sufficient to compensate for the infringement and an injunction may not serve the public interest. In addition injunctive relief may have different consequences for the burgeoning number of patents over business methods, which were not of much economic and legal significance in earlier times. The potential vagueness and suspect validity of some of these patents may affect the calculus under the four-factor test.

While permanent injunctions go hand in hand with the principle of property rights associated with intellectual property rights, and typically with patents, they have proved to be both problematic and contentious, as the BlackBerry patent infringement case between NTP, Inc. and Research in Motion (RIM) shows. According to NTP, a patent-holding company, RIM, the provider of the popular BlackBerry wireless email device, had infringed several of NTP's patents. A jury found in favour of NTP's claims and NTP asked the court for an injunction against RIM to stop selling BlackBerry devices. RIM immediately faced a lot of pressure and the invidious choice it had to make between settling the case or a shutdown of the BlackBerry service. In March 2006, RIM paid $612.5 million to NTP to settle the case, thus reflecting the strong bargaining position NTP obtained by being granted the injunction to close the BlackBerry service but not the underlying value of NTP's patented technology. The eBay ruling followed shortly after the BlackBerry one.

(Continued)

(Continued)

The IT sector, including computer hardware and software, Internet business methods, semiconductors and telecommunications products, is particularly concerned with injunctions in patent cases. Shapiro (2010) provides six reasons for this concern. First, there has been an avalanche of patenting of software and business methods over the past 10 years (Bessen and Hunt, 2007) with often limited shelf lives for these products and services. Second, there have been widespread complaints about patent quality, and especially about vague and what has been perceived as unnecessarily broad patents in this area (Federal Trade Commission, 2003; Jaffe and Lerner, 2004; National Academies of Science, 2004). Third, the incremental nature of software innovations results in quick sequential innovation (Cohen and Lemley, 2001). Fourth, software and hardware products tend to be complex, which can lead to a single product potentially infringing many patents (Heller and Eisenberg, 1998; Hall and Ziedonis, 2001; Shapiro, 2001). Fifth, software and hardware are generally sold at prices well above marginal cost, which enables appropriate returns to be obtained on R&D and other investments. Finally, working to avoid possible and real infringement claims means redesigning products, which can be both costly and time consuming. Unsurprisingly, a large number of firms in the IT sector supported the judgment in the eBay case and lobbied hard for the reform of patent laws. Software patents can hinder technological progress and encourage monopolisation. Equally they can add massively to costs through the creation of patent thickets, as the phenomenon of patent trolls demonstrates.

Patent trolls are a major new development in the innovation game and are often described as patent-assertion entities. They use the threat of legal injunction to hold up product-producing companies in patent suits. Although, as Chien and Lemley (2012) state, the US Supreme Court's 2006 decision in *eBay Inc.* v. *MercExchange, LLC* more or less stopped that practice in federal courts, it has unintentionally driven patent trolls to a different environment, namely the International Trade Commission (ITC), where the ITC has tended to grant injunctions because it is an administrative agency, not a federal court, and therefore cannot award monetary damages.

Sources: Shapiro (2010); Chien and Lemley (2012)

Often the public-good characteristics of certain goods and services, such as education or blue sky research and development, mean that there is not enough room for their trade or exploitation in the marketplace. These goods and services are provided rightfully for the benefit of all in society with the state as the custodian of such provision. Without such custodianship there might be too many inequalities in society, preventing certain groups of people from accessing these goods and services (Blöndal, 2003).

NON-MARKET RESOLUTIONS

Not all market failures can be resolved by extending the activities of the market. For example 'hold-up and exploitative problems' leading to opportunistic behaviour are often best resolved by business networks, associations and works councils. In other cases, knowledge spillovers, patents and other forms of intellectual property rights (IPR) can help firms to internalise the benefits from the protection offered by IPR. It should also be recognised that certain types of specialised economic activity are probably more inclined to generate market failures than others. Highly complex products using non-standard technologies (as, for example, customised software or specialist advanced manufacturing equipment) are more likely to be associated with specialist know-how and different levels of information and knowledge among firms and their customers. This specialist knowledge is often guarded zealously during outsourcing operations when outsourcing firms are required to maintain separate silos of services for individual clients. In these circumstances market failures are best avoided by non-market solutions, such as having board membership in client firms or the other way round.

Many of the non-market solutions to market failures emanate from the codes and customs or institutions governing behaviour, attitudes and evolving business culture. They become part of systems, but then these systems are also prone to setbacks and failures.

SYSTEMIC, INSTITUTIONAL AND CAPABILITY FAILURES

We have discussed different systems of innovation (national, regional, local) in Chapter 3 relying on both the standard work on the subject (Lundvall, 1992; Nelson, 1993; Freeman, 1995; Edquist, 1997) and the rationales for their development (Lipsey and Carlaw, 1998; Smith, 2000; Chaminade and Edquist, 2006). These systems are often prone to failure because of systemic imperfections that block spillover effects and interactive learning (Woolthuis et al., 2005); we touched on some of these failures in that chapter too. Here we explore the topic in a bit more detail and especially how these failures prompt policy development.

A distinction is often drawn among infrastructure problems, transition and lock-in problems, institutional, organisational and network problems, information and coordination problems or problems arising from shared resources, complementarities or diversity of capabilities (Carlsson and Jacobsson, 1997; Hauknes and Norgren, 1999; Smith, 2000; Rodrik, 2004; Woolthuis et al., 2005; Chaminade and Edquist, 2006) and negative spillover effects.

Take spillover effects. Firms in one region may benefit from the new knowledge generated by a first mover, from expertise from R&D activities of other firms and from high rates of specialist employee turnover. These spillovers and their value are not reflected in market prices and are often referred to as 'untraded dependencies' (Storper, 1997). Here we are dealing with what is customary in agglomerations where there is a concentration of similar or related firms and supporting institutions. In these environments the results are not necessarily negative, as an implicit mutuality of purpose may contribute to the development of the producer firm generating new knowledge as well as the receiving firm or the beneficiary of the spillover. Reciprocation by firms consequent upon similar levels of capability or expertise and involvement in the same industry can reinforce trust. Firms in this situation take advantage of network externalities.

Network externalities emanate as a function of the geographical proximity of firms to complementary or related firms, individuals and institutions. These complementary firms tend to be found in abundance in business clusters. However, such a concentration of clustered and networked resources is inevitably limited to some regions, and those areas which do not have a rich density of firms are inevitably burdened with considerable barriers to entrepreneurship. As Audrestsch and Keilbach (2007) argue, the expected value of any recognised opportunity is correspondingly lower in regions where there is no such agglomeration of firms. Moreover, if mistrust is an issue then other deficiencies in the receiving firm may result in its not being able to reciprocate, and even in a flagrant abuse of the knowledge 'stolen' from the other (Mitra, 2012).

Chaminade et al. (2008) argue that while systemic problems occur in different scenarios as in developed, emerging and developing economies, the nature and type of the problems can be rather different in those contexts. They suggest that firms are likely not to have the minimum capabilities to engage in interactive learning or that the connections between them may not be strong enough within their systems of innovation. In short, the weakness of institutions is too significant to allow for effective systemic value to be derived by the players in those systems. These weaknesses can be described as capability, networking and institutional problems or failures (Intarakumnerd et al., 2002; Giuliani and Bell, 2005; Chaminade and Vang, 2006).

Unfortunately, some of the arguments referred to above bear the hallmark of rather restricted and narrow conceptions on capabilities, networks and systems in different contexts. It is likely that institutions, as seen in terms of formal arrangements and organisations, may be weak in developing countries, but that does not preclude networking capabilities or informal systems from developing, often acting as alternative and responsible conduits of relevant and localised innovation activities and institutional fragility. Consider the emergence of M-Pesa and the financial remittance arrangements in Kenya built on the back of informal connections being supported by mobile telephony, suggesting the role that new technologies can play in leapfrogging a linear model of institutional development and formal networked linkages. In these environments it is the role of government to work around and with these informal institutions and use technology applications to foster innovation and job creation for economic development.

In fact, in most countries we witness the coexistence of separate systems and modalities of innovation. Regions within countries differ in terms of the stock of innovative forms, local absorptive capacities, the mix of indigenous and transnational firms and the skills base. Nuanced regional policy making becomes more important than a one-size innovation agenda dictated by national priorities (Abubakar et al., 2012; Mitra and Tardios, 2015).

MARKET AND OTHER FAILURES AND GOVERNMENTS

So what can government do to address market and other failures that hinder innovation? This question is particularly important when we examine the view of most free-market economists who believe that markets should be essentially left alone, and that it is not the government's role to intervene in the workings of the market. People are rational, they have perfect information, they know what they are or should be doing, and the best interests of people or the organisations in which they work and share similar interests can only be compromised by freedom-restricting governments. So ideally markets do not really fail; they simply go through periods of readjustment, and, therefore, market failure occurs only rarely. Ironically even Milton Friedman, the doyen of free-market economists, had relented by admitting that markets can fail in some circumstances. As Chan notes, pollution is a good example:

> People 'over produce' pollution because they are not paying for the costs of dealing with it. So what are regarded as optimal levels of pollution for individuals (or individual firms) add up to a sub-optimal level from the social point of view. (2010: 169)

The cost of pollution constitutes what is referred to as a negative externality and is not accounted for by companies that are responsible for the pollution. In these circumstances our free-market economist friends would argue that a good way of tackling the problem of over-pollution is by introducing a market for it, as in 'tradable emission rights' which let people buy and sell the right to pollute based on their needs within a socially agreed optimal maximum.

A non-market facilitating government can only make things worse because governments do not always have the right information to rectify market problems, and politicians and bureaucrats only promote their own interests anyway (Chan, 2010). So the best form of intervention is to find new markets for dealing with market failure. Going back to the pollution example, the introduction of a new carbon-trading market may indeed be considered to be a Schumpeterian style of innovation, but here is a good model of form overtaking substance. In other words, the form of a new market, in terms of trading between higher- and lower volume-carbon-emission producers, is innovative, but the substance of the innovation is in fact a blow for emission reduction because there is no effective reduction of such emissions. What the world needs by all scientific accounts to date is innovative ways to reduce the economic, social and environmental costs of emissions, not the maintenance of the status quo.

Part of what governments in most countries do is attract private investment to make, create and provide for the goods and services people want. But if the social returns on any investment outweigh the private returns on such investment, then private investors are reluctant to make that investment. In other words, in such situations the market fails to protect the private interest and the social or public gain is deemed more important. Basic education and basic research are good examples because they are public goods which generate public gain. However, as Mazzucato (2013: 4), referring to Mowery (2010), argues eloquently:

> Big visionary projects – like 'putting a man on the moon' or creating a vision behind the Internet – required much more than the calculation of social and private returns.

THE CASE FOR PUBLIC INTERVENTION FOR INNOVATION – FOR OR AGAINST?

Engaging in big visionary projects which can stimulate innovation and economic advancement suggests that governments can legitimately occupy that space in the innovation process, which, as Keynes (1926) had remarked, people or organisations do not do at all (as opposed to what they do already or what they may not be doing that well!). So while it is understood that individuals and firms will invent, develop and improve products and services, usually within the realms of what we know about market needs, it is possible that we may anticipate discoveries or experiment with possibilities also based on what we know but which the market does not necessarily understand. To do so governments can take a proactive role in identifying and harnessing the technology, sector and product or service-specific skills together with the talent and expertise with which to make that space productive, indeed to commercialise it where appropriate. Referring to both DARPA (the agency for the US Department of Defense) and ARPA-E (the US agency for the Department of Energy), Mazzucato (2013) points out their ability to recruit such expertise to invent and then drive the commercialisation of the Internet (DARPA), and now direct and experiment with green investments (ARPA-E). In Brazil it is the state banks that have led on both countercyclical lending and directing investments in new areas such as biotech and clean energy while earning huge, productive returns (21.2% in 2010), which they could then reinvest in public goods and services such as education and health. The Chinese Development Bank is yet another example of enlightened public interest, investing in the green economy and other sectors where private firms with their short-term, shareholder dividend predications fear to tread (Mazzucato, 2013).

The state has not been found wanting when we look at some of the most groundbreaking innovations (radical new drugs, solar panels, lithium batteries, wind turbines and the Internet). In fact it has often proved to be a far more reliable investor than the private sector. The short-term time horizons for returns on investment by venture capitalists and other finance houses fail to appreciate what is required by either start-ups or growth, especially in new industries.

The trade-off for the state is between playing a purely administrative role and that of a proactive catalyst or interventionist role. The trade-off may fluctuate from time to time given the stage of economic development or the prevailing economic conditions (as in recessionary or stable economy conditions). So the argument could run as follows: in the good times of growth, the government would have done enough for the market and the private sector to activate incremental forms of innovation and look for efficiencies in terms of economies of scale and scope. In a knowledge economy there is likely to be more disruption within and across different sectors, but it may be best to leave the private players and the market to allow for dominant innovation strategies to emerge. In recessionary conditions governments could look at fiscal and monetary measures to ease the macroeconomic conditions to allow for new but cautious investment.

However, the proactive role of government does not always surface in inclement times. Variations occur as budget cuts often result in R&D expenditures, necessary for the visionary role of government referred to above, being reduced or abandoned by the private sector. Further, the problem with the argument referred to in the previous paragraph is that it relies entirely on an ideological view of the market and the state which claims that governments cannot be selective about strategies because they are inefficient at picking winners through industrial policies. They do not have sufficient information about technologies, markets or talent, and the absence of a motivation for profit makes them irresponsible about outcomes.

Whether governments believe proactive intervention is necessary remains a moot point, especially when dramatic changes occur in the economy. The latest global economic crisis in the latter half of the first decade had a significant and almost deleterious impact on R&D expenditures and the prospect of sustained innovation. It was

TABLE 4.3 Gross domestic R&D expenditure: from crisis to recovery

Countries with no fall in GERD during the crisis that have expanded since 2013

Country	Crisis		Recovery			
	2008	2009	2010	2011	2012	2013
China	100	124	145	166	193	218
Turkey	100	111	121	134	147	157
Hungary	100	108	110	116	122	137
Russian Fed.	100	111	104	105	112	113
France	100	104	105	108	110	110
Italy	100	99	101	100	102	99

Countries with fall in GERD but above pre-crisis levels in 2013

Country	2008	2009	2010	2011	2012	2013
Slovakia	100	97	132	147	181	188
Estonia	100	94	110	176	170	139
Netherlands	100	99	102	114	116	116
Germany	100	99	103	109	113	115
Japan	100	91	93	96	97	102
USA	100	99	99	101	105	n/a

Countries with GERD below crisis levels in 2013

Country	2008	2009	2010	2011	2012	2013
UK	100	99	98	99	96	98
Finland	100	97	99	99	92	88
Greece	100	90	82	83	80	88
Romania	100	75	73	81	79	66
Singapore	100	82	88	100	96	n/a
South Africa	100	92	83	85	88	n/a

Source: OECD MSTI, February 2015, data used: gross domestic expenditure on R&D (GERD) at constant 2005 Purchasing Power Parity (PPP)$, index = 2008 (selected countries only); cited in *The Global Innovation Index, 2015*

Note: The 2013 data is either provisional or underestimated.

only after the discovery of some green shoots of recovery following global economic stagnation that we started to see combined public and private R&D expenditure begin to increase by 3.7% in 2010, 5.3% in 2011 and 5.6% in 2012, falling slightly to about 4.3% in 2013, thus suggesting a path of constant growth. However, gross domestic expenditures of R&D (or GERD) increased by 1.4% in 2010, 3.6% in 2011 and 3% in 2012, but then fell to 2.6% in 2013. While the slowdown after 2011 was caused by the continuation of diminishing public R&D expenditure in the OECD countries, we can also observe that the growth in overall and global R&D expenditure was due probably to commitments to R&D expenditure outside the domestic environment, by both public and private organisations. The levels of R&D expenditure were not uniform across all countries, thus suggesting conflicting priorities for innovation in different countries. We find three types of countries:

(a) Countries with no fall in GERD and subsequent rise in such expenditure.
(b) Countries with a fall in in GERD but still above pre-crisis levels.
(c) Countries where GERD is still below pre-crisis levels.

Table 4.3 shows a selective snapshot of GERD in all three types of countries from 2008 to 2013, with 2008 as the base year indexed at 100.

THE STATE AND MORE THAN R&D

R&D funding is of course not the be all and end all for supporting and promoting innovation. R&D is at best an input expenditure and there is no guarantee that either such expenditure or patents (an intermediary output) on products developed as a result of such expenditure lead to innovation and absorption in the marketplace. So can the state play a role that is bigger and more direct in enabling innovation? Mazzucato (2013) makes some interesting observations on this. She argues that the state can become involved in proactive and interventionist strategic and functional roles. First, as a catalyst for developing 'systems of innovation', it can create the economic conditions, networks, research frameworks and financial and non-financial support mechanisms for innovation. Second, and crucially, it can get involved directly or in partnership with the private sector, at the commercial viability stage. These two actions can help to create and shape the markets that are required for start-ups and innovative incumbent firms to develop sustainable business models. In this sense the state might be seen to be best placed as an institution to 'pick winners', supporting the work of the gazelle firms. Mazzucato refers to the development of the most popular Apple products to show how, from the Internet and GPS to the touch-screen display and new voice-activated personal assistant (SIRI), not a single key technology behind the iPhone emerged without the government's funding and entrepreneurial spirit.

What Mazzucato points to, is that in our modern world innovation in the supply side of the equilibrium requires a system of support that the free market is unable to provide. Mazzucato also challenges some of the new growth theories which point out that innovation is an endogenous outcome of investment in R&D, with the positive impact of R&D investment on growth being examined only at the level of the firm. New growth theories, therefore, undermine the importance of the state's involvement in technological change, and by implication Schumpeter's argument about innovation flowing from collaborating and competitive firms of different types being embedded in different systems at the local, regional and national levels. It is this approach to growth as being mostly driven by a system of innovations which justifies the state's involvement in the economy.

THE MARKET OVER THE STATE

The critique of the argument about the state backing winners, and therefore being a principal investor in high-risk projects with uncertain outcomes, is a strong one. Various heterodox economists referring to the idea of neo-liberalism suggest a new role for the capitalist economy, one that relies on market forces but also on new political and theoretical (especially economic theory) ideas which revisit the old neo-classical ones (Saad-Filho and Johnston, 2005; Duménil and Lévy, 2011)

The supplier of the new economic theory, the Chicago School of Economics, stresses the efficiency of market competition, the role of rational individuals in determining economic outcomes, the distortions associated with government intervention and the regulation of markets (Vertova, 2014). Here the state has diminished responsibilities for development or for welfare. Financial institutions forge new relationships with non-financial sectors but to the benefit of the former. Mergers and acquisitions are favoured to speed up capital accumulation together with the strengthening of central banks and their fundamental role in ensuring price stability, and a pronounced imperative to drain resources of the periphery in favour of the centre (Duménil and Lévy, 2005). The state thus has a reduced role in the shaping and implementation of industrial and innovation policies, its primary purpose being that of developing regulation that creates an environment conducive to innovation. We are not a million miles away from the ideas of older advocates of the importance of a 'lesser state', such as Hayek, who believed that any government intervention in the hallowed freedom of the market would put at risk Adam Smith's invisible hand and its mystical ability to create a state of equilibrium where supply would perfectly match demand. But does the 'hand' of Smith need to remain invisible all the time?

A bigger problem with the arguments about the positive role of the state, as promoted by Mazzucato, is their dominant focus on technology, and especially on the early stages of technological invention. Let us consider the iPhone and iPod again. The touch-screen displays, semiconductors, hard drives and even the MP3 protocol were originally backed by public money, but it is probably a bit short-sighted to rely on the development of these technologies as being the only source of innovation in these Apple products. It misses out, for example, the role of development – the D in R&D – in making inventions useful. Apple's real achievement involved integrating the different technologies, improving them to make them more user-friendly, reliable and portable. Their organisational endeavour also includes brokering deals with cellular carriers and record labels so iPhones could make calls and download songs, which could be easily affordable. It also omits the non-technological aspects of innovation that form the basis of most technological products. Referring to another case, the University of Sheffield's Richard Jones recently observed that IBM's role in applying the principle of giant magnetoresistance to hard drives was as significant as the publicly funded discovery of the principle itself (NESTA, 2015).

CRITICAL CONTEXTS AND PUBLIC POLICY

Much of the discussion above with its particular focus on advanced technologies and western countries misses out on the variations in approaches to public policy for innovation in different countries. The variation occurs because of contextual differences. While technology is a common factor for development, the type of technologies used and the innovations that make a difference to particular economies reflect different stages of development of those economies. Referring particularly to entrepreneurship and innovation policy, Acs (2008) identifies policy variations commensurate with three stages of development and the set of priorities that may prevail in these countries.

TABLE 4.4   Framework condition priorities of an economy according to stage of development

Less developed countries	Developing countries	Developed countries
Strengthen small and medium-sized sector before focusing on entrepreneurial framework	More balanced between the national and the entrepreneurial framework	Focus on strengthening the entrepreneurial framework conditions; focus on change
Policies focused on firms	Strengthen conditions for and improve quality of entrepreneurial environment for established firms	Strengthen technology transfer
Financial and management assistance	Rule of law and labour market flexibility	Make early-stage funding available
Training and reducing regulatory burdens	Infrastructure, financial market efficiency and management skills	Support entrepreneurial activity at the state, corporate and educational levels
Focus on bringing in FDI	This will attract FDI that will enable employment, technology transfer, exports and tax revenues	Focus on high value added, high technology, innovation and technology commercialisation
Strong commitment to education	Strong commitment to education	Higher education system plays an important role in R&D, technology commercialisation and education

Source: Adapted from Acs (2008)

As Table 4.4 indicates, there are certain essential ingredients or activities that enable innovation, and differentiated policies are often a manipulation of these ingredients determined by the context in question. Thus a strong commitment to general education and the strengthening of the small-firms base could be a priority for developing countries, while a focus on higher education and R&D and an enhanced entrepreneurial framework may be more appropriate for a developed country (for more on what applies to different environments see Chapter 2).

DIFFERENTIATED POLICY AGENDAS

Acs's differentiated model for public policy interventions is a useful helicopter view of contextually specific activities. National policy frameworks can be designed taking these factors into consideration. There is an assumption that the differences between the three categories rests primarily on institutional conditions prevailing in those countries. So, for example, the 'developed countries' box in the table does not differentiate between the roles and functions of small, medium and large firms presupposing that the strengths of each in the innovation process are fully understood and accounted for. Consequently the only overarching action necessary is to provide for better facilitative conditions for new knowledge creation and their rapid application. In contrast, for less developed countries the key issue is that of addressing capability failures (training and education), foreign sources of capital and both hard and soft infrastructure. In the middle stand the developing nations whose priorities are expected to focus on the strengthening of facilitative institutions (law and order, education) and the improvement of entrepreneurial framework conditions.

Realistic propositions would, however, account for the variations in size, complexity and regional differences of nations in any of the three categories. A national policy on innovation in a country as large as India, China or Nigeria would require many regional caveats to reflect the considerable differences in innovation capacity, skill sets of people and the availability of financial, human and social capital between, say, Bihar and Bangalore in India, Xinjian and Shanghai in China, and Kano and Lagos in Nigeria. It requires little imagination to note that policies relevant for California would not necessarily hold for Detroit. The landlocked environment of Burkina Faso in West Africa would have difficulty in adopting policies appropriate for Rwanda. There are other realities which impugn standardised approaches. The destination attracting the largest share of FDI, for instance, is the USA, thus suggesting that investment patterns are more likely to follow activities supporting either capital accumulation or high-risk advanced technology advancement, and not necessarily development. So across all 'development' categories we would expect to see variations in policy design and implementation.

Another major issue affecting the prospects of innovation policy is the more open, networked or closer to production strategies for R&D-based innovation adopted especially by larger, multinational firms. Firms with headquarters in North America are leaders in corporate R&D, but where they spend their R&D funds has changed dramatically in the 8 years since the last big recession (i.e. between 2007 and 2015).

Asia is currently the biggest attractor of global corporate R&D spending, accounting for 35% of the global total for the 207 largest spending companies, beating both the USA (33%) and Europe (28%) in the game. This proportion includes both spending by local firms and R&D spending from other countries. While in 2007 domestic spending constituted the majority of R&D spending in North America, Europe and Asia, in 2015 a significant shift in the balance of such spending occurred in Asian countries (mainly China and India) where 52% of R&D spending was imported (Jaruzelski et al., 2015). Table 4.5 shows the changes in 'in-country' (or domestic plus imported spending) R&D spending at two points in an 8-year period, 2007 and 2015, for countries where more than US$10 billion was spent on corporate R&D in 2015.

The numbers suggest a certain ramping up of globalised forms of innovation based on more liberal approaches to FDI and R&D capital investment by foreign corporates. While the USA continues to lead the table partly because of increased European R&D investment in that country, collectively a larger share of R&D is now being conducted in Asia than in North America or Europe.

Two key points may be worth noting. First, liberalism in policy appears to be accompanied by corporate strategies denoting a shift in R&D-based innovation investment to countries and regions in which the manufacturing and sales of those companies are growing fastest. Second, the shift in business and innovation strategies of roaming corporates is due as much to the pragmatic approaches for doing business as it is to deregulation and the ease of doing business in emerging economies. Therefore, for policy makers the need for designing and implementing innovation policies is a function of both the imperative for economic growth and the changing strategic priorities of globally networked businesses. Whether governments are making sense of these two developments remains to be seen, but if we accept these two dimensions of policy making, we could argue that policies for innovation can perhaps best be realised when the needs and aspirations of governments and innovative firms

TABLE 4.5 Domestic and imported R&D spending (US$) by firms

Countries	2007	2015
USA	109	145
Japan	40	50
Germany	28	32
China	25	55
India	13	28
Canada	9	10
Italy	8	11
South Korea	7	13
Israel	7	11
France	20	16
UK	23	22

Source: Adapted from Jaruzelski et al. (2015)

are intertwined. We should note also that the function of government policy making is to generate and augment social good. So alongside the imperative for economic growth and meeting the globally networked interests of firms, policy can really be effective if the social effects are also built into policy agendas.

Given that there are huge regional variations, especially within large countries but also between economies grouped in any one of the three categories (developed, developing and less developed countries), regional policy issues may not mirror national policy priorities. At the country level it does not necessarily make sense for all the BRICS (Brazil, Russia, India, China and South Africa), for example, to try and emulate the 'Made in China' model to promote innovation as much as there being any purpose in benchmarking Silicon Valley for developing local innovation systems. In the first case China's state-driven model to date does not have any correspondence to the models in the democratic institutional environments of India, South Africa or Brazil, irrespective of the virtues of any system. These differences in governance structures allow for innovation to grow and for innovation to be thwarted using very different approaches to policy and practice. At the regional systems level, major technological developments in Silicon Valley could meet advanced manufacturing or service industry needs for the development of niche products, but this may not be particularly useful for mass manufacturing of, for example, car components.

It is not simply a matter of technology and the use of so-called relevant technologies for different environments. Advanced technologies for eye surgery have made considerable differences in the lives of the destitute in India, and modern mobile technologies have transformed the lives of the poor in many parts of Africa. On the other hand, smart use of local resources, such as the calibrated marshalling of solar power, has helped rural villagers to overcome limited grid access to electricity in the developing economies of India, Mali, Nicaragua and Tanzania. The key policy issue here is that of identifying prospects and needs together with the harnessing of commensurate technologies and the design of policies that can foster innovation.

POLICY, GOOD INTENTIONS AND EXCLUSIVENESS

What tends to happen sometimes with policy measures that identify good prospects for development is the unintended consequence of exclusion from the use and benefits of the innovation. Expensive, complex or long-drawn-out application procedures before any rewards are secured can affect firms, and especially the smaller firms, adversely. The granting of IP rights, for example, with their huge enforcement costs (legal and management costs plus time for litigation – see the above vignette on patents) act as a barrier to small firms. Previous success with funding or other rewards from similar policies tend to favour incumbents who can also benefit if the deadlines are too tight or there is only a limited amount of publicity for these schemes. The incumbency advantage is attractive to policy makers, who can then avoid the risk associated with potential future success. This can make a mockery of, for example, R&D funding for universities, businesses and other organisations when incumbency is associated with apparent excellence precluding novel approaches to both research and their commercialisation for the future. Using past track records for future potential is often the only, fallacious approach to funding allocations in limited time horizons. When policies target specific sectors or particular social challenges, these may result in a spatial concentration effect excluding regions that do not have those sectors or do not face those challenges. The concentration problem is augmented if more developed regions are able to use their reserves to match direct project funding (OECD, 2015).

Referring to the data above on corporate R&D funding, it is not surprising to see the growth of R&D spending by large firms. These firms are likely to have greater access to critical sources of innovation, including finance, human and intellectual capital, and an organisational infrastructure which enables them to internalise these sources by setting up R&D labs or 'skunk works'. Their smaller counterparts tend to rely on external resources, which makes it more difficult to organise them for innovation projects. This gap is exacerbated by poor business framework conditions. Liberalisation in India since 1991, for example, tended to benefit larger firms. While private investment in R&D grew from around 3% in the 1980s to 27% in 1999, there was a 14% increase in the probability of greater R&D investment by larger firms but a corresponding decrease by 8% of similar R&D investment by smaller firms (OECD, 2015).

Assuming that national governments have an interest in good innovation practice and economic development across countries, it would be incumbent on them to develop inclusive innovation policy that addresses both local needs and capacity building where necessary. This is particularly significant with less developed and developing countries where the early rollout of context-specific innovation heralds an approach to the much vaunted notion and practice of inclusive policy making.

INCLUSIVE POLICY MAKING

Inclusive policy making tends to be associated with policy matters affecting developing countries, mainly because of the gap between the rich and poor and the relatively low income levels caused by significant levels of poverty. Inclusive policy-making activities are, therefore, meant to offer opportunities for lower-income and excluded groups. This discrepancy, resulting from an excessive share of the economic riches being concentrated in the hands of the few, is of course not a developing economy prerogative. Income and wealth inequalities have attracted much attention in the developed economies in particular since the last economic recession began in 2008, so much so that the vocabulary of inclusion is as powerful in advanced economies as it is in poorer nations. The reasons are different, and the absolute levels of poverty or indeed wealth and high income also vary considerably between these two categories of nations. Let us focus attention on the more conventional agenda for inclusive policy making, which finds particular purchase in emerging and developing economies.

Poverty and social exclusion account for an estimated 4.3 billion (2010 figures) people, or approximately 62% of the world's population who live on less than $5 per day (OECD, 2015; World Bank, 2014). The exclusion of vast swathes of the population from the market, from goods and services, from adequate levels of access to basic utilities, food and shelter, is a missed economic opportunity in terms of adequate provision for a large community of people. Crucially it is also a social indictment and a moral outrage because of the egregious scrambling for resources and its concomitants of war, the displacement of people, environmental degradation and a perpetuation of unacceptable levels of inequality. Innovation and policies promoting innovation cannot necessarily address the big inequality question, which in the latter part of the twentieth and in the first decade of the twenty-first century has been entrenched by rates of return on capital exceeding the rate of growth of output and income, as they did in the nineteenth century (Piketty, 2014). However, an inclusive approach to innovation policy can work towards the partial alleviation of arbitrary and unsustainable inequalities and restore the meritocratic values of democratic societies. It can do so by focusing on market failures that exclude certain groups of people from participation in the economy, the better provision of public policies which can address the needs of the poor, and proactively to engage the poor in the marketplace as both consumers and producers. This approach suggests a mix of welfare economics with market imperatives, a key role for the state as an innovator, together with the creation of new producers or entrepreneurs who are enabled to seek opportunities for innovation.

But what do we mean by inclusive innovation policy? The currency of inclusive innovation policy is best understood in terms of how it improves the welfare of lower-income and excluded groups of people. To this end the OCED (2015) refers to two types of inclusive innovation: pro-inclusive and grassroots. The two variations of inclusive innovation attempt to address a range of market and systemic failures. These include typically a lack of or barriers to information about markets and customers, difficulties in accessing basic infrastructure utilities like energy sources, and the unavailability of credit, generally for the poor and the excluded, or the failure of institutions to coordinate demand and supply for these goods and services. Mendoza (2011) suggests that these deficits impose a 'poverty penalty', leading often to the poor paying more for these goods and services because the cost of supplying these goods becomes higher too! In some cases there are missed opportunities as both producers and the poor are excluded from these 'missed markets' (OECD, 2015).

Pro-inclusive and grassroots innovation policies can make sense if they help to create opportunities for lower-income people to jump the poverty line and advance their escape. Poverty is often just one illness away, one dowry payment away, or one death away for many who escape the immediate threshold. Krishna (2011) narrates the story of a 50-year-old woman, Chandibai, whose husband owned a general purpose shop in the village square in the prosperous state of Gujarat in western India. They were also owners of a house and agricultural land which they leased out for a share of the crop. Then a spate of events accelerated a downward spiral. First it was the husband's illness and subsequent death, which meant assets had to be sold and debt incurred to pay for medical bills. Then 2 years later, the oldest daughter's marriage, in keeping with middle-class traditions, helped to accumulate the debt to levels equivalent to 2 years' income at the official minimum wage (not forgetting the interest that helped to double the amount owed every year). The land was sold. Work on construction sites at below minimum wages and only limited or poor quality food was eaten because Chandibai had no credit in the local shop. If cheaper and effective health care, the proper enforcement of laws related to inheritance for women, easier availability of credit, the removal of dowries and ostentatious weddings in fact a reversal of the chain of events that induce chronic poverty – could have been possible, then Chandibai's descent into poverty would have been avoided.

The narrative above illustrates what is needed to intervene and how best to help communities overcome the interconnected social and institutional barriers to inclusive innovation and economic development. This necessitates an understanding and application of appropriate ecosystems and not rigid or standardised models developed in very different socio-economic environments. Based on the discussion that we have had so far we can identify five distinctive rationales:

1. Overcoming various types of market, system and capacity failures.
2. Augmenting innovation in the design and delivery of public services and public-good creation activities.
3. Empowering low-income groups to be active producers and consumers of innovative products and services that are consumed by all communities of interest.
4. The extension of the idea of growth to address both economic growth and social development.
5. Incorporation of *ex ante* and *ex post* evaluation metrics that capture social innovation outcomes alongside those for economic ones for general innovation policies.

As stated earlier, inclusive innovation policies tend to be associated with developing and especially the larger emerging economies where advances in wealth creation may have allowed some slack for an early consideration of inclusive policy making. One of the reasons is the need to slow down or recalibrate the pace of growth for the few, which fuels inequality. Disparities between the rich and the poor exaggerated by the adoption of the dominant logic of the market acquire a poignancy that demands a greater urgency of action, not least because of the large numbers of people who are left behind somewhere between abject poverty and a vulnerable hiatus just above the line of escape from poverty.

Different countries interpret inclusive policy making based on priorities that they have set for themselves, as Table 4.6 shows.

The overall Global Entrepreneurship Index (GEI) score measures the quality and scale of the entrepreneurial process in 132 different countries. The Global Entrepreneurship Development Index (GEDI) methodology collects data on the entrepreneurial attitudes, abilities and aspirations of the local population and then weights these against the prevailing social and economic 'infrastructure'; this includes aspects such as broadband connectivity and the transport links to external markets. This process creates 14 'pillars' which GEDI uses to measure the health of the regional ecosystem (GEDI, 2016).

The GEDI scores are included here simply to examine an association between 'needs' and the 'entrepreneurial capability' (as measured by the GEI) of a country. Significantly, all countries bar one in the table are in the middle-ranking category of 'efficiency-driven economies' or countries that have made sufficient strides in terms of economic growth to deliver efficient manufacturing industries and the apparent

TABLE 4.6 Approaches to inclusive innovation and Global Entrepreneurship Index scores

Country	Approach to policy	Typical initiatives	Global Entrepreneurship Index growth category	Overall Global Entrepreneurship Index score
China	Science- and technology-based innovations for public well-being/poverty alleviation through science and technology	Focus on growing urban population; the supply of affordable health care, education and sanitation	Efficiency-based economy	34.9
India	Innovation solving problems of people at bottom of pyramid	National Innovation Foundation providing institutional support to grassroots innovators and traditional knowledge providers	Factor-driven economy	24.9
Indonesia	Incremental innovation emphasising process innovations	No specific policy but involvement of several ministries and non-ministerial government institutions	Efficiency-driven economy	22.8
Colombia	Aligning economic development to social development; innovations that resolve social problems	National Node on Social Innovation; intergovernmental cooperation	Efficiency-driven economy	44.8
South Africa	Empowerment of excluded people; exclusion in terms of poverty, race, gender and disability	Inclusiveness both in terms of outputs and processes with access to basic services, the involvement of science councils and grassroots innovation	Efficiency-driven economy	38.5

Sources: Adapted from OECD (2015); GEDI (2016)

enrichment of their population. The higher the score, the greater the chances of eco-nomic equality as measured by correlating GEI scores against the Gini coefficient measure (GEDI, 2016).

Inclusive innovation policy making is not easy to secure because it inevitably involves cross-institutional collaboration. Typically, agencies responsible for poverty alleviation, health, education, infrastructure, and science and technology, among oth-ers, need to cooperate with each other because of overlaps occurring as a result of tackling economic growth with social development. Governance structures beyond national levels and across disaggregated regions where larger numbers of the excluded live and work are critical for identifying need, generating data and addressing con-flicting priorities (as between what happens at the national level and what impacts on local communities). Coordination of multiple agencies at different levels becomes important in the management and coordination of disparate needs while ensuring cor-respondence between national policy guidelines and local engagement (OECD, 2015).

Inclusive policy development necessitates inclusive policy design and involvement in the innovation processes directly. While individual firms may be able to achieve such outcomes with specific products (as in the case of the Amul Dairy cooperative in India and the rural women suppliers of milk), it is not easy to wade across bureaucratic currents at the governmental, institutional and spatial divides to coordinate design, production and delivery with the involvement of various excluded communities. The creation of an active ecosystem of players becomes a major requirement, quite often involving government departments, NGOs, universities, research institutions, private sector partners and the financial sector, working in tandem with grassroots innova-tors, low-income groups and consumers. Colombia's Social Innovation Policy is a good example of clear inclusive policy-making intent, as explained in Vignette 4.2.

VIGNETTE 4.2   COLOMBIA'S SOCIAL INNOVATION POLICY

Developed alongside the National Development Plan of 2010–14, the Colombian Social Innovation Policy (SIP) identified innovation as the critical variable in the country's productive sector and for social and sustainable development with good governance. The SIP also aims to create an inclusive innovation system drawing on all sectors of society, including non-profit organisations, academic institutions, the private sector and the wider communities themselves.

The Centre for Social Innovation (CIS) was created in June 2011 with the aim of connecting the public and private sectors to provide for innovative, sustainable, scalable solutions to the problem of extreme poverty. The type of social innovation policies that it has generated include mapping the inclusive innovation sector (Project Hilando). The project searches for social innovation initiatives across the country and records them in an online directory to facilitate access and contacts among different innovators and other interested parties.

The Somas mas 'Spinning with the Community' project offers a virtual platform that has 1,519 active members working together to strengthen the ecosystem of social inno-vation to overcome extreme poverty. The mission is to create a collective intelligence social ecosystem, to meet challenges that can only be solved by others. The project has helped to develop route services for social innovators, namely, Atlantic, Antioquia, Bolívar, Cundinamarca, Valle del Cauca, Huila, Chocó, Magdalena, La Guajira, Meta, Boyacá, Nariño, Caldas and Risaralda. The route services are developed from the collective design investigative tools. The information that is collected is analysed in terms of significant moments that pass through innovative initiatives and the sequential relationships between the initiatives and the people involved with them. This has resulted in 460 people turning their collective intelligence workshops, 807 services being identified for social innovators in 14 municipalities, and 614 projects participating in the web platform.

Other projects include the promotion of 'projectya Colombia', for public–private partnerships, with the involvement of Socialab academic partnerships for social innovation projects, for example between the Faculties of Design at the University of the Andes, Jorge Tadeo University and Universidad Pontificia Bolivariana.

In partnership with the National Agency for Overcoming Extreme Poverty (ANSPE), Colcinncias, the Administrative Department of Science, Technology and Innovation, developed another project, the Ideas Para el Cambio, which selects a priority area for intervention, consulting with local communities about specific challenges in the priority area, and then issues a call for solutions to the problems based on consultations with the scientific and innovation community. With an overall budget of US$550,000 the project has generated solutions such as ceramic filters for water sanitation and solar pumps for water provision.

Sources: Colciencias (2014); ANSPE (2014) cited in OECD (2015); Somas mas (2016)

International cooperation extends the scope of governance while enabling wider reach, publicity and additional resource mobilisation. The Global Research Alliance, a network of nine research institutions from the USA, South Africa, Australia, Denmark, Germany, Malaysia, the Netherlands and Finland, works for example with the Council of Scientific and Industrial Research (CSIR) in India (among others) to grant-aid work on herbal medicine, the use of ICT for agricultural development, alongside support for peer learning. The alliance's aim is to improve the livelihoods of the world's poorest through science and technology, through partnerships and the involvement of end users, local stakeholders and the private sector (OECD, 2015).

Policy development for innovation is dependent on adequate regulatory frameworks. Yet regulation often bypasses informal and grassroots innovators and especially the poor end users or producers. The absence of official data on informal activity makes it difficult to identify projects worthy of support through proper frameworks, and then there is the additional problem of scaling up the many grassroots initiatives that suffer from the liability of smallness, poor access to formal sources of finance, and lack of skills, especially in the use of key technologies. Poor timing of legislation, anti-competitive product market regulation, and the absence of IPR protection can also have an adverse effect on grassroots-based activities. The latter issue is a critical element in the development of effective policies by, for example, the National Innovation Fund and the Honey Bee Network in India (OECD, 2015).

INCLUSIVENESS AND THE EXCLUSIVENESS IN DEVELOPED ECONOMIES – NEW CHALLENGES TO INNOVATION POLICY

The complexity of the inclusive innovation policy agenda suggests that it is far removed from standard innovation policy development, especially that found in advanced economies with their domain focus on science, R&D and technology. Yet we can see that even in these scenarios organisational innovations involving people as producers, end users and consumers are a necessary concomitant of technological innovations. Paradoxically, we also see major institutional failures. These divergent strands in the social and economic fabric of advanced countries can be seen in four different developments. The developments stem from the perpetuation of previously unresolved social dysfunctionalism, many years of economic practice based on a combination of neo-classical notions of the rational man and capital accumulation and militaristic hegemony, and the pressures of technological breakthroughs which challenge the way we manage the innovation process.

First, when inequality (the 1%–99% divide) becomes embedded in the economy, and a failure to carve out any substantive recovery following a recession becomes the norm (as it has been since the start of the recession in 2007–8 until now, in 2016), then the travails of the disadvantaged are magnified and become more entrenched. Second, inequalities in wealth and income simply entrench other inequalities of class, race and gender (as in the continuity of lower proportions of black and working-class students entering our universities, or women finding similar jobs to men but being paid less than the latter, or economically-driven social engineering that makes it impossible for the poor to find housing in growing metros such as London because they remain poor). Third, the misallocation of resources underlined by ideological priorities (as between large amounts of military spending on foreign wars, visa restrictions on the mobility of workers, a failure to manage the refugee crisis when even the demographics demand a morally responsible response) is often accompanied on the one hand by the bunker mentality of the privileged few who protect exclusive innovations, and on the other by the growing community of the disenfranchised many who seek the immediacy of protection of their own declining resources. In many respects this kind of development reflects a cyclical economic outcome. Fourth, against the scenarios depicted above we also find technology disrupting structural and institutional arrangements in, for example, the way we shop and consume (Internet shopping and environmentally conscious consumption, downloading music and video), how we could organise what and how we pay for goods and services (free services, recognition of the value of blockchain technology and the use of bitcoin currency that call into question the value of price mechanism), and how we learn or make products (massive, online open courses (MOOCs) and open source).

All of the above scenarios call for innovative policy solutions to the problems. Much of what is occurring in terms of the search for these solutions can be found in the alternative third space of community-based initiatives, social enterprises and networked-based commercial endeavour. Inclusive public policy in these conditions needs to reorient itself to support the technological and social innovations on the ground. Here, clear analytical policies need to be developed to differentiate between the rent-seeking innovations (e.g. many 'apps-based' innovators such as Uber or Twitter, which try to create short-term value from the scraps of information that engulf us) and the productive innovations of Apple, Google, Snapdeal, Alibaba and Didi (who also need to pay their taxes!) which can change the way we improve our lives.

Grassroots innovation and inclusive innovation policy development only has purchase when an ecosystem of key players and institutions is established and supported. This leads to a democratisation of the innovation process that is now also apparent in networked-based, open innovation architectures for modern product development projects involving leading manufacturing and technology firms across the world. In fact, a distinctive factor in the inclusive innovation development process is this producer–user–institutional nexus coupled with the conjoined technological–economic–social imperatives, not whether the innovation is new to the firm or to the world, which is how standard innovations are measured.

CONCLUDING OBSERVATIONS

The function of innovation policy is to provide direction, offset for market and other failures, and facilitate conditions in which innovations appropriate to the economy and society in question can be made possible. The activities that define policies are various and numerous but they do not all obtain in different environments. Neither do they seek to achieve similar goals. As we have seen already, the competitive advantage that nations seek tends to rely on technologies, skills, knowledge, people and institutions pursuing similar goals. While this may be possible across countries with similar economic and social profiles (as in advanced or emerging or low-income countries), they are not universal. They are also not universal for two other reasons that call into question general comparisons even among countries with similar characteristics. The first explanation centres around questions of spatial and territorial differences across and within countries. Regional differences, especially in large countries (the USA, China, India, Nigeria, Brazil) but also in small nations (the UK), make it difficult to apply national policy agendas. While physical differences in the former often account for economic differences, poorly designed institutional arrangements exacerbate differences in smaller counties. The north east in England, for example, struggles with innovative capacity not because of the lack of innovative people, but due to the lack of institutional support mechanisms for industry, housing and social needs, resources for which are concentrated in the south and south east of the country.

Second, the priorities for innovation for countries with dissimilar economic and social environments will differ. The difference will be found not only in terms of the scale of economic activity or social development, but also in terms of alternative pathways for growth or transformation of the existing state of affairs. For example, inclusive innovation policies consider not only pro-poor, socially-oriented approaches, but also, prospectively, an alternative to linear models of growth that predicate social development on economic outcomes.

In short, context matters. Comparisons offer possibilities of learning and adaptation, but despite popular ideas of technological and economic convergence, it is inconceivable that any amount of catching up could lead to any real convergence. Markets thrive on differences, and exploitative firms can abuse these differences since the reality of practice is not determined by rational man. Add to that geographical, some cultural and institutional factors that distinguish countries and regions, and it is not too difficult to see why inequalities at worst and variations at best explain how economies follow specific routes and how policies reflect these differences.

Nuanced approaches to policy development suggest that more can be achieved if targets are set within particular ecosystems by makers and users and by policy agents and communities. Nuanced approaches also means that government policy is not simply reduced to addressing system or market failures. Proactive government intervention can also help to create and promote the work of Apple and the Honey Bee Network in varied environments. Finally, nuanced approaches can help to embrace inclusivity which not only assists in different types of innovation (new to market, product, process and organisational), but also generates impact-oriented outcomes.

After studying the first four chapters we can now see how technical change prompts innovation, and how such innovation obtains in different environments, evolving as a result of systems and institutions, and the various ways in which governments interact with these systems to support business and their innovation activities. This then is the macro picture. It is the big canvas on which business paints the various hues of innovation through the ingenuity of its people and the effectiveness of its organisations. People and organisations form the micro component of the business of innovation, and it is to this part that we turn next, first by examining how innovative organisations work. We then dig deeper, to explore what is at the heart of these organisations – its people.

 SELF-ASSESSMENT QUESTIONS

1.   Why do we need policies for innovation?

2.   What do we mean by demand- and supply-side activities and policies?

3.   What are market, systemic and capability failures?

4.   Can government create proactive policy and engage in proactive intervention for innovation?

5.   What is inclusive innovation, and how and why do countries need inclusive innovation policies?

 **REFERENCES**

Abubakar, Y.A., Trstenjak, J. and Mitra, J. (2012) 'Regional disparities in entrepreneurial activities in the United Kingdom and their impact on regional employment growth rates between 2004 and 2009', Paper presented at the 35th ISBE Conference on Creating Opportunities through Innovation: Local Energy, Global Vision', Dublin, 7–8 November.

Acs, Z.J. (2008) *Entrepreneurship, Growth and Public Policy: Prelude to a Knowledge Spillover Theory of Entrepreneurship.* Cheltenham: Edward Elgar.

Akerlof, G. (1970) 'The market for "Lemmons": quality uncertainty and the market mechanism', *Quarterly Journal of Economics*, 84(3): 488–500.

ANSPE (2014) 'Agency for overcoming extreme poverty', Centre for Social Innovation. Available at: www.anspe.gov.co/es/programma/que-es-el-centro-innovacion-social

Audretsch, D.B. and Keilbach, M. (2007) 'The theory of knowledge spillover entrepreneurship', *Journal of Management Studies*, 44(7): 1242–54.

Barbaroux, P. (2014) 'From market failures to market opportunities: managing innovation under asymmetric information', *Journal of Innovation and Entrepreneurship*, 3: 5. Available at: www.innovation-entrepreneurship.com/content/3/1/5 (last accessed 23 November 2015).

Bergek, A., Jacobsson, S., Carlsson, B., Lindmark, S. and Rickne, A. (2008) 'Analyzing the functional dynamics of technological innovation systems: a scheme of analysis', *Research Policy*, 37(3): 407–29.

Bessen, J. and Hunt, R.M. (2007) 'An empirical look at software patents', *Journal of Economics & Management Strategy*, 16(1): 157–89.

Blöndal, J.R. (2003) 'Budget reform in OECD member countries', *OECD Journal on Budgeting*, 2(4): 7–25.

Carlsson, B. and Jacobsson, S. (1997) 'Diversity creation and technological systems: a technology policy perspective' in C. Edquist (ed.), *Systems of Innovation: Technologies, Institutions and Organizations*. London: Pinter Publishers. pp. 266–94.

Chaminade, C. and Edquist, C. (2006) 'From theory to practice: the use of systems of innovation approach in innovation policy', CIRCLE Electronic Working Paper Series, Paper No. 2005/02.

Chaminade, C. and Vang, J. (2006) 'Innovation policy for Asian SMEs: exploring cluster differences', Paper presented at the DRUID Summer Conference on Knowledge, Innovation and Competitiveness: Dynamics of Firms, Networks, Regions and Institutions, Copenhagen, 18–20 June. p. 6.

Chaminade, C., Intarakumnerd, P. and Sapprasert, K. (2008) 'Measuring systemic failures in innovation systems in developing countries using innovation survey data: the case of Thailand'. Available at: http://citeseerx.ist.psu.edu/viewdoc/download?doi=10.1.1.468.1621&rep=rep1&type=pdf (last accessed on 25 November 2015).

Chan, H.-J. (2010) *23 Things They Didn't Tell You About Capitalism*. London: Allen Lane.

Chien, C.V. and Lemley, M.A. (2011) 'Patents and the public interest', *New York Times*, 13 December. Available at: www.nytimes.com/2011/12/13/opinion/patents-smartphones-and-the-public-interest.html (last accessed 1 October 2016).

Chien, C.V. and Lemley, M.A. (2012) 'Patent holdup, the ITC, and the public interest', *Cornell Law Review*, Stanford Public Law Working Paper No. 2022168, 9 October. Available at: http://papers.ssrn.com/sol3/papers.cfm?abstract_id=2022168 (last accessed 23 November 2015).

Cohen, J. and Lemley, M.A. (2001) 'Patent scope and innovation in the software industry', *California Law Review*, 89: 1–57.

Colciencias (2014) Ideas para el Cambio website, www.ideasparaelcambio.gov.co (last accessed 27 January 2017).

Duménil, G. and Lévy, D. (2005) 'The neoliberal (counter) revolution', in A. Saad-Filho and D. Johnston (eds), *Neoliberalism. A Critical Reader*. London: Pluto Press. pp. 9–19.

Duménil, G. and Lévy, D. (2011) *The Crisis of Neoliberalism*. Cambridge, MA: Harvard University Press.

Edler, J. (ed.) (2007) *Internationalisierung der deutschen Forschungs- und Wissenschaftslandschaf* [Internationalization of the German research and science landscape]. Karlsruhe: Fraunhofer Institute Systems and Innovation Research.

Edler, J. (2007) *Nachfrageorientierte Innovationspolitik* [Demand Oriented Innovation Policy]. Berlin: Edition Sigma.

Edler, J. (2010) 'Demand-based innovation policy', in R. Smits, S. Kuhlmann and P. Shapira (eds), *The Theory and Practice of Innovation Policy: An International Research Handbook*. Cheltenham: Edward Elgar.

Edler, J. and Georghiou, L. (2007) 'Public procurement and innovation – resurrecting the demand side', *Research Policy*, 36(7): 949–63.

Edler, J., Ruhland, S., Hafner, S., Rigby, J., Georghiou, L., Hommen, L., Rolfstam, M., Edquist, C., Tsipouri, L. and Papadakou, M. (2005) *Innovation and public procurement: Review of issues at stake*. Karlsruhe: Fraunhofer Institute Systems and Innovation Research.

Edquist, C. (1997) *Systems of Innovation: Technologies, Institutions and Organisations*. London: Pinter.

Edquist, C. (1999) 'Innovation policy – a systemic approach', Department of Technology and Social Change, Linköping University. Available at: https://www.researchgate.net/profile/Charles_Edquist/publication/228866782_Innovation_PolicyA_Systemic_Approach/links/548177b70cf20f081e727cb4.pdf (last accessed 10 December 2015).

Edquist, C. (2005) 'Systems of innovation: perspectives and challenges', in J. Fagerberg, D. Mowery and R.R. Nelson (eds), *The Oxford Handbook of Innovation*. Oxford: Oxford University Press.

Edquist, C. and IFRIS (2011) 'Innovation policy design: identification of systemic problems', Centre for Innovation, Research and Competence in the Learning Economy (CIRCLE), Lund University, and Institut Francilien Recherche Innovation Société (IFRIS), Université Paris-Est.

Federal Trade Commission (2003) *To promote innovation: the proper balance of competition and patent law and policy*, a Report by the Federal Trade Commission. Collingdale, PA: DIANE Publishing.

Freeman, C.A. (1995) 'The "National System of Innovation" in historical perspective', *Cambridge Journal of Economics*, 19: 5–24.

Galli, R. and Teubal, M. (1997) 'Paradigmatic shifts in national innovation systems'. Available at: http://ifise.unipv.it/Publications/Paradigmatic.pdf (last accessed 25 November 2015).

GEDI (2016) 'Research'. Available at: http://thegedi.org/global-entrepreneurship-and-development-index/ (last accessed 15 February 2016).

Giuliani, E. and Bell, M. (2005) 'The micro-determinants of meso-level learning and innovation: evidence from a Chilean wine cluster', *Research Policy*, 34: 47–68.

Hall, B.H. and Ziedonis, R.H. (2001) 'The patent paradox revisited: an empirical study of patenting in the US semiconductor industry, 1979–1995', *RAND Journal of Economics*, 32(1): 101–28.

Hauknes, J. and Norgren, L. (1999) *Economic Rationales of Government Intervention in Innovation and the Supply of Innovation-Related services*, STEP Report 08. Oslo: STEP Group, downloadable from www.nifu.no.

Heller, M.A. and Eisenberg, R.S. (1998) 'Can patents deter innovation? The anticommons in biomedical research', *Science*, 280: 698–701.

Intarakumnerd, P., Chairatana, P. and Tangchitpiboonet, T. (2002) 'National innovation system in less successful developing countries: the case of Thailand', *Research Policy*, 31: 1445–57.

Jaffe, A. and Lerner, J. (2004) *Innovation and Its Discontents: How Our Broken Patent System Is Endangering Innovation and Progress, and What to Do About It*. Princeton, NJ: Princeton University Press.

Jaruzelski, B., Schwartz, K. and Staack, V. (2015) 'The Global Innovation 1000: Innovation's new world order', *Strategy + Business*, Issue 81, Winter.

Johnson, A. and Jacobsson, S. (2003) 'The emergence of a growth industry: a comparative analysis of the German, Dutch and Swedish wind turbine industries', in S. Metcalfe and U. Cantner (eds), *Transformation and Development: Schumpeterian Perspectives*. Heidelberg: Springer.

Keynes, J.M. (1926) *The End of Laissez-Faire*. London: L. & V. Woolf.

Kirzner, I. (1997) 'Entrepreneurial discovery and the competitive market process: an Austrian approach', *Journal of Economic Perspectives*, 35(1): 60–85.

Krishna, A. (2011) *One Illness Away: Why People Become Poor and How They Escape Poverty*. Oxford: Oxford University Press.

Lipsey, R.G. and Carlaw, K. (1998) 'Technology policies in neo-classical and structuralist-evolutionary models', *STI Review*, 22: 31–73.

Liu, X. and White, S. (2001) 'Comparing innovation systems: a framework and application to China's transitional context', *Research Policy*, 30: 1091–14.

Lundvall, B.A. (1992) *National Systems of Innovation: An Analytical Framework*. London: Pinter.

Mazzucato, M. (2013) *The Entrepreneurial State: Debunking Public vs Private Sector Myths*. London: Anthem Press.

Mendoza, R.U. (2011) 'Why do the poor pay more? Exploring the poverty penalty concept'; *Journal of International Development*, 23(1): 1–28.

Miller, D. (2003) An asymmetry-based view of advantage: towards an attainable sustainability'. *Strategic Management Journal*, 24(10): 961–976.

Mitra, J. (2012) *Entrepreneurship, Innovation and Regional Development: An Introduction*. Abingdon: Routledge.

Mitra, J. and Tardios, J.A. (2015) 'A nuanced approach to supply side factors affecting innovation, opportunity development and employment growth in English regions: a case study of the Thames Gateway Region in Essex', Paper presented at the 38th ISBE Conference on Internationalisation, Innovation and Leadership, Glasgow, 10–12 November.

Mowery, D.C. (2010) 'Military R&D and innovation', in B.H. Hall and N. Rosenberg (eds), *Handbook of the Economics of Innovation*. Amsterdam: North Holland.

National Academies of Science (2004) *How People Learn: Brain, Mind, Experience, and School*, Commission on Behavioral and Social Sciences and Education, National Research Council. Washington, DC: National Academy Press.

Nelson, R.A. (1993) *National Innovation Systems: A Comparative Analysis*. Oxford: Oxford University Press.

NESTA (2015) 'Some thoughts on *The Entrepreneurial State*'. Available at: www.nesta.org.uk/blog/some-thoughts-entrepreneurial-state#sthash.HtyYHX3J.dpuf (last accessed 6 October 2016).

OECD (2011) *Demand-side Innovation Policies*. Paris: OECD Publishing.

OECD (2013) 'Supply side policy instruments for innovation in firms'. Available at: http://innovationpoli cyplatform.org/content/supply-sidepolicy-instruments-innvation-firms (last accessed 23 November 2015).

OECD (2015) *Innovation Policies for Inclusive Growth*. Paris: OECD Publishing. Available at: http://dx.doi.org/10.1787/9789264229488-en (last accessed 27 January 2017).

Picard, P. (1987) 'On the design of incentive schemes under moral hazard and adverse selection', *Journal of Public Economics*, 33(3): 305–31.

Piketty, T. (2014) *Capital in the Twenty First Century*. Cambridge, MA: Belknap, Harvard University Press.

Rodrik, D. (2004) 'Industrial policy for the twenty first century', CEPR Discussion Paper No. 4767, Centre for Economic Policy Research, November.

Saad-Filho, A. and Johnston, D. (eds) (2005) *Neoliberalism: A Critical Reader*. London: Pluto Press.

Shapiro, C. (2001) 'Navigating the patent thicket: cross licenses, patent pools and standard setting' in A. Jaffe, J. Lerner and S. Stern, *Innovation Policy and the Economy 1*. Cambridge, MA: NBER/MIT Press. pp. 119–50.

Shapiro, C. (2010) 'Injunctions, hold-up, and patent royalties', *American Law and Economics Review*, doi: 10.1093/aler/ahq014. Oxford: Oxford University Press.

Smith, K. (2000) 'Innovation as a systemic phenomenon: rethinking the role of policy', *Enterprise and Innovation Management Studies*, 1(1): 73–102.

Somos mas (2016) 'Spinning in the community'. Available at: https://somosmas.org/project/hilando-comunidad-de-innovacion-social-2 and https://somosmas.org/nosotros/ (last accessed 15 February 2016).

Spence, M. (1976) 'Informational aspects of market structure: an introduction', *Quarterly Journal of Economics*, 90(4): 591–7.

Stiglitz, J. (2000) 'The contributions of the economics of information to twentieth century economics', *Quarterly Journal of Economics*, 115(4): 1441–78.

Storper, M. (1997) *The Regional World: Territorial Development in a Global Economy*. New York: Guilford Press.

The Global Innovation Index 2015: Effective Innovation Policies for Development, ed. S. Dutta, B. Lanvin and S. Wunsch-Vincent. Johnson Cornell University, INSEAD and World Intellectual Property Organisation.

Vertova, G. (2014) 'The state and national systems of innovation: a sympathetic critique', Working Paper No. 823, Levy Economics Institute of Bard College, Annandale-on-Hudson, NY, December.

Woolthuis, R.A., Lankhuizenb, M. and Gilsing, V. (2005) 'A system failure framework for innovation policy design approach in innovation policy', *Technovation*, 25(6): 609–19.

World Bank (2010) *Innovation Policy: A Guide for Developing Countries*. Washington, DC: The International Bank for Reconstruction and Development/The World Bank.

THE CHARACTERISTICS AND FEATURES OF INNOVATIVE ORGANISATIONS

5

SCOPE AND OBJECTIVES

- The meaning and scope of innovative organisations (IOs), their varied features, component parts and styles.
- A discussion based on the question: what is an IO and what does it represent?
- Do all IOs have similar features and are they able to maintain them to help develop sustainable IOs?

INTRODUCTION

Understanding what innovation means to society and to our economies requires us to look beyond innovative individuals to organisations where such individuals work or with whom communities of innovative people interact. Understanding what innovation means in an organisational context helps us to identify and appreciate firms that survive and grow by making new products and services and those that create spaces and conditions for productive change. It also helps us to appreciate how these firms represent change and the ability to adapt as dynamic organisations in continually transforming environments. But changing to adapt to different demands in the wider economy is not enough. Innovative organisations (IOs) change to progress, to move forward proactively, going beyond adaptation to realise transformation in the products and services they provide, in their business models and organisational structures, in the mindsets of all its stakeholders, and sometimes even in the economies and societies in which they are embedded. This may sound like a grand claim, especially as transformation is not easy to achieve. Contexts matter, as do the varied types, features, structures, objectives and dynamics of such organisations.

IOs are adaptive and entrepreneurial organisations. For these firms ambidexterity, adaptability and agility, as measured by the ability to manage markets and resources using both traditional business models and novel ones, constitute the norm. Instead of stability and adherence to tried and tested standards of practice they navigate the randomness and diversity associated with uncertainty and disruptiveness in technology life cycles, market fluctuations and unusual opportunities in unknown and complex environments. In being ambidextrous, adaptable and agile they often make new combinations of existing resources in unusual ways.

Complexity in uncertainty environments requires more from organisations than ambidexterity and new combinations. Complexity in the environment and in production processes often leaves firms ill-equipped or deficient in managing the various processes, diverse sets of people, and multiple projects that they need to organise. Networking has emerged as a strategic tool for organisations which now make products and provide services based on inter- and intra-firm alliances and relationships. Networked firms are concentrations of business units connected with each other and coordinated by market and non-market mechanisms. The evolution of these firms and the key drivers of innovation in these firms now find new directions in the changing landscape of innovation in a globalised world. They include new firms, small firms, medium-sized and large firms, and their quest for meaningful and sustainable competitive advantage.

New organisations are most likely to be small organisations, but they do not necessarily take the form of totally independent small firms. Crucially, larger firms often demonstrate the ability to reinvent themselves to pursue entrepreneurial activities. These innovative organisations identify and create new business models with which to carry out new activities and generate revenue streams which were not imagined before. Other types of organisations have completely radical missions, such as the fulfilment of social objectives through their business activities. These are the so-called social or community enterprises. All of these organisations:

- create different forms of economic, social, cultural and personal value; and
- contribute to the social and economic development of the regions in which they are located.

As the introduction to this chapter suggests, the subject of IOs is both complex and voluminous. IOs have specific features and then, as we have mentioned above, there are different types of IOs. We cover both features and types in our exploration of IOs and to this end we organise our exploration over two chapters. The study of IOs is the centrepiece of this book and this point alone justifies the extended coverage.

Our focus here is on the innovative *business* organisation – its characteristics and key features. Such an organisation is not necessarily a *new*, small firm. *Existing* firms which are able to adapt, change and create value through new products, new services, new markets and organisational transformation can also be regarded as exemplars of entrepreneurial activity (Mitra, 2012). The exploration also raises questions of the characteristics, constraints and approaches to innovation, their relative strengths and weaknesses according to the sectoral context in which they operate, and quite importantly the way they collaborate and network to optimise their innovative potential.

What IOs represent and what they do are to a great extent determined by the forms of innovations they pursue – product, process and organisational – and by the structure and context of their organisations, which includes their size and the economic environment in which they operate. In summary, there are different ways to look at and analyse IOs. We can examine them in terms of:

- features and characteristics;
- types, size and models; and
- processes and methods.

In this chapter we study the first aspect of IOs. Understanding the different features and characteristics helps us to locate the processes that they pursue. Recognising the types of IOs provides us with different contexts in which to examine the features and characteristics and which of these hold in specific contexts. The process aspect of innovative firms is wide and complex and deserves separate scrutiny.

But first, what are organisations and what makes an innovative one? How they create value, their constructs and purpose, and their role in economic development are what we explore in this chapter. This exploration takes in a quick overview of organisations and what we understand about the organisational process – the organising component – that distinguishes different and especially the standard organisation from the IO.

ORGANISATIONS

Intuitively, we all know that Ford Motor Company is as much an organisation as Tata Steel or Samsung, or even Wikipedia. But do they represent the universal organisation? What makes one of them new and innovative and the other traditional?

Before we go any further it is worth reminding ourselves what organisations are all about, and then discover what makes some of them more innovative than others.

The original roots of the word 'organisation' can be found in the Greek word *organon*, which is a variation of the word *ergon* meaning 'organ' or a vehicle for a particular job. A wide range of researchers and analysts (Weick, 1969; Whetten and Aldrich, 1979; Burton and Obel, 1984; March and Simon, 1993; Scott and Falcone, 1998) have all provided useful conceptualisations of organisations and what they represent. These definitions go beyond the explanation of an organisation as physical form, or as entities made up of people, machinery and other assets and legal instruments. A higher level of abstraction helps to identify an organisation as a collective of people sharing the same goals and where there is a sense of control over the actions that achieve those goals and a systematic structure for doing so. Let us look at a few definitions.

According to Bedeian and Zammuto (1991), organisations can be considered to be:

social entities that are goal directed, deliberately structured activity systems with a permeable boundary.

The 'deliberately structured activity systems' enable organisations to divide systematically complex tasks among a wide range of people and/or units of activity to achieve a common purpose. The idea of the 'permeable boundary' is an abstract and conceptual boundary (apart from the physical fencing) that explains or defines what or who is part of an organisation.

March and Simon (1993: 2) offer the following, comprehensive definition:

> Organisations are systems of co-ordinated action among individuals and groups whose preferences, information, interests or knowledge differ.

The two definitions, and indeed many others, share four common features of:

- multi-agency;
- identifiable boundaries;
- system-level goals; and
- the coordination of efforts to make a contribution to the achievement of that goal. (Puranam et al., 2014)

These features can be studied from a variety of perspectives. For example, a *process-related perspective* looks at how tasks or actions are constituted within an organisation and how they are reset to serve different interests or goals. A *functional perspective* focuses on how a business organisation is similar to a government agency or a not-for-profit entity, and how each of them evolve over time following their own goals and using their specific systems. A third perspective can be referred to as the *institutional perspective* where attention shifts to the structure of an organisation and the particular context in which that structure is built and made operational. The three perspectives can of course be connected, in that any one organisation may be studied from all three perspectives and there are overlapping elements in each perspective which enable the connection.

Implicit in the explanation above is the notion of 'organising'. Organisations exist because they 'organise', but as Weick (1969) reminded us, 'organisations' and 'organising' are not the same thing. The latter may be regarded as a problem-solving process, with the problems requiring a solution which are those of the division of labour and the integration of effort (Mintzberg, 1979; Burton and Obel, 1988; March and Simon, 1993). Inherent in the divergent 'division of labour problem' are two practical and universal problems, 'task division' and 'task allocation', while the convergent problem of 'integration of effort' accommodates the two other practical and universal problems of 'reward provision' and 'information provision' (Puranam et al., 2014). Figure 5.1 attempts an encapsulation of the ideas of organisation and organising in theory.

Given what we know now about organisations from the brief overview above, what then are IOs?

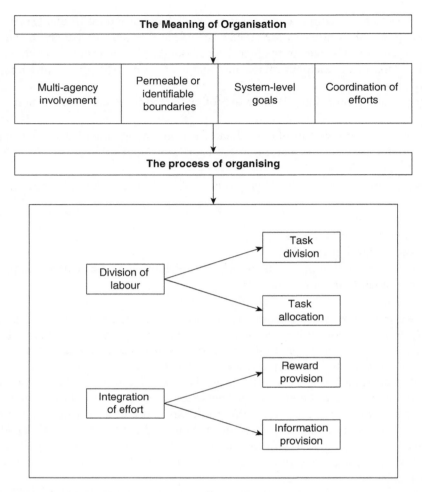

FIGURE 5.1   Features of organisations and organising

THE INNOVATIVE ORGANISATION AND INNOVATIVE ORGANISING

Assuming an acceptance of the idea of innovation as something new or novel, it can be argued that IOs are those that identify, practise and realise novel or new forms of organising by exploring solutions to the universal problems referred to above. Their approach to problem solving can then be compared with existing non-innovative organisations (Puranam et al., 2014).

Let us look at two vignettes of IOs at two different ends of the technology spectrum: the rookie innovator (or the start-up) and the innovative turnaround of a larger and established business.

INTRODUCTION

The Raspberry Pi is a credit-card-sized educational computer that is 'open source', 'adaptable' and 'hackable'. It is available on the market for £16! It has no keyboard or screen but you can do coding on it. It has acquired global fame within the first 12 months of its inception, in which time 12 million units have been sold. In the process it has been used to 'operate a teething toy chicken, create a cocktail-pouring robot and send pictures of a mini Tardis from the edge of space'. Behind it is a small organisation based in Cambridge in the UK which includes a hardware and a software engineer, an educational development leader, a designer and a three-in-one Jedi entrepreneur, angel investor and computer science academic from Cambridge University where the idea was spun off and developed.

THE FRUIT IN THE MACHINE

What makes Raspberry Pi an attraction is its malleable nature and its evolution from a niche education product to its success in acting as a symbol of new manufacturing in the UK and of infusing a new culture of 'making' things there. The motivation behind its creation was a deep concern about the fall in the number of students studying computer science at British universities together with the quality of students who were taking it up as an undergraduate subject. There was concern too over the tendency to download information for consumption instead of learning how to make things using a computer and computer programming. Set against this concern was the experience of a success story from the past (the 1980s) of the BBC Microcomputer at a Cambridge-based firm, Acorn, which Jack Lang, Chairman of Raspberry Pi, was also instrumental in creating.

THE GOOD OLD DAYS

The BBC Acorn experience was 'pivotal' for many people growing up in the 1980s, according to Eben Upton, Executive Director and Founding Trustee along with Jack Lang. You could do programming with that computer. You could, for example, write the two-line program

    10 I am the best

    20 GO TO 10

and then type 'run', and the screen would show in full 'I am the best'. Education and programming were, therefore, antecedents for the Raspberry Pi, which was built to educate a new community of computer science undergraduates who could work on basic problem solving.

(Continued)

(Continued)

THE BUSINESS MODEL

On the business front, the crucial issue for making the Raspberry Pi work in the market for education was that of price. The trade-off was between a cheap price, somewhere between £15 and £23, and reduced levels of functionality. Then there was the question of technology and especially high-quality graphics, because handing it over to students meant competing with iPhones and Xboxes. The Ethernet connection was of significance because it allowed the machine to be used for a variety of purposes that have made it popular today. Organising an optimum mix of items to get both design and the price was not easy, and initially, obtaining the necessary interface, the power management unit and the memory meant that prices shot up to somewhere in the region of £75. The consequence was a return to the drawing board. Only when they had access to the Broadcom microchip (BCM2835), which was designed originally for a Nokia smart phone, could the Raspberry designers work on a three-chip solution. The only thing missing at this time was the 'ability to port open source software'. What came to the rescue was technology from ARM Ltd, another Cambridge high-tech firm. Uptin, who had left his job at Cambridge to join Broadcom, managed to persuade his employer that the new Raspberry Pi Charitable Foundation should be able to buy the BCM2835 at a discount even though the initial sales projections indicated sales of only 10,000 units.

GETTING STARTED

The absence of a defined market meant that the finance necessary to produce the machine was not easily available. A proposal to the regional development agency was turned down for this very reason. The founding trustees' own money was not sufficient, and the only way out was family support. The initial capital raised was a modest £150,000, with the only guarantee being that the best outcome possible would be a return of that money!

What followed the first stage of bootstrapping provides material for the perfect new venture creation case study. Typically, there was a garage (Lang's) which stored the inventory, the latter soaking up all the capital that had been invested in the business. The absence of financial leverage was capped by the lack of any manufacturing capability for the boards that were to be built because the arrangements for doing that had fallen through. When a Taipei-based sales representative of Broadcom offered to help by finding an electronics production and assembly facility in Shenzhen, China, they found that it sent the chips only via a forwarding agent in Hong Kong because of restrictions against direct transfer in China. The transfer that did take place in January 2012 consisted of £30,000 (about $50,000) in cash and the same amount in chips, with the first Pi sets being promised to consumers within weeks. It was not until March that the first box of 10 Pis turned up, fully wrapped with a serious problem, namely a jack that did not work. Instead of an integrated jack, what arrived was a connector, so there was no way in which the network jack could be used. Overcoming the manufacturing stalemate required an innovative solution. This the founders did by copying the strategy of the erstwhile Arm Ltd, another offshoot of Acorn and another highly successful Cambridge-based firm.

THE NEW BUSINESS MODEL

Arm's unique business proposition lies in its ability to license the design of chips instead of making them. It has achieved huge success from this business model with the likes of Samsung, Cisco, Apple, Amazon and Sony. Adopting similar strategies, Raspberry Pi found two businesses, Premier Farnell, an electronics manufacturer and a distributor, and a separate distributing company, RS Components, to whom they granted licences. The speed of the productive rearrangements was a forerunner of things to come. First, there was the fixing of the jacks with new ones being sourced. Second, and by the third week of March, Lang's garage started receiving the first set of Raspberry Pis, all 1,950 of them. All the Pis worked and a new computer company had started. In less than a week in May, a YouTube video clip had been watched by 40,000 viewers. Since 2012 all Rasberry Pis have been made in the UK, in the little town of Pencoed in Wales. What made this possible was the availability of highly skilled people and a supportive infrastructure which allowed for an economic case to prevail over any patriotic fervour about British manufacturing!

CONCLUSION: THE SPREAD OF CREATIVITY

The $35 credit-sized computer has unleashed an extraordinary amount of creativity in the domestic, commercial, scientific and educational arenas. It has made possible the development of miniature arcade games and a computerised balloon that has travelled as far as the brink of the Earth's atmosphere. It has allowed a hacker to make an iPhone-operated garage door opener. A micro-brewery management system called BrewPi lubricates many a beer-drinking Pi enthusiast, while a cocktail dispensing machine called Bartendro was inspired by the Pi. Not to be outdone, a nature-loving academic has put a Rasberry Pi inside a bird box to take photos and send real tweets when birds enter the box. Various other small businesses have emerged around Pi, including a Pi logo designer and a Pi case maker. Crucially, the availability of the computer in schools and colleges, due to the sponsorship of Google and others, is expected to open up possibilities for a new era of computer literacy as a bedrock for education. What has made this possible is the use of the open architecture design model which enables a wider form of diffusion through its use in various platforms. Online feedback has also made it possible to incorporate new features including, for example, the installation of a camera.

Sources: Adapted from *Wired* and from informal conversations with Jack Lang

The Raspberry Pi story reveals numerous aspects of novel forms of organising, including the creation of a structure for accommodating and enabling this novelty to take shape and generate outcomes. The decline in the availability of computer-literate young people with programming skills was a spur for the originators of the business. Even as a start-up the multi-agency involvement of different stakeholders and interest groups helped to inaugurate the process of forming an organisation with an adequate set of novel resources. When traditional approaches to making the computer failed, novel forms of task allocation and task division, through licensing and open sourcing, created unique opportunities for the development and diffusion of the product across multiple arenas of economic and social activity. The open architecture model has provided for new ways of information provision, with sources of ideas, technologies and applications being available from both within and outside the firm, creating new ways in which people's efforts are integrated and rewarded.

Let us now examine a larger organisation climbing back from disaster territory in business terms to a fresh lease of life and success through innovation.

VIGNETTE 5.2   BRICKS OF INNOVATION – THE LEGO WONDERLAND

INTRODUCTION

LEGO, one of the world's biggest and much loved manufacturers of colourful, interlocking bricks, emerged in the last century during the Great Depression of the 1930s, When the construction sector collapsed in 1932 in Denmark, Ole Kirk Christiansen, a carpenter, found himself out of work and with only wood scraps in the Danish town of Bilkund. Instead of despair Christiansen chose to make toys from the wood scraps. Gradually, and with the improvement in the economy, he found that he had established a foundation for a new business and that he was rather successful with his work. It was time to give his business an identity and a name – LEGO – after the Danish words *leg godt*, which mean 'play well'.

EARLY GROWTH STORY

With the growth of the business Christiansen decided to move from wood to plastic toys. Plastic had already become popular with manufacturers of both industrial and domestic products. Christiansen was an early entrant in plastic technologies, buying his country's first plastic injection machine which he soon followed in 1958 by patenting the interlocking bricks that have since become part of children's play time and the creative adult psyche. LEGO did not simply rely on the success of its wooden toys, but used its technology gatekeeping skills to shift its materials base from wood to plastic and make a genuinely new offering to its customers (Mitra, 2012).

DOWN THE HARD ROAD

Times have moved on for LEGO in more ways than one. Visitors to Billund are now welcomed by a mural of Jorgen Vig Knudstrop, the current Chief Executive, a former McKinsey consultant who succeeded Christiansen's grandson as CEO in 2004. The mural is a tribute to the new man who resurrected the company after it took a nose dive in the early part of this century. At the time of what was the worst crisis for the firm in its 79-year history, the company posted $350 million in losses in 2004! Analysts had written it off as a 'casualty of the digital era'. Its supply chain and its inventory were in a mess as the firm tried to keep nearly 14,000 unique elements in stock. Deadlines were missed and retailers found their agents both agnostic and aloof. LEGO was bleeding $1million in cash a day and recording huge deficits. No one really knew where, how and why the problems occurred. The company had tried different solutions, such as the 'Click-its' (snap jewellery for girls) that were a far cry from the plastic bricks. Focus groups suggested bigger blocks for boys because competitors made them, and the whole environment swirled in negativity (Bradley, 2014).

THE RECOVERY: LEGO BRICK BY LEGO BRICK

Seven years later the many doubts that plagued LEGO's survival chances were all dispelled with gusto. Turnover rose more than a third to DKr16 billion ($3 billion) and net profits went up to DKr3.7 billion ($700 million). Together with these numbers the company saw its market share rise to nearly 6%.

Turning round a relatively low-tech business in first a recession and second in a world dominated by the virtual kingdom of the Internet and 'high-tech' toys is by all standards a remarkable achievement. LEGO's tactile toys may be a far cry from the virtual, 'high-tech' toys that are thrust upon children these days. 'People theorise that's it all going to be "virtual play" in future but kids are always going to want to run after a soccer ball and build things with LEGO bricks', said Knudstrop in an interview with the *Financial Times*. In a difficult economic climate it is often the traditional, tried and tested products which still give pleasure to customers. Parents are keen to save money but not deprive their children of fun. The opportunity cost of a trip to Disney World can be forgone given the availability of the cheaper but attractive alternative of LEGO toys.

There are several explanations for the turnaround that beat the 7-year itch! A rigorous focus on the bottom line and on cash flow was part of a major restructuring of the business and the brand. This involved a shift in focus on the type of user, the business model and the operational aspects of the business. Rather than follow the usual short-term approach of increasing sales, there was a refocusing of the product line on core consumers – the 'serious builders' of LEGO. Knudstrop introduced higher levels of efficiency in the firm's logistics, reducing by half the amount of unique pieces that were produced by the factories.

The change was not without the painful measures that were taken at the time. In the small town of 6,000, hundreds of people were laid off and some manufacturing typically went offshore to Eastern Europe and Mexico. Legoland theme parks were sold off and the refocusing embraced the classic bricks and mini-figures. While the business struggled for a few years, it was well prepared for the recession that hit the market around 2008. LEGO 'sailed through it like it was no problem', according to a toy industry analyst at Needham and Co.

Beyond the financial tightening and the operational efficiency, the real change came in the reorganisation of the product and business models. Instead of relying on the classic studded bricks for its success, the company shifted from selling construction toys to marketing highly developed models, even an entire 'toy world' where the interlocking blocks narrate stories or enable children to build stories in the same way as books spur the imagination of the readers. Selling themed boxes, rather than individual plastic brick toy components, was now the better marketing option. This process had already started in 1999 with its first licence deal to produce sets based on the *Star Wars* movies. Licensed products account for approximately a quarter of the sales in

(Continued)

(Continued)

the toy industry and LEGO has continued to offer products based on Batman, Harry Potter, Bob the Builder, Indiana Jones and Spongebob Squarepants. Then smack in the middle of the worst economic crisis in the world, LEGO announced a multi-year partnership with Disney in 2009 with LEGO acquiring the rights to produce sets based on a wide range of the company's intellectual properties. By 2011 new products based on *Toy Story*, *Prince of Persia* and *Cars* had been introduced to the market.

Toy building and story building became part of the new operational norm of LEGO. You can have 'every license you want in the toy industry' (according to Lutz Muller of Klosters Trading Corp.), but creating your own story lines is another experience. 'Atlantis' is a deep-sea adventure series which is sold online with a 22-minute movie, mini games, a 3-D website and augmented-reality content. Children are provided with triggers for them to play in the form of the main points of the plot, the important battles and the discovery of the city. As LEGO makes the product available on the Web, it networks with developers who continue to update it with new features as part of an open architecture of production.

LEGO ON THE NET

The LEGO website attracts 20 million unique visitors each month who can use a program called 'DesignbyMe' to put together a virtual LEGO creation, then order a real, physical copy together with an automatically generated building guide that they can print off from the site.

LEGO on the Web has generated a new adult following. There is now a cult following among engineers and software developers and, bearing this in mind, LEGO launched a new series of architectural models of skyscrapers designed for LEGO bricks by a web-centred LEGO admirer and fan! LEGO's 74 red and yellow retail units across the world stock building kits for helicopters, rockets and trains alongside contemporary products such as the LEGO Alien Conquest, 'a daffy War of Worlds scenario with spaceships and laser canons, and "LEGO Ninjago", a "spinjistzu" warrior-themed product line heavy on martial arts and supernatural powers' (Wieners, 2011).

LEGO's online experience may not quite match that of its work with physical toys. But the spirit of innovation does not shy away from a challenge. The firm is now engaged with the creation of 'LegoUniverse', a multi-user online rolling game in which participants mutate into LEGO figurines fighting evil in a world overtaken by a dark energy called 'Maelstrom', while combat, collection and the completion of missions form the major part of the game, though users are also able to design their personal space. These developments are all part of the plan to move the business to an era where a reliance on freestyle construction and the little plastic brick can be transformed to undertake new challenges in the form of the industry, the technologies and the demand in the market for toys and games.

THE LEGO KIDS

Some have argued that LEGO's focus on boys through its focus on spatial, mathematical and motor skills was part of a deliberate strategy which helped it to increase its revenue by 105% over a 5-year period since 2006. The 'boy focus' has left many parents frustrated because they feel their daughters have missed out on LEGO. Sensitive to changing customers, after 4 years of field research LEGO is now embracing ideas drawn more from cultural anthropology than focus groups, and cultivating LEGO Friends in its larger markets.

Boys or girls, for the many or the few, LEGO unfurled a new commitment to children and learning in August 2013 with the new LEGO School in Billund. Christiansen's dream is to place the town on the world map as the 'capital of children'. Headed by a British physicist turned school teacher and focusing on creativity and play, to think and do, and on enquiry-based learning, the International School of Billund will combine a free and easy approach to learning with LEGO's research into child development. The school, the construction of a church, community facilities, a library, a theatre, and the building of Denmark's second largest airport, are all part of the LEGO bricks ecosystem for a town of 6,000 people.

CONCLUSION

The shift in the type and range of products is marked by changes in the management architecture. Restructuring was accompanied by a ruthless private-equity-type management style. This has now given way to growth orientation of the kind favoured by public companies, thus allowing the introduction of a professional culture into the world's fourth largest toymaker. It was once a small family-owned firm which grew out of a small town carpentry workshop. The big decisions of investment have been positive ones, and in the last 5 years the firm has grown to 8,000 employees with growth in traditional markets being supported by expansion into developing economies. LEGO has never made an acquisition in its 80 years and the family firm virtues have not necessarily been discarded, especially because family ownership makes it possible to 'think long term but act very fast', according to Knudstrop. This is also in keeping with the founder Christiansen's motto: *det bedtse er ikke for godt* ('only the best is good enough').

Source: Adapted from Wieners (2011)

We can read the LEGO story as a good turnaround narrative of reorganisation using standard tactics of cost cutting, a leaner workforce and a shift to new markets. Much of those routine turnaround tactics were taken up by LEGO especially after 2004, but the company's evolving toy experience adventure is more of a creative adventure involving a mix of innovation, adaptability, the management of routines, and networks. This creative mix has enabled the firm to adopt varied management strategies to rebuild the organisation and to move to a new, virtual world of games without compromising the essence of the plastic brick that provides its essential value. What we find in this embrace of the digital age is a real sense of adaptability with a clear focus on the innovative use of key products. LEGO's adaptability has probably inspired engineers and architects to design and build buildings and other constructions which pay tribute to colourful bricks.

THE FEATURES OF INNOVATIVE ORGANISATIONS

If some firms are innovative then there are others which are different from them. The distinctiveness is achieved by how these organisations are structured and how specific contexts and conditions shape them to become conduits for change and progress. Taking Raspberry Pi as an example, organisations are created and resources are mobilised to realise an opportunity and vision for making a difference in the specific context of computing education. A social cause and a motivation for making a difference in the skill sets of young people generated a successful business project. The success rested on two key counts: the development of a unique and affordable computer where people could learn programming; and the mobilisation of resources in novel ways, a key feature of entrepreneurial outcomes. Raspberry Pi is a start-up story where innovation defines the organisation – the new product, the novel blend of social cause with the mobilisation of resources necessary to run an organisation (finance talent and technologies), and the networks necessary to obtain leverage for those resources. The structure of the organisation is an evolving one as one would expect of a start-up where much is learnt through experimentation and a capacity for following unexpected directions in the development of the business.

The very different story of LEGO shows us how a real turnaround in business fortunes of an existing company is made possible through a combination of a strong values-based foundation with a strict management discipline. This mix of management vision and strategy is buttressed by the tactical focus on developing new products and processes for a different time and a changing client group. LEGO's organisational structure changes and adapts itself first to the downturn from which it has to recover. But the company cannot simply depend on standard cost-cutting measures to do so. An initial bout of lean management has to give way to a form of reinvention of the company so that it can take up the challenges of mobilising resources for a digital era. Experimentation also features strongly, accompanied by serious research into technologies, markets and new customer groups using novel methods.

THE THREE 'A'S OF INNOVATIVE ORGANISATIONS

We focus on three critical features which distinguish IOs, as shown in Figure 5.2. Taken together as an aggregate, the three 'A's are indissoluble components of an IO. Losing any one of those elements could easily displace the others, making it difficult for the IO to maintain its status.

ADAPTABILITY

Relevant, flexible structures enable IOs to manage the complex management of the innovation process in organisations. This includes the 'identification of an objective, exploration and exploitation of ideas and resources, search and routines, forecasting and implementation, learning and diffusing, all in highly uncertain environments with no clear linear trajectories of activity' (Mitra, 2012). What we do know is that

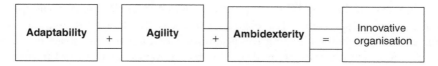

FIGURE 5.2 The three 'A's of innovative organisations

innovation occurs in an organisation if it has a culture and relevant structures to support innovation. This makes the IO more than the opposite of a non-IO. The appropriateness of such structures and mechanisms are contingent upon the type of innovation the organisation is able to produce and the industrial sector in which it operates. If we accept that IOs can be both start-ups and existing businesses, then by definition they cannot be homogeneous units following routine processes. Their uniqueness is a function of their plans and actions in different environments. The innovation that occurs is found not only in the new products and services, but also in the management processes and even in the recreation of the style and adequate business models used to earn revenues.

The discussion above suggests adaptability and a preparedness to allow for changes either as new or existing organisations and in terms of the demands of the marketplace, buyer behaviour and external factors. This is what we can expect from such firms. The greater the uncertainty of the environment, the higher the level of flexibility or agility that is required in changing structures and processes. This in turn creates opportunities for new product and service development as well as the restructuring of businesses.

AGILITY

Agile firms are those organisations that are able to respond quickly and flexibly to variations in the environment by adopting innovative strategies (Bessant et al., 2001). Agility is also seen as being crucial for the performance of firms in a fast-changing environment (Braunscheidel and Suresh, 2009; Bottani, 2010). We find a good deal of evidence of such agility in the electronics, IT and biotechnology sectors which appear to have highly adaptive and organic modes of operation. Their counterparts in the traditional industries are often regarded as being the opposite, although the evidence suggests that agility is not the prerogative of high-technology firms. Agility as a concept embracing the notion of dynamic capability is increasingly becoming a feature of the contemporary business environment (Roberts and Grover, 2012).

The idea of agile manufacturing was introduced by a group of scholars at the Iacocca Institute of Lehigh University in the USA (1991), and it has since then attracted considerable attention among researchers and practitioners (Bottani, 2010).

Agile firms often need to have twin and differentiated structures within the organisation with specialist groups to meet the needs of a diverse marketplace (Bessant, 2013).

Agile IOs stretch the scope and content of existing markets. All new products and services open up possibilities for imitation and incremental improvements, and offer choices in terms of the use of different products and services. Some firms adopt 'Blue Ocean' strategies (Kim and Mauborgne, 2005; 2014), identifying markets which do not exist either by challenging the boundaries of existing industries or through operations in new industries created by new technologies such as the Internet. Kim and Mauborgne (2005) refer to the creation of a new market space in a declining market by a Canadian firm, Cirque du Soleil, a circus industry firm established by street performers who achieved a level of revenue in 20 years that the industry global champions took 100 years to achieve. Given that the original market was fading, a switch to corporate customers and adults as opposed to the expected traditional audience of children and their parents helped the firm to identify new market opportunities for success. By moving out of the common space occupied by most circuses the firm made its competition irrelevant (Mitra, 2012). Being agile to a differentiated set of opportunities in a new marketplace enabled Cirque de Soleil to share something in common with LEGO – innovative leadership practices facing new market realities (Kim and Mauborgne, 2014). The structure of the firm evolved from an honest appraisal of decline in the traditional market and untapped opportunities in alternative markets for the same product.

AMBIDEXTERITY

What we can bank on so far is the idea that an IO is one that is specifically designed for that purpose. Its structures, processes, rewards and people are combined in a special way to do something for the first time. Other organisations also have structures, processes and reward systems. They too manage people effectively. But whereas their goal is to produce more of the same (perhaps with some modifications), the IO creates and manages opportunities for producing goods and services for the first time. In typically large organisations there is a need to do both, to manage an 'operating organisation' which looks after routine production and an IO which develops new lines of activity (Galbraith, 2004). Often new lines evolve into standard products and services over time and their development then becomes the preoccupation of the 'operating' firm.

Managing the two types of organisation makes a single organisation an ambidextrous organisation (Tushman et al., 1997), the type of organisation necessary to emerge as a knowledge-creating company (Nonaka and Takeuchi, 1995).

We can add a whole string of features as we explore in depth the wide range of components of IOs, but the three 'A's mentioned above are good overriding labels that help to describe IOs and create models for their further analysis.

THE INTEGRATED SET OF COMPONENTS AND CAPABILITIES

Summing up the characteristics and features of IOs may be a difficult proposition given the complexity of these firms and their operations in different contexts. Fortunately, Tidd and Bessant (2013) offer a neat solution to the problem when they argue that the innovative organisation is characterised by an 'integrated set of

TABLE 5.1 Components of innovative organisations

Component	Key features	Meaning and scope	Fit with the three 'A's
1. Shared vision, leadership and the will to innovate	Clearly articulated and shared sense of purpose; stretching strategic intent; 'top management commitment'	The idea and practice of innovation is not limited to a few people – for example, managers and technocrats – but shared across all levels and encouraged through different types of activities	Agility; shared vision contributing to a dynamic organisation; inclusive leadership
2. Appropriate structure	Organisational design which enables creativity, learning and interaction. Not always a loose 'skunk works' model; key issue is finding appropriate balance between organic and mechanistic options for particular contingencies	Adapting and experimenting with varied forms, structures, mechanisms and responsibilities to allow for proper understanding of change through new products, services and organisational practice	Adaptability: flexible structures and connected decision makers at all levels within and outside the organisation
3. Key individuals	Promoters, champions, gatekeepers and others who energise or facilitate innovation	Believers, supporters, providers and implementers of innovation who facilitate and make innovation happen	Agility: shared belief in innovation among disparate individuals affording agile thinking
4. Effective team working	Appropriate use of teams (at local, cross-functional and inter-organisational level) to solve problems requires investment in team selection and building	Individuals working within groups and across different functional activities to harness capabilities to deal best with the varied pressures of uncertainty	Agility: effective teams harnessing diverse talent and creating agile work content
5. High-involvement innovation	Participation in organisation-wide continuous improvement activity	Together with structure to keep innovation on a level of meaningful alertness at all levels of business activity	Ambidexterity: high-level innovation allowing for conflicting or multiple visions, ideas, tactics to work
6. Creative climate	Positive approach to creative ideas, supported by relevant motivation systems	Generating, harnessing and using creative ideas through tensions and cooperation of people across the organisation and through networks within which organisations operate	Ambidexterity: different creative ideas often at odds being managed and high-tolerance thresholds for creative tension
7. External focus	Internal and external customer orientation; exclusive networking	Recognising and valuing the role of the organisation within its sector, its geographical location, its network of stakeholders, as part of its strategic and operational focus, imbibing ideas from outside and influencing the external environment with ideas generated within the firm	Adaptability: absorbing externalities; making connectivity with co-creators and other agents

Source: Adapted from Tidd and Bessant (2013)

components that work together to create and reinforce the kind of environment which enables innovation to flourish' (p. 101). They identify seven components which represent a second order of the features or capabilities of IOs as shown in Table 5.1. We adapt this table and identify the ways in which the components can be encapsulated within the three 'A's described above.

Of course it would be impossible to find in any organisation the set of seven components identified above being available in equal measure. The literature refers to 'skunk works', informal environments, adaptive cultures, networked organisations and even well-managed structures, all as examples of IOs working through their particular operating contingencies. These are all examples of different structures that are created to accommodate and promote innovation. They also reflect the climate or environment in which innovation occurs and the focus a firm has to give to the world outside the immediate organisation to augment its capacity for innovation. We argue that what binds them as a 'category' of firms, as IOs, are the three 'A's (or higher order features) of adaptability, agility and ambidexterity. These three dimensions raise issues about how firms organise the process of innovation, a subject which we will explore in Chapter 9.

SOME FIRMS ARE INNOVATIVE WHILE OTHERS ARE NOT?

But why do some firms do better than others? Resource- and knowledge-based theories of the firm suggest that successful innovative firms establish and build unique and inimitable resources, capabilities and structures. These resources include tangible and intangible assets as well as explicit and tacit knowledge, skills and competencies, and networks of relationships with other organisations. These unique resources are available to firms and they mould and direct the opportunities that they confront. Firms which deploy these resources and use such capabilities may benefit from a breakthrough new product which in turn provides both the incentives and the pressure to scale up production and entry into new markets. They develop specific routines over time and the choices they make over what new products to make reflect their past. Decisions become path dependent. Consequently, different firms in their response to the pressures of competition and new challenges start from different places in terms of their unique, firm-specific capabilities and knowledge (Martin and Eisenhardt, 2001; Teece, 2007).

Unique, inimitable resources define individual firms and how they use their knowledge and capabilities. But knowledge does not always remain within organisations. Knowledge spills over and contributes to innovation, productivity and growth (Audretsch and Lehmann, 2005; Gilbert et al., 2008; Piekkola, 2010), often combining with the unique firm-specific resources. Knowledge from universities producing public goods through their research can spill over for the benefit of existing firms, while codified knowledge can be transferred through journal publications, seminars and workshops. Tacit or hidden knowledge is often converted to explicit and codified knowledge through regular face-to-face exchange among co-workers or in concentrations of firms in industrial districts or clusters. Finally, the mobility of human capital evinced in people moving from one job to another is also a mechanism for the transmission of knowledge.

One way of knowing which firms innovate more than others is through empirical observation and analysis using appropriate measurement tools. We do need calibration tools with which to gauge the type, volume and value of change generated by innovation, and the impact that innovation has on the firm, the industry in which it operates and the economy in which it is located. It is to these aspects of measurement that we now turn our attention.

MEASURING INNOVATION

A generalised debate on the relative innovation capabilities of different-sized firms becomes sterile unless we introduce nuanced arguments which consider the importance of measurement of different forms and rates of innovation.

We can calculate innovation activity by 'input' measures such as R&D. R&D does not often lead to innovation and it may not be possible for most firms to secure budgets to implement R&D. This makes comparisons between small, medium and large firms difficult, if not impossible. As we have noted above, R&D budgets attract early cuts whenever the economic conditions put a squeeze on costs. Overall, therefore, it is not a particularly good measure despite its widespread use in research and policy formulation.

Intermediate measures such as patents can also be considered but the results are somewhat ambiguous. Not all patents lead to innovative outcomes, and the attention that has been given recently to the abuse of patents is well worth noting. The USA can be regarded as the leading country in the world for the filing of patents. Filing a patent can be regarded as important as seeking an IPO on Nasdaq. The US Constitution gives Congress the power to give inventors the exclusive right to their discoveries and inventions for a limited amount of time (around 20 years). During this time competitors cannot sell similar products, and without this protective incentive the value of innovation (or at least the invention) could be called into question. Without such protection granted by patents we would not have had such ground-breaking technologies as the cotton gin, Morse code, the Yale lock, the Hula Hoop, the Xerox machine, the laser and the Siri (Levy, 2012).

Patents are also regarded as assets. Inventors who obtain patent rights are allowed to sell them in the open market, enabling the new owner of the patent to create new products. This was seen as further facilitation of the innovation process. The original inventors could at least make money if they did not possess the entrepreneurial nous to commercialise their inventions, while the buyer could develop products for the market. In reality, however, anyone could buy these patents. Over time lawyers have virtually scooped up patents and have used their legal expertise to sue other inventors for infringement of intellectual property rights (IPR). Companies have been created simply to enforce their IP ownership, costing US firms $29 billion in 2011 alone (from under $7 billion in 2005). Referred to as 'patent troll cases', the number of defences in troll cases has gone up from 1,401 in 2005 to 5,842 in 2011. The impact on innovation and new product development is a negative one as patents and patent trolls have emerged as an implicit tax on innovation. A Google vice-president once remarked that 'patents were meant to encourage innovation ... but lately they are being used as a weapon to stop it' (Levy, 2012).

Beyond input and intermediate measurement devices, there is the direct measure of innovative output, or the actual products and services that are created. Using such a measure could be a complex exercise but we have the benefit of obtaining tangible outcomes. Here too there are variations in the ability of different-sized firms to make certain types of innovative products. We find that entrepreneurial firms contribute more to innovation according to the industries to which they belong. For example, small firms generate more innovations in computers and process control instruments, while large firms are the main innovators in pharmaceuticals and the aircraft industries where significant capital outlay for new product development is essential (Acs and Audretsch, 2005).

A more reliable measure of innovative activity in firms is the total innovation rate, which is the total number of innovations per thousand employees in each industry (Acs and Audretsch, 2005). For larger firms it is the total number of innovations made by firms with at least 500 or 250 employees (depending on whether we are referring to the US or Europe, for example) divided by the number of employees (thousands). For small and medium-sized firms the reference is made to firms with less than 500 or 250 employees divided by the number of employees (thousands) in small firms. This latter category could be further subdivided into measures for small firms (say up to 50 employees) and medium-sized firms (from 50 to 250 employees) using European standards. This calculation provides us with a more accountable measure of innovation in large- and small-firm innovation relative to the number of these firms in different industries. In other words, if we are to obtain value from measuring innovative activity then it is important to factor in the context of the industry and the overall size of the stock of large, medium and small firms.

We explore how innovation is or can be measured in more depth in Chapter 11.

CONCLUDING OBSERVATIONS

Organisations evolve over time and as they do they acquire new features and shed some of their older ones. The development of new products, new market entry and organisational forms engender this process of change. This change is represented and measured by the levels of turnover, profit or employment. But it is difficult to state whether non-innovative firms remain non-innovative or whether they transform into innovative organisations. Conversely, innovative firms may cease to be innovative or entrepreneurial once they start growing and acquire a coveted share of the market. The likes of Microsoft, Dell, Wipro and Sony are all examples of firms that were heralded for their innovative capabilities for a long time until they started to recede from those frontiers some time ago.

Do all firms share similar features and characteristics? To answer this question we need to shift the discussion to a consideration of the various types and sizes of firms and their ability to innovate. An examination of the typology of firms can help us to assess whether all types of firms share common characteristics or whether the organisational contexts define their features. We turn in the next chapter to a detailed investigation of different types and sizes of firms and the evidence backing up their ability to grow through innovation.

 SELF-ASSESSMENT AND RESEARCH QUESTIONS

1. What are the essential features of an innovative organisation?

2. What are the three 'A's of innovative organisations and how would you use them to explain how IOs carve out their capabilities for innovation?

3. What are the differences in terms of features and characteristics between small and large innovative firms?

4. Why do some firms innovate while others do not?

5. How best can we measure the innovative capacity of firms?

 REFERENCES

Acs, Z.J. and Audretsch, D.B. (2005) 'Entrepreneurship, innovation and technological change', in *Foundations and Trends in Entrepreneurship*. Hanover, MA: now publishers.

Audretsch, D.B. and Lehmann, E.E. (2005) 'Does the knowledge spillover theory of entrepreneurship hold for regions?', *Research Policy*, 34(8): 1191–202.

Bedeian, A. and Zammuto, R.F. (1991) *Organisations: Theory and Design*. London: Thompson Learning.

Bessant, J. (2013) 'Innovation in the twenty-first century', in R.J. Owen, J. Bessant and M. Heintz (eds), *Responsible Innovation: Managing the Responsible Emergence of Science and Innovation in Society*. New York: John Wiley & Sons. pp. 1–26.

Bessant, J., Caffyn, S. and Gallagher, M. (2001) 'An evolutionary model of continuous improvement behaviour', *Technovation*, 21(2): 67–77.

Bottani, E. (2010) 'Profile and enablers of agile companies: an empirical investigation', *International Journal of Production Economics*, 125(2): 251–61.

Blöndal, J.R. (2003) 'Budget reform in OECD member countries', *OECD Journal on Budgeting*, 2(4): 7–25.

Bradley, R. (2014) 'How LEGO got hot … again', *Fortune*, 27 February.

Braunscheidel, M.J. and Suresh, N.C. (2009) 'The organizational antecedents of a firm's supply chain agility for risk mitigation and response', *Journal of Operations Management*, 27(2): 119–40.

Burton, R.M. and Obel, B. (1984) *Designing Efficient Organisations: Modelling and Experimentation*. Amsterdam: Elsevier.

Burton, R.M. and Obel, B. (1988) 'Opportunism, incentives, and the M-form hypothesis: a laboratory study', *Journal of Economic Behavior & Organization*, 10(1): 99–119.

Galbraith, J.R. (2004) 'Designing the innovating organization', in K. Starkey et al., *How Organizations Learn: Managing the Search for Knowledge*. Andover: Cengage Learning. pp. 202–23.

Gilbert, B.A., McDougall, P.P. and Audretsch, D.B. (2008) 'Clusters, knowledge spillovers and new venture performance: an empirical examination', *Journal of Business Venturing*, 23(4): 405–22.

Kim, W.C. and Mauborgne, R. (2005) 'Blue ocean strategy: from theory to practice', *California Management Review*, 47(3): 105–21.

Kim, W.C. and Mauborgne, R. (2014) 'Blue ocean leadership', *Harvard Business Review*, 92(5): 60–72.

Levy, S. (2012) 'Going with the flow: Google's secret switch to the next wave of networking', *Wired*, April: 17.

March, J.G. and Simon, H.A. (1993) 'Organizations revisited', *Industrial and Corporate Change*, 2(1): 299–316.

Martin, J.A. and Eisenhardt, K.M. (2001) 'Exploring cross-business synergies', *Academy of Management Proceedings*, 2001(1): H1–6.

Mintzberg, H. (1979) *The Structuring of Organization: A Synthesis of the Research.* Englewood Cliffs, NJ: Prentice Hall.

Mitra, J. (2012) *Entrepreneurship, Innovation and Regional Development: An Introduction.* Abingdon: Routledge.

Nonaka, I. and Takeuchi, H. (1995) *The Knowledge Creation Company: How Japanese Companies Create the Dynamics of Innovation.* New York: Oxford University Press. p. 304.

Piekkola, H. (2010) 'Intangibles: can they explain the unexplained?', University of Vaasa Department of Economics Working Paper, 15.

Puranam, P., Alexy, O. and Reitzig, M. (2014) 'What's "new" about new forms of organizing?', *Academy of Management Review*, 39(2): 162–80.

Roberts, N. and Grover, V. (2012) 'Investigating firm's customer agility and firm performance: the importance of aligning sense and respond capabilities', *Journal of Business Research*, 65(5): 579–85.

Scott, P.G. and Falcone, S. (1998) 'Comparing public and private organizations an exploratory analysis of three frameworks', *The American Review of Public Administration*, 28(2): 126–45.

Teece, D.J. (2007) 'Explicating dynamic capabilities: the nature and microfoundations of (sustainable) enterprise performance', *Strategic Management Journal*, 28(13): 1319–50.

Tidd, J and Bessant, J. (2013). *Managing Innovation: Integrating Technological, Market and Organisational Change.* Chichester: John Wiley.

Tushman, M.L., Anderson, P.C. and O'Reilly, C. (1997) 'Technology cycles, innovation streams, and ambidextrous organizations: organization renewal through innovation streams and strategic change', *Managing Strategic Innovation and Change*, 3: 23.

Weick, K.E.K.E. (1969) *The Social Psychology of Organizing.* Reading, MA: Addison-Wesley.

Whetten, D.A. and Aldrich, H. (1979) 'Organization set size and diversity: people-processing organizations and their environments', *Administration and Society*, 11(3): 251–81.

Wieners, B. (2011) 'Lego Is for Girls: Inside the world's most admired toy company's effort to finally click with girls', *Financial Times*, 28 July. Available at: https://www.bloomberg.com/news/articles/2011-12-14/lego-is-for-girls (last accessed 20 August 2014).

INNOVATION AND THE TYPES AND SIZE OF FIRMS

6

SCOPE AND OBJECTIVES

- An enquiry into the different types, sizes and structures of innovative firms and the changing landscape of their activities in local and global spaces.
- Types that produce different models in different contexts.
- Importance or irrelevance of size.
- Networks of innovative firms.
- Citizen innovation.

INTRODUCTION

In the preceding chapter we found evidence of innovative firms which have features that distinguish them from their non-innovative counterparts. They are also different structurally in terms of size and operations and they are found in different sectors and contexts. So, various types of firms can be considered to be innovative. But do they all function and operate in the same way? Does size make a difference? Intuitively we would agree that the very fact that size is a function of resources makes firms behave differently. Ergo, the innovation processes in such firms will vary too.

But is size the only consideration? Is there any difference in the age of firms and their ability to accumulate knowledge and experience which could provide them with a greater advantage to innovate? To help us answer such questions let us examine some of the ideas and the evidence relating to different types and the varied size of firms.

FIRM SIZE AND INNOVATION

INNOVATION AND LARGE FIRMS

Large IOs feature prominently in the innovation literature. Researchers argue that larger firms are able to accommodate large and complex activities because they can demonstrate their ambidexterity by running parallel activities of a highly technical or specialised nature involving new technologies, new products or services alongside routine business practice. They can also work with other firms in networked modes of production or use supply chains involving many operators, all as part of a net-worked environment. They can take advantage of large R&D investments, secure their intellectual property and practise economies of scale and scope. Both venture capital and private equity funds seek out the stable, mid-to-large organisations. Their market power, networks and reach help them to diffuse the innovation and obtain handsome returns on investment where necessary. Conventional and received wisdom accept the innovative capability of larger firms. In his Mark II days Schumpeter argued that:

> There cannot be any reasonable doubt that under the conditions of our epoch such superiority is as a matter of fact the outstanding feature of the typical large-scale unit of control, though mere size is neither necessary or sufficient for it. These units not only arise in the process of creative destruction and function in a way entirely different from the static schema, but in many cases of decisive importance they provide the necessary form for the achievement. (1942: 101)

Schumpeter was referring to the larger firm in the context of monopolies in the burgeoning capitalist economy of the USA. The monopolist firm is likely to generate a larger supply of innovations even when the market may not be ready for them because there is limited competition. Large, monopolist corporations were more likely to push for industrial technology because of better levels of access to capital and their ability to pool risks in terms of scale and scope, especially in the maintenance of R&D. Equally, in such situations monopolist firms may well be averse to innovation because of the absence of competition. This suggests that unless a firm dominates a market it cannot undertake the risks and uncertainties associated with innovation.

LARGE FIRMS AND R&D INVESTMENT FOR INNOVATION

The evidence backing the superiority of larger firms in innovation is particularly strong when the R&D aspect of technological change is considered. Scherer (1984) found increasing returns to scale for about 20% of the industries he studied, constant returns to scale for a little less than 75%, and diminishing returns in less than 10% of them. R&D-focused studies differ in their findings from those examining the case of patents. According to Scherer (1984), the Gelman Research Associates' large database of major innovations shows that small firms are relatively more likely to make major innovations with firms with fewer than 1,000 employees, being responsible for 47.3% of key innovations. This proportion is greater than their 41.2% share of total employment. Businesses with over 10,000 employees are responsible for 34.5% of the innovations and 36% of total employment. This data suggests that the ability of larger firms to innovate varies roughly in proportion to size. Smaller firms innovate out of proportion, and medium-sized firms do not do much by way of innovation.

In a separate sample of significant innovations in the USA (reported in *Industrial Research & Development*), Scherer (1984: ch. 11) found that 72% of the major innovations came from profit-seeking firms, 12.9% from government laboratories and 10.7% from other non-profit organisations. The Federal Trade Commission's (FTC's) line-of-business survey noted that large firms contribute to 73% of both business-financed and federal contract industrial R&D expenditures, 55–60% of manufacturing sales and 55% of the major innovations. There is no strong evidence to suggest that size leads to more innovation. The large firms in the FTC data account for only 61% of all patented inventions, a smaller segment than their 73% share of the R&D expenditures. Other studies, including one by Scherer (1982), show that the number of patented inventions increases less than proportionately with firm size.

The findings from a statistical analysis of the FTC's line-of-business data by Cohen et al. (2002) and Levin et al. (1987) show that as business-unit size has no effect on the R&D intensity (R&D as a percentage of sales) of firms conducting R&D, it does affect the probability of engaging in R&D. Moreover, business-unit and firm size collectively explain less than 1% of the variance in R&D intensity, in contrast to industry effects, which explain nearly half the variance.

Using sophisticated statistical techniques to control for the underreporting of R&D, Bound et al. (1984) found that R&D expenditures grew with turnover and gross plant size in 1976. A 1% increase in sales causes a 0.7% increase in R&D. But the impact of size is not straightforward. It is in fact non-linear. Small and very large firms are more R&D intensive than average-sized firms. Small firms that do research tend to patent more per R&D dollar than larger firms, and firms with large R&D programmes tend to have a constant ratio of patenting to R&D. According to Jensen (1987), who studied the pharmaceutical industry, there are no advantages or disadvantages accruing from the placing of an R&D programme in a larger firm. Holmes et al. (1991) found that R&D intensity varies with firm size in some industries but not in others, and where such variations did take place they may be negatively or positively related to size. These analytical results call into question the Schumpeterian hypotheses about large firms and R&D.

Investment in R&D, patents and ambidexterity, all taken together, appear to give the larger firms the edge over their smaller counterparts in innovation. But is this a specifically American phenomenon? When we look at the range of products and services that companies such as Samsung in Korea, Huawei in China, Foxconn in Taiwan or indeed LEGO in Denmark, and until recently Nokia in Finland, we note that innovative larger organisations dominate the industrial landscape. So what then can we make of the medium-sized or the smaller firm?

INNOVATION AND THE MEDIUM-SIZED FIRM

The 'M' in 'SME' refers to medium-sized firms, and although they are distinct entities they are often referred to as similar units of operation. Lumping them together challenges an analytical perspective because the markets for these firms are often different. Also different are their methods and capacities for innovative production or service provision, their management processes and the use of functions and routines.

A good test of the capability or resilience of different types of firms is to examine them under testing conditions such as in an economic recession. Acording to Nicolaou et al. (2015), UK revenue growth for mid-sized firms (the mid-market) moved up to 3.9% in the last year, this rate being significantly above the UK GDP growth rate of 2.8%. Growth is ushering in employment with it, with a 2.5% increase in the mid-market workforce over the last 12 months, the highest rate in the major economies of Europe. These firms have a very positive attitude and belief about the future and they had demonstrated consistent growth as reflected in their shared values: they all had long-term growth strategies and strong management capabilities focused on their customers. These findings contradict the ones generated by Bound et al. (1984) if we accept that their reference to average firms is a proxy for medium-sized businesses.

If research evidence is often confusing then we have two options to consider. One of them is to study firms sector by sector and perhaps size by size and obtain independent results that are of relevance to those units of analysis. The other is to examine firms in depth through case studies or ethnographic observations.

MID-SIZED FIRMS AS THE HIDDEN CHAMPIONS OF INNOVATION

Simon (2009, cited in Mitra 2012), in his detailed study of what he refers to as the 'hidden champions', found that countless mid-size firms are world leaders in exports. Approximately 80% of all mid-size world market leaders come from the German/Scandinavian countries and the exporting success of German-language and Scandinavian countries is a measure of the innovative capability of these firms. Success stories can also be found across the world and especially in the USA, Brazil, Japan, South Africa, Korea and New Zealand. Borrowing from Simon (2009), Table 6.1 lists some of these mid-size leaders across the world.

A consideration of the sectors in which such mid-sized firms operate suggests that they are spread across a large cross-section of industries. These are not the much vaunted and sexy sectors of IT or nano- and biotechnology. They are the 'hidden' ones of manufacturing and services, the component suppliers dealing with fishing lines, laminated tubes, cork products and the rest. Embraer's regional jets are one of the few in the list above which are likely to attract immediate attention from the average person because of the type of industry it represents. Yet all such products and services are essential for the manufacture of products deemed necessary for our lives.

Simon (2009) refers to the firms above as successful export-oriented firms in terms of:

TABLE 6.1 Mid-size global leaders in their field

Country	Names of firm	Product/service
Iceland	Baader	Fish processing systems
USA	McIlhenny	Pepper sauce ('Tabasco')
	3B Scientific	Anatomical teaching aids
Singapore	International SOS	International emergency services
Sweden	Tetra	Aquarium and pond supplies
New Zealand	Gallagher	Electric fences
Norway	Tandberg	Video conferencing technology
UK	De La Rue	Printer and maker of security paper
Germany	Arnold & Richter, Sachtler	ARRI camera and tripod
	CEAG	Charging devices for cell phones
France	Petzel	Harnesses, rope-blocking snap links, front lamps, etc., for sports such as rock climbing, mountaineering and cave exploration
Italy	Technogym	Fitness equipment
India	Essel Propack	Laminated tubes for toothpaste and similar substances
Austria	Plansee	Manufacturer of high-performance materials made with refractory metals and composites
	Jungbunzlaeur (Austrian-Swiss)	Citric acid supplier for Coca-Cola
South Africa	Sappi	Coated fine paper and dissolvable pulp
Brazil	Embraer	Regional jets
Japan	Nisha	Small touch panels
Portugal	Amorim	Cork products and cork flooring

Source: Adapted from Simon (2009, cited in Mitra, 2012)

(a) their position in the global market – they are either number one, two or three, or number one on their continent;
(b) their revenue being below $4 billion; and
(c) the low level of public awareness of these firms.

Eschewing popularity, these firms rely on two critical aspects of exporting: diversification and globalisation. Organic growth is preferred over growth through acquisitions, and this form of growth is informed by innovation, internationalisation and diversification.

Underpinning the innovation process are the organisational arrangements for technological, process, information and management systems, export-focused marketing, services, high levels of R&D intensity, early patenting and the production of products with high revenue margins. We will discuss the tactics and processes deployed by such firms in other chapters, but we could argue that medium-sized firms occupy a special place in the innovation space. Organic growth is made possible because of three critical factors: export orientation of relatively obscure but highly important products and services; smart organisational management focusing on key internal resources; and innovation. Few countries match the success of the innovative mid-sized firms (known as the Mittelstand) of Germany.

VIGNETTE 6.1   THE GERMAN MITTELSTAND

INTRODUCTION

The particular excellence of the German mid-sized manufacturers who are collectively known as the Mittelstand has now generated considerable interest among policy makers and researchers. These generally family-owned firms, located in small towns, form the backbone of the fourth largest economy in the world. They benefit from clever relationships with schools, Fachonschulens (or technical schools), and between the board room and the unions, that is between capital and labour.

CHARACTERISTICS

A unique contribution of the Mittelstand is the notion of inclusiveness, namely that of firms with deep local roots and a strong apprenticeship system which inspire loyalty among their workers and customers. This sense of inclusiveness is a direct riposte to the negative impressions of the capitalist system. According to an academic at the University of Mannheim in Germany, Professor Winifred Weber, 'the combination of medium sized companies with deep local roots and a strong apprenticeship system means that in Germany only 7.8% of those aged 25 or under are unemployed, compared with 22.1% in Sweden and 54% in Spain' (Schumpeter, 2014: 68). These firms attract loyal employees with an average of only 2.7% of them leaving each year, which compares with a rate of 30% for large American firms.

EXPORTING THEIR WAY TO SUCCESS

Mid-sized German firms are big-time exporters. This is one good reason why Germany, together with China, is the only large country gaining share in world trade. Germany has over 10% of the global export market share in sectors stretching from medical devices to lighting and electrical equipment, processed food, prefabricated enclosures and structures, aerospace and defence, machine equipment, automotive components, plastics, and analytical instruments. The largest number of the world's market-leading companies is in the machine equipment sector. Of the 1,500 or so companies, 1,300 of them are family owned (Venohr and Meyer, 2007).

MANAGEMENT MODEL

What distinguishes these Mittelstand companies is their unique management model. The three key, linked dimensions of the model include strategies for dominating global niche markets, a governance system based on enlightened family capitalism, and operational effectiveness which translates as being world class in key processes (Venohr and Meyer, 2007). In common with other innovative firms, the Mittelstand community does not stand still in its glory! Despite being part of the family structure for many generations, these firms have begun to produce globally and hire talent from outside Germany. A good example is the Freudenberg Group, which makes lubricants, filters and seals. The group has been owned by the Freudenberg family for over eight generations, but that did not stop it from hiring an Iranian-born American, Moshen Sohi, as becoming its chief executive (Schumpeter, 2014). The global adventure does not compromise the Mittelstand firm's local roots; rather it confirms the paradox that characterises successful and innovative firms and clusters of firms in highly innovative regions – picking and mixing ideas, technologies, talent and resources and remixing them into productive combinations.

Sources: Adapted from *The Economist* (2013); Marsh (2012)

TYPES OF MID-SIZED HIDDEN CHAMPIONS

In the UK, a typical mid-sized business has a turnover ranging from £25 to £500 million: £25 million is the upper limit for small firms, the 'S' in 'SME', while £500 million is the cut-off point for larger firms (those with over 250 employees). According to the UK *Mid-Sized Business Growth Review* (Grant Thornton, 2012) over half of these businesses have no more than 250 employees. Table 6.2 provides a snapshot of the profile of mid-sized businesses in the UK. Growth in the mid-market has meant

TABLE 6.2 Profile of mid-sized businesses (MSBs) in the UK

Profile features	Value
No. of MSBs	33,700
No. of people employed by MSBs	4.1 million
Annual turnover of MSBs	£628 billion
Exports by MSB	£36 billion (they have increased their exports by 4.3%)
Jobs created	52,000 in 12 months
Turnover per employee	18% higher than UK average
Value added (sum of profits, wages and taxes on production)	£249 billion
Money injected by MSBs into finances of UK households (through wages and salaries)	£133 billion
Contribution to UK GDP (out of total of £1.5 trillion in 2011 prices)	£285 billion

Source: Grant Thornton (2012)

new jobs. In 2015 alone, 60% of firms increased the size of their workforce, and only 12% shrunk their numbers of employees. The overall growth was 2.5%, higher than the rate in 2014 or 2013. The UK now leads the major European economies in mid-market job creation (Nicolaou et al., 2015).

Their population, their significant annual turnover and the contribution they make to the labour market in the private sector all suggest a buoyant marketplace for these firms. As opposed to large firms, they are agile enough to respond quickly to opportunities and, unlike small firms, they have the infrastructure to manage innovation and change. This is evinced in the faster annual growth (4.1% turnover growth and also in gross profits earned and sales volume) on average than both the average of all firms and the UK economy as a whole in 2011. Manufacturing takes the largest share of the MSB population, with more than 840,000 workers being employed in the sector which turns over £131 billion. This sector also shows some of the fastest productivity growth of any sector over the past 10 years. In comparison with European counterparts, the UK MSBs make up 19.7% of private sector turnover (German MSB's share is 31.7% while the figure is 32% for Finland). But the UK comes a close second to Germany in terms of MSB's share of employment (21.2% and 23.2% respectively). Yet another measure of growth, namely exports, shows that MSBs have outperformed both large and small firms with 4.3% (£35.5 billion at the start of 2011) compared with 3.8% for small employers and 3.7 % for the larger firms. Figures provided to the Confederation of British Industry (CBI) in 2011 by NESTA reveal that just 6% of MSBs create 60% of all the new jobs created by the sector. If more firms could reach their potential to grow, this could help achieve an extra £20–£50 billion by 2020, a major boost to the UK's GDP.

The unique combination of size, the flexibility afforded by not being too large or too small, the growth in turnover, profits, share of employment and productivity, together with exports, suggests that underpinning these metrics is the ability of MSBs to innovate. A CBI survey in 2011 suggested that a relatively high proportion of MSBs place a good degree of importance on innovation (63% being innovation active compared with 60% for large firms and 57% for small businesses). The larger ones, that is those with employment levels above 250 and less than 500 employees, are particularly active in protecting their intellectual property and much more so than smaller firms in most cases and large firm counterparts in some situations. Revenues generated from innovation are also higher than the two other categories of firms. Approximately 13.5% of MSBs applied for patents while another 18.2% registered a trademark, 5.9% for registering an industrial design and 12.2% for the production of materials eligible for copyright (compared with 2.3% of small firms with less than 50 employees and 7% of large firms for patents; and 4.4% and 310.8% for trademark registration, 1.0% and 3.3% for industrial design, and 5.4% and 8% for copyright, respectively).

Although MSBs are supposed to be the leading group of innovators in the UK, a 2008 European Community Innovation Survey and the GE Capital report (Nicolaou et al., 2015) show that they are either falling behind their German and French counterparts or that the latter are catching up. Only 62.5% describe themselves as innovating relative to 84% for the Germans and 67% in France. R&D expenditure also falls behind the same two countries, and while collaboration is deemed important for innovation, not many MSBs connect with universities, government research laboratories or private research organisations. The fragmented ecosystem for innovation in the UK may, therefore, put UK MSBs behind those of other developed countries.

INNOVATIVE MID-SIZED FIRMS IN EMERGING AND DEVELOPING ECONOMIES

We can expect a stronger profile for MSBs in advanced economies, and perhaps fewer mid-sized players in less developed countries. The reality is somewhat different. Emerging economies which continued to grow in spite of the recession have done so because of the resilience and innovative capability of their MSBs.

A profile of the top 500 mid-sized firms in 2009 in India includes 200 listed companies, 200 unlisted public companies and 100 privately held businesses. They represent diverse industrial sectors including IT and IT-enabled services (11.6% of all 500 firms in the top 10 sectors), food manufacturing and consumer goods and steel (8.2%), pharmaceuticals and engineering (7%), construction and real estate (6.4%), capital goods (6%), textiles (5.8%), infrastructure (5%) and chemicals (4.8%). Their 3-year compound annual growth rates (CAGR) vary from well over 40% for the construction and real estate, engineering and IT firms to around 35% for the fast-moving consumer goods (FMCG), steel and textiles sector (Inc 500, 2009). Five major Indian businesses – Asian Paints (rank 18), Hindustan Unilever (31), Tata Consultancy Services (66), Sun Pharma (73) and Larsen & Toubro (89) – were ranked among Forbes's list of 'The World's Most Innovative Companies' for 2016. The firms were ranked by their innovation premium, which represents the difference between their market capitalisation and the net present value of cash flows from existing businesses. The computation of this premium is based on a proprietary algorithm from Credit Suisse HOLT (Forbes, 2016).

MSBs in the BRICS (Brazil, Russia, India, China and South Africa) appear to play equally powerful roles in the development of their respective economies as their counterparts in Europe and the USA. Some of the most successful and innovative firms in Brazil include mid-sized companies such as Bematch, Fotosensores, Reivax and Opto.). Based on data from PINTEC-2000 (Industrial Research on Technological Innovation-2000) and using a non-parametric statistical procedure, Kannebley et al. (2005) found that the four major drivers or predictors of innovation were exporting orientation, firm size, foreign capital origin and inter-industry differences, in decreasing order. Export orientation and foreign or mixed capital origin were the main determinants for introducing a new process or a new product in the market. In another analysis of a comprehensive nationwide, government-sponsored innovation survey (PINTEC), involving more than 30,000 companies and 34 industrial sectors, Frank et al. (2016) show that Brazilian industry tends to adopt two very different innovation strategies: market-orientation and technology-acquisition. The first strategy prioritises R&D, both internal and external, together with commercialisation and new product launch activities. Such a strategy leads to a positive effect on innovation output. The technology-acquisition strategy based on industrial machinery and equipment acquisition, however, had a negative effect on innovation output; the export orientation of MSBs is common to most of them across the world.

Reports filter in about the Mittelstands of Germany being bought out by Chinese investors representing a mix of large and mid-sized Chinese firms. Chinese direct investment in Germany grew from €46 million to €68 million between 2012 and 2013. As the industrial sun rises in the east, the tradition of family succession in Germany is beginning to crumble, reflecting the ageing population of the latter country. Specialists such as the fork-lift manufacturer Kion, semiconductor firms such as Prema and car door latch maker Kiekart have all passed into Chinese ownership (*The Local*, 2014).

INNOVATION AND THE SMALL FIRM

Over time various pieces of research have found compelling explanations for the innovation advantage that small firms have over large firms. The management structures of small firms where there is less bureaucracy (in comparison with larger organisations) and a smaller decision-making team are conducive to a culture of innovation in the firm. There are financial, production and general managerial decisions necessary with the use of certain technologies and markets that may not be of interest to the larger firm. As Acs and Audretsch (2005), referring to Scherer (1988), point out:

> many advances in technology accumulate upon a myriad of detailed inventions involving individual components, materials and fabrication techniques. The sales possibilities for making such narrow, detailed advances are often too modest to interest giant corporations. An individual entrepreneur's juices will flow over a new product or process with sales prospects in millions of dollars per year, whereas few large corporations can work up much excitement over such small fish, nor can they accommodate small ventures easily into their organisational structures. (p. 20; cited in Mitra, 2012)

Where the small firm scores over the large firm is often in the initial indifference of its larger counterparts to specific products and processes and markets. Differences in expectations in the value of an invention between the technical or scientific inventor in a large firm and the management of the firm could leave the creator disenchanted and lead him or her to prospect a new firm spin-off, especially if the costs of doing so are lower than the return from the prospective innovation. The inventor acquires knowledge at his or her place of work which can then be used to spin off a commercial venture.

For some time now there has been much talk and some evidence about knowledge created in universities spilling over to private firms for eventual commercialisation or indeed leading to the creation of university spin-offs by staff or students. Acs et al. (1992) have argued that spillovers from universities contribute more to innovation in smaller firms. This contrasts sharply with the work of larger firms which can be more active in university-based or sponsored research (Link and Rees, 1990). KPMG's recent investment in Imperial College of $20 million for a Big Data Centre in London is a case in point.

Different sectors are likely to show different levels and factors affecting the success of small-firm innovation. Underpinning these success stories are the relative behavioural advantages of flexibility and speed of response to market changes that small firms enjoy over their larger counterparts, which tend to rely on resource advantages (Rothwell and Dodgson, 1994). Rogers (2004) suggests that smaller firms have access mainly to smaller pools of knowledge and human capital, but the smaller high-technology firm can overcome part of this problem by obtaining value in information exchange, acquisition of resources, technology transfer and risk management from cooperative R&D to improve their competitiveness and innovative capabilities with other small and larger firms (Noteboom, 1994; Rogers, 2004). However, collaboration is not easy and the outcomes are often patchy, varying according to sector, the technologies and the innovations involved (Freel, 2003).

Size restricts smaller firms from easily accessing the critical technologies, finance, competencies and capabilities sometimes necessary for innovation. Scale and scope tilt the advantage towards large firms and help them to manage innovations, especially where specialised teams or high-value machinery is needed (Cohen and Klepper, 1992).

An OECD (2010) report found that the environment for innovation has changed and the importance of new and small firms to the innovation process has increased. What characterises the new environment is the combination of new technologies, niche forms of market demand and increasing incomes. These factors may have reduced the 'structural disadvantages' of flexibility, quick decision making and autonomy in the marketplace, of the smaller firm. Open and distributed forms of innovation, and greater reliance on non-technological forms of social and organisational innovation, have generated new challenges. Globalisation has created new opportunities especially for domestic knowledge to be exploited overseas together with possibilities for tapping into knowledge generated abroad. SMEs have begun to make smart use of 'Knowledge-Intensive Service Activities' (KISA) by bringing in outside firms and consultants to enable the implementation of change in operational matters such as quality control, marketing and product development.

SMALL, HIGH-IMPACT INNOVATIVE FIRMS

However, there appears to be an uneven distribution of small-firm innovation between a few high-impact or high-growth firms and a vast majority of SMEs that innovate less. OECD data also indicates that SMEs innovate less than large firms across a range of categories, including product, process, non-technological and new-to-market product innovation. They also appear to occupy a smaller share of collaborative innovation activities. The OECD report on SMEs, entrepreneurship and innovation (2010) shows, for example, that in Sweden only one in five SMEs (compared with nearly one-half of larger firms) had introduced a product innovation in the last 3 years. Even after adjusting for size there is a marked difference, albeit the gap is smaller (8% of turnover for SMEs compared with 14% for larger firms).

Bessant (2013) has also challenged some of the findings on small-firm innovation which showed that, when adjusted for size, smaller firms made more new products than larger firms. Methodological shortcomings in those studies consist of problems associated with the inclusion of subsidiaries and divisions of larger firms in the count, and inappropriate weighting of the technological merit and commercial value of innovations or the firms. There is no strong link between formal R&D and growth and profitability. Other factors, such as the founder's level of managerial experience and technological know-how, proactiveness and propensity to engage in innovation, have stronger associations with innovation performance (see below for a fuller discussion on high-impact firms).

SMALL FIRMS, LARGE FIRMS – VALUE, IMPACT AND GROWTH

The relative value of large and small firms is found in discussions centred around the link between size, survival and growth and the implicit connection that is made between innovation, impact and growth. This debate takes place in the context of industry life cycles, the different types of innovation, the various sectors in which they operate and the state of the economy.

Who does what type of innovation provides clearer insights into what different firms do than generalised observations about innovation. They also help to explain how the structures of IOs are determined by what they do. As the UK Community Innovation survey results show, innovation occurs as a result of a wide variety of business practices. A range of indicators can be used to measure its level within the enterprise or in the wider economy as a whole. These include, for example, resources allocated to innovation which measures the level of effort and investment made for innovation, and the number of new or improved products and processes introduced over a specific period of time, which calibrates achievement levels. Table 6.3 shows a selection of the different types of innovation activity over a 3-year period, 2008–10.

UK innovation activity is defined in broad Schumpeterian terms and follows those adopted by Eurostat:

- the introduction of a new or significantly improved product (good or service);
- engagement in innovation projects not yet complete or abandoned;
- new and significantly improved forms of organisation, business structures or practices and marketing concepts or strategies; and
- acquisition in areas such as internal R&D, training, acquisition of external knowledge or machinery and equipment linked to innovation activities.

Only the first three sets of activities make a business 'innovation active', and therefore the definition excludes expenditure and activities linked to innovation. This exclusion is in keeping with the EU-wide definition of 'innovation active'.

If a business is engaged in all four activities identified above then it is referred to as a 'broader innovator'. A 'wider innovator' is a business that has been involved in organisational processes, structural changes and marketing for innovation.

During the period under review both product and process innovations fell, but note that nearly 50% of all product innovations were novel or new to the market while approximately 25% of the process innovations were also considered to be novel. In terms of size, it is clear that the proportion of large firms involved in all types of innovation was higher than those for SMEs.

TABLE 6.3   Enterprises engaged in innovation by size and activity (2008-10)

Type of activity	Size of enterprise, 2011			Size of enterprise, 2009		
	No. of employees (%)			No. of employees (%)		
	10-250	250+	All	10-250	250+	All
Innovation active (revised)	37	42	37	38	49	38
Innovation activity (old definition)	36	41	36	58	60	58
Broader innovator	39	44	39	60	64	61
Wider innovator	31	35	31	26	38	27
Activities	33	38	33	55	55	55
Product innovator	19	23	19	24	30	24
(of which share with new-to-market products)	46	50	46	45	43	45
Process innovator	10	17	10	12	18	13
(of which share with new-to-industry processes)	27	24	26	29	30	29
Abandoned activities	4	6	4	4	6	4
Ongoing activities	7	9	7	6	9	6
Both product and process innovator	7	13	8	9	14	9
Either product or process innovator	22	28	22	27	35	28

Source: Adapted from BIS (2013)

Any commentary on the type of data referred to above would be incomplete without taking the context into account. The period in question (2008–10) has now been well recognised as one that was marked by fluid and unfavourable conditions associated with a recession. Although it would be difficult to make direct comparisons between the two years because of the fluid economic conditions, what is worth noting is that there was hardly any change in the number of innovation-active firms. This suggests that innovative firms can be more resilient than other firms during inclement economic times because they have the capacity to create and sell new products in tune with the changing needs of the market.

INNOVATION AND THE GROWTH OF FIRMS

Firms grow because they innovate, and their ability to innovate may have something to do with their size! It could also be argued that the relationship between innovation and growth could have something to do with how firms learn to grow. In writing specifically about new firms facing the costs problem, Jovanovic (1982) suggested that costs are not simply random; they vary according to different sectors and across firms. Typically an entrant does not know its own cost structure but it gains its relative efficiency through a process of learning and discovery from the actual marketplace. Survival is possible if the entrants' abilities exceed their expectations. One way in which they can demonstrate how their grasp (abilities) can surpass their reach (expectations) is by occupying strategic niches in specific industries. In fact smaller firms may not need to grow to survive because they can be spared the trials and tribulations of survival if they remain small in strategic industrial niches (Caves and Porter, 1977; Porter, 1979). It is possible that in the formative stage of a life cycle there is no dominant design or product. Firms can experiment through short production runs, making changes in response to feedback from customers. Things are likely to change at a mature stage in the life cycle of an industry. The product is expected to be more standardised as markets grow at a more predictable rate. Innovations tend to be limited and connections between suppliers and customers can absorb any volatility in the market as firms develop routines with which to combat market pressures (Utterback and Abernathy, 1975; Winter, 1984).

The data in Table 6.3 above shows that when it comes to introducing new products to the market or new processes to industry, the smaller and medium-sized firm cannot really be seen as a laggard. It is not simply a matter of large or small firms being more innovative than the other. What matters in terms of a firm's ability to innovate are:

(a) the type of innovation – different types of products, services processes;
(b) the industrial sector in which the innovation is taking place;
(c) the measure of technological change generated by innovation; and
(d) the management processes in those firms that help to nurture and support innovation.

Knowing whether a firm has distinctive capabilities and competencies and understanding the contexts in which innovation occurs are important. But does such innovation have any impact on the organisation, and on the industry and the economy in which it is located?

HIGH-IMPACT, HIGH-GROWTH AND HIGHLY INNOVATIVE FIRMS

Measurement helps us to ascribe a value to innovative achievement and to determine whether innovation has an impact on firms, industries and the economy. The higher the level of impact, the better it could be for all three units of economic activity. High impact means fast growth in terms of turnover, productivity and the employment of people. Higher levels of turnover are attractive to firms not least because of their potential contribution to cash flow and profitability. Increased levels of productivity are of significance to firms because of their effect on expenditure levels and profitability, while enhanced job creation is a boon to governments because of its importance for economic development and political popularity. Together with job creation, high-growth firms also help with improving the stock of businesses in the economy (Birch and Medoff, 1994; Davidsson and Henrekson, 2002). Researchers have also argued that firm growth, however heterogeneous, is positively related to economic growth (Delmar et al., 2003; Fleischer et al., 2010). Examining the growth rate of firms has become an important part of government policy (Kemp and Verhoeven, 2002). This is because of the belief that only a small minority of high-growth firms do most to boost the economy. The year of 1994 was good for researchers arriving at similar conclusions. Birch and Medoff (1994) found that firms which move from a small to a larger size quickly (known as 'gazelles') account for almost all the job creation in the economy (Birch et al., 1997, concluded that 3% of the gazelles generated over 70% of the jobs in the USA between 1992 and 1996). Then Kirchhoff (1994) noted that 4% of firms formed in 1977–8 created 74% of the cohort of firms with employment growth 6 years later. Storey (1994) showed that 4% of surviving firms were responsible for 50% of jobs created 10 years later. So there is a case for facilitating an increase in the share of fast-growing firms, not least because there are spillover effects of rapid firm growth on the growth of other businesses and on economic and social development in both the regional and national economies.

But what are high-impact firms? This is not an easy question to answer. First, there is the confusion over terminology. They are referred to as 'high-growth firms' (Delmar et al., 2003), 'rapid growth firms' (Fischer and Reuber, 2003), 'gazelles' (Birch, 1979; 1987), 'gorillas' (Owen, 2004), as plain 'high impact' (Acs, 2013) and as highly innovative firms (Coad et al., 2014). We will use these terms interchangeably for the rest of this chapter. What they are not are the coffee shops, the home-based or lifestyle businesses and the legions of the self-employed!

Lifting the veil of terminology, we find greater clarity in some of the explanations. Based on this definition and some of the points above we find that there are probably two definitional categories of high-impact firms (Goedhuys and Sleuwaegen, 2010). The first group captures a certain proportion of firms in the economy and the second refers to the levels of growth in terms of turnover, employment and value added or productivity. Barringer et al. (2005) and Delmar et al. (2003) have argued that a 10% growth in employment was the defining characteristic of high-impact firms, while others have focused their attention on turnover with a minimum of 20% to 25% per year of sales growth for a period of 3–5 years as an explanation of high-growth firms (Fischer and Reuber, 2003; Nicholls-Nixon, 2005).

The OECD defines high-growth firms in more conciliatory terms as those with 10 or more employees and which have recorded average annual growth rates of 20% or more in either employment or sales. This is corroborated by Acs et al. (2008), Brandt et al. (2012) and Eurostat–OECD (2008). A quote from the Eurostat–OECD business demography manual is worth considering:

> All enterprises with average annualised growth greater than 20 per cent over a three year period, and ten or more employees in the beginning of the observation period, should be considered as high-growth enterprises. Growth can be measured by the number of employees or by turnover.

Sustaining high levels of growth over any period of time could be attributed to innovation. Mason and Brown (2013) and Anyadike-Danes et al. (2009) suggest that the ability of high-growth firms to beat other non-innovative firms in the business game is due in great part to successful innovation. They find innovative firms in the UK grow twice as fast, in both employment and sales, as firms that do not innovate. The former do so because of their earlier investment in resources for innovation and the nurturing of innovation-related capabilities. The business decision to invest continues even after the initial period of growth. A firm introducing a product innovation in 2002–4 enjoyed, on average, a 4.4% employment growth rate from 2004–7 (Mason et al., 2009). This growth rate compares favourably with the 2% average growth rate of non-innovating firms (10% and 5.8% respectively when sales growth is taken into account).

SIZE AND AGE OF HIGH-IMPACT FIRMS

The discussion so far does not distinguish between types or the size of high-impact firms. In fact age may be more significant a factor for growth than the size of the firms. According to Mason et al. (2009), the distribution of high-impact firms by size in terms of employment, turnover and average turnover by employee are not that different from the overall size distribution of firms with 10 or more employees. However, firms less than 5 years old are overrepresented in all three measures stated above. Notwithstanding this last point, Mason et al. (2009) note that most high-growth firms are more than 5 years old. In the USA, the average age of high-impact firms is 25 years (Acs, 2008). The Acs et al. definition indicates that high-impact firms are those whose sales have doubled over a 4-year period and in which period an employment growth quantifier is two or greater over the same period. The employment growth quantifier is measured as the product of a firm's absolute change and percentage change in employment expressed as a decimal. This contrast between UK and US firms is a feature of differences in methodological issues. What is clear, however, is that in both cases the average age of high-impact firms is still lower than those of low-impact firms. Henrekson and Johansson (2008) found unambiguous evidence of high-impact firms being younger than other firms, and Coad (2007) concluded that, minus a few exceptions, a key feature of industrial dynamics is the negative dependence of growth rates on age.

Three issues are of critical importance:

1. Size is of less importance to the innovation process, especially when measuring the value of high-impact firms. This means that small, medium and large firms all contribute to high impact through innovation.
2. The age of firms is a significant factor in considering the type of firm that makes a high impact.
3. The relationship between firm growth and innovation is a two-way process, in that while investing in innovation can be considered to be one of the drivers of growth, high-impact firms are also better equipped to innovate.

But are all high-growth firms (HGFs) also highly innovative firms (HIFs)? There is an argument that suggests that the relationship between growth and innovation is at best unclear. Coad et al. (2014) define HIFs as the top 20% of firms in terms of R&D spending and the top 20% of firms with sales from new-to-market products and services (operationalised as firms with sales of more than 11% from new-to-market products and services). Their definition of HGFs is the top 5% of firms by employment and sales growth.[1] The authors find that there is very little overlap between HGFs and HIFs. Of the 12,689 firms that they investigated, only 101 were both HGFs and HIFs. But this data does not fully explain whether HGFs can also be highly innovative. The results emanating from survey work and the use of descriptive, univariate and multivariate statistical analysis techniques show that the correlation varies by different waves of surveys and measures used. Only about 8%–23% of HGF firms are also HIFs and the proportions are not statistically different from those firms which are not HGFs. HGFs are also less likely to be HIFS than non-HGFs. Small biotech firms which invest heavily in R&D can be very innovative but they do not necessarily grow significantly. Firms that have already introduced products to the market are more likely to derive value from their innovations than firms focusing on R&D. Over time and successful waves of innovation, HIFs maintained their high levels of innovation and only a small percentage of non-HIF firms converted to become highly innovative. Path dependency may have a lot to do with firms being innovative or not (Coad et al., 2014).

THE EMERGENCE OF NEW TYPES OF ORGANISATION FOR INNOVATION

New forms of organisation are spurring and enabling innovations in the marketplace and in society. These are the networked firms that make the interdependency between larger, medium and smaller firms a structural necessity for manufacturing and services across the world. It is therefore appropriate to conclude this chapter with a reference to these new species of firms and their claim to be the harbingers of new knowledge creation in the global economy.

Inter-firm alliances, networks and collaborative arrangements are often the main sources of innovation, according to von Hippel (2007). Networking activities by firms within and across borders have grown sharply over the past two decades (Hagedoorn, 2002). The absence of any real resolution about any specific model of innovation or the innovative firms means that they operate outside the rational logic of growth. Knowledge spills over, technology and its component parts are developed in different parts of the world, innovation processes embrace both open and closed forms, allowing the free flow of knowledge to complement proprietary knowledge-creating platforms. The outcome is the phenomenal growth of networked firms and organisations.

Networked firms can be defined as clusters of business units coordinated by market mechanisms. They replace layers of management and multiple decision makers within a single organisation (Snow et al., 1992). They are less reliant on centralised planning and control and on scale economies, focusing instead on economies of scope and a project-driven business agenda. The truly networked organisation explores opportunities and resources globally and maximises returns on assets dedicated to a linked unit of business organisations irrespective of whether they are owned by their firm or by partners, associates or even competitors. They perform functions for which they have specific expertise and competencies, often outsourcing activities that can be performed more efficiently and more effectively. Castells (2000; 2011) refers to them as

> the organisational form built around business projects resulting from the co-operation between different components of different firms, networking among themselves for the duration of a given project, and reconfiguring their networks for the implementation of each project. (2000: 67)

As Table 6.4 shows, there is a mix of external and internal forces or imperatives that have driven changes in the structure and type of organisation best suited to innovate in the twenty-first century. Snow et al. (1992) predicted these changes back in 1992

TABLE 6.4　Organisation responses to the new business environment

The new competitive reality	
Driving forces:	**Interactive forces**
Globalisation:	Deregulation:
Strong new players at every stage of the value chain (upstream and downstream)	Legal and policy change produce uncertainty and increase competition
Competition has reduced all margins – no slack left in most economic systems	Public services are being privatised
Technological change and technology transfer:	**Changing workforce demographics:**
Shorter product life cycles	Domestic workforce is becoming more mature, diverse and less well trained and educated
Lower barriers to entry	Global workforce is becoming more mobile
Economies of scope as well as scale	
	Facilitating forces:
	CAD/CAM and other manufacturing advances
	Faster, lower-cost communications and computer technologies (the Internet)
	More social and political freedom
Organisational imperatives	
Product and service demands:	**Managerial requirements:**
Focus on distinctive competency	Building smaller, better-trained permanent workforces
Reduce costs and accelerate innovation	Develop and use links to part-time and temporary human resources
Hold only productive assets	
Reduce overall time cycle	Develop and use links to global technological resources

and the issues remain as important today as when the authors first articulated how organisations were beginning to respond to structural, legislative, demographic and technological changes.

NETWORK STRUCTURES

Snow et al. (1992) refer to three types of network structures – internal, stable and dynamic – each appropriate for particular competitive environments. In common with organisational structures in general, network-based structures are dependent on the context of their operations. *Internal networks* are found within firms to enable managers of different units and assets to work to the common logic of the market. Here the belief is that innovations are more likely to take place as a result of the unique inimitable resources of the firm and also from the pressures on internal units to operate with market-based prices instead of artificial transfer prices. *Stable networks* are characterised by allowing firms to introduce a certain degree of flexibility in the overall value chain of a business. This is made possible through outsourcing. Assets can be owned by many firms, but they are dedicated to a particular business which allows for the ownership of assets and associated risks to be distributed across independent firms. The result is an inevitable trade-off between close cooperation and scheduling, for example against the costs of mutual dependence and some loss of flexibility. *Dynamic networks* can be described as meta networks of discontinuous, innovative and highly competitive environments. Here, extensive outsourcing is common among, typically, firms in the film, music, publishing, fashion, electronics and advanced manufacturing businesses. The lead firms in the dynamic network rely on a core skill (such as manufacturing, R&D, design, assembly or brokering) identifying and assembling assets owned by other companies.

Globalisation has raised the stakes of dynamic networking by and between firms. Networking is being facilitated by flows of capital, technologies and talent across borders in a cluster of industries often related to each other through common and transferable technologies and skills. Dynamic networking is probably most apparent in manufacturing, as evinced in the rise of the global production networks in the Pearl River Delta in the Far East where multiple layers of firms of varied size form part of a huge network of operators engaged in the manufacture of electronic gadgets, instruments and other related products (Yang and Liao, 2010). We could argue that these firms are simply part of any network in any production value chain. We could also argue that the purchasing of components from outside suppliers instead of making them in a vertically structured organisation is not to organisational theory and practice. Larger firms have separated different production functions across multiple sites since well before the Second World War, and the consecration of the concept of value chains occurred over 20 years ago when Michael Porter wrote in his book *The Competitive Advantage of Nations* (2011), 'A firm's value chain is an interdependent system or network of activities connected by linkages', and that the effective management of these linkages is an essential source of competitive advantage. Things have changed. What we knew about connectivity and networks has undergone radical transformation.

First, we note the increased density of the new networks with higher levels of fragmentation of activities as technology and capital flow from one point to another, and as different units of activity are established across multiple sites. Decision-making powers devolve across countries and regions as the different, spatially dispersed units of production become responsible for producing specific components or even whole products for different markets. Marsh (2012) identifies four different stages in the evolution of production industries, with interconnected manufacturing representing the fourth stage of this evolution beginning around the year 2000. The stages are as follows:

Stage 1: 1850–1930 Manufacturers make products in one place and sell goods around the world through overseas marketing offices. Exports define global reach. A good example is Siemens in Germany which was established in 1847 and which developed an international perspective from the very beginning by setting up marketing offices in the UK and Russia since the 1850s. Local manufacturing gave way to multiple site manufacturing because it became easier to sell goods locally if one also produced locally and to avoid restrictive import tariffs.

Stage 2: from around 1930 Broader and more extensive series of manufacturing outside the home countries. Ford set up the 'Detroit of Europe' plant in Dagenham in east London in the UK, its first big plant outside the USA, followed by another plant in Cologne. General Motors, General Electric and many others followed the same path. The Industrial Revolution had come full circle. These plants remained independent of the manufacturers' home base but goods were sold primarily in the so-called developed parts of the world.

Stage 3: from the early 1980s Economic growth, especially in developed nations, encouraged plant building, which became a global phenomenon. Growth, as Robert Solow understood it, was being made possible through the establishment of plants globally. Emerging economies showing signs of fast growth would also provide lower-cost environments alongside rising incomes among its citizens, thus providing for ease of manufacturing and a ready market for sales. Foreign direct investment (FDI) grew from $50 million in 1980 to $1,900 million in 2007, a staggering increase of 3,700%, just before the recent economic recession.

Stage 4: The 'now' period Marked by the convergence of technologies, quality standards across a wider group of manufacturing nations enabled by digitisation, together with divergences in disposable incomes, consumer spending habits, technological capabilities and the levels of human capital. Although the divergences allowed for low-cost manufacturing, production decisions are not simply reliant on manufacturing costs. If high-volume production together with minimal changes in design between production runs is the order of the day, then manufacturing in low-cost countries might make sense. Consequently businesses operating and selling in different countries have opted for a hybrid form of manufacturing, so called because of the decision to combine low- and high-cost manufacturing plants in different countries at the same time. This ambidexterity calls for different levels of competencies appropriate for the different contexts in which these plants are located. There is also a clear exchange of learning from each other and the development of new competencies because of this spillover effect. When Siemens, for example, found that its interventional X-ray machines used in operating theatres was too expensive for the Indian market, its technology centre in India developed a local replacement costing only $500 (as opposed to the $2,000 price tag of the original product) by focusing attention on the camera in the scanner which was redesigned from scratch. It is more than likely that the huge saving of costs and price would mean that the machine would also find markets in the developed economies of the USA and Europe. (Marsh, 2012)

The advent of open forms of innovation and open standards in supply chain relation-ships is particularly manifest in the electronics industry. As Marsh (2012) notes, a supplier that has found a novel way to make printed circuit boards is generally free to use the same technology in selling goods and services to all the firms in the sup-ply network. In the semiconductor business fewer companies are running their own plants. Fabrication-less or 'fabless' models mean that these businesses concentrate on activities in design while leaving the production to specialists. Suppliers provide the innovative product technologies. We will discuss open innovation together with the complementary approach of user-led innovation and related ideas as part of the array of different innovation processes in other chapters of the book.

Worth noting is the emergence of different business models which are reli-ant on what Prahalad and Krishnan called the connections between the 'various architectural elements that create an entrepreneurial and innovative culture in a firm' (2008: 236). There are two key architectures: the social architecture and the technical architecture. The pillars that are supporting these two architectures are personalised co-created experiences, and global access to resources and talent, enabled by flexible and resilient business processes and focused analytics. This is because, the authors predicted, the real competitive advantage of firms lies in con-necting consumers and resources seamlessly while managing the needs for efficiency and flexibility. What consumers will demand increasingly will be the unique quality of their experiences at the lowest possible cost. Prahalad and Krishnan's analysis is predicated on two important factors changing the dynamics of business and busi-ness architectures in a digital economy: the impossibility of firms of any size to satisfy varied individual consumer experiences at any one time, and the demand for personalised experiences of different consumers. This means firms building capabilities to access resources from a large variety of many different firms as part of an ecosystem of resource providers, and firms learning how to individualise the product or service experience of different consumers. Vignette 6.2 below offers a glimpse into how dynamic networked services optimising the value of digitisation and connectivity are changing the education market.

VIGNETTE 6.2   THE CHANGING MARKET AND ORGANISATIONAL STRUCTURE OF EDUCATION

INTRODUCTION

Students wanting tuition for their homework are generally dependent on one form of learning system at a given time and place. Tutor Vista, a tuition provider from India, offers students the opportunity to chose the time of learning, organise the priority of their learning needs, and identify any teacher to provide that learning experience from anywhere in the world. It was founded in 2005 by two Indians in Bangalore, namely Krishnan and Meena Ganesh, together with three other founding partners. The early introduction of venture funding of over $10 million by Sequoia Capital and Lightspeed Venture Partners placed the organisation on a sound financial footing.

THE ORGANISATIONAL MODEL

Although the tutors are spread around the world, each of them is bound by common standards of behaviour, quality and ethics. These tutors test a student's understanding of the subject and then help to develop a tailor-made course for the student. Resources are obtained from a global pool while remote connectivity is enabled by digitisation of the learning platform. Apart from individualised one-to-one tutoring using interactive whiteboards, the learning platform offers 24/7 tutor availability, unlimited tutoring with the same tutor, help with assignments, preparation for tests and detailed reports about performance.

The model of providing unique learning experiences for students using global pools of knowledge and resources testifies to the power of networked organisations challenging traditional industries such as education. At a more practical level, examples such as those of Tutor Vista in India and the Khan Academy in the USA challenge the management practices connected especially to secondary education and talent management, product development of learning resources, pricing structures, logistics and marketing. We find similar challenges being posed to higher education through the development of MOOCs (massive, online open courses).

OVERCOMING DIFFICULTIES, NETWORK-BASED GROWTH AND TAKEOVER

What contributed to initial difficulties was overcoming the fear of distant learning by unknown teachers from various parts of the world. Establishing cognitive legitimacy with the students, and especially their parents, made for edgy beginnings. However, the business has grown. It first acquired Edurite, an education provider, in 2007, and then established a partnership with American Book Company in 2009. Six years after its formation, Pearson, the major global publishing and education company, first acquired 76% of the shares of Tutor Vista for $127 million before buying the remaining 20% in 2013.

It remains to be seen whether Tutor Vista has really changed secondary education by offering an alternative platform for learning. Its acquisition by a large company suggests that its original, innovative, networked-based and entrepreneurial endeavour may have been compromised.

Sources: Prahalad and Krishnan (2008); Tutor Vista website www.tutorvista.com (last accessed 20 August 2014); Wikipedia

CITIZEN INNOVATION: SHARING AND GIVING INNOVATIVE ORGANISATIONS

Where then are the Airbnbs, the Blablacars and the Truilas of the world – the leading advocates of what this author refers to as 'citizen innovation and entrepreneurship'? By citizen innovation entrepreneurship I refer to a unique democratisation of innovation which allows consumers, intermediary users and producers to share knowledge, resources, ideas and technologies both as 'units' of economic activity and as citizens engaged in social and community participation. This convergence of economic and social action is part of the emergence of what is referred to as the 'sharing economy'. The development of new products and services is 'shared' in the process of creation, production and consumption. Digitisation and the use of smart phones and tablets make possible the availability of data, the spread of entrepreneurial outcomes in business and in society, and a proper set of measurement tools and analytics for evaluation (Brynjolfsson and McAfee, 2014).

The innovation that occurs is both social in orientation (citizens as investors and entrepreneurs) and economic in outcomes (growth in the stock of entrepreneurs, firms, employment). Opportunities are found in the marketplace, but also in the conscious movement of attitudes and aspirations that makes citizens act as consumers, entrepreneurs, donors and beneficiaries of these new opportunities. Digital technology enables both the giving and sharing as more data and information are made available, which in turn facilitates the scaling up of individual businesses and the spread of many others often in unknown environments. Borrowing Weitzman's (1998) ideas for new growth theory we may refer to the technologies as 'fixed factors' in an economy which are augmented by the 'seed ideas' or knowledge obtained in venture philanthropy and the sharing economy. This manifests itself in the form of new ventures where

> we are hopping into strangers' cars (Lyft, Sidecar, Uber) welcoming them into our spare rooms (Airbnb), dropping off our dogs at their houses (DogVacay, Rover) … This is not just an economic breakthrough. It is a cultural one, enabled by a sophisticated series of mechanisms, algorithms and finely calibrated systems of rewards and punishments. (Tanz, 2014)

The combination of economic and cultural phenomena enables a democratisation of entrepreneurship and innovation based on new digital technology, trust and attitudinal change, which is radical, building on the person-to-person type of marketplace created by eBay (Tanz, 2014). Zuboff (2011) refers to it as a form of distributed capitalism which does not destroy old-style production and manufacturing-based capitalism entirely, but opens up opportunities for a greater number of people to carve out their own form of capitalist endeavour. New networks emerge as people change roles and functions, and the possibilities of new institutions are created because of the opening up of entrepreneurial opportunities through giving and sharing.

A sharing economy's well-being is afforded by the conscious intervention of all parties to economic and social development both within an organisation and without. Much of this is achieved locally with the use of local skills and knowledge. A better appreciation and use of locally available skills, for example, helps outweigh the cost of training and possible sourcing or even relocation elsewhere. The same problem could occur in the absence of a regional supply chain. Instead of purely short-term measures and a passive reliance on the production of skills by schools, universities and technical colleges, a proactive engagement with those institutions in curriculum development, mentoring and creating factories with in-built classrooms (e.g. Southwire in rural Carrollton, GA). Others (John Deere, Caterpillar and Harley-Davidson) offer in-person courses or online resources, dedicated staff and joint projects with each other, thereby lowering the costs of logistics, enabling rapid problem solving and easier joint innovation (Porter and Rivkin, 2012).

The sharing economy emerges as a genuine ecosystem when sharing and giving in production and knowledge creation are complemented by the sharing and giving of money. The idea of crowdfunding is a unique capacity for network ideas generation, knowledge dissemination, peer production and funding, as Wikipedia, Twitter, Facebook, Linux, and now Kickstarter have demonstrated. At the centre of this is collaboration on a large scale with the necessary technological tools and collaborative infrastructures, including Internet telephony and open source infrastructure, to create, value and compete, thus liberating people, as Tapscott and Williams (2008) suggest, to participate in innovation and wealth creation within every sector of the economy and society. Crowdfunding now extends that possibility of mass participation in philanthropy with a defined mission. Here the demarcation line between social activism and business becomes fuzzy, suggesting more by way of convergence of thought and action rather than a confusion of values. This is evinced particularly in how Kickstarter raises funds. As the highest profile website for the crowdfunding of new ideas, from technology gadgets to art movies, and watchbands that allow you to strap iPod Nanos to your wrist, Kickstarter has less of an interest in becoming a quasi-venture-capital firm or a start-up factory than caring about enabling creative people to pay for one-off projects with a clearly defined mission, a beginning and an end, irrespective of their ability to become profit-making ventures. Backers provide advice, engage in the cause behind the venture and obtain gifts, but do take equity holdings steering clear of direct competition with venture capitalists. Other websites such as Indiegogo and CircleUp have started proliferating with perhaps more of an accent on start-ups, and President Obama's JOBS Act is attempting to relax securities regulations to encourage crowdfunders for venture funding of businesses (McCracken, 2012). According to the CF Crowd Funding Industry Report, crowdfunding platforms have raised $2.7 billion (an increase of 81%) and provided funding for 1 million campaigns in 2012.

The expectations are that this sum is likely to increase by approximately 100% to $5.1 billion (crowdsourcing.com, 2013)! The ability to raise funds through crowdfunding opens up considerable opportunities for scaling up donations by ordinary individuals because it is in the substantiveness of the offering that there is hope in the sustainability of endeavour. Crowdfunding represents a type of hybrid form of social and economic value creation which supports social causes and new business creation.

CONCLUDING OBSERVATIONS

Organisations evolve, and with their evolution we see the emergence of different strategies and tactics for innovation. This is to be expected in any dynamic situation. What we may not be able to guess is the necessary direction of travel for these firms, especially in relation to their innovation strategies. The various types of firms that inhabit the changing world of markets, hierarchies and networks need to respond to different situations, and it is not always clear whether innovation alone determines change. We will explore more of these developments, and crucially the processes which underpin the emergence of new structures, types and modes of innovation, in the chapters that follow. For now we know that behind structures, features and types are people. We could even argue that the distinguishing features and structures of firms are determined or shaped by the people who work in those organisations and others who interact with them. These are the innovative people, and it is them to whom we turn in the next chapter.

 ——— SELF-ASSESSMENT AND RESEARCH QUESTIONS ———

1. How do networked organisations operate and in what way are they different from other types of innovative organisations?

2. Does size matter? Or are different types of firms noted for their own innovative capabilities?

3. Describe the changing landscape of innovation and the role of entrepreneurial organisations in this landscape.

4. What do we mean by high-impact firms? Does size influence the capability of firms to have a high impact?

5. Discuss critically the emerging organisational types and how they reflect a democratisation of innovation and entrepreneurship in society.

NOTE

1. The research evidence was drawn from four waves of the Community Innovation survey in the UK for the years 2004, 2006, 2008 and 2010.

 ——— REFERENCES ———

Acs, Z. (2008) *Foundations of High Impact Entrepreneurship*. Boston: now Publishers.

Acs, Z.J. (2013) 'High-impact firms: gazelles revisited', in Z.J. Acs and D.B. Audretsch (eds), *Handbook of Research on Entrepreneurship and Regional Development: National and Regional Perspectives*. New York: Springer. p. 133.

Acs, Z.J. and Audretsch, D.B. (2005) *Entrepreneurship, Innovation, and Technological Change*. Boston, MA: now Publishers.

Acs, Z.J., Audretsch, D.B. and Feldman, M.P. (1992) 'Real effects of academic research: comment', *American Economic Review*, 82(1): 363–7.

Acs, Z.J., Desai, S. and Klapper, L.F. (2008) 'What does "entrepreneurship" data really show?', *Small Business Economics*, 31(3): 265–81.

Anyadike-Danes, M., Bonner, K., Hart, M. and Mason, C. (2009) 'Measuring business growth: high growth firms and their contribution to employment in the UK'. Strathprints Institutional Repository, University of Strathclyde. Available at: http://strathprints.strath.ac.uk/16124/ (last accessed 10 September 2016).

Barringer, B.R., Jones, F.F. and Neubaum, D.O. (2005) 'A quantitative content analysis of the characteristics of rapid-growth firms and their founders', *Journal of Business Venturing*, 20(5): 663–87.

Bessant, J. (2013) 'Innovation in the twenty-first century', in R. Owen, J. Bessant and M. Heintz (eds), *Responsible Innovation: Managing the Responsible Emergence of Science and Innovation in Society*. Chichester: Wiley. pp. 1–26.

Birch, D. (1979) *The Job Generation Process: Final Report to Economic Development Administration*. Cambridge, MA: MIT Program on Neighbourhood and Regional Change.

Birch, D. (1987) *Job Creation in America: How our Smallest Companies Put the Most People to Work*. New York: The Free Press.

Birch, D.L. and Medoff, J. (1994) 'Gazelles', in L.C. Solmon and A.R. Levenson (eds), *Labor Markets, Employment Policy, and Job Creation*. Boulder, CO: Westview Press.

Birch, D., Haggerty, A. and Parsons, W. (1997) *Who's Creating Jobs?* Cambridge, MA: Cognetics.

BIS (Department for Business, Innovation and Skills) (2013) *First Findings from the UK Innovation Survey 2013: Science and Innovation Analysis*. London: BIS.

Bound, J., Cummins, C., Griliches, Z., Hall, B. and Jaffe, A. (1984) 'Who does R&D and who patents?', in Z. Griliches (ed.), *R&D Patents and Productivity*. Chicago, IL: University of Chicago Press.

Brandt, L., Van Biesebroeck, J. and Zhang, Y. (2012) 'Creative accounting or creative destruction? Firm-level productivity growth in Chinese manufacturing', *Journal of Development Economics*, 97(2): 339–51.

Brynjolfsson, E. and McAfee, A. (2014) *The Second Machine Age: Work, Progress, and Prosperity in a Time of Brilliant Technologies*. New York: W.W. Norton.

Castells, M. (2000) 'Materials for an exploratory theory of the network society', *The British Journal of Sociology*, 51(1): 5–24.

Castells, M. (2011) 'Network theory: a network theory of power', *International Journal of Communication*, 5(15): 773–87.

Caves, R.E. and Porter, M.E. (1977) 'From entry barriers to mobility barriers: conjectural decisions and contrived deterrence to new competition', *Quarterly Journal of Economics*, 91(2): 241–61.

Coad, A. (2007) 'Testing the principle of "growth of the fitter": The relationship between profits and firm growth', *Structural Change and Economic Dynamics*, 18(3): 370–86.

Coad, A., Daunfeldt, S.O., Hölzl, W., Johansson, D. and Nightingale, P. (2014) 'High-growth firms: introduction to the special section', *Industrial and Corporate Change*, 23(1): 91–112.

Cohen, W.M. and Klepper, S. (1992) 'The anatomy of industry R&D intensity distributions', *American Economic Review*, 82(4): 773–99.

Cohen, W.M., Nelson, R.R. and Walsh, J.P. (2002) 'Links and impacts: the influence of public research on industrial R&D', *Management Science*, 48(1): 1–23.

Davidsson, P. and Henrekson, M. (2002) 'Determinants of the prevalence of start-ups and high-growth firms', *Small Business Economics*, 19(2): 81–104.

Delmar, F., Davidsson, P. and Gartner, W.B. (2003) 'Arriving at the high-growth firm', *Journal of Business Venturing*, 18(2): 189–216.

Eurostat–OECD (2007) *Eurostat–OECD Manual on Business Demography Statistics*. Paris: OECD.

Eurostat–OECD (2008) *Eurostat–OECD Manual on Business Demography Statistics*. Paris: OECD.

Fischer, E. and Reuber, A.R. (2003) 'Support for rapid-growth firms: a comparison of the views of founders, government policymakers, and private sector resource providers', *Journal of Small Business Management*, 41(4): 346–65.

Fleisher, B., Li, H. and Zhao, M.Q. (2010) 'Human capital, economic growth, and regional inequality in China', *Journal of Development Economics*, 92(2): 215–31.

Forbes (2016) 'The world's most innovative companies', Forbes Media LLC. Available at: http://www.forbes.com/innovative-companies/#2e331371f172 (last accessed 1 December 2016).

Frank, A.G., Cortimiglia, M.N., Ribeiro, J.L.D. and de Oliveira, L.S. (2016) 'The effect of innovation activities on innovation outputs in the Brazilian industry: market-orientation vs. technology-acquisition strategies', *Research Policy*, 45(3): 577–92.

Freel, M.S. (2003) 'Sectoral patterns of small firm innovation, networking and proximity', *Research Policy*, 32(5): 751–770.

Goedhuys, M. and Sleuwaegen, L. (2010) 'High-growth entrepreneurial firms in Africa: a quantile regression approach', *Small Business Economics*, 34(1): 31–51.

Grant Thornton (2012) 'Agents of growth: How UK mid-sized businesses are beating the market'. Grant Thornton LLP Report.

Hagedoorn, J. (2002) 'Inter-firm R&D partnerships: an overview of major trends and patterns since 1960', *Research Policy*, 31(4): 477–92.

Henrekson, M. and Johansson, D. (2008) 'Competencies and institutions fostering high-growth firms', IFN Working Paper No. 757. Research Institute of Industrial Economics, Sweden Papers. ssrn.com.

Holmes, J., Hutton, P.A. and Weber, E. (1991) 'A functional-form-free test of the research and development/firm size relationship', *Journal of Business and Economic Statistics*, 9(1): 85–90.

Inc. 500 (2009) 'Our annual ranking of the fastest-growing private companies in America'. Available at: http://www.inc.com/inc5000/list/2009/ (last accessed 20 July 2016).

Jensen, E.J. (1987) 'Research expenditures and discovery of new drugs', *Journal of Industrial Economics*, 36: 83–95.

Jovanovic, B. (1982) 'Selection and the evolution of industry', *Econometrica: Journal of the Econometric Society*, 50(3): 649–70.

Kannebley Jr., S., Porto, G.S. and Toldo Pazelloa, E. (2005) 'Characteristics of Brazilian innovative firms: an empirical analysis based on PINTEC – industrial research on technological innovation', *Research Policy*, 34(6): 872–93.

Kemp, R.G.M. and Verhoeven, W.H.J. (2002) 'Growth patterns of medium-sized, fast-growing firms: the optimal resource bundles for organisational growth and performance. Research Report H200111 (part of the research programme SMEs and Entrepreneurship, which is financed by the Netherlands Ministry of Economic Affairs).

Kirchhoff, B.A. (1994) *Entrepreneurship and Dynamic Capitalism: The Economics of Business Firm Formation and Growth*. Santa Barbara, CA: ABC-CLIO.

Levin, R.C., Klevorick, A.K., Nelson, R.R., Winter, S.G., Gilbert, R. and Griliches, Z. (1987) 'Appropriating the returns from industrial research and development', *Brookings Papers on Economic Activity*, 18(3): 783–831.

Link, A.N. and Rees, J. (1990) 'Firm size, university based research, and the returns to R&D', *Small Business Economics*, 2(1): 25–31.

Marsh, P. (2012) *The New Industrial Revolution: Consumers, Globalization and the End of Mass Production*. New Haven, CT: Yale University Press.

Mason, C. and Brown, R. (2013) 'Creating good public policy to support high-growth firms', *Small Business Economics*, 40(2): 211–25.

McCracken, H. (2012) 'The Kickstarter economy', *Time Magazine*, 1 October. Available at: www.time.com/time/magazine/article/0,9171,2125023,00.html (last accessed 21 July 2016).

Mitra, J. (2012) *Entrepreneurship, Innovation and Regional Development: An Introduction*. Abingdon: Routledge.

Nicholls-Nixon, C.L. (2005) 'Rapid growth and high performance: the entrepreneur's "impossible dream"?', *Academy of Management Executive*, 19(1): 77–89.

Nicolaou, N., Roper, S., Waters, J. and del Beato, I. (2015) 'The UK mid-market 2015: Delivering on growth: leading from the middle', Championing UK Growth, GE Capital Bank Ltd. Available at: www.gecapital.co.uk (last accessed on 14 May 2016).

Noteboom, B (1994) 'Innovation and diffusion in small firms: theory and evidence', *Small Business Economics*, 6: S327–47.

OECD (2010) *OECD Science, Technology and Industry Outlook 2010*. Paris: OECD Publications.

Owen, G. (2004) 'Where are the big gorillas? High technology entrepreneurship in the UK and the role of public policy', Entrepreneurship and Public Policy Project, Diebold Institute for Public Policy Studies, London.

Porter, M.E. (1979) 'The structure within industries and companies' performance', *Review of Economics and Statistics*, 61(2): 214–27.

Porter, M.E. (2011) *The Competitive Advantage of Nations: Creating and Sustaining Superior Performance*. New York: Simon and Schuster.

Porter, M.E. and Rivkin, J.W. (2012) 'The looming challenge to U.S. competitiveness', *Harvard Business Review*, March. Available at: https://hbr.org/2012/03/the-looming-challenge-to-us-competitiveness (last accessed on 16 July 2016).

Prahalad, C.K. and Krishnan, M.S. (2008) *The New Age of Innovation: Driving Cocreated Value Through Global Networks*. New York: McGraw Hill Professional.

Rogers, E.M. (2004) 'A prospective and retrospective look at the diffusion model', *Journal of Health Communication*, 9(S1): 13–19.

Rothwell, R. and Dodgson, M. (1994) 'Innovation and size of firm', in *The Oxford Handbook of Industrial Innovation*. Oxford: Oxford University Press. pp. 310–24.

Scherer, F.M. (1982) 'Inter-industry technology flows and productivity growth', *The Review of Economics and Statistics*, 64(4): 627–34.

Scherer, F.M. (1984) 'Using linked patent and R&D data to measure interindustry technology flows', in Z. Griliches (ed.), *R&D, Patents, and Productivity*. Chicago, IL: University of Chicago Press. pp. 417–61.

Scherer, F.M. (1988) 'Corporate takeovers: the efficiency arguments', *Journal of Economic Perspectives*, 2(1): 69–82.

Schumpeter, J.A. (2014) 'Measuring management', *The Economist* (18 January) p. 68.

Schumpeter, J.A. (1942) *Socialism, Capitalism and Democracy*. New York: Harper and Brothers.

Simon, H. (2009) *Hidden Champions of the 21st Century: Success Strategies of Unknown World Market Leaders*. New York: Springer.

Snow, C.C., Miles, R.E. and Coleman, H.J. Jr (1992) 'Managing 21st century network organizations', *Organisational Dynamics*, 20(3): 5–20.

Storey, D.J. (1994) 'Understanding the small business sector', University of Illinois at Urbana–Champaign's Academy for Entrepreneurial Leadership Historical Research Reference in Entrepreneurship.

Tanz, J. (2014) 'How Airbnb and Lyft finally got Americans to trust each other', *Wired*, 23 April. Available at: https://www.wired.com/2014/04/trust-in-the-share-economy/ (last accessed 20 September 2016).

Tapscott, D. and Williams, A.D. (2008) *Wikinomics: How Mass Collaboration Changes Everything*. Harmondsworth: Penguin Books.

The Local (2014) 'China woos Germany's heirless "Mittelstand"', *The Local* (de), 15 June. Available at: http://www.thelocal.de/20140615/china-woos-germanys-heir-less-mittelstand (last accessed 15 June 2016).

Utterback, J.M. and W.J. Abernathy (1975) 'A dynamic model of process and product innovation', *Omega*, 3(6): 639–56.

Venohr, B and Meyer, K.E. (2007). 'The German miracle keeps running: how Germany's hidden champions stay ahead in the global economy'. Available at: http://www.klausmeyer.co.uk/publications/Venohr_Meyer_The_German_Miracle070331.pdf (last accessed 27 January 2017).

Von Hippel, E. (2007) 'Horizontal innovation networks – by and for users', *Industrial and Corporate Change*, 16(2): 293–315.

Weitzman, M.L. (1998) 'Recombinant growth', *Quarterly Journal of Economics*, 113(2): 331–60.

Winter, S.G. (1984) 'Schumpeterian competition in alternative technological regimes', *Journal of Economic Behavior & Organization*, 5(3–4): 287–320.

Yang, C. and Liao, H. (2010) 'Backward linkages of cross-border production networks of Taiwanese PC investment in the Pearl River Delta, China', *Tijdschrift voor Economische en sociale Geografie* [*Journal of Economic & Social Geography*], 101(2): 199–217.

Zuboff, S. (2010) 'Creating value in the age of distributed capitalism'. Available at: http://glennas.files.wordpress.com/2010/12/creating-value-in-theage-of-distributed-capitalism-shoshana-zuboff-september-2010.pdf (last accessed 1 January 2016).

INNOVATIVE PEOPLE

7

SCOPE AND OBJECTIVES

- People as innovators.
- The human capital factor.
- Characteristics of creativity, higher levels of skills and competencies, the talent quotient.
- Individuals and teams.
- Sources of creativity.
- Leadership that galvanises innovative people.

INTRODUCTION

The basic premise of this book indicates that all three factors that contribute to innovation, namely innovative people, the innovative organisation and the innovative environment, are inextricably connected to each other. The difficulty lies in separating them and their influence over or co-relationship with each other. However, it is this problem that demands a separate understanding of each of these factors if only to consider a synthesis at the end. In this chapter we examine innovative people.

To refer to innovative people as innovators causes a degree of confusion. Innovators include organisations as well as individual people, and in common parlance creative organisations generating new products and services are often referred to as innovators. This is one of the reasons why people do not receive much attention in typical textbooks on innovation. Entrepreneurs have a better press, at least in terms of their roles in identifying opportunity and creating new firms. At best innovators are often confused with white-coat-wearing scientists, techno-babbling nerds, or Steve Jobs. But Jobs was also seen as an entrepreneur! So is the innovator also an entrepreneur?

INNOVATIVE PEOPLE, ENTREPRENEURS AND THE DISTINCTION BETWEEN ENTREPRENEURSHIP AND INNOVATION

Before it all starts becoming even more confusing, it is perhaps important to posit simple explanations that help to distinguish entrepreneurship and innovation. If by innovation we mean the development of new products, new services, new forms of organization and new business models, then we could argue that entrepreneurship is associated with the identification of opportunities for all these new forms and their value in the marketplace or in society. Add to that the necessary mobilisation of resources (including firm creation) to implement such value creation, and we have a measure of the difference between the two concepts. This explanation helps to distinguish between entrepreneurship and innovation which are often viewed synonymously, as in Shane and Venkataraman's definition of entrepreneurship as the study of

> how, by whom and with what consequences opportunities to produce future goods and services are discovered, evaluated and exploited. (2000: 218)

The distinctiveness is afforded by the acknowledgement of an organisational component, namely the formation of new organisations. It is this organisational context that distinguishes innovation from entrepreneurship (Acs and Audretsch, 2005). So it could be argued that the innovator creates new, out-of-the-box ideas, products or processes while the entrepreneur spots the commercial opportunity to take them to the market by organising resources and taking risks to start and grow an enterprise. Just as the risk taker could be both the creator of a new product and the resource provider to enable the product to be taken to the marketplace, the qualities of the entrepreneur and the innovator can also be found in one person. Argued another way, innovation can be regarded as the creation of new capacities for wealth creation, while entrepreneurship is the exploitation of these capacities using the vehicle of a new organisation. The convergence of these qualities may be afforded by separate people, or can occur at different intervals during a person's journey through life in business or social activity. Others argue that innovation creates change, but this can be outside the realm of business creation or new firm formation. Here innovation manifests itself in terms of activity which can cause a change to society, but this action may have nothing to do with starting or growing a business. A politician, such as the first Prime Minister of Israel, Ben Gurion, realising the need for change in a nation besieged by both an inclement natural and a hostile political environment, sought self-sufficiency and political strength through a reliance on technological innovations and economic strength. He too was an innovator (Senor and Singer, 2009; Mitra, 2012).

Although we can make these distinctions between the entrepreneur and the innovator, they quite often end up in a restatement of the connection between the two or the equation of concepts with many other issues. For example, there is a generally held belief that entrepreneurship is associated with any business activity and often with self-employment. In this melee there is not much room for analytical thought. So it may be better to overcome this problem of articulating the difference by accepting that the lines are blurred, and that there is not much gain to be had from making any distinction between the two. Alternatively, and perhaps more importantly, it may be useful to strip away the multiple associations of entrepreneurship with any business activity and focus instead on entrepreneurship as the necessary corollary to innovation. Fortunately, there is help at hand with Schumpeter (1942), who equated entrepreneurship with the concept of innovation and applied it to a business context. In his view the entrepreneur is the same as the innovator because he or she enables and implements change within markets through the carrying out of new combinations. These new combinations can take at least five different forms: (1) the introduction of a new good or an improvement in its quality; (2) the introduction of a new method of production; (3) the finding or opening of a new market; (4) the conquest of a new source of supply of new materials or parts; and (5) the carrying out of the new organisation of any industry (Schumpeter, 1942).

Schumpeter's definition allows us to concentrate attention on the process of making new combinations – from the making of a new good to the building of a new organisation. Taken together, the several forms can involve many different people with perhaps different entrepreneurial and innovative attributes. Looking at the forms independently, we can also surmise that each of those processes can involve a variety of individuals. The literature on entrepreneurship covers a range of psychological and behavioural characteristics of entrepreneurs who are sometimes identified as innovators or craft workers or even business managers. Sometimes these characteristics are often traced to innovators as well.

For the purpose of this chapter we take the view that the business of innovation is best understood when we can find market-based outcomes for new products, new services and new ways of creating and managing organisations. In other words, the business of innovation is carried out in the field of entrepreneurship. So even if there is a distinction to be drawn between the capacities necessary for making or serving something new in the market and the exploitation of those capacities, there is a symbiotic connection between the two. From an analytical perspective we concern ourselves here with the new or recombined capacities that help to create new products, services, business models and organisations. Inherent in this approach is the identification and use of different forms of human, social and organisational capital that reside within a number of individuals who are sometimes connected with each other as part of a team of innovators.

CAPACITY DEVELOPMENT AND INNOVATION

Accepting the relationship between innovation and entrepreneurship but distinguishing between developing capacities for making something new and exploiting those capacities, we concentrate in this chapter on capacities. Capacities can include a range of tangible and intangible, human and technological resources, and hard and soft infrastructure. Our interest here is in the human factor in capacity building. We explore the role of human capital in fostering innovation – talent, creativity, ingenuity and teams of innovators – together with the analytical distinctions between different forms of human, social, organisational and intellectual capital that are often regarded as central to the innovation process.

HUMAN CAPITAL AND INNOVATION

KNOWLEDGE, EXPERIENCE AND SKILLS

By human capital we are referring to a set of knowledge, capabilities, skills, competencies and expertise that people possess and which can be developed or improved
over time. The use of these skills and the knowledge base of individuals could generate economic returns (Schultz, 1961; Becker, 1964; 1993). This set can be acquired
through formal education and informal means of experiential, societal learning.
Becker (1964) argued that the levels of human capital and their mutation can change
the way people act (Gradstein and Justman, 2000). Both broad labour market experience and vocational experience, used productively, can be a source of competitive
advantage to individuals, organisations, economies and societies (Coleman, 1988;
Honig, 1996; Gimeno et al., 1997; Reynolds, 1997; Zucker et al., 1998; Reynolds
et al., 1999; Acs and Armington, 2004; Abubakar and Mitra, 2007; Mitra et al.,
2011). This can take place in terms of, for example, growth in regional economies
through new firm formation or indeed their dissolution (because of a lack of such
capital); in businesses, through new products and services; and for individuals,
through enhanced capacity for effecting change in their lives (Pennings et al., 1998).

The link between human capital and innovative outcomes can be examined at the
level of the individual, the firm and the industry, so it is important to distinguish how
human capital is interpreted at these different levels.

FIRM-SPECIFIC HUMAN CAPITAL

When we refer to firm-level human capital we are attending to skills and knowledge
that are obtained in a specific firm. These firm-specific skills can confer an advantage over competitors because they are inimitable or non-transferable (Penrose,
1956; Grant, 1996). Firms nurture the skills of their employees or have high levels
of absorptive capacity (Cohen and Levinthal, 1990) to acquire skills and knowledge from outside, but their firm-specific boundaries mean that they can have only
a limited amount of impact on overall innovative activity within a region or the
wider society.

INDUSTRY-SPECIFIC HUMAN CAPITAL

Industry-specific human capital is associated with the aggregate skills of all firms in
a particular industrial sector. These skill sets have a shared meaning, often evolving
from tacit know-how within the sector which may or may not be transferable to
other sectors. Researchers have argued that the knowledge created and shared from
experience within an industry can have an impact on the creation of new ventures or
the growth and improved economic performance of innovative firms which are able
to absorb knowledge generated across that industry (Siegel et al., 1993; Kenney and
von Burg, 1999; Bianchi, 2001). Saxenian (1999) argued that the success of Silicon
Valley is partly related to the presence of an intensive flow of tacit know-how among
local firms and a culture directed at open communication, which ultimately resulted

in a steady process of incremental knowledge development within that region. The problems facing the Route 128 area, however, may be explained by a local culture of secrecy and limited inter-firm cooperation.

INDIVIDUAL-SPECIFIC HUMAN CAPITAL

Individual-specific human capital refers to knowledge that is applicable to a broad range of firms and industries; it includes general managerial and entrepreneurial experience (e.g. Pennings et al., 1998), the level of academic education and vocational training (Hinz and Jungbauer-Gans, 1999).

We focus here on human capital that pertains to an individual or teams of individuals.

Becker's (1964) idea of the transformational value of human capital can be linked to Bourdieu's (1983) theory of 'conversions', which posits the argument that various forms of capital can be converted into resources and other economic dividends. A kind of linear argument promotes the idea that the more educated a person is, the more time, energy and money they spend in improving their knowledge or skill sets and the more equipped they are to derive increased benefits for themselves. But does that make people innovative? If conversion of a basic stock of knowledge and skills is to take place, is there any necessary correlation between an innovative outcome and the development of capability or the pursuit of a specific activity?

If we regard innovation as a knowledge-intensive activity, then what we mean is either the creation of new knowledge for economic or social benefit, or the combination of existing bodies of knowledge for similar outcomes. These outcomes are measured in terms of increased productivity or heightened competitiveness. What researchers argue is that on-the-job training and education and continuing investment in such activities help to increase productivity at the organisational or societal level and higher intellectual capacity at the individual level (Black and Lynch, 1996; Cannon, 2000). Overall growth in both individual intellectual capabilities and economic terms drives the need for new products, new processes and new forms of organisations.

Knowledge-intensive activity enables people to adapt to, integrate with and make sense of new situations (Weick, 1996). As we have argued elsewhere, both explicit and tacit knowledge (often referred to as uncodified, know-what) or explicit knowledge (codified in procedures, formal manuals and written documents, formal education) as explained by Polanyi (1967) are integral parts of knowledge-intensive activity which include complex problem solving and creative decision making. Embedded as they are in social structures and belief systems, these activities have the highest impact in the situations and locations where they are carried out, with the knowledge spillover effect either consolidating such knowledge locally or transferring it elsewhere. Both are theoretically predicted to increase human capital. Previous knowledge and previous entrepreneurial experience are significantly related to innovative or entrepreneurial activity, particularly when controlling for factors such as industry and gender (Robinson and Sexton, 1994; Bates, 1995; Gimeno et al., 1997).

The apparent positive relationship between human capital and innovative activity is, however, undermined by conflicting results from various empirical studies. Gimeno et al. (1997) found that human capital can increase performance, but not persistence. Moreover, it is likely that different types of human capital may be necessary at different stages in the innovation process or for varied types of innovation. R&D for example may require higher levels of education, while the implementation of a specific process in new product development may require high levels of experiential know-how. Similarly, incremental innovation may depend more on work experience, while radical innovation is best found from scientific or technological experimentation first in research laboratories.

WEAKNESSES IN THE TRADITIONAL ARGUMENTS ABOUT THE LINKS BETWEEN HUMAN CAPITAL AND INNOVATION

There are a number of other weaknesses with the argument of accumulation of individual human capital and their implications for innovation.

First, even if we were to acknowledge the view that more human capital is generally always better, social structures and systems might bias individuals either to invest excessively or to under-invest in such capital. The notion of carrying an undergraduate degree loan over one's lifetime may discourage the relatively poorer section of communities in the UK to consider alternatives to higher education if they were available. How much and when they invest in such capital may influence life career choices, including attitudes towards both entrepreneurial activity and innovation in different ways. There are, for example, many arguments about over-investment in higher education, discouraging risk taking among graduates (Davidsson and Honig, 2003).

Second, ignoring the social structures of organisations and social networks reduces our understanding of factors impacting on human capital outcomes. Although a high proportion of knowledge and skills required for innovation may reside with individuals, most modern innovations are complex. These modern innovations demand a combination and integration of multiple strands of this knowledge and skills. The conception of a new idea may well be an individual activity, but developing, testing, market search, implementation and evaluation are a collective achievement (Van de Ven, 1986; Hill et al., 2014; Isaacson, 2014). Within organisations, structures, systems and routines are created to accumulate individual knowledge for collective current and future use, create new product development teams and formal product development processes, facilitate communication, group formation and interactions that can streamline individual contributions and convert them into flowing streams of innovative outputs and outcomes (Cooper, 2001). See Chapters 5 and 6 on innovative organisations for details of how these processes work within an organisation.

Third, human capital is an aggregate measure which counts the stock of skills, qualifications and knowledge of a body of people within an organisation. Aggregate measures are useful for economists, but there is an unfortunate outcome in looking at the talent and ingenuity of people in terms of a commodity that can simply be bought and sold in the market or added or reduced in an organisation to secure profits. Fortunately, good research on human capital does not fall into this trap. What we need to understand is:

- the huge variety of people who make up such a stock, and their mindsets, attitudes and capabilities; and
- how these different capabilities and mindsets are harnessed by organisations and their leadership so that people are then willing and able to innovate when brought together to facilitate innovation. (Hill et al., 2014)

CAPABILITIES AND MINDSETS FOR INNOVATION

Let us look at mindsets and capabilities first. These are often associated with leaders who pioneer or enable innovation or with entrepreneurs who implement the innovations in the market. But this need not be the case. It is often the coming together of disparate competencies in different types of networks that makes for innovation. Leadership may of course bind these competencies together, and take it down a particular route to market.

At one end there is this notion of a 'higher set' of attitudes and motivation of people who translate intentions into results. We sometimes find examples of these 'heroes' in glitzy, 'how to do it' airport books on management practice, but also in more reasoned, research-based volumes such as Narang and Deviah's *Orbit-Shifting Innovation* (2014). As opposed to linear-mode thinking for creating, for example yet another 'app', orbit-shifting innovators identify a need to create something new and not follow history. The breakthrough that is achieved has a transformative impact on organisations, the economy and wider society. Tim Berners-Lee with his World Wide Web can be regarded as one such pioneer.

Using the planetary metaphor of gravity and orbits, Narang and Deviah explore both the impediments of culture (the 'cultural gravity' of arrogance or subservience) and the enabling factors of, for example, lateral thinking in a range of cases from cataract surgery to TV quiz shows, and cultural backdrops ranging from Korea to India. They begin by challenging the barriers that hold them and others back instead of accepting or living with the situation. In other words, they confront some manufactured gravitational pull that can hold innovations back – mindset gravity, organisation gravity, industry gravity, country gravity and cultural gravity. They identify six characteristics of 'orbit-shifting' innovation:

1. An ability to seek personal growth which is the motivation for taking up a challenge. Here it is the *size of the challenge*, not the size of the organisation or the monetary reward, but rather the difference (the 'size of the difference') it can make which is more appealing. In taking up such a challenge they are keen to move out of their comfort zone and into realms of uncertainty and the unknown.

2. The change and adoption of the *new direction* necessary for making a difference becomes the challenge and not necessarily the final destination. Stepping into the unknown does not promise definable outcomes. The mechanics, the instruments and the process of transformation are seen as more attractive for innovators than a performance goal or the metrics associated with the goal. These characteristics may be shared with many others in the business of creative activity, including academic researchers. The latter group is less concerned, for example, with the impact of their research, and is perhaps motivated more by the process of enquiry. However, innovators differ from researchers in that they do want to see an impact – technological, economic and social – which changes the way we think, do and create new openings. Unlike status quo maintenance managers, they are less interested in protecting legacies and more attracted to legacy creation. They ignore failures and are constantly looking at the progress made. They treat innovations reviews like performance reviews.

3. Seeking challenges and new directions is necessarily accompanied by a discovery-oriented mindset characterised by *fresh insights that emanate from a desire to ask questions*, but not always answers. In doing so these innovators move away from doing the same and seeking the immediate legitimacy of their peers (unlike academic researchers!). They are convinced by their art of finding value in every experience, and in every conversation. Possibilities of what could happen are a better proposition than the use of prescriptions to determine outcomes.

4. *Collaborating with stakeholders* is the key to their search for new possibilities. This is different from simply making a pitch to funders and marketing to consumers. These stakeholders are connected to the vision and realities of work of the innovator, often as end users, crowdsourced idea generators or problem solvers. As a result the stakeholders often adopt, co-own and extend the idea, the product or the service. Collaborating often involves dissent, and overcoming this through shared problem-solving platforms while synthesising different approaches forms part of the search for new directions.

5. The use of a *non-linear approach*, that is identifying the problem first rather than their individual capabilities, helps innovators to convert problems to opportunities. The ideas stem from the identification of the problem, and in asking 'what-else?' questions they allow for the original idea sometimes to grow bigger than the initial concept.

6. They combine their romantic visions for change with *realism in execution* by seeking challenges and new directions, collaborating with stakeholders and dealing with problems. They may be self-efficacious but the efficacy is evinced later in the outcomes. Non-innovators are perhaps more realistic about the vision and hence easy buyers of the idea of what cannot be done, let alone be executed.

Let us look at an example.

VIGNETTE 7.1   EXCEPTIONAL PASSION, TALENT AND TECHNOLOGY

INTRODUCTION

Nkosinathi Maphumulo (NM) dreamt about being a DJ in South Africa. He used to sketch Technics SI-1200 turntables as a child. But this dream was nearly shattered at a time when his country was participating in a bigger dream about the future with the release of Nelson Mandela from prison in 1990. On the very day (11 February) that Mandela was released, crowd violence in NM's own town in Durban led to the dislocation of this 14-year-old boy's shoulder very badly. The doctors had even considered amputation.

A BIO SKETCH

Born on 11 March 1976 in Durban in KwaZulu-Natal Province, NM is now a South African multi-award-winning record producer and DJ. He commenced his music career back in 1994 and has released four albums and one live DVD using his Johannesburg-based record label, Soulistic Music. NM majored in Jazz Studies at Technikon Nata, and then worked as a backup singer for Madala Kunene together with his two school-mates, Mnqobi Mdabe (Shota) and Thandukwazi Sikhosana (Demor). The three of them formed an Afro-pop trio called SHANA, short for 'Simply Hot And Naturally African', and were signed under Melt 2000, then headed by Robert Trunz. By 2007, as 'Black Coffee' NM had become a household name in the country's DJ scene, as he both fired up and seduced audiences with his tribally infectious, vocal-laced beats. In the same year he released his second studio album titled *Have Another One*, which topped local charts. Now at 39 he is a flourishing DJ/producer! He is probably one of the most influential musicians on the African continent after having obtained his big break soon after being chosen as a participant for his country in the 2004 Red Bull Music Academy held in Cape Town. In September 2015 he was selected as the 'Breakthrough DJ Of The Year' on Awards at Ibiza, only a little over 2 weeks after his latest album, *Pieces Of Me*, was released. The main instruments in his repertoire are vocals, keyboards, sampler, percussion and a synthesiser.

EMBRACING TECHNOLOGY, OVERCOMING ADVERSITY

Where and how did it all begin for a young man who suffered such a shattering injury? NM ignored his physio's advice and taught himself how to use the music production software Cakewalk, and managed to get his dream turntables at the age of 22. What appeared to constrain him were the doubts about his mainly disabled and immobile left arm. He would worry about carrying a crate of records, taking a record out with one hand, playing it and then returning it into its cover. This is where his awareness and adoption of modern technology came to the rescue.

THE INNOVATION

NM uses a custom rig with bespoke Pioneer 350-CDJs, including USB sticks, to ena-ble him to do the mixing with one hand while he puts the hand of his damaged left arm in his pocket. With technology at his disposal NM makes 'soulful live instrumentation with Logic-created rhythms'. This is 'Black Coffee' music, with NM producing his new album for the influential dance label, 'Ultra'. Alongside his music production NM has also a created retail app for South African music called 'GongBox', motivated by the need to fill a gap in the market for South African music. As he states, 'You can't find South African music anywhere online. I couldn't even find my debut album there!'.

FUTURE DIRECTIONS

Where can Black Coffee go in the future? Would he be South Africa's answer to Spotify or even Apple? This will be his challenge, as will the need to persuade an emerging

(Continued)

(Continued)

Internet country to buy MP3s. It seems NM's evolution as a music-producing, high-tech entrepreneur has its own riff in Mandela's comment: 'It always seems impossible until it's done!'

Quote from Red Bull Studios:

Considering his meteoric rise to fame, it would be easy to stereotype Black Coffee as just another black diamond, a BEE beat magnet out to mine the insatiable upwardly mobile urban house-party market. But as he proved on his South African Music Award-winning album Home Brewed, this DJ and producer defies convention. Sidestepping Afro-house clichés and stage-managed highs in favour of restrained sophistication, Black Coffee's penchant is for true Afropolitan house: home-brewed but trendsetting, fashion-conscious and future-focused. Expect almost sculptural balance and beauty'. (www.redbull studios.com)

Source: Morris (2015)

For Maphumulo, a passion for playing and making music as a DJ was the challenge, especially when we factor in the disability that he suffered from his accident at a time of high euphoria in his country. Instead of succumbing to his disability he asks 'what else?' and collaborates with the technology providers, and social media, not only to produce his music, but crucially to put exciting new music on the new media map. Not only does he take new directions in terms of technology, but he uses the technology to extend the music platform (the app) and to challenge potentially the big label global incumbents by providing a platform for African dance music. This is not simply a story of overcoming disability, but one of creating music in a new form using relevant new technology. The Mandela quote probably sums up best the arguments used by Narang and Deviah (2014).

What is being referred to above is not limited to individual capability or a flash of genius. The set of six behavioural characteristics is a complex compendium of attitudes, behaviour and action. We can see this being manifest in the solo efforts of an individual innovator such as Maphumulo and also in larger creative organisations.

Maphumulo's story illustrates an unusual capacity to fight the odds as an individual and to achieve the heights of excellence not seen in common situations. In adapting himself to his circumstances he takes a non-linear approach, defying expectations of limitations traditionally associated with disability. His dreams may be part of his romantic vision, but a focused realism of execution can be found in both his dedication to his muse and to the effective way he sets about organising a music label and working towards cultivating a digital music community in South Africa.

Maphumulo's innovation narrative may reflect best the realisation of the creative abilities of an individual. In organisations, especially in larger firms, routines and established modes of conduct may not have room for the flowering of such talent. But then this view precludes organisations from building on and harnessing talent. If we assume that organisations can be innovative, then part of that identity is derived from the roles individuals play in those organisational arenas individually and as a collective. So let us see if we can find the mix of creative capabilities in an organisational setting, where individually carrying people both inside (fellow workers) and outside (customers, suppliers distributors, partners) the organisation is part of the creative process making innovation come alive. How does the innovative person navigate his or her way through set structures, routines, the rigours of quarterly returns and other constraints?

VIGNETTE 7.2   GAMING AND THE REAL, INNOVATIVE MASTER CHIEF

INTRODUCTION

Take Bonnie Ross, a 48-year-old woman in charge of Microsoft's gaming franchise, *Halo 5: Guardians*, considered to be one of the biggest game releases of 2015. She runs a studio within Microsoft, called 343 Industries, where she manages 600 staff and oversees a budget of more than $100 million for *Halo 5* alone. In *Halo 5*, Microsoft is betting on a comeback in games and recouping the investment it made in the Xbox One which never quite caught up with Sony's PlayStation 4. Both the Halo and the Xbox emerged in 2001 with the former being responsible for Xbox's survival, according to Microsoft executives.

Microsoft has licensed the Halo name to a wide range of products, from special editions of Monopoly to a full body armour suit (that sold for $450), and even a novel entitled *Halo: The Fall of Reach* which was published before the first game was available on the market. Over the past 14 years consumers have spent $4.6 billion on these Halo products, about 25% of them on non-game merchandise.

BIO SKETCH

Bonnie Ross arrived in the video games business by chance. Having given up her interest in volleyball because her father wanted her to something 'useful', she studied technical communications and computer science at Colorado State University in the USA. During this time she acquired an internship at IBM, and on graduating applied for jobs at three major organisations, of which NeXT and Apple did not respond. Microsoft did, and in 1989 Ross started work there, but quickly lost interest in drafting manuals to forage instead with a team developing a basketball game for Microsoft's early-stage game business. Her knowledge of sports was probably the motivation and the draw for this involvement and indulgence in creative work. Her first titles were developed for the PC and then the Xbox, and included a portfolio of games called *Fusion Frenzy* that debuted with the original Xbox console. Having managed a number of games after that, Ross eventually chose to focus on Halo in 2007.

(Continued)

(Continued)

OVERCOMING STEREOTYPES AND CONSTRAINTS

At the time of Ross's entry into the world of Halo, most of her colleagues were not entirely comfortable with Halo, thinking it was the end of the franchise and worrying about whether she had taken the right decision for a young person with considerable future career prospects. Could this reservation have been anything to do with stereotypical assumptions about the occupations and ambitions of women? Ross stuck to it and demonstrated a determination to make things work. 'The thing I asked for was: If I take it over, I want to be George Luca. I want to know everything, and I want to do things differently', Ross reflected during an interview with *Bloomberg*.

THE INNOVATION

The studio that created Halo in 2000 was called Bungie. Creative tensions led to this studio being spun out of Microsoft, but the latter held onto Halo and formed 343 studios to run it instead. The creative 'deserters' in Bungie did not quite give up and have gone on to make the video game *Destiny*, which is one of Halo's key competitors. The world of video games, with its stereotypical anti-establishment and non-corporatist approach to work, assumed that the large corporate culture of Microsoft would kill Halo. When a guy called O'Connor who had moved to Bungie helped Microsoft with the transition, he was surprised at Ross's depth and breadth of knowledge of the narrative of the fiction and the games. Indeed, O'Connor left Bungie and returned to Microsoft to work with Ross in the new studio which was named after a deadly piece of artificial intelligence that appears in many Halo games.

The team started a new lease of life in what was previously a hardware store in Kirkland, a suburb of Seattle and near to Microsoft's headquarters at Redmond. The team believe in the building which they consider to be just about perfect for their work, especially the coding in an open floor plan but with little natural light. Ross makes a telling comment about how the ambience is conducive to creative team work: 'During game development you can feel the pulse. You can walk in and tell if we're off or not, and whether morale is up or down, because we all act as one.' While the headquarters has room for about 230 people only, the rest of 343's employees operate from another building down the block. The full roster of people at 343 includes computer programmers or designers, cloud computing experts, a professional team of competitive game players, and a psychologist who works with user interfaces. A group of people are dedicated to sound only because most of the noises are customised for the game. Typically, these sound engineers are known to have gone to a gun range in California to record bullets whistling past their ears! A visit to a concert hall in Prague was made with the intention of obtaining a proper angelic chorus for the 'big moments', and a hot spring in Iceland provided the right kind of extraterrestrial ambient sounds.

Ross's attention to detail is well captured by the *Bloomberg* interviewer. He refers to her meetings with the consumer-products team and the way she makes choices about materials and products that are outside her direct interest in gaming, especially when she seeks reassurance about possible manufacturing shortages. Ross is a rare species, a woman in the games industry, which is dominated by men. Internet trolls routinely and mercilessly harass women in the industry. She feels that her job is to remind her colleagues that girls also play video games, and she has insisted that the fully formed female characters play prominent roles in *Halo 5*. Equally, she has ensured that the Halo T-shirts are made in cuts for women too.

One constant feature of Ross's style of working on constant innovation practice is to confer openly and readily with equal partners in their specific areas of excellence. Interacting with colleagues like O'Connor, who runs Halo's fiction business, enables her to understand better the connections between content (the story) with the spin-off game and the iPhone app that followed. While O'Connor suggests that there may not be much to worry about in respect of mainstream acceptance of the 'novelistic stylings' in a multibillion-dollar product, Ross acknowledges the value that lies in creating greater awareness of the game which she likens to 'world-building'. Then there are the regular tests and experiments with the creative director and the involvement of guest players. As a sports fan, Ross has given the Seattle Seahawks an open invitation to come and engage in multiplayer combat with her in-house team of gamers. Multiplayer gaming and getting it right are considered essential for 343.

In November 2014, *Halo: Master Chief Collection* was released. Making available a single disc for the new console with remastered versions of the first four games was a smart way to allow fans to play on the new Xbox while generating more revenue from the old games. Routine interactions and taking the games to be tested in employees' homes also allow Ross and her team to work out why simple mistakes occur, such as scheduling a time for people to log in when there is football on TV. This is where Ross as both a gamer and a sports fan trumps the 'nerdy' preoccupations of gamers. Being aware of the world in which consumers will use the innovation that is launched is as important as the fine tuning of the technical and financial aspects of the product.

REFLECTIONS

Each Halo launch has been larger than before but there are now fewer Xbox ones. This compares with more Xbox 360s when *Halo 4* was released onto the market. So this could potentially reduce sales, something which makes Ross and her executives not too confident about the strength of *Halo 5*. Perhaps Microsoft has waited too long to develop and launch it.

Source: Adapted from *Bloomberg* (2015)

Bonnie Ross's Microsoft journey shows us that creative talent can be nurtured in larger organisations too. Here, the effort that is made to secure innovative outcomes centres around the coalescence of multiple levels of expertise, a willingness to learn from others, and a strong motivation for connecting one's goals and objectives with the capabilities of various others in the organisation. We can reflect on Bonnie Ross and find in her career path how innovative people find expression of their strong personal interest by marrying a set of key capabilities with the environment in which they deploy them. A strong sense of new directions for the Xbox, especially under highly competitive circumstances, is based on an equally strong desire for personal growth and mixed with a good understanding of collaborative work with key internal stakeholders and prospective customers. A commitment to realism in execution is also seen in the various ways in which she tests the new game to ensure that it plays out best for Microsoft's future in this sector.

We can reconfigure the set of six behavioural characteristics of Narang and Deviah (2014) in terms of generic skills and attributes that underpin innovative behaviour, which are drawn from the literature on trait theories (supporting the idea of what comes from within us) and social cognitive approaches (focusing on behaviour and attitudes and emphasising what can be learnt).

SKILLS AND ATTRIBUTES

In developing a tool – the Youth Innovation Skills Measurement Tool – for NESTA in the UK, Chell and Athayde (2009) refer to five generic skills underpinning innovative behaviour. These include:

(a) 'creativity (imagination, connecting ideas, tackling and solving problems, curiosity);
(b) self-efficacy (self-belief, self-assurance, self-awareness, feelings of empowerment, social confidence);
(c) energy (drive, enthusiasm, motivation, hard work, persistence and commitment);
(d) risk propensity (a combination of risk tolerance and the ability to take calculated risks); and
(e) leadership (vision and the ability to mobilise commitment).

Interestingly, many of these attributes are also found among entrepreneurs, lending credence to the confusion between entrepreneurship and innovation which we reflected upon at the beginning of this chapter. What is missing from this list is opportunity identification and resolution and the mobilising of resources, as distinctive attributes of an entrepreneur, which if added to the list above could potentially exacerbate the confusion.

In examining attributes and characteristics, trait theorists may concede the view that people are not necessarily born with specific skills. They do, however, assume that attitudes, aptitudes, abilities and behaviour are formed early in life and stay with people because personality is a fairly stable variable and also because interactions between genetic make-up and experience occur early on in life Thus innovators are born and we cannot increase the supply of innovators artificially. Judging by the fact that major, radical, orbit-shifting innovations do not occur every day or regularly, one may be inclined to endorse the born-innovator concept. But then what innovations are we referring to and why do we assume that radical innovations are the only source of transformation in societies? Is all behaviour neutral and do environmental conditions or political factors affect what we innovate and where? Radical innovations do not fall like manna from heaven, but are often the unseen, breakthrough outcomes after many years of accumulated incremental innovation. As Pringle (2013) notes, human creativity 'simmered for hundreds of years before reaching a boil'.

The idea of accumulated creativity and innovation, the different forms of innovation emerging at different times, suggests that the human endeavour necessary to make innovation work has a social function.

SOCIALISING HUMAN CAPITAL

Social factors underpinning human, innovative endeavour include beliefs, attitudes, values and skills. They are influenced by social interactions among people and in or across cultures, in various institutions that stretch from the temple to the neighbourhood club. If interactions lead to a change of behaviour as a result of the influence then that means that a certain amount of learning takes place. Bandura (1986) refers to this form of learning as 'social learning' which, as Chell and Athayade (2009) state, matches the set of evolving attitudes and values with behaviour and goals. The lack of such a match results in cognitive dissonance (Festinger, 1957). But can we expect consistency in matching behaviour and beliefs or could cognitive dissonance allow for new creative tensions as beliefs get ruptured or behaviour deviates from the norm? Whichever way we look at these issues we find that innovative behaviour that leads to economic and social development is informed by a cognitive process, based on the experience and ability of creative people to use their ideas, knowledge and skills to develop something new or novel of value to themselves and, crucially, others.

In both the cases discussed so far, the navigation of the contexts and the environment in which innovative people find themselves is perhaps the overriding skill which draws on creativity, energy, risk taking and the other attributes listed above. It would be erroneous to suggest that either Maphumulo or Ross necessarily operated in the most conducive environments. In both cases there were possibly greater impediments of different kinds than entirely favourable conditions. Maphumulo worked through his personal constraints, but crucially in an economic and social climate that was not conducive to the fulfilment of his interests. Who knows whether Ross would have achieved more at Sony, and what about her role as a female leader in a world of mainly male gamers? We do not as yet know whether *Halo 5* will rescue Xbox from stagnation. Each person had their particular conditions and their own set of constraints. More than their attributes, it is in their use and application for achieving specific goals that we find innovative people creating, making possible and enabling the emergence of something new.

We may debate endlessly about the right or optimal mix of skills and attributes necessary for innovation. Creativity, which subsumes imagination, is often regarded as the key attribute among innovators. Generating an idea needs both imagination and skill, but spotting an opportunity for that idea to work in the market needs a social context. If there is insufficient self-efficacy or effectuation, then the creative spirit may disconnect with the opportunities, and if there is a low threshold of tolerance of risk then calculated risk taking may not be possible to see through the creation of a new product. Then there is leadership which marshals all the four other attributes and works with a disparate talent grouping to drive the innovation process. Various tropes of abstraction and sampled reality have offered insights and speculated on their universality, more so because of the simple recognition that we are seemingly hardwired to create something new and desirable. What we do know is that the full set of skills is constantly applied in experimentation with technology, whether that be improving designs to creating spacecraft in the USA or making little gifts or souvenirs representing the Loch Ness monster in Scotland.

Inherent, but not necessarily explicit, in the innovation process and in the capability of people to engage with this process, is the unique ability to stretch the imagination, to mix, for example, sardines with white chocolate as Ferran Adria thinks is eminently possible in a world of meaningful change. We turn to another vignette to see how such 'stretch works'.

VIGNETTE 7.3   MIXING SARDINES WITH WHITE CHOCOLATE

INTRODUCTION

Ferran Adrià is a chef. He closed down his world-famous restaurant to start a foundation for innovation in 2000, asking, 'who says you can't mix sardines and white chocolate?'. Ferran works with a handful of web developers and user-interface designers and a creative team from his celebrated restaurant 'elBulli' in his *taller*, or workshop, in an eighteenth-century building in Barcelona. His vision is to create an online database that will host every possible item of gastronomic knowledge ever collected together – 'La Bullipedia'.

THE CREATIVE MIND AND TECHNOLOGY

How does Ferran look at products and information, which in his case is essentially about food? He refers to working with white asparagus as a scientific process and asks questions about what you can do with asparagus creatively. You can inject it with truffle oil, you can cut it up into little pieces and never identify them afterwards. Then within the website one can move forwards and backwards and curiously think of rhubarb and imagine how that vegetable can be injected. The focus here is on the technique, which is also the starting point, the chemistry, biology, physics and mechanics, rather than the product or its ingredients, the same creative focus which was behind the enormous success of his elBulli restaurant. The *Restaurant Magazine* had voted elBulli the best in the world in 2002 and subsequently 4 years on the trot from 2006 to 2009. In 2011, 2 million people sought a table at the restaurant, and there were at least 6,000 applications for internship for every stage in his kitchen. Over 24 years he and his team had created 1,846 dishes. Three Michelin stars and an appellation as 'undoubtedly the most brilliant creator in the world' by Joël Robuchon, the 26 Michelin star chef, crown his achievements.

CONSTANT INNOVATION

A life of endorsements, branches across the world and television appearances as 'super celebrity' chef would have been expected of Ferran following the extraordinary success of his restaurant. Instead, in 2010 he announced that elBulli was to close down. The industry and general press, including the *Financial Times*, concluded that 'la cocina de vanguardia' – the new wave of Spanish molecular gastronomy – was at an end. For Ferran, however, the limit of innovation in haute cuisine had been reached. The announcement of the closure of elBulli was followed within weeks of another pronouncement, namely his intention to set up the elBulli Foundation, a centre for innovation where digital technology would remake and rethink haute cuisine and offer a road map for innovation for other activities.

Some 8,000 pages of the elBulli General Catalogue contain the 'genome of cuisine', a huge compendium providing details of Ferran Adrià's repertoire. In order to innovate he felt the need to move away from the concept of the restaurant to work out procedures for collaboration and address the nature of creativity by asking questions about the source of ideas and how they could be generated. Ferran's working life as a chef offers some clues to the answer to these questions.

Since the nineteenth century, gastronomy has been concerned with the perfection of dishes, with most kitchens operating along the lines of 'brigade de cuisine', which is a hierarchical system of specialisation where the kitchen is divided into sections supervised by a chef de cuisine. When Spain became the heart of the gastronomic world in the 1990s with chefs such as Ferran Adrià and Joan and Jordi Roca, they wondered, in common with most innovators, how things could be changed and improved from the way the incumbents were running the industry. Ferran was offered the opportunity to move to Barcelona by a customer, the sculptor Xavier Medina-Campeny, in 1992. It was the start of a 'revolution'.

For the first time chefs came together not to prepare dishes, but to study and commit themselves to theoretical work that would extend the scope of thinking and imagining what could be accomplished with food. All aspects of the discoveries they made were recorded in minute detail, photographed at each stage of evolution of any one dish. All ingredients were purchased fresh daily from the la Boqueria market and the chefs were also sent to hardware stores. Young chefs passing thought the town could walk in and find out what was being made as they were welcomed in a spirit of openness to and networking with the trade, unlike the secretive practice and tendencies of most chefs. The sharing of ideas was considered important for the continuous improvement of processes and products. The aim was to deconstruct whatever went before, to take chicken curry and treat each ingredient differently and remake it with new textures. Liquid would be mixed with alginic acid to create new spheres of different textures and consistencies such as 'caviar of melon', or to discover hidden tastes and smells. More a research project than a kitchen, the instruments and tools were more likely to be candyfloss machines, soda siphons, liquid nitrogen, dehydrators and syringes.

The Foundation is conceived as a place for experimentation 'by processes, efficiency and a way of auditing creativity', dealing with cuisine as discourse and communicating with other disciplines of science, the arts, philosophy and technology, presenting the findings through the Internet and producing creativity and talent. This vision of creativity is also to be found in the design of the Foundation complex. A number of new carbon-free buildings include a brainstorming area shaped like a gourd which doubles up as a cinema. An archive is found on top of the kitchen, an 'idearium' accommodates reference materials and workstations, and there is a plan to build an observatory of coral.

THEORY AND EMPIRICS

Underpinning the creativity is a search for a rigorous theoretical framework to help build the culinary database. The framework is divided into five areas, all as part of

(Continued)

(Continued)

an evolutionary map of eBulli's discoveries – organisation and philosophy, products, technology, elaborations, and styles and characteristics. This is consolidated with a highly imaginative taxonomy including the following:

- Products with soul.
- What is a sauce?
- Parmesan serum.
- Provocation, play, irony, decontextualisation.
- Smell, an overlooked sense.
- Sequences as micro-menus.

Underlying this creative experiment is serious empirical work that Ferran has carried out with, for example, a professor of experimental psychology at Oxford University, Charles Spence, on augmenting the taste and flavour of a dish by matching how, and on what, food is offered. Strawberry mousse is supposed to taste 10% sweeter when served on a white plate than on a black one. There is more than a hint of interest, and perhaps serious work, in neuroscience or 'neurogastronomy' according to Charles Spence.

The *Modern Gastronomy A to Z: A Scientific and Gastronomic Lexicon* that Ferran and his brother tried to produce is a major compendium of a cookbook that scrutinises ingredients at their chemical level. A periodic table at the centre of the book focuses on how food reacts under specific conditions and the different uses to which it might be put. An example helps to explain this work. Instead of a recipe for mayonnaise we find an entry for emulsion. This describes the condiment made from egg yolk, oil and vinegar as a 'colloidal dispersion of two immiscible liquids'. Every entry is accompanied by the title of the ingredient, the chemical code, a definition, and the various uses and practical information for cooks. In the latter half of the 1990s, Ferran took a keen interest in the way food was served and eaten. The displays of metal, glass, paper and slate dishes, and of multi-coloured plasticine maquettes representing the size and position of elements in elBulli dishes on the plate, bear testimony to this interest. So does the offering of some courses in some of his restaurants where knives and forks are not available and the food is eaten with one's hands.

Much of Ferran's fare could be described as an extraordinary mix of art and science. There is art and magic in molecular gastronomy. At the same time, frying an egg is also a chemical process, while cuisine stretches as a transversal discipline across homes, restaurants, hospitals, schools, airports, fashion and new technologies!

Ferran's Foundation is designed by a Catalan architect, Enric Ruiz-Geli, and his advisory group of thought leaders include the economist and Nobel laureate Joseph Stiglitz. Telefónica is a sponsor, supervising the technology following a relationship that started in 2010 when the telecoms company hired Stiglitz as an ambassador, and opened Ferran's eyes to the wonders of technology alongside his interest in chemistry and physics.

The technology platform is an extension of the Foundation's creative agenda. Together with data from elBulli, LaBullipedia uses open data and visualisation to investigate where innovation could take place next. A distribution network generates video content daily, allowing users to post ideas for food pairing and suggestions for apps. The elBulli archive is available online, while food blogs are catalogued within the site. While the chefs curate recipes the technology team builds an archive using semantic technology. This helps users to discover relationships which they could not have found otherwise.

At the heart of a fantastic journey of food with algorithms, the opening of new restaurants and bars which serve liquid ravioli, spherical olives and water melon infused with sangria, the lecturing at Harvard, and even the movie, *El Bulli: Cooking in Progress*, showing worldwide, and the connection of the digital world to the physical one, is Ferran's all-consuming interest – the human emotion. Like many other celebrities, he has used both the power of fame and innovative thinking to move from one creative direction to another. Schwarzenegger switched from acting to politics, P.Diddy and Jay Z from music to sports clothing and spirits.

CHALLENGES AND FUTURE DIRECTIONS

Nothing stirs the innovative Ferran more than food and the technology in a constantly changing environment. This is particularly relevant for Ferran as he faces the biggest challenge in his new frontier, and that is actually to make the Foundation work. Stacked against him are local environmentalists who are deeply concerned about the possible impact of his grand scheme on the landscape of Catalonia, the thousands of tourists who are expected to throng his foundation and the locale. It is unclear whether he wants to run his Foundation as another start-up. Existing as it does in the sphere of ideas it is uncertain how he will translate his ideas into a viable project. For now, knowledge and creativity are his two main strands of creative destruction. Knowledge creates while creativity deconstructs the process by which knowledge is created.

But what about the reality of such a 'dream'? At the conclusion of one of many long monologues, Mr Adrià was asked what he expected the Foundation's budget to be for 2015. He took a breath. 'One million euros,' he said. In response to a quizzical expression of doubt – moments earlier, he said he intended to have a staff approaching 75 – he explained: 'We will hire a lot of interns.'

In the meantime, projects abound with each leap in the knowledge creation and deconstruction processes. The El Bulli Lab is the Barcelona-based office where people with creativity and knowledge (the El Bulli DNA) do their work. Then there is 6W Food, which is expected to operate as a cross between a science museum, an art museum and a house of culinary innovation. A search engine known as SeaUrching (named in part for the delicacy) is complemented by a language to describe gastronomy known as Huevo (Spanish for egg) which could eventually become a digital language coded for use by refrigerators or other kitchen appliances. In the meantime he is working on a side project as a consultant with Cirque du Soleil, stating that 'We are helping create a restaurant that is not a restaurant.'

Innovation beckons as Ferran Adrià conjures up food in a future of algorithms and creativity.

Sources: Adapted from Williams (2012) and Borden (2015)

Ferran Adrià's story is not a common story of innovators. The original list of skills and attributes, referred to by Chell and Athayde (2009), appear to fall a bit short in capturing the essence of innovative capability of an unusual and extraordinary creative person such as Ferran Adrià. Perhaps any reductionist approach at modelling innovative behaviour would fail, not least because many such people are outliers, and outliers are all different not only from the norm but from other outliers too. But then innovators do not always share common stories. Our analytical search for common characteristics offers possibilities for comparison but not recipes for cloning! The greater the variety of innovators in any organisation or even in an economy, the greater the possibility for change through innovation.

Ferran Adrià's story does, however, illustrate clearly the evolution, including the stops and starts and the unexpected directions taken in the process of evolution of the innovative mindset. To understand the evolution of this mindset and the portfolio of innovative skills and competencies we may benefit from insights from history and archaeology. Innovation is often associated with thinking outside the box, so it may be useful to stretch our thinking beyond the traditional ramparts of academic disciplines that provide our sources of knowledge and understanding of the subject of innovation. Stretching our learning back to trace the history of innovative people could offer unique insights.

THE EVOLUTION OF INNOVATIVE PEOPLE

Historians and archaeologists argue that our early ancestors left little or no visible record of innovation for nearly 3.4 million years. Livelihood and sustenance were made possible with digging or jabbing sticks to obtain food. Acts of ingenuity of an extraordinary kind probably occurred 2.6 million years ago in Ethiopia when wandering hominids began to flake cobblestones worn by water to create cutting tools. They were able to do this with hammer stones. Researchers have not found anything beyond minor incremental advances to the handheld axe for nearly 1.6 million years, which they then followed with a long-held view that about 40,000 years ago, in the Upper Palaeolithic period, *Homo sapiens* suddenly went on a creative, inventive spree in Europe, decorating cave walls with paintings of Ice Age animals, making shell-bead necklaces, and breaking into pieces a range of new stone and bone tools. This inventive surge was attributed to a random genetic mutation which sparked off a huge leap in cognitive capability and ignited a creative 'big bang'. New evidence from archaeologists in South Africa suggests, however, that art and advanced technology have antecedents going back to a time before the emergence of *Homo sapiens*, 200,000 years ago. What we refer to as the force of innovation today is likely to have evolved over hundreds of years due to a mix of biological and social factors (Pringle, 2013).

Perhaps about 77,000 years ago the occupants of Sibudu Cave, about 40 kilometres from Durban, South Africa, used an astonishing knowledge of local vegetation to create a brittle form of bedding with rushes and other plants for sitting and sleeping on. To make these beddings the occupants used leaves from *Cryptocarya woodii*, a tree which contained natural insecticides and larvicides that are effective against malaria-carrying mosquitoes. These creative Sibudu people crafted bows and arrows, and researchers have found that the cave occupants were probably also 'competent chemists, alchemists and pyrotechnologists' (Wadley et al., 2011, cited in Pringle, 2013), who were probably the original standard bearers of technical ingenuity. So were the hunter–gatherers from 100,000 and 72,000 years ago, and the Neanderthals who 300,000 years ago made birch-bark-tar glue to fasten stone flakes to wood handles and fabricated hafted tools.

Something else, however, distinguishes the depth and range of innovation that modern humans have shown to be capable of when compared with our remote forbears. That has to do with brain size, with scientists claiming that even 100,000 years ago *Homo sapiens* had a mean capacity of 1,330 cubic centimetres and 100 billion neurons transmitting information across approximately 0.15 quadrillion synapses, demonstrating the connection between intellectual productive gain and the size of the brain. The large size of the brain allowed for free association of different stimuli and the encoding of multiple messages from a specific episode.

Crucially, what helped with survival was not simply the free association of stimuli but analytic thought, which enabled them to move from one mode of thought to another. What lies beyond such analytic capability is referred to by anthropologists as cultural ratcheting, the ability to take the ideas of others and 'put their own twist on them, adding one modification after another until we end up with something new and very complex', from one individual to another and from one generation to another. At the heart of this cultural ratcheting are the social skills and various cognitive abilities referred to earlier in this chapter. The crunch came with demography, according to evolutionary geneticists such as Mark Thomas of University College London (Pringle, 2013). The larger the group of people, the greater the chance of an individual learning an innovation, suggesting that, much more than the ability of the smart individual, it is the group of connected individuals who lead on the innovation front. This sense of a demographic network now enjoys almost unlimited collective advantage with the use of the World Wide Web, especially in urban regions where more and more people crowd together sharing ideas, inventions, resources and passions.

Just as the larger brain enables free association of stimuli, so indeed does the larger physical space in which we connect and engender creativity and innovation for the community. The complexity of the mind is associated with the connectivity of networks of people to help innovation thrive. It is in the mix of different innovative people and in the layering of their capabilities across both space and time that we find the essence of innovation and the value of innovative people. The management of the innovation process can, therefore, be read as the management of collective genius.

MANAGING COLLECTIVE GENIUS

So far, in whatever we have examined about innovative people, we find that it is in the social process and the social interactions among different people that innovation is obtained within an organisation, the economy and wider societies. What makes this possible is the appropriate blending and management of the varied mindsets, skills and resources. We could, therefore, argue that in referring to innovative people we are really reflecting on the collective dynamics of multiple individuals in specific contexts.

Let us consider how innovative people are organised and managed in innovative organisations. This not only helps us to connect people to organisations, but also emphasises the point about innovative organisations being different from others because of innovative people, and how they come together to make innovative products, services and business models that underpin their high-impact productive value.

VIGNETTE 7.4   ANIMATING CREATIVITY

INTRODUCTION

Hill et al. (2014) explain the significance of this issue with reference to Pixar Animation Studios and how they have managed to produce blockbusters continually for nearly 20 years now, commanding the respect of technologists, the business community and, crucially, film makers. Pixar's success is attributed less to the solitary, inspirational genius of Steve Jobs, who bought the original company, Lucas Film, in 1986, but more to the hundreds of people, their wealth of ideas, their work, and the massive amounts of investment and, critically, the unique environment that Ed Catmull, the computer animation pioneer, helped to create. Catmull is known for his clever and dexterous approach to management, some of the secrets of which he shares with the world in his best-selling book, *Creativity Inc*. (2014).

THE CATMULL CREATIVE COLLECTIVE

As President of Pixar, Catmull provided a form of leadership that fostered and enabled innovation. This he continues to do with John Lasseter, the Chief Creative Officer, of both Pixar and Disney Animation Studios (Disney acquired Pixar for $7.4 billion and installed Lassater and Catmull to shape the creative culture on Disney's own shaky creative studio).

It is impossible to extricate the leadership of Catmull from the work of the creative collective at Pixar. This is because every aspect of any film that Pixar produces – 'everything, down to the tiniest speck of dust or the subtle flow of a shadow across a character's face' – is selected, created, invented, inserted and implemented by each one of the hundreds of people involved. Figure 7.1 shows a summary of the overall process.

THE INNOVATION PROCESS

The editorial process involves the director's idea of a story and the working out of the story through many revisions in the story department for between 12 and 18 months. The ensuing description of the story leads to a script, which is then translated into images or individual storyboards which in turn are cut to produce reels. The art department works on the 'look' and realisation of 'characters', while the editor together with the director cut the storyboards and create reels that bind the art, the dialogue and

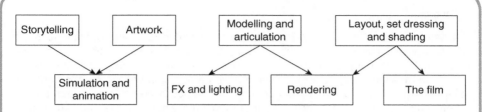

FIGURE 7.1 Pixar and the film-making process

the music, with the reels being updated and refined at every stage of the production process. Once the work moves to various groups of artists and technicians, they use design software to create many thousands of digital components that make up the final film, with each group being entrusted with different creative activities such as digital settings, digital models of the characters of the stories, and layout work scoping how the characters and different objects will be shot. While lighting experts will manage the amount of light to fall, animators will define and specify the precise movements of the characters. Then there are those who create the surface textures (skin and hair, for example), the way in which light interacts with those surfaces, and simulators who produce the digital versions of the movements or actions of the characters, not forgetting the special effects people working on complex movements of objects and characters. Finally, hundreds of computers 'render' or use the instructions for the earlier stages to work out each movie frame (over 100,000 frames), frame by frame, at 24 frames per second (Hill et al., 2014).

Creativity is expected to prevail at every step of the process described above, and the leader is dependent on all the creative people's actions at each step. The creative production act is a synthesis of the creative actions of all the people involved. What the leader does is create an environment for:

- collaboration – allowing for the mix of talent and for the necessary interaction of ideas, using a number of instruments such as staff watching and discussing presentations of work in progress;
- engagement in discovery-driven learning – working through a messy process by solving problems;
- encouragement of integrative decision making – experimenting with and integrating ideas, making integrative choices based on the mix of those ideas, combining and recombining them as appropriate.

ORGANISATIONAL PLURALITY

Appropriate mechanisms with unusual organisational arrangements need to be in place to optimise the value of collaboration, engagement in discovery-driven learning and integrative decision making. In Pixar, this mechanism is called the Braintrust. Braintrust is a kind of rolling collective of the best of the creative brains supporting and guiding every film during the development phase. The membership of the group changes, but it grew out of a core team of highly distinguished directors, including

(Continued)

(Continued)

Lasseter, Andrew Stanton, Peter Docter and Le Unkrich (directors of films such as *Finding Nemo, Monsters Inc.* and *Toy Story 3*). Catmull and Lasseter describe the Braintrust in eloquent terms. They speak of a group that gets together to address a problem, meeting every 12 weeks, starting with a screening of the most recent cut of a film, and then providing notes on what is deemed acceptable and what needs improvement. But the notes are not seen as 'mandatory notes'; rather they are instruments of open and constructive feedback. Their notes do not carry any more weight than those of the animators. No one owns an idea exclusively, and they all rely on stimulating each other with their range of ideas. As Lasseter notes in his interview by Franklin-Wallis of *Wired*, 'At the end what you have is this feeling that everybody has shared ownership and being proud of the whole thing'.

The notion of a plural identity underpins the capabilities of Pixar's innovative people.

Sources: Adapted from Hill et al. (2014); Franklin-Wallis (2015)

These three dimensions – collaboration, engagement in discovery-driven learning and encouragement of integrative decision making – permeate the work of all the organisations that Hill et al. (2014) studied, including HCL Technologies, eBay, Pentagram, Google and others. Isaacson finds the same strength of collaboration among hackers, geniuses and geeks in the creation of the protocols of the Internet which, as he states, 'were devised by peer collaboration and the resulting system seemed to have embedded in its genetic code a propensity to facilitate such collaboration' (2014: 4). In common with other breakthrough innovations, such as the printing press, the idea of collaboration (open networks in the case of the Internet) has opened up opportunities for citizen innovators not circumscribed by traditional or restrictive gatekeepers of knowledge. As Isaacson notes, collaborative and networked creativity marks the interaction between humans, between humans and machines, and between arts and sciences. Here too we find the idea of cultural ratcheting as we found among *Homo sapiens* of 100,000 years ago.

We can count on collaboration and networking skills to be at the forefront of the list of competencies, behaviour and actions of innovative people. It is in the identification of different capabilities that organisations can best harness diverse talent for innovative outcomes. Assessing the human capital of people is one approach, but there is a tendency here to use a definitive set of exemplary attributes that pertain to 'special people' (think of Steve Jobs or Jack Ma) and to try and measure capabilities on, for example, a scale of 'poor to excellent' attributes. Doing so does not help to realise the different capabilities that are brought to bear on an innovation. As the Pixar study shows, it is the identification and mobilisation of a range of capabilities that facilitate innovation. Examining, assessing and evaluating actual abilities of various individuals both to use their capabilities and find the opportunity to do so form part of what we can consider to be a capabilities approach to promoting innovation.

CAPABILITIES APPROACH TO INNOVATION

If innovation leads to change in terms of new products and services, and new ways of organising firms, then developing a framework for the evaluation and assessment of individual well-being and social arrangements, the design of policies, and proposals about such change, can be useful. The capabilities approach can be traced back to, among others, Aristotle, Adam Smith and Karl Marx, but its most prominent, modern form has been pioneered by the economist and philosopher Amartya Sen (1980; 1984; 1985a; 1985b; 1987; 1988; 1989; 1990b; 1992; 1993a; 1999), followed by some significant development of the ideas by the philosopher Martha Nussbaum (2000; 2011) and others such as Deneulin and Shahani (2009).

Although this approach has been tested in a wide range of fields, in particular in development studies, welfare economics, social policy and political philosophy, it has by and large been ignored in the innovation and entrepreneurship literature. Yet if collaboration, engagement, discovery-driven learning and integrative decision making were to be effective in innovative organisations, then exploring the well-being of people, not simply in terms of what they possess but of what they can choose to do in particular environments, can be deemed an essential requirement.

Allowing for the necessary freedoms individuals can have to pursue their own learning, improve their self-efficacy and sharpen their perceptions about what they could achieve would be important considerations for managers of organisations. The focus here is less on personal utility, the acquisition of specific assets, reputation or wealth and overcoming restrictions on rights, and more on the capability to function or the turning of capability to 'functionings'. As Sen explains:

> Functionings represent parts of the state of a person – in particular the various things that he or she manages to do or be in leading a life. The capability of a person reflects the alternative combinations of functionings the person can achieve, and from which he or she can choose one collection. The approach is based on a view of living as a combination of various 'doings and beings', with quality of life to be assessed in terms of the capability to achieve valuable functionings. (1993b)

With respect to innovation, functionings can include work–life balance, being technically literate, being creative, being healthy, being part of a community of interest, being respected and having space to generate new ideas and solutions to problems. The distinction between functionings and capabilities is between 'the realised and the effectively possible; in other words, between achievements on the one hand, and freedoms or valuable options from which one can choose on the other'.

In the context of innovation, and given the assumptions about the positive value of collective endeavour in organisational innovation, we can argue that ensuring that people can have the space to choose to function innovatively is critical to innovative outcomes. Supporting innovative people in their effective opportunities to undertake the actions and activities that they want to engage in, and be whom they want to be on an innovation platform, need to be factored into organisational policy and practice. Removing barriers in their work so that they have more freedom to function creatively to deploy their skills, to generate new ideas and to fulfil objectives (their own and those of the organisation), so that they have a reason to value what they do and can do, is part of the evaluation process. The end objective of an innovation outcome and the recycling of the innovation process have intrinsic importance. The means are instruments to achieve the ends. This is one reason why no de facto minimum architecture for innovation in an organisation may work as a standardised project for innovation. Crucially, an emphasis on organisational routines that can corral people to operate effectively in only one gnostic way may actually deter innovation. In reality, ends and means may blur because some ends are simultaneously means to other ends (e.g. the capability of being technologically savvy could be an end in itself, but it may also be a means to achieve the capability for innovation practice).

This brief reference to the capabilities approach is a very modest attempt to apply a much broader, more detailed and highly philosophical set of theories to ways in which we can best understand and support innovative people. Researchers on the subject may well consider a proper appreciation of the approach and a systematic application to innovation management through empirical work. What we can draw from this synopsis is an understanding of the reality of managing innovative people, a reality which impugns straitjacketed management ideas of goal congruence, routines, shared vision and systems thinking. The capabilities approach also helps to disentangle firms from people, and the idea of a firm's capacity to rely on a stock of inimitable resources of human capital to innovate from the individual capabilities for innovation in that stock. As we have seen from the Pixar example and from our observations of and insights into innovative organisations (see Chapters 5 and 6), management practices that rely less on managing people as 'commodities' (uniform stock of people evaluated in terms of set criteria of achievement), and more on managing different levels of capabilities-based on gender, ethnicity and other forms of diversity, tend to derive the gains from innovative advantage. Encouraging employee involvement and innovative behaviour in organisations can, therefore, be considered a worthwhile objective for managers.

THE INVOLVEMENT OF INNOVATIVE EMPLOYEES

A focus on capabilities inevitably leads to the question of involvement of people in the innovation process in organisations. Various studies have tried to articulate the role of employees in contributing to innovation outcomes in firms (Feldman and Pentland, 2003; Kristiansen and Bloch-Poulsen, 2010). Such involvement tends to vary across sectors. De Jong and Vermeulen (2006) found that knowledge-intensive industries accommodate more innovative employees than others. This may be due to a concentration of highly skilled technical jobs in those organisations, thus reflecting a possible bias towards technology-oriented firms and the normative association between technology and innovation. Manufacturing firms, with their division of labour, project-based and shift-work patterns, and various occupational divisions, can restrict innovative behaviour among employees (Aaltonen and Hytti, 2014).

One way of identifying innovative behaviour is to observe different aspects of practice. Innovation can be seen as a phenomenon that is formed and reformed through the practice of individuals (Corradi et al., 2010). Here individual actors navigate their way through institutional routines, discern the embeddedness of work in the organisational culture, and absorb knowledge from within and from outside the firm. In terms of activities, this takes the form of conceptualisation, effectuation, application of both codified knowledge and heuristics, problem identification and solutions, and resolution of issues individually and collectively. In large firms these activities may play out among different groups, between groups and collaboration with end users, ending with integrative decision making (Hill et al., 2014). In smaller firms there is the added difficulty of balancing the owner–manager's multitasking capabilities, the emotional attachment to processes and outcomes, and the internal locus of control which may prevent employee involvement. Curiously, however, it is in this very controlled environment of the small firm that the employee is also expected to 'muck in', to work alongside the owner–manager and deal with all eventualities, self-organising the diversity of practices that would otherwise be divided among several individuals in a larger business.

This chapter on innovative people cannot be complete without special reference to the gender dimension to the subject of innovative people. So many debates in management and organisational psychology, and increasingly in entrepreneurship, are addressing the specific roles and contributions of women that we would be remiss not to refer to their innovative leadership functions. More importantly, obtaining an understanding of the gender dimension could help us to acquire a sharper and nuanced understanding of the breadth of innovative endeavour.

INNOVATIVE PEOPLE AND THE GENDER DIMENSION

Various studies on entrepreneurship and gender argue that the phenomenon of entrepreneurship is gendered (Minniti, 2009) and that gender is embedded in processes, meanings and experiences (Carter and Shaw, 2006; Ahl and Nelson, 2010). These studies form part of the discourse and empirical work in the field of entrepreneurship. Gender does not enjoy a high status in the innovation literature mainly because, as we stated at the beginning of this chapter, innovative people do not get good press. If process, systems and organisation are seen as the principal building blocks for the study of innovation, then people, let alone women, become more or less invisible and under communicated (Brannback et al., 2012). Considering people helps us to understand the human capital, skills and capabilities that drive innovation. Considering gender enables us to comprehend the richness of different forms of innovative endeavour among people.

What can we find in the literature that sheds some light on our understanding of the gender perspective?[1]

THE GENDER PERSPECTIVE

Comparative studies on gender differences and similarities in innovation dominate the rather sparse literature on gender and innovation. Quantitative studies of innovation in male- and female-owned businesses, together with the literature on gender differences on standard measurable inputs and outputs such as patenting and commercialisation, suggest that male researchers are more likely than female researchers to engage in industry cooperation (Azagra-Caro et al., 2006; Bozeman and Gaughan, 2007). A study by Whittington (2011) showed that 'academic mothers' are less likely to take out patents, probably because of the uneasy relationship between family responsibilities and workplace achievements that may impede women's ability to innovate. Interestingly, Foss et al. (2013) found that women are equally innovative in generating new ideas compared with men, but that women's ideas do not travel well in terms of implementation, often because of a lack of collegiate support (Poutanen and Kovalainen, 2013). If organisational practices and the glass ceiling of gender bias are factors, then the trouble lies with those organisations that are unable to derive value from the work of creative women.

The same gender bias is also evident in the deployment of research grants, not least because policy and research on innovation suffer from this deficit of bias (Viner et al., 2004). There appear to be layers of stereotypes, assumptions about the innovation construct itself, separate roles and consequent discrimination: women are typecast as being interested in work in industries that favour women; women do not tend to implement ideas because their role as 'mothers' can inhibit them from realising their working goals; women are only interested in 'feminine' issues, and so on and so forth. Consequently, comparative studies of men and women in innovation may be inherently biased because of possible assumptions. As Wikhamn and Knights (2013) have indicated, there is a need for some vigilance on the part of researchers when notions of femininity and masculinity are attached to women and men.

Feminist studies have pointed out that the innovation concept is in itself replete with male connotations (Blake and Hanson, 2005; Nahlinder et al., 2012), resulting in public support for innovation or R&D for men by men. Notions of masculinity underline the scientific, technological and engineering fields (Wajcman, 2010; Dautzenberg, 2012). Even ostensibly less institutionalised forms of innovation, such as open innovation, are swayed by male-oriented organisational practices (Wikhamn and Knights, 2013).

The issues highlighted in this part of the chapter are those emanating from a notion of disadvantage that is the result of the inadequacies of men. The literature is even more limited on the role, function and achievements of women such as Bonnie Ross (described above) and their endeavours that overcome the dysfunctional constraints of male hegemony.

But instead of dwelling on the imposed barriers and the assumed ontological differences in our understanding of female innovators, it may be worth examining women in practice, together with their objectives, behaviour and how they make new products, provide services and create new forms of organisations.

That women excel in as diverse a set of areas as robotics, finance, biomedical engineering and education is not in doubt. In these pursuits such women have not only entered previously male bastions of technology, but also earned their rightful place as leaders. However, real leadership is probably being demonstrated through a different model of operation which defies standard business models and expectations in the marketplace. If there is anything that is crying out for change it is in the way business is conducted in the face of dramatic conditions that are affecting our environment: social structures due to rising inequality; demographic imbalances with rapid ageing of the population, especially in developed economies; water and food shortages; and the cul de sacs of growth that are holding back economies across the world as scarce resources defy economic equilibrium arguments. It is here, perhaps, that women are taking up a real challenge in taking new directions for doing business.

Female innovators are increasingly being seen to adopt a humanistic approach to enable positive change. This humanism considers people and the problems they face first, before relying on applying a known set of skills to any given situation. The innovation is in the actions taken to mix 'hard' technology' with 'soft' humanism to run socially conscious enterprises that work towards earning social returns on investment as strongly as they pursue economic surpluses. This notion of organising resources, structures and processes around social and economic goals is in itself innovative. The use of technology and creativity simply enhances the innovation.

VIGNETTE 7.5   OF WOMEN, BY WOMEN, FOR THE WORLD: TWO MINI CASE STUDIES

SANGEETA BHATIA

Take the case of a graduate of MIT and Harvard, a biomedical and mechanical engineer, physician, professor, inventor and entrepreneur, Dr Sangeeta Bhatia, who fights disease through innovation. Recognised as one of the most innovative young scientists worldwide and one of the 100 most creative people in business, Dr Bhatia is the co-founder of biotech start-ups Zymera and Hepregen. She won the 2014 Lemelson-MIT Prize of $500,000 for her ground-breaking inventions in miniaturised biomedical technologies and youth mentorship.

THE APPROACH

Dr Bhatia sees herself as being an impatient inventor. She looks at the size of a challenge knowing well that there are really big problems out in the world today, and her motivation appears to be seek to move beyond what has been found already. The two inventions which have singled her out as a champion in her field(s) are the synthetic biomarkers that detect cancer through a paper urine test and a human microliver built to fight infectious disease by predicting drug toxicity and interacting with human pathogens. The microlivers provide a basis for an engineered liver that may one day replace the need for transplants in patients with liver disease. Her portfolio of

(Continued)

(Continued)

inventions reflects this. In addition to drug toxicity and cancer therapeutics, she has addressed problems in the areas of tissue regeneration, non-invasive diagnostics and infectious disease.

Dr Bhatia's education and skills no doubt put her in a very good position to work towards successful outcomes. However, it is in her mentors and in the diversity of interests and experience that she finds an explanation for her own success. They 'saw more for me than I saw for myself'. There is a strong recognition of how innovation occurs when different disciplines collide. Her own training in miniaturisation as an engineer made her understand that alongside the big field of microfabrication, which was invented for making computer chips, there was also the other world of nanotechnology, a materials science invention. At the interface of these two technologies lies the possibility for medical applications. According to Dr Bhatia, combining these fields helps scientists to leapfrog in advances, something which she and her team have been trying repeatedly with diverse teams of people with varied perspectives and experiences.

OVERCOMING CONSTRAINTS

One of the struggles that Dr Bhatia had to contend with was finding women who had the life she thought she wanted. Having not found many examples as she honed her talents, she has dedicated herself to the advocacy of STEM (Science, Technology, Engineering and Mathematics) fields for women, and to try and find more women who could pursue high-tech entrepreneurship.

SOFIA APPLEGREEN

Sofia Applegreen, a Swedish entrepreneur, launched a company called Mitt Liv in 2008 to help immigrants into Swedish society, to help create a platform for people from around the world so that they can be part of an inclusive society. Her objective was to find a way to solve the problem of what she describes as the two doors for immigrants coming into Sweden. A generous immigration policy welcomes migrants through an open door, while a closed labour market door shuts them out of employment. Applegreen's solution is to pair smart, keen and capable young immigrant women with mentors who offer advice on job résumés, applications and interviews, through her company. But Mitt Liv is not a charitable organisation. Large Swedish corporations pay Applegreen's firm to take on mentees and also to advise the companies on diversification of the workforce. This business model has helped Mitt Liv to grow from 40 to 400 people who are mentored every year from September to June.

Applegreen finds solutions rather than dwelling on problems, focusing more on what people can achieve in terms of their capabilities than on what they perceive themselves to be or how they are perceived by others. It is through this sense of determination that she has built her reputation and enjoyed success. She runs Mitt Liv from offices in Gothenburg, Stockholm, Malmö, Linköping and Norrköping, and has plans to set up more offices elsewhere in Sweden, with the hope that the success of her work in integrating immigrants better will eventually drive her out of this business!

Sources: '6 Innovative Women to Watch in 2015', www.entrepreneur.com/slideshow/240845; Gibson (2015)

In Sangeeta Bhatia's and Sofia Applegreen's stories we find unique, innovative qualities which at first glance may not be attributable to gender. The fact that they both seek new directions, work collaboratively in a non-linear way across disciplines or with seemingly intractable problems, have remarkable energy, and are realistic about implementing specific actions makes them as innovative as any of their male equivalents. It is probably in the choices they make, the wider social objectives they set, in their use of economic instruments and, importantly, in their humanistic approach to solving problems that we find differences in approach (from males) to performing innovative actions. It is, however, difficult to claim that they are doing anything which men cannot or do not do. Their actions do not reveal a female prerogative, but it is possible that the motivations which guide them distinguish these women as a different set of leaders who inject a greater sense of humanism into the world of innovation. If by focusing strongly on a social objective to the generally technology-oriented projects of innovation they compel us to recreate a different set of beliefs and attitudes, then that in itself could be a harbinger for a meaningful gender-based definition of the innovation process.

CHOICE, PREFERENCE, KINSHIP AND THE USE OF PERSONAL NETWORKS FOR INNOVATIVE OUTCOMES

Access to bastions seen as traditional reserves of men and redefining approaches to work as entrepreneurs are not the only way women carve out their unique role as innovators. Empirical evidence suggests that the choices that women make and the preferences that they show for managing early-stage growth of their ventures can be uniquely innovative. The innovativeness is expressed in their motivations for growth, heuristically-oriented but conscious preferences for specific types of partnerships in particular economic and social environments, a departure from normative patterns of growth trajectories of female entrepreneurs and, in some cases, a culturally complex and collective sense of growth which emphasises the benefits for the collective over the individual firm's interests.

Take the case of established second-generation Pakistani female entrepreneurs in European societies. They represent a unique constituency for research. In the UK they represent British women entrepreneurs. As ethnic female entrepreneurs they are regarded as 'voluntary entrepreneurs' in terms of the choices they make as women and as members of their communities with better access to opportunities, information and resources than their immigrant counterparts (Peters, 2002; Sahin et al., 2007; McPherson, 2010). While their Islamic identity distinguishes them from members of other minority communities, the presence of the new immigrants – Bangladeshi, Turkish and Arabic migrants – encourages new alignments with other Muslim female entrepreneurs. Ethnic, religious and gender heterogeneity are often exhibited by way of the generational differences in entrepreneurial intentions (Sullivan et al., 2009) within various ethnic groups, their motivations (Levent et al., 2003; Rušinovi, 2006), the choice of business sector (Gersick, 1997) and in their growth aspirations (Kourilsky and Walstad, 1998; McGregor and Tweed, 2002). These combinations can affect positively or adversely the growth of their ventures and the organisational innovativeness that is evinced in the outcomes of their endeavours (Rauf and Mitra, 2016).

The literature on growth and gender suggests that business performance influences the self-perception of women entrepreneurs and their abilities to realise business growth, given the social desirability and legitimacy attached to successful business outcomes (Anna et al., 2000). As businesses grow, women develop similar networks to those of men (Klyver, 2007; Klyver and Foley, 2012). Others note that that the results are inconclusive (de Bruin et al., 2006; 2007). Negotiating these networks is often a function of trust that is embedded in the structures of social networks in the form of strong or weak ties (Granovetter, 1973). For second-generation Muslim female entrepreneurs, trust is a function of ethnicity, gender and religion played out through weak and strong kinship, friendship and business ties, but mostly through personal and social networks, including the emotional and financial support provided by the family (Baines and Wheelock, 1998; Aldrich & Cliff, 2003; de Bruin et al., 2006).

Rauf and Mitra (2016) found that, despite exposure to the wider relationship domains, the personal networks of second-generation Pakistani female entrepreneurs are a product of gender and religion which permeate ethnicity, kinship, friendship and business or professional ties. Kinship and ethnicity are kept at bay, while religion appears to underpin their gendered business activities, based on notions of trust. The maintenance of dense gendered networks results in the slower growth of the business and therefore in a brake on the aspirations that they may have for their enterprises. However, this conventional view is countered by the idea of growth as a female community issue where the lower growth of individual businesses is compensated in collective form by the growth of many businesses in the network. A critical counterpoint to growth theories based on the growth of individual firms can be found in how young Muslim female entrepreneurs link their aspirations for growth to the benefits derived from social correspondence with other Muslim female entrepreneurs. So while slower growth may be the outcome of operating in dense gendered networks for individual entrepreneurs, the social value of collective benefit outweighs the loss of individual gain. Both the process of using personal networks selectively and the socially beneficial outcome are manifestations of a form of innovative socialisation of growth. Whereas individual growth of any one firm is often accompanied by the loss experienced of others in terms of trade-offs, here we find the slower growth of many compensating for the random, fractured and unsustainable and normative patterns of growth. The innovation is in the complexity that underpins simple choices and the navigation of personal networks guided by preferences for processes, people and cultural institutions that enable growth.

CONCLUDING OBSERVATIONS

It is not uncommon to find few chapters in recognised texts with sufficient reference to the role of people, as individuals, as teams or as networks. Good trade and other business or technology magazines tend to reveal much more through interviews, snippets and stories. It is difficult to keep track of the large variety of people and cohorts who drive, engineer and make innovation possible. Their behaviour often challenges received wisdom and theories. We know that we can study them from economic, sociological, managerial, psychological and other perspectives, but the innovative mind probably cuts across all of these theoretical domains. Part of this difficulty of labelling people in conceptual terms may be due to the fact that the attitudes, capabilities and competencies of innovative people find true expression in the contexts in which they operate, in their organisations, in networks and in the wider environment. We examined how these attitudes, capabilities and behaviour contribute to the innovative character of organisations in Chapters 5 and 6.

 —— **SELF-ASSESSMENT AND RESEARCH QUESTIONS** ——

1.   Do innovators have the same characteristics as entrepreneurs?

2.   Why are innovative people generally 'invisible' in the literature on innovation?

3.   Are we better able to understand the innovation process by examining innovative people?

4.   Does the examination of a gender dimension to innovation help us to understand better the role of men and women in the innovation process?

5.   How do organisations manage innovative people?

NOTE

1.   Some of the references in this section are drawn from the article 'Gender and innovation: state of the art and a research agenda' by Alsos et al. (2013).

 —— **REFERENCES** ——

Aaltonen, S. and Hytti, U. (2014) 'Barriers to employee driven innovation: a study of a regional medium sized bakery', *International Journal of Entrepreneurship and Innovation*, 15(3): 159–68.

Acs, Z.J. and Audretsch, D.B. (2005) *Entrepreneurship, Innovation and Technological Change*. Boston, MA: now publishers.

Ahl, H. and Nelson, T. (2010) 'Moving forward: institutional perspectives on gender and entrepreneurship', *International Journal of Gender and Entrepreneurship*, 2(1): 5–9.

Aldrich, H. and Cliff, J. (2003) 'The pervasive effects of family on entrepreneurship: toward a family embeddedness perspective', *Journal of Business Venturing*, 18: 573–96.

Alsos, G.A., Ljunggren, E. and Hytti, U. (2013) 'Gender and innovation: state of the art and a research agenda', *International Journal of Gender and Entrepreneurship*, 5(3): 236–56.

Anna, A., Chandler, G., Jansen, E. and Mero, N. (2000) 'Women business owners in traditional and nontraditional industries', *Journal of Business Venturing*, 15(3): 279–303.

Azagra-Caro, J.M., Archontakis, F., Gutiérrez-Gracia, A. and Fernández-de-Lucio, I. (2006) 'Faculty support for the objectives of university-industry relations versus degree of R&D cooperation: the importance of regional absorptive capacity', *Research Policy*, 35(1): 37–55.

Baines, S. and Wheelock, J. (1998) 'Reinventing traditional solutions: job creation, gender and the micro-business household', *Work, Employment and Society*, 12(4): 579–601.

Bandura, A. (1986) *Social Foundations of Thought and Action: A Social Cognitive Theory*. Englewood Cliffs, NJ: Prentice-Hall.

Becker, G. (1993) *Human Capital: A Theoretical and Empirical Approach with Special References to Education*. Chicago, IL: University of Chicago.

Becker, G.S. (1964) *Human Capital*. Chicago, IL: The University of Chicago Press.

Bianchi, T. (2001) 'With and without co-operation: two alternative strategies in the food-processing industry in the Italian South', *Entrepreneurship & Regional Development*, 13: 117–45

Black, S. and Lynch, L. (1996) 'Human-capital investments and productivity', *American Economic Review,* 86: 263–8.

Blake, M.K. and Hanson, S. (2005) 'Rethinking innovation: context and gender', *Environment and Planning A*, 37(4): 681–701.

Bloomberg (2015) 'Can the Woman Behind Halo 5 Save the Xbox?', *Bloomberg Businessweek,* 22 October. Available at: http://www.bloomberg.com/features/2015-halo-5-bonnie-ross/ (last accessed 15 January 2016).

Borden, S. (2015) 'Ferran Adrià feeds the hungry mind: the former ElBulli chef is now serving up creative enquiry', *New York Times*, 2 January. Available at: http://nyti.ms/1Dcgl75 (last accessed 30 October 2015).

Bourdieu, P. (1983) 'Forms of capital', in J. Richardson (ed.), *Handbook of Theory and Research for the Sociology of Education*. New York: Greenwood Press. pp. 241–58.

Bozeman, B. and M. Gaughan (2007) 'Impacts of grants and contracts on academic researchers' interactions with industry', *Research Policy*, 36(5): 694–707.

Brannback, M., K. Berglund and A.L. Carsrud (2012) 'Understanding the entrepreneur and innovator nexus as basis for the coming of the science of the artificial', Paper presented at RENT – Research on Entrepreneurship and Small Business Conference, Lyon, 21–3 November.

Brustein, J. (2015) 'Bonnie's Army: Can HALO 5 save the Xbox – the career of one of gaming's most powerful women is riding on it', *Bloomberg Businessweek*, 26 October–1 November: 44–9.

Cannon, E. (2000) 'Human capital: level versus growth effects', *Oxford Economic Papers*, 52: 670–7.

Carter, S.L. and Shaw, E. (2006) 'Women's business ownership: recent research and policy developments'. Strathprints Institutional Repository, University of Strathclyde. Available at: http://strathprints.strath.ac.uk/8962/ (last accessed May 2016).

Catmull, E. (2014) *Creativity, Inc.: Overcoming the Unseen Forces That Stand in the Way of True Inspiration*. New York: Penguin, Random House.

Chell, E. and Athayde, R. (2009) 'The identification and measurement of innovative characteristics of young people: development of the Youth Innovation Skills Measurement Tool'. Research Report, July, London NESTA.

Cohen, W.M. and Levinthal, D.A. (1990) 'Absorptive capacity: a new perspective of learning and innovation', *Administrative Science Quarterly*, 35: 128–52.

Coleman, J. (1988) 'Social capital in the creation of human capital', *American Journal of Sociology*, 94: S95–120.

Cooper, A.C. (2001) 'Networks, alliances and entrepreneurship', in M.A. Hitt, S.M. Camp and D.L. Sexton (eds), *Strategic Entrepreneurship: Creating a New Integrated Mindset*. Oxford: Blackwell.

Corradi, G., Gherardi, S. and Verzelloni, L. (2010) 'Through the practice lens: where is the bandwagon of practice-based studies heading?', *Management Learning*, 41(3): 265–83.

Dautzenberg, K. (2012) 'Gender differences of business owners in technology-based firms', *International Journal of Gender and Entrepreneurship*, 4(1): 79–98.

Davidsson, P. and Honig, B. (2003) 'The role of social and human capital among nascent entrepreneurs', *Journal of Business Venturing*, 18(3): 301–31.

de Bruin, A., Brush, C. and Welter, F. (2006) 'Towards building cumulative knowledge on women's entrepreneurship', *Entrepreneurship Theory and Practice*, 30(5): 585–94.

de Bruin, A., Brush, C. and Welter, F. (2007) 'Advancing a framework for coherent research on women's entrepreneurship', *Entrepreneurship Theory and Practice*, 31(3): 323–39.

De Jong, J.P.J. and P.A.M. Vermeulen (2006) 'Determinants of product innovation in small firms: a comparison across industries', *International Small Business Journal*, 24(6): 587–609.

Deneulin, S. and L. Shahani (2009) *An Introduction to the Human Development and Capability Approach: Freedom and Agency*. London, Earthscan/IDRC.

Feldman, M. and Pentland, B. (2003) 'Reconceptualising organisational routines as a source of flexibility and change', *Administrative Science Quarterly*, 48(1): 94–118.

Festinger, L. (1957) *Cognitive Dissonance Theory. Primary Prevention of HIV/AIDS: Psychological Approaches*. Newbury Park, CA: SAGE Publications.

Foss, L., Woll, K. and Moilanen, M. (2013) 'Creativity and implementations of new ideas: do organisational structure, work environment and gender matter?', *International Journal of Gender and Entrepreneurship*, 5(3): 298–322.

Franklin-Wallis, O. (2015) 'How Pixar embraces crisis', *Wired*, December: 132–45.

Gersick, K.E. (1997) *Generation to Generation: Life Cycles of the Family Business*. Cambridge MA: Harvard Business School Press.

Gibson, M. (2015) 'Next generation leaders', *TIME*, 186(13): 36–43.

Gimeno, J., Folta, T., Cooper, A. and Woo, C. (1997) 'Survival of the fittest? Entrepreneurial human capital and the persistence of underperforming firms', *Administrative Science Quarterly*, 42: 750–83.

Gradstein, M. and Justman, M. (2000) 'Human capital, social capital, and public schooling', *European Economic Review*, 44: 879–91.

Granovetter, M.S. (1973) 'The strength of weak ties', *American Journal of Sociology*, 78(6): 1360–80.

Grant, R.M. (1996) 'Toward a knowledge-based theory of the firm', *Strategic Management Journal*, 17(S2): 109–22.

Hill, L.A., Brandeau, G., Truelove, E. and Lineback, K. (2014) *Collective Genius: The Art and Practice of Leading Innovation.* Boston, MA: Harvard Business Review Press.

Hinz, T. and Jungbauer-Gans, M. (1999) 'Starting a business after unemployment: characteristics and chances of success (empirical evidence from a regional German labour market)', *Entrepreneurship & Regional Development,* 11(4): 317–33.

Honig, B. (1996) 'Education and self-employment in Jamaica', *Comparative Education Review*, 40(2): 177–93.

Isaacson, W. (2014) *The Innovators: How Groups of Hackers, Geniuses and Geeks Created the Digital Revolution*. London: Simon and Schuster.

Kenney, M. and Von Burg, U. (1999) 'Technology, entrepreneurship and path dependence: industrial clustering in Silicon Valley and Route 128', *Industrial and Corporate Change*, 8(1): 67–103.

Klyver, K. (2007) 'An investigation of gender differences in social network dynamics', Paper presented at the Academy of Management Conference, Philadelphia, August.

Klyver, K. and Foley, D. (2012) 'Networking and culture in entrepreneurship', *Entrepreneurship & Regional Development,* 24(7–8): 561–88.

Kourilsky, M.L. and Walstad, W.B. (1998) 'Entrepreneurship and female youth: knowledge, attitudes, gender differences, and educational practices', *Journal of Business Venturing*, 13(1): 77–88.

Kristiansen, M. and Bloch-Poulsen, J. (2010) 'Employee Driven Innovation in Team (EDIT)-Innovative potential, dialogue, and dissensus', *International Journal of Action Research*, 6 (2–3): 155–95.

Levent, T. B., Masurel, E. and Nijkamp, P. (2003) Diversity in entrepreneurship: ethnic and female roles in urban economic life. *International Journal of Social Economics*, 30(11): 1131–61.

McGregor, J. and Tweed, D. (2002) 'Profiling a new generation of female small business owners in New Zealand: networking, mentoring and growth', *Gender, Work & Organization*, 9(4): 420–38.

McPherson, M. (2010) 'An outsiders' inside view of ethnic entrepreneurship'. Paper presented at the 33rd Annual Conference of The Institute for Small Business and Entrepreneurship (ISBE), London, 2–4 November.

Minniti, M. (2009) *Gender Issues in Entrepreneurship*. Hanover, MA: now publishers.

Mitra, J. (2012) *Entrepreneurship, Innovation and Economic Development: An Introduction*. Abingdon: Routledge.

Mitra, J., Abubakar, Y. and Sagagi, M.S. (2011) 'Graduate entrepreneurship education and training: knowledge creation, human capital and development', *Education + Training*, 53(5): 462–79.

Morris, A. (2015) 'Black Coffee's house blend', *Wired*, UK edn, 15 November. Available at: https://en.wikipedia.org/wiki/Black_Coffee_(DJ) (last accessed 7 October 2015) and www.redbullstudios.com/capetown/artists/black-coffee (last accessed 7 October 2015).

Nahlinder, J., Tillmar, M. and Wigren-Kristoferson, C. (2012) 'Are female and male entrepreneurs equally innovative? Reducing the gender bias of operationalisations and industries studied', in S. Andersson, K. Berglund, J.G. Torslund, E. Gunnarsson and E. Sundin (eds), *Promoting Innovation – Policies, Practices and Procedures.* Stockholm: VINNOVA.

Narang, R. and Deviah, D. (2014) *Orbit-Shifting Innovation: The Dynamics of Ideas that Create History.* London: Kogan Page.

Nussbaum, M.C. (2000) *Women and Human Development: The Capabilities Approach*. Cambridge: Cambridge University Press.

Nussbaum, M.C. (2011) *Creating Capabilities: The Human Development Approach*. Boston, MA: Belknap, Harvard University Press.

Pennings, J.M., Lee, K. and van Witteloostuijn, A. (1998) 'Human capital, social capital, and firm dissolution', *Academy of Management Journal*, 41: 425–40.

Penrose, E.T. (1956) 'Foreign investment and the growth of the firm', *Economic Journal*, 66: 220–35.

Peters, N. (2002) 'Mixed embeddedness: Does it really explain immigrant enterprise in Western Australia (WA)?', *International Journal of Entrepreneurial Behaviour & Research*, 8(1/2): 32–53.

Polanyi, M. (1967) *The Tacit Dimension*. London: Routledge & Kegan Paul.

Poutanen, S. and Kovalainen, A. (2013) 'Gendering innovation process in an industrial plant – revisiting tokenism, gender and innovation', *International Journal of Gender and Entrepreneurship*, 5(3): 257–74.

Pringle, H. (2013) 'The origins of creativity', *Scientific American*, 308(3): 36–43.

Rauf, A. and Mitra, J. (2016) 'The gift of young muslim women entrepreneurs and their personal networks: second generation muslim female entrepreneurs in the UK: growth aspirations and social sustainability'. 61st Annual World Conference of the International Council for Small Business, Conference Proceedings, New York, 17–18 June.

Reynolds, P. (1997) 'Who starts firms? Preliminary explorations of firms in gestation', *Small Business Economics*, 9: 449–62.

Reynolds, P.D., Hay, M. and Camp, S.M.(1999) *Global Entrepreneurship Monitor*. Kansas City, MO: Kauffman Center for Entrepreneurial Leadership.

Robinson, P.B. and Sexton, E.A. (1994) 'The effect of education and experience on self-employment success', *Journal of Business Venturing*, 9(2): 141–56.

Rušinovi, K. (2006) *Dynamic Entrepreneurship: First and Second-Generation Immigrant Entrepreneurs in Dutch Cities*. Amsterdam: Amsterdam University Press.

Sahin, M., P. Nijkamp and T. Baycan-Levent (2007) 'Migrant entrepreneurship from the perspective of cultural diversity', in L.-P. Dana (ed.), *Handbook of Research on Ethnic Minority Entrepreneurship: A Co-Evolutionary View on Resource Management*. Cheltenham: Edward Elgar. pp. 99–113.

Saxenian, A. (1999) 'Comment on Kenney and von Burg "Technology entrepreneurship and path dependence: Industrial clustering in Silicon Valley and Route 128"', *Industrial and Corporate Change*, 8: 104–10.

Schultz, T.W.(1961) 'Investment in human capital', *The American Economic Review*, 51(1): 1–17.

Schumpeter, J. (1942) *Capitalism, Socialism and Democracy*. New York: Harper and Brothers.

Sen, A. (1984) *Resources, Values and Development*. Cambridge, MA: Harvard University Press.

Sen, A. (1985a) *Commodities and Capabilities*. Amsterdam: North Holland.

Sen, A. (1985b) 'Well-being, agency and freedom', *Journal of Philosophy*, 82(4): 169–221.

Sen, A. (1987) 'The standard of living', in G. Hawthorn (ed.), *The Standard of Living*. Cambridge: Cambridge University Press.

Sen, A. (1988) 'The concept of development', in H. Chenery and T.N. Srinivasan (eds), *Handbook of Development Economics*. Amsterdam: Elsevier Science. pp. 9–26.

Sen, A. (1989) 'Development as capability expansion', *Journal of Development Planning*, 19: 41–58.

Sen, A. (1990a) 'Gender and cooperative conflicts', in I. Tinker (ed.), *Persistent Inequalities*. New York: Oxford University Press. pp. 123–49.

Sen, A. (1990b) 'Justice: means versus freedoms', *Philosophy and Public Affairs*, 19: 111–21.

Sen, A. (1992) *Inequality Reexamined*. Cambridge, MA: Harvard University Press.

Sen, A. (1993a) 'Capability and well-being', in M.C. Nussbaum and A. Sen (eds), *The Quality of Life*. Oxford: Clarendon Press. pp. 30–53.

Sen, A. (1993b) 'Introduction', in M. Nussbaum and A. Sen (eds), *The Quality of Life*. Oxford: Clarendon Press.

Sen, A. (1999) *Development as Freedom*. New York: Knopf.

Senor, D. and Singer, S. (2009) *Start-Up Nation: The Story of Israel's Economic Miracle*. New York: Twelve.

Shane, S. and Venkataraman, S. (2000) 'The promise of entrepreneurship as a field of research', *Academy of Management Review*, 25: 217–21.

Siegel, R., Siegel, E. and Macmillan, I.C. (1993) 'Characteristics distinguishing high-growth ventures', *Journal of Business Venturing*, 8(2), pp. 169–80.

Sullivan, S.E., Forret, M.L., Carraher, S.M. and Mainiero, L.A. (2009) 'Using the kaleidoscope career model to examine generational differences in work attitudes', *Career Development International*, 14(3): 284–302.

Van de Ven, A.H. (1986) 'Central problems in the management of innovation', *Management Science*, 32(5): 590–607.

Viner, N., Powell, P. and Green, R. (2004) 'Institutionalized biases in the award of research grants: a preliminary analysis revisiting the principle of accumulative advantage', *Research Policy*, 33(3): 443–54.

Wadley, L., Sievers, C., Bamford, M., Goldberg, P., Berna, F. and Miller, C. (2013) 'Middle Stone Age bedding construction and settlement patterns at Sibudu, South Africa', *Science*, 334: 1388–91.

Wajcman, J. (2010) 'Feminist theories of technology', *Cambridge Journal of Economics*, 34(1): 143–52.

Weick, K. (1996) 'Drop your tools: an allegory for organizational studies', *Administrative Science Quarterly*, 41: 301–14.

Whittington, K.B. (2011) 'Mothers of invention? Gender, motherhood, and new dimensions of productivity in the science profession', *Work and Occupations*, 38(3): 417–56.

Wikhamn, B.R. and Knights, D. (2013) 'Open innovation, gender and the infiltration of masculine discourses', *International Journal of Gender and Entrepreneurship*, 5(3): 275–97.

Williams, G. (2012) 'Ferran Adria: the chef without a restaurant has big ideas', *Wired*, UK edn, October: 100–9; and 'Ferran Adria: elBulli chef has big new ideas'. Available at: www.cnn.com/2014/06/23/travel/ferran-adria-new-venture/ (last accessed 30 October 2015).

Zucker, L.G., Darby, M.R. and Armstrong, J. (1998) 'Geographically localized knowledge: spillovers or markets?', *Economic Inquiry*, 36(1): 65–86.

TYPES OF INNOVATION

8

┌─────────── SCOPE AND OBJECTIVES ───────────┐

- The characteristics of innovation embodied in types of innovation.
- The uses and application of technology, the context of organisations and the location of their use to explain types of innovation; various types and their meaning for organisations.
- Integrated models of innovation.

INTRODUCTION

We have explored how innovation is enabled and affected by people, organisational and environmental factors. But not all innovations are influenced by identical factors (Jansen et al., 2006). Different innovations are generated, adopted and diffused variously at organisational and spatial levels (Abernathy and Utterback, 1978). The specific purpose or focus of innovation together with the resources in hand, the specific stage in the business cycle of the organisation and the eventual outcomes of the innovation also create many types of innovation, as in Zaltman et al.'s (1973) 20 types. Distinctions are sometimes made between technological (technical) and organisational (administrative or management) innovations (Lam, 2005; Birkinshaw, 2008). This has led to the idea of different types of innovation, generally and popularly understood in terms of product and process innovations (Abernathy and Utterback, 1978).

In this chapter we explore the different types of innovation that have evolved over time. We start with an explanation of traditional approaches to the question of classification and then distinguish both the distinctive and the overlapping categories that show how many types of innovation impact on organisations in various ways.

Any discussion on types of innovation comes with a 'health warning': not only are there many types, but in trying to identify these types we often have to tread carefully to distinguish between semantics and the reality of differentiation. Moreover, typology-based distinctions can obscure the real purpose of those innovations and adversely affect decision making. So some care and caution is recommended.

Why do we need to know about types of innovation and what can we gain from an understanding of different types of innovation? Some writers such as Damanpour (1987) have argued that the differentiation between various types of innovation is critical for constructing appropriate and realistic theories of organisational innovations. The suggestion here is that there are so many intricacies associated with the different types (technologies, products, processes, contexts, organisational culture, skills) that it is difficult to develop an overarching theory. The need to value all types of innovation is regarded by Kelley and Littmann (2006) as being essential for the establishment of a proper framework of types of innovation. This is because all organisations not only need to compete with an excellent, highly innovative product, but are also required to have organisational arrangements in place to create the most conducive environment for creative outputs.

We distinguish between types and forms of innovation. Types represent characteristics that explain the constituent elements of innovation. Different types have different characteristics. When these innovation types take shape in a specific context, for example within a specific organisation or in a particular geographical environment, where they are affected by some set of processes that give them shape and meaning in a organisation or wider economic context, then they begin to acquire forms. These forms impact on the business model or the structure of an organisation. So we can consider product and process or radical and incremental innovations as types of innovation. When these types intermix or give shape to business activities and the way these activities are conducted, then we find the innovations impacting on business models, the design of an organisational architecture, and strategic approaches to the innovation activities in forms such as open innovation or frugal innovation.

Understanding types and forms of innovation matter, if only to help us obtain more calibrated insights into the innovation process as it evolves in different organisations and contexts. Linked to this is the question of performance. Do firms improve their performance when they concentrate on certain types of innovation? Are certain types more useful than others as far as economic and social value creation are concerned? These may be difficult questions to answer unless comparisons are made within specific categories and only when we can make connections between organisational objectives, contexts and the type of innovation in question. Our purpose here is to explain the different types, especially the ones which have particular currency in our times. In this chapter we focus on the types that characterise innovation.

The text that follows examines the forms that shape innovation in organisations together with the innovation process that uses different types and forms to push innovation forward. We should assert that many of the types we may regard as 'modern' or 'contemporary' all have their roots in some of the original thinking on this topic. We turn our attention, then, to some of those original foundations first with specific reference to the different types of innovation.

THE EVOLUTION OF IDEAS OF TYPES OF INNOVATION

PRODUCT, PROCESS, MARKETS AND ORGANISATIONS

In defining innovation as new combinations of existing resources, Schumpeter (1934) drew attention to five different types of innovation: new products, new methods of production, new sources of supply, the exploitation of new markets, and new ways to organise business. In most respects this typology has influenced classifications made by researchers over time.

However, as Fagerberg (2006) argues, most economists have tended to focus attention on new products and new methods. By distinguishing between 'product technology' and 'production technology', for example, Schmookler (1966) defined the former category as the knowledge required to create and improve products, and production technology as the knowledge about how to produce them.

Product and process innovations involve a series of scientific, technological, organisational, financial and commercial activities, and the firm introducing the innovation is one that has implemented technologically new or significantly techno-logically-improved products or processes during the period under review.

An institutional analysis of the types of innovation provided by what are known as the Oslo Manuals (1996; 2005) (Eurostat OECD, 2005) relies on the Schumpeterian categorisations. By differentiating between innovations that occur in different contexts and focusing primarily on innovations that are implemented by business organisations, the OECD explains product, process, and marketing and organisa-tional innovations. Marketing innovation includes changes to the design and look of products or the introduction of sales strategies, such as the issue of loyalty cards. Organisational innovations are novel forms of product sourcing, development or management information systems, or even new workplace configurations, imple-mented to allow for transformations in the way the organisation manages its business either because of the introduction of new products or because of the discovery of unique ways of running the organisation irrespective of what is offered in the market (Eurostat and OECD, 2005; Galindo-Rueda, n.d.).

In effect, the ability of a firm to judge whether any novelty has been introduced is dependent on significant improvements to the product or process evidenced by the performance of those products or processes. Fraught as it is with difficulty, it is important to tease out the specific added value generated by the innovation to the sales and profit margins of the business. This is made worse when we search for improvements objectively in service industries. For example, it is easier to under-stand and apply performance criteria to goods and services that are traded between manufacturing firms. It is relatively simple to construct a set of performance char-acteristics for machinery, computers and software to evaluate new or improved characteristics that can be understood by the producer and the user. But imagine applying objective measures to identify the newness in or improvements of a design of a new fashion garment, or a restaurant meal. How would producers identify the specific improvement and its contribution to outcomes? How could users base their decision to acquire such goods and services on particular performance characteris-tics? While it may be problematic to answer these questions, what we do know is that the real value of the innovation lies in both the improved performance of the firm (or producer) and the improved satisfaction of the user. It is just that it is not easy to measure them systematically.

RADICAL AND INCREMENTAL

Schumpeter's other great contribution was to differentiate between radical and incremental innovations. Radical innovations occur as a result of the introduction of new machinery for the first time or a clustering of critical innovations which have a far-reaching impact. The latter sort is described in terms of technological waves or revolutions. They also have a close relationship with general purpose technologies (GPTs), which were discussed in Chapter 1. Incremental innovations are marginal improvements to products and services often associated with process innovations. Improvements in Microsoft Windows operating systems or the introduction of a new app in a bundle of others on our mobile phones are examples of incremental innovations.[1] Which of these two types could be more important than the other? This is an almost impossible question to answer, and by asking such a question we land ourselves in a morass of conditions and circumstances.

A serious product innovator company such as Apple or Google might lay greater store in radical innovations, whereas a car manufacturer may rely more on incremental innovations. Here again we find that contexts matter. Moreover, it is now part of received wisdom that the real economic benefits of radical innovations can only be realised after a series of incremental or complementary innovations have occurred. As for incremental innovations, the cumulative effect may well lead to a radical innovation at a later point in time and even perhaps to greater economic benefits. Having noted the difference between radical and incremental innovations, it is not inconceivable also to regard them as attributes of different types because they represent the nature and scope of the change occurring from the deployment of a particular type of innovation. Thus we could have radical product and service innovations and incremental process innovations (Rowley and Sambrook, 2011).

ORGANISATIONAL INNOVATIONS

Organisational innovations can be introduced as a by-product of product or process innovation. For example, the production of shampoos in sachets for customers at the bottom of the pyramid in small village groceries can engender very different marketing and selling techniques than would be the case for a business selling shampoos in bottles in a supermarket. The introduction of e-commerce channels by a book store will inevitably result in alternate or parallel but different channels of communication, sales and after-sales services, which could result in 'channel conflict'.[2]

Another type of organisational innovation may have nothing to do with specific products or services, but rather with different ways to codify knowledge created in the organisation or deliver training for employees, supply chain and quality management systems. Popular organisational innovations have been linked to ideas of re-engineering, lean production, incentive schemes, and external relations with customers as producers. These may be referred to as non-technical innovations (Colecchia 2008).

PRODUCTS, PROCESSES, ORGANISATIONS, PEOPLE

Another early proponent of different types of innovation was Knight (1967), who identified four types of innovation:

1. Innovations associated with the new product or service an organisation offers, or *product or service innovation.*
2. Innovations that deal with changes to the operations and production processes of an organisation stemming from technological changes, or *production or process innovations.*
3. Innovations in the business architecture, management and operational structures, including personnel rewards and incentives management, management information and communications, or *organisational structure innovation.*
4. Innovations linked to changes in roles and functions and levels of staffing, behavioural norms, shifts in culture generated by innovation, or *people-based innovation.*

We find very similar categories to those proposed by Schumpeter above and, as we will see below, by various others that have followed since. The notable distinction is the category of innovative people, a curious piece of omission from so many tomes written on the subject, as if processes, organisations, inputs and outputs had very little to do with the people making those innovations happen in the first place (see Chapter 7).

EXTERNAL AND INTERNAL FOCI

Various scholars have attempted to establish typologies and taxonomies of innovation based on the distinctions Schumpeter identified and on ideas that economics as a discipline has courted. Edquist et al. (2001) and Meeus and Edquist (2006), for example, distinguished between goods and service innovations (categorised as product innovations) or technological and organisational innovations (grouped under process innovations). However, product and service innovations have tended to be treated as being part of the *external* focus of a business, which means that these innovations are essentially market driven, with the clients' demands determining new products or services or managers creating new products or services for existing markets (Damanpour and Gopalakrishnan, 2001; Damanpour et al., 2009). An internal focus on innovation generates process innovations. The innovation here is aimed at improving or increasing the efficiency and effectiveness of processes for making products or facilitating services within the organisations, to create a better offering for the customer. Examples of efficiencies and effectiveness include the reduction of production costs or in delivery time and increases in operational speed or flexibility. This is often made possible due to the introduction of new technologies, although there is evidence to suggest that innovative organisational arrangements can also lead to such efficiencies and effectiveness (Birkinshaw et al., 2008; see also Chapters 5 and 6 in this book). Hamel (2006) separated innovations in operational processes, such as in customer services, logistics and procurement, from those which he regarded as management process innovations, as in strategic planning, project management and employee assessment.

ECONOMIC AND SOCIAL IMPACT

Another distinction between product and process innovation is based on the assumption that there might be differences in the *economic and social impact* of these two types. The introduction of new products could, for example, have a direct positive impact on employment or income growth. A process innovation, on the other hand, given its emphasis on cost cutting and resource efficiency outcomes, may not have any clear, unambiguous effect. It may take a long time before the incremental benefits turn into major changes in which a firm carries out its business, or creates new product platforms. Moreover, the product innovation of one firm may well turn out be the process innovation of another.

CONTEXTS AND TYPES

Differences in the application of product or process or other types of innovation are often dependent on contexts. But how do we account for contexts to distinguish between different types of innovation? Where an innovation is introduced can help to define whether an actual innovation has taken place or whether imitation of a similar product or process introduced somewhere else has occurred. We are clear about labelling the introduction of a new product for the first time anywhere as a genuine innovation, but we fight shy of equating imitation with innovation. Yet imitation can sometimes lead to new innovations because of the diffusion process which allows for significant improvements to and adaptations of original products. A case in point is the Chinese mobile handset market where the Shanzhai phenomenon has made considerable contributions to the availability and modification of phones through adaptive imitation. Sometimes imitation as diffusion is equated with technology transfer, generally from developed countries to less well-off economies. This equation offers only a partial explanation of both the value of imitation and technology transfer. Imitation is not simply about copying what has been developed before. Forgeries in, for example, art, or with Armani suits or cash bills, also constitute a form of imitation. However, imitation as innovation takes existing products to different heights or levels appropriate for users in different locations and sometimes to changes in organisational structures (Godhino and Fagerberg, 2005) and forms of governance (Mitra and Chunlin, 2010). We will discuss imitation later in Chapter 9 on forms and processes.

HYBRID TYPES

Where innovation types cross over they can be considered to be hybrids. Hybrid types are a mix of product and service (Velamuri et al., 2008) innovations providing a form of integrated solution to technological, production and organisational problems. These types have emerged as businesses have sought to integrate products and services to meet specific client needs. For example, the sale of a surgical instrument to a hospital can be combined with the sale of both anti-contamination equipment and the know-how concerning the use of any software related to the use of such equipment. In many cases the allied firms may come together to provide such joint, hybrid innovation services.

Nike's range of product services stretches from shoes to calorie measurement devices, the distance someone runs wearing those shoes, and the pace at which they run, all integrated with the shoes. Here the product becomes the service.

Let us look in Vignette 8.1 at a critical new technology that is beginning to change processes and methods in banking and financial organisations. We select this example for our mini case study because of the turbulence that has rocked the financial industry since the last recession started in 2008, with few signs of satisfactory mitigation 8 years after its recognised starting point.

VIGNETTE 8.1   BITS OF TYPES OF FINTECH INNOVATION

INTRODUCTION

For good or bad the health of our banking and financial industries has a significant impact on our economies. Although captains of the industry, such as Andrea Orcel, President of UBS Investment Bank, believe that the banking system is a lot more robust than it was before (implying possibly the lead-up to the last recession and the few years thereafter), there are serious problems such as trying to obtain appropriate risk-adjusted returns given the fragile state of the economy, the growing canon of regulation and the continuing uncertainties in markets. These in turn have an effect on the push for transformation of business models and cost structures that can help to manage the external challenges better. Commentators suggest that these sets of internal and external challenges are surpassed by the bigger challenge of 'fintech' which is affecting various aspects of finance, including investment advice, retail payments and back office payments. In fact the potential to 'upend the status quo' (Tett and Kaminska, 2016) translates into the possible cessation of cash as a currency medium of monetary transaction.

VIRTUAL MONEY

Fintech represents the new world of virtual currency. It uses the new and controversial blockchain technology, which is like a ledger enabling electronic payments. Fintech refers to specific types of technology start-ups that are disrupting payment systems of the banking and finance industry in general and sectors such as mobile payments, money transfers, loans, fundraising and asset management in particular.

An Accenture report found that global investment in fintech has exploded from $930 million back in 2008 to over $12 billion by the beginning of 2015. Europe has been the seat of this explosion with the highest growth rate, with an increase of 215% to $1.48 billion in 2014. In its wake it has unleashed a series of challenges to financial regulations, new innovations and customer behaviour, prompting leading financial institutions in major heartlands of finance, such as London, to ramp up the technology and its applications. One way the UK financial sector intends to maintain its leadership position in the finance industry is by recruiting talent to develop fintech into a financial fine art.

ALTERNATIVE SOURCES AND METHODS

The rise of fintech reflects the considerable changes in the way technology has enabled new businesses to seek alternative sources of finance, methods of payment and indeed the ways firms go about their daily business. As the traditional high street bank has failed to make access to finance easy for, especially, new business, the alternative, and in particular the online alternative, finance industry has grown in strength. A recent NESTA report indicates that the online alternative financial market grew on a year-on-year basis by 83.91%, with loans, investments and donations totalling £3.2 billion compared with the industry total of £1.74 billion in 2014 (NESTA, 2016).

From peer-to-peer consumer lending to peer-to-peer business lending, invoice trading, equity, reward and donation-based crowdfunding and mobile payments, the choice of relatively cheaper sources of money has witnessed an unprecedented rise in the fintech market for entrepreneurs.

THE TRAJECTORY OF FINTECH GROWTH

The absence of traditional overheads and their agility, a corollary of innovative activity, helps fintech firms to pass on savings to customers. What has enabled fintech to make rapid progress is the range of tools, from cheap storage to cheap computing, and phenomenally big data-based analytics. These technologies have ushered in changes to the regulatory environment, how people manage their money and do business online, and how financial and retail organisations cope with the necessary amendments to organisational structure and processual change.

Munch (n.d.) refers to staggering claims made by Goldman Sachs which estimates that fintech upstarts could secure up to $4.7 trillion in annual revenue, and $470 billion in profit, from established financial services companies. Seizing on this prospect, Goldman Sachs has launched its own online lending operation.

Although the International Monetary Fund (IMF) points to the very small scale of virtual currencies ($7 billion in market value, which contrasts with $1.4 trillion of US paper currency) in circulation, they are ramping up very fast, forcing bankers and policy makers to take note of the explosion in the market. New fintech firms are 'cashing' in on the new technology revolution to disrupt the incumbent banks, in a classic case of radical or strategic innovation managed by new 'upstart' organisations upsetting incumbents and compelling the latter to develop their own fintech technologies and to

(Continued)

(Continued)

collaborate with smaller technology start-ups to combat the disruption. J.P. Morgan, for example, expects to use the blockchain technology to commence procedures to settle loan trades.

Blockchain's reputation as a technology has been partly sullied because of the apparent failure of bitcoin and the hackable vulnerability of programming and software associated with the latter. Therefore, scepticism about the blockchain technology continues to be propagated by bankers and economists who may find it difficult to make the necessary adjustments to their models of this radically new, open source technology. Given security concerns on the one hand and an acknowledgement of the power of the technology to cut costs and change both processes and the emergence of a new currency product on the other, the ensuing debate is about the introduction of regulatory controls for the new fintech innovators that would be the same as those for others in the business of finance.

Sources: Tett and Kaminska (2016); Apspan (n.d.); Munch (n.d.)

The fintech vignette outlines how innovations can occur on the product, process, radical and integrated fronts almost simultaneously. When this happens we find genuine disruption to firms, industrial sectors, markets and the ways in which they affect customer behaviour and even legislation. We see not only a hybrid formulation of innovation, but one that encourages us to examine the various layers of impact that a mix of innovations has on numerous stakeholders. One way of examining this is to consider integrated forms of innovation.

As the above summary shows, we have in our midst a cornucopia of studies elaborating on the different types of innovation. Many of the explanations tend to highlight the binary division or dwell on variations to the binary construct of product and process: radical and incremental, and technical and administrative innovations. It is when we begin to search for meanings that we find that there are underlying factors, such as innovations having an external or internal focus and making a social or economic impact. Consideration of these factors leads us across pathways that crisscross each other. Managing crossroads can be confusing, and too many convergences and divergences could be disastrous for any navigator of traffic! To help allay some of these concerns various writers have attempted to provide integrative models showing both the distinctions and the overlaps between the different types of innovation. Let us look at some of these integrated models.

INTEGRATIVE MODELS OF TYPES OF INNOVATION

Markides and Geroski (2003) organise separate categories or patterns of the different types of innovation and offer suggestions for their possible impact on the market based on the effect that they have on two sets of dependencies: the effect of innovation on the competencies and complementary assets of established firms;

and the effect of innovation on consumer habits and behaviours. The patterns are classified in terms of hierarchical quadrants of incremental, strategic, major and radical innovations (see Figure 8.1), while the integration is achieved by measuring the effects on consumers and on established firms.

RADICAL INNOVATION

The 'highest' form of innovation, or *radical innovation*, has a major effect on consumer habits and behaviours while destroying the competencies and complementary assets of incumbent firms. The invention of the motor car, for example, was based on the different sets of scientific and technological principles than the prevailing horse-drawn vehicle. They had a disruptive effect on both customers and producers and they created new, inchoate markets which demanded new consumer behaviours.

STRATEGIC INNOVATIONS

Smaller cars, by contrast, from the Mini to the Nano car, fall into the category of *strategic innovations*. They are referred to as strategic because they tend to have a dramatic effect on competition even if the actual production or technological changes are relatively small. The real effect is on the competition, and businesses introducing these strategic innovations are required to change their business models in order to generate new income streams and capture the best value from different customer segments. Customers continue to drive cars so we can expect only minor changes in customer behaviour. What these strategic innovations have in common, however, is that they both have drastic and destructive effects on other established firms although in the case of the Nana car the results have gone in the opposite direction.

MAJOR INNOVATIONS

Contrasting radical innovations with 'major' innovations, Markides and Geroski (2003) show that the latter enhance the effect on established firms' competencies and complementary assets. A typical major innovation, such as a speed camera, can have an enhancing effect in that the speed camera producers or installers may actually use the assets and competencies of existing firms by finding another use for the camera. For the consumer the same major innovation has led to significant changes in the behaviour of car drivers who now have to drive with much greater care on roads with speed restrictions so that they do not fall foul of the law.

INCREMENTAL INNOVATIONS

Incremental innovations tend to have the least immediate impact on competitors or on consumers because they simply tend to extend the existing proposition through minor changes in the make-up or the use of a product or service. As for the existing firm, the resulting enhancing effect is based on the improvement of current products and assets. As we have noted, however, over time incremental innovations can lead to major or even radical innovations, often through the mediation of design.

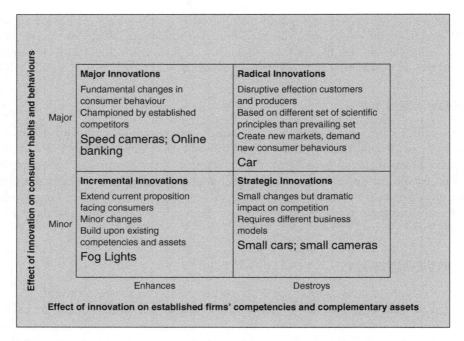

FIGURE 8.1   How different types of innovation have an effect on the market: an integrated model of types of innovation

Source: Adapted from Markides and Geroski (2003)

Integrated models tend to be dependent on how we interpret the connections between the types of innovation or by finding overarching themes that bind the various types and organise them in terms of their implications for the market, the consumer and the competition. Through this process authors have identified a number of dimensions in an innovation space (Tidd and Bessant, 2013). Taking product and process as the essential types of innovation they create a framework map for all types of organisation, adding two other dimensions – position innovation and paradigm innovation – to this framework. We have already discussed product and process innovation earlier. Their interesting proposition is made through the introduction of the other two types.

POSITION INNOVATION

Position (or repositioning) innovation can take the form of an established product or process and repositioning its perception in a different user context. Tidd and Bessant (2013) refer to the glucose-based drink developed originally in 1927 for children and convalescents that was relaunched as a health drink in response to the growing fitness market. We do not find any reference to any technological or incremental change here. All that has taken place is the identification of a market which others might interpret as a marketing innovation.

PARADIGM INNOVATION

The other form of encapsulation of types of innovation that Tidd and Bessant (2013) refer to is 'paradigm innovation'. They refer to the Ford motor car as an example of paradigm innovation because of the fundamental transformation that occurred in mass-produced car making. The shift from craft-style handmade cars to mass production is considered to be a revolutionary paradigm shift. Paradigm shifts induce changes in mental models and often kill off previous models of business operation. Other examples cited by the same authors include low-cost airlines and online insurance. The 'mental models' that changed were the ones we have had of, in this case, air travel (expensive and with all the frills of pre-booking seats and on-board catering services included in the price of tickets) and the use of brokers in insurance. Our perceptions of air travel and insurance payments have changed dramatically, although the reality of low-cost travel is that of hidden extra costs that add to the price of our tickets when we seek the basic comforts associated with air travel. Paradigms shift, but in this case they have a habit of returning (Kuhn, 1962). We find some connection with 'radical' innovations which we discussed earlier, which offers a simpler explanation of innovation that has a major and destructive impact on consumer behaviour and the competencies of existing firms.

Talk of paradigms invokes the greatness of Kuhn's challenge of the views of scientific progress as 'development-by-accumulation' of received wisdom – the past of accepted facts and theories. Kuhn's argument for the episodic model which allowed for the interruption of continuity in thought, discovery and invention by revolutionary science made room for the discovery of anomalies or outliers. It is these anomalies that impugn old data and old science which leads to paradigm shifts and changes in the rules of the game. We referred in an earlier chapter to the emergence of M-Pesa and its revolutionary mobile phone-based payment system, which has transformed payment and even banking systems in developing economies and introduced tariff segmentation in billing, an innovation that found its way from Africa to Europe and is now part of the billing systems for different types of utilities. We can refer to this as an example of a paradigm shift. Science may not have contributed directly to any paradigm shift in this case, but a novel form of thinking did disrupt both telecommunications and banking systems.

CONCLUDING OBSERVATIONS

Inherent in any integrated model of types of innovation is its fluidity. Depending on the context of the process of innovation we can find some types interacting with others or merging with each other. In our understanding we try to create analytical constructs that can sometimes enlighten and at other times confuse us. Take for example the extended vocabulary of innovation types that includes experiential innovation, strategic innovation, paradigm innovation, revolutionary innovation, value innovation, application innovation (Sniukas, 2009) and even conceptual innovation (*Aesthetica*, 2015). These types take shape in organisations and in the wider economy in the form and use of business model innovation, user-led innovation, distributed innovation, inclusive

innovation and designer-led innovation, to name but just a few. We find in these forms
the mix of various types which cover the making, financing, offering and delivery of
products and services in distinctive fashion for different organisations across disparate
industries. It is to these forms and processes that we turn in the next two chapters.

 —————— **SELF-ASSESSMENT AND RESEARCH QUESTIONS** ——————

1. What do we mean by types of innovation?

2. Why is it important to study different types of innovation?

3. Identify the main types of innovation and reflect on where the boundaries between different innovations are fuzzy.

4. How do integrated models of different types of innovation help with our understanding of innovation?

NOTES

1. But note the app in itself could be a 'new product' innovation which becomes a process innovation for the mobile phone manufacturer or service provider.
2. Tensions or conflict arising from direct sales channels (as in traditional sales formats) and electronic ones for the sale of similar products.

 —————— REFERENCES ——————

Abernathy, W.J. and Utterback, J.M. (1978) 'Patterns of industrial innovation', *Technology Review*, 80: 40–7.

Aesthetica (2015) 'Tailored innovation: ode to Dutch fashion'; *Aesthetica*, Issue 66, August/September: 78–83.

Apsan, M. (n.d.) 'Why fintech is one of the most promising industries of 2015', Inc. 5000. Available at: www.inc.com/magazine/201509/maria-aspan/2015-inc5000-fintech-finally-lifts-off.html (last accessed 12 March 2016).

Birkinshaw, J., Hamel, G. and Mol, M. (2008) 'Management innovation', *Academy of Management Review*, 33: 825–45.

Colecchia, A. (2008) 'Defining and measuring non-technical innovation: Oslo Manual and lessons learnt from innovation surveys 1', OECD, Karlsruhe, 16–17 October. Available at: www.6cp.net/downloads/1_Colecchia.pdf (last accessed 7 March 2016).

Damanpour, F. (1987) 'The adoption of technological, administrative and ancillary innovations: impact of organizational factors', *Journal of Management*, 13(4): 675–88.

Damanpour, F. and Gopalakrishnan, S. (2001) 'The dynamics of the adoption of product and process innovations in organizations', *Journal of Management Studies*, 38: 45–65.

Damanpour, F., Walker, R.M. and Avellaneda, C.N. (2009) 'Combinative effects of innovation types and organizational performance: a longitudinal study of service organizations', *Journal of Management Studies*, 46(4): 650–75.

Edquist, C., Hommen, L. and McKelvey, M. (2001) *Innovation and Employment: Process versus Product Innovation*. Cheltenham: Edward Elgar.

Eurostat and OECD (2005) *Oslo Manual: Guidelines for Collecting and Interpreting Innovation Data*. Paris: Organisation for Economic Co-opeation and Development (OECD)

Fagerberg, J. (2006) 'Innovation: a guide to the literature', in J. Fagerberg, D.C. Mowery and R.R. Nelson (eds), *The Oxford Handbook of Innovation*. Oxford: Oxford University Press. pp. 1–27.

Galindo-Rueda, F. (n.d.) 'The Oslo Manual: Main Issues', International Training Workshop on R&D and Innovation Statistics, OECD. Available at: https://www.hse.ru/data/2011/06/10/1213023771/GalindoRueda_The%20Oslo%20Manual.pdfso (last accessed 7 March 2016).

Godhino, M. and Fagerberg, J. (2005) 'Innovation and catching-up', in J. Fagerberg, D. Mowery and R. Nelson (eds), *The Oxford Handbook of Innovation*. Oxford: Oxford University Press.

Hamel, G. (2006) 'The why, what and how of management innovation', *Harvard Business Review*, 84: 72–84.

Jansen, J.J., Van Den Bosch, F.A. and Volberda, H.W. (2006) 'Exploratory innovation, exploitative innovation, and performance: effects of organizational antecedents and environmental moderators', *Management Science,* 52(11): 1661–74.

Kelley, T. and Littman, J. (2006) 'The ten faces of innovation: IDEO's strategies for beating the devil's advocate and driving creativity throughout your organization', *Research Technology Management*, 49(1): 62–3.

Knight, K.E. (1967) 'A descriptive model of the intra-firm innovation process', *The Journal of Business,* 40(4): 478–96.

Kuhn, T.S. (1962) *The Structure of Scientific Revolutions* (50th Anniversary Edition, 2012). Chicago, IL: University of Chicago Press.

Lam, A. (2005) 'Organizational innovation', in J. Fagerberg, D.C. Mowery and R.R. Nelson (eds), *The Oxford Handbook of Innovations.* Oxford: Oxford University Press. pp. 115–47.

Markides, C. and Geroski, P. (2003) 'Teaching elephants how to dance and other silly ideas', *Business Strategy Review*, 14(3): 49–53.

Meeus, M.T.H. and Edquist, C. (2006) 'Introduction to Part I: Product and process innovation', in J. Hage and M. Meeus (eds), *Innovation, Science, and Institutional Change.* Oxford: Oxford University Press. pp. 23–37.

Mitra, J. and Chunlin, S. (2010) Innovation, entrepreneurship and governance: the shanzhai handset business. In *ICSB World Conference Proceedings*, 55th International Council for Small Business (ICSB) Conference. Cincinnati, OH, 24–7 June.

Munch, J. (n.d) 'What is fintech and why does it matter to all entrepreneurs?', *Hot Topics.* Available at: https://www.hottopics.ht/stories/finance/what-is-fintech-and-why-it-matters/ (last accessed 12 March 2016).

NESTA (2016) 'Pushing the Boundaries: The 2015 UK Alternative Finance Industry Report' by B. Zhang, P. Baeck, T. Ziegler, J. Bone and K. Garvey; National Endowment for Science, Technology and the Arts (NESTA) and Cambridge Centre for Alternative Finance.

Rowley, J. and Sambrook, S. (2011) 'Towards an innovation-type mapping tool', *Management Decision*, 49(1): 73–86.

Schmookler, J. (1966) *Invention and Economic Growth*. Cambridge, MA: Harvard University Press.

Schumpeter, J. (1934) *The Theory of Economic Development*. Cambridge, MA: Harvard University Press.

Sniukas, M. (2009) 'Defining innovation types', PowerPoint presentation. Available at: www.slideshare.net/sniukas/the-innovation-map-a-framework-for-defining-innovation-outcomes (last accessed 10 October 2016).

Tett, G. and. Kaminska, I. (2016) 'Blockchain eclipses Basel III as fintech sets Davos abuzz', *Financial Times*, 22 January, p. 10.

Tidd, J. and Bessant, J. (2013) *Managing Innovation: Integrating Technological, Market and Organisational Change*, 5th edn. Chichester: Wiley.

Velamuri, V., Neyer, A.K. and Moeslein, K.M. (2008) 'What influences the design of hybrid products? Lessons learned from the preventive health-care industry', Paper presented at the EURAM Annual Conference, Ljubljana, May.

Zaltman, G., Duncan, R. and Holbek, J. (1973) *Innovations and Organizations*. New York: Wiley.

THE PROCESS OF INNOVATION

9

SCOPE AND OBJECTIVES

- Process as the crucial link between types and forms of innovation.
- Components of the process of innovation.
- Stages of readiness; strategy and cultural alignment governing the process of innovation.
- Execution and strategy.
- Process leading to forms of innovation.

INTRODUCTION

When we refer to the interplay of people, technologies and contexts we are drawing attention to the process of innovation with which business engages to enact renewal or the development of something new or novel. This process of innovation leads to the emergence of forms. So it is helpful to try to obtain an understanding of what we mean by the process of innovation. The two chapters on types and the features of innovative organisations would have captured part of what we know about the processes of innovation. However, in those chapters our interest was in the organisational constructs and outcomes of innovative activity of different types of innovative firms. Here we focus on the actual process or the actions taken by managers and employees of firms to fulfil their innovation goals. These actions lead to the emergence and use of specific forms of innovation activity.

The interplay that we refer to above entails the discovery, creation and development of ideas, followed by their refinement into useful forms. These forms can take the shape of innovative business models, open innovation systems, frugal innovation and reverse innovation, among many other forms. The forms are then used to sustain regular revenue streams, earn profits, increase efficiency, reduce costs and diffuse the outcomes. In this chapter we examine the processes that firms tend to follow in general under different situations and the forms of innovation they accommodate to pursue their innovation goals.

THE INNOVATION PROCESS

If we accept that at its most generic state innovation supports survival and growth for firms, especially in a very competitive environment, then we can find (following Tidd and Bessant, 2013) specific underlying processes such as the following:

1. *Search* – The exploration of the internal environment of the firm and the wider economic and social environment to pick up signals about possible opportunities, threats of early entry by competitors and the prospects for change.
2. *Selection* – Here, following search, the idea is to make strategic choices about the technologies, the resources, the markets and the processes by which a firm can respond to the 'search signals'.
3. *Implementation* – Implementing the strategic decision in terms of well-defined tactics and operations, including human capital management, for launching a new product or service in both internal and external markets in uncertain environments through a series of events.
4. *Value generation* – Capturing economic value in terms of a successful launch of a product or service over a specified period of time, sustainability of those products or services based on their adoption and diffusion in the market, measuring the economic and social impact of the innovation, and generating some learning capability from the change or improvements.

It is not necessarily a straightforward jump from one step to another. The search process cannot really begin unless the managers have established an innovation strategy for the business and made a specific commitment in relation to time, resources and talent. Between search and selection, there is also information orientation and generation for the organisation and its employees. Selection does not automatically lead to implementation. Certain aspects of the choices could be mothballed for a time, and organisational arrangements need to be in place for the implementation to take place. At any point in the process of innovation there could be provision for built-in *ex ante* rejection points. Crucially, the adoption of any process will depend on the type of firm in question. A large pharmaceutical business is expected to be heavily R&D search oriented as opposed to typical retailers, although in our Big Data age, clever analytics are enabling retailers to work out different innovative ways to offer multiple buying and sales channels (physical stores, Internet and inclusion in third-party platforms). Engineering firms may seek opportunities for innovation in project management. Innovative firms will also concentrate on what forms to adopt as in the use of an open innovation process or the construction of innovative business models for new revenue streams. Firms develop a learning capacity for both the processes that best suit their interests and the forms they adopt for the implementation of innovation.

The proper management of the innovation process, including the efforts invested in learning, is a function of the innovation-oriented culture of the firm, the acceptance of strategic formulation of innovation as a key plank of business activity, the harnessing of specific competencies and the marshalling of resources, all as part of a critical, holistic appreciation of the business. This capability will vary between firms and will be dependent on what they do in each market. Innovative manufacturing firms operating in global markets may be dependent on global networks, ideas generation, and sourcing of solutions through open innovation practices and outsourcing. We have already seen in the discussion of different types of firms how small, medium and large firms will navigate their survival and growth in rather different ways. Processes have evolved over the years, from linear models, a hangover from the 1960s, to complex 'fifth-generation', highly fragmented models requiring high levels of integration among different players often in different parts of the world (Rothwell, 1992). None of these processes is used in the abstract, divorced from the reality of the environment and, for business, commercial imperatives. Much of what takes place is either a reaction to or proactive anticipation of the market. Being able to respond is also a function of 'push' and 'pull' factors in the market.

In internalising the factors affecting the innovation process, can a firm follow specific steps to achieve successful outcomes? Given the different contexts and prerogatives of culture, style and vision, not to mention technologies and human capital, how do different innovation processes work? Could we find something generic that helps us to obtain a critical overview of the innovation process? We can try to achieve our objective by scanning the literature on the subject.

The industry-based literature points to the need for:

- getting into the correct mind set;
- working with the right people;
- identifying and securing the best financial resources;
- managing your cash flow; and
- understanding your market place. (The Centre for Process Innovation (CPI), 2014)

If the above principles are followed then specific steps can be taken to ride safely through the 'valley of death', a much vaunted phenomenon which refers to the plethora of ideas that do not survive the 5–10 years of dedicated effort to reach technology readiness levels. The UK's Technology Strategy Board (TSB) argues that this death gap occurs generally between technology readiness levels 4 and 7, that is between completion of the research to prove a feasibility stage and the beginning of the market launch and commercialisation stage (see Figure 9.1 for a diagrammatic representation of the stages of innovation, or the innovation chain, as understood by the TSB in the UK and NASA in the USA).

The diagram shows the three key stakeholders and their strategic roles in generating new knowledge, developing technology applications and commercialisation. While

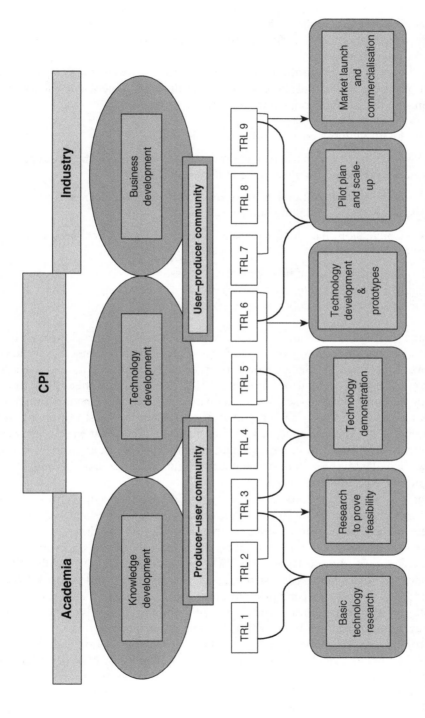

FIGURE 9.1 Stages of innovation for technological readiness – the TSB and NASA approach (TRL = Technology Readiness Level)

Source: Adapted from citation in CPI (2014)

these may correspond to expected roles and functions, the innovation process seldom offers possibilities for the linear packaging of such roles. What we find instead are overlapping functions where the producers of knowledge are often creating knowledge with users, and the users are feeding into both the development and production of new knowledge.

The managers of an organisation are responsible for processes for seeing an idea through to prototyping, setting the cost and value of the products, and identifying and recognising the available opportunities. This entails:

Step 1 – Identifying the goals or problems to be solved.

Step 2 – Analysis of the markets, customers and the fitness of the product or services to them plus a close review of competitors.

Step 3 – Development and design based on the information gleaned from the analysis, followed by modelling and prototyping.

Step 4 – Conversion that enables translation of the idea into real products or services for the market.

Step 5 – Commercialisation involving the post-testing or conversion phase and taking and diffusing the product or service in the marketplace. This could include actions for subcontracting or outsourcing.

If we assume that an organisation is seeking renewal or making a breakthrough in a competitive market through innovation, then most of the requirements that we have stated above – the individual elements of strategy, capabilities and technologies – hold true. However, according to Jaruzelski et al. (2011), the culture of the organisation, its DNA, or the sum total of its self-sustaining patterns of acting, behaving, thinking, sense making and believing stitched together are probably the most important. Yet Jaruzelski et al. (2011) states that only half of all firms argue that their corporate culture reflects their innovation strategy and that their innovation strategy is not adequately aligned with the overall strategy. The extent and degrees of this alignment or misalignment are shown in Figure 9.2.

The idea of culture being important for a firm does of course apply to business strategy in general as much as it does to innovation strategy in particular. A culture of interdependence, collaboration and co-dependence across the firm, its branches and all its collaborators (including customers) characterised 3M's business and innovation strategies, according to Palnesky of 3M (Jaruzelski and Dehoff, 2010). What supports such a strategic approach is strong customer orientation and product definition as evinced in a sense of strong pride in the superior quality of its products.

Interestingly, most companies in the Booz and Company (Jaruzelski and Dehoff, 2010) study found tolerance of failure in the innovation process to be the lowest ranked attribute of their innovation culture. This flies in the face of academic discourse which suggests exactly the opposite, in that highly innovative firms have a high tolerance threshold when failure is at stake. Does it mean that firms are essentially risk averse? If so, is their innovation culture ephemeral? Some care has to be taken with 1-year surveys as they do not necessarily demonstrate a robustness of the empirical evidence.

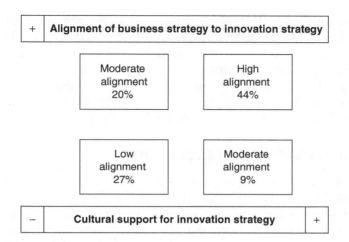

FIGURE 9.2 Innovation strategy and cultural alignment

Source: Adapted from Jaruzelski et al. (2011)

Booz and Company's classification of firms into 'need seekers', 'market readers' and 'technology drivers' allows us to consider different approaches that firms take to developing innovation strategies. 'Need seekers' have a high customer (both existing and prospective) orientation in that they work with both groups to develop new products and services, articulating often unspecified or unarticulated needs which give them an edge in terms of market entry. 'Market readers' are also customer oriented but they tend to rely on cautious forms of incremental innovation, preferring

TABLE 9.1 The culture of firms and their innovation goals

Innovation goals 'Need seekers'	'Market readers'	'Technology drivers'	All strategies
Distinct innovation goal			***Common innovation goals***
Advantaged products and services	Customised products for local markets and geographies	Developing technology-driven and low-cost products	Superior product performance Superior product quality
Distinct cultural attributes			***Common Cultural Attributes***
Openness to new ideas from customers, suppliers, competitors and other industries	Culture of collaboration across different functions and geographies	Reverence and respect for technology, knowledge and talent	Strong identification with the customer and overall orientation towards the customer experience Passion and pride in the products and services offered

Source: Adapted from Jaurzelskie and Dehoff (2010)

to act as 'fast followers'. 'Technology drivers' are essentially technology and R&D reliant, often serving unarticulated needs through new technology solutions. These arguments overlap with others discussed in the chapter on types of firms, and we also find them mirroring some of the discussion on types of innovation such as radical and incremental innovation. Our point here is to find out how these categories of firms and their cultures adopt certain processes that lead them to specific forms of innovation practice. Table 9.1 lists the distinctive and common goals and cultural attributes.

FILLING THE GAP BETWEEN EXECUTION AND STRATEGY

In reality, firms find it difficult not only to align business and innovation strategies, but also to fill the gap between the development of a strategy and its execution. The consequence of this failure in implementation can mean that firms miss out on major opportunities in the market. Leinwand et al. (2016) refer to Strategy & Business (PwC's strategy consulting business), which shows that more than 50% of 4,400 of their respondents were not sure of having a winning strategy, with 9 out of 10 of 500 senior executives acknowledging that they were excluding themselves from serious market opportunities, according to another PwC survey. The challenges for any firm could be a mix of external forces and internal factors such as misaligned strategies. Those who do close the gap manage to grow successfully, as demonstrated by their revenue curves, profit margins, and crucially their association with their customers and collaborators.

The Natura case study in the vignette below reinforces the point about the importance of strategic objectives for the process of innovation. The processes adopted by any firm will need to meet these objectives and it is the latter which enables a certain structure to the process. Table 9.2 shows how different types of processes can be used against different objectives of any given firm and its interest in securing strategic advantage. For example, a business offering a new product or service will seek to ramp up novelty in the making of its products. Others looking to obtain a competitive advantage through a radical new solution to a problem or a breakthrough new product will probably find that they need to ensure that the right set of competencies is available across the firm, to research, develop, produce, market, sell and provide after-sales services to ensure proper diffusion of the innovation. The more complex the technology, the greater the need might be for engaging in new learning and overcoming entry barriers.

TABLE 9.2   Aligning processes with objectives

• NOVELTY	⟶	• New offering
• COMPETENCE CHANGE	⟶	• Changing rules of competitive game
• COMPLEXITY	⟶	• Difficulties in learning & high entry barriers
• ROBUST DESIGN	⟶	• Stretching basic model
• INCREMENTAL	⟶	• Continuous change

Different researchers have attempted to account for the sources and nature of the innovation process by focusing on the drivers of innovation, what innovation helps to achieve and the outcomes of different processes. Drucker's (1985a, 1985b) famous encapsulation of the different sources of innovation shows the wide variety of conscious, directed and serendipitous ways in which innovation works. Innovation occurs in unusual and unexpected situations where incongruities can generate positive outcomes; it secures competitive advantage; it takes place in both large and small firms; and it has a place-based context. Bessant (2013), Birkinshaw et al. (2008) and Mol and Birkinshaw (2009), for example, differentiate between discontinuous innovation where new developments arise, as in continuous forms of innovation, and independent and external sources leading sometimes to game-changing outcomes. The sector may remain the same, but the uses of a product may be disruptive. Good examples can be found in the advent of:

- mobile telephony replacing landlines and generating multiple uses of the phone, from calls (including free calls) to chats to transmitting pictures and transferring money; and
- PCs in the 1970s which spawned a flotilla of new firms such as Apple, Microsoft and Sun Microsystems, which left the old supercomputer industry behind in terms of routine usage, while enabling new ways of data processing for both corporates and users. Ironically, supercomputers have made a welcome return, especially for corporates and their need to both mine and analyse Big Data.

Lienwand et al. (2016) point to several firms such as the well-known brands of Apple, Haier, LEGO, Qualcomm and Starbucks as exemplars, although it is questionable as to whether these firms can tick off all that is on a list of good businesses to work for in typical, periodical rankings conducted by *Fortune* or *Bloomberg*. The authors provide a fine example of a Brazilian firm which has achieved this convergence between strategy and execution to secure an innovation advantage, together with rapid growth, by committing itself to the development of a specific identity, humanising strategy from the abstract to the everyday routine, valorising the culture of the organisation and keeping a sharp eye on operations. Vignette 9.1 provides details of this firm's approach to strategic innovation and business strategy for growth.

VIGNETTE 9.1 INNOVATIONS IN PERSONAL CARE AND STRATEGY

Natura Cosmeticos is better known in Latin America than in the rest of the world. This limited fame is unfortunate because what it does and what it has achieved to date deserve widespread global attention. This Brazilian firm has done so by turning

(Continued)

(Continued)

conventional wisdom on its head. By electing to commit to an identity, it has focused attention on translating the strategic function to an everyday operation with loops of learning feeding back into the strategy. Natura Cosmeticos produces and sells high-quality, ecologically friendly, socially conscious, natural, personal care products. It has carved out an identity with a far-sighted Portuguese slogan *'bem estar bem'* ('well-being; being well') and the celebration of health and quality of life at every age. Instead of purveying the association of beauty and good health with youth, and the image of a forever-young ideal of beauty, it seeks to find and promote beauty and good health in all people's lives.

Direct sales consultants of over 1.5 million have close working relationships with the women of Brazil who are visited every few weeks by these consultants. But what would these visits be worth if they were not supported by a constant output of new products meeting the needs of the women? To do so with respect for the environment and by way of development of the local community (sourcing materials from remote villages in the Amazonian rainforest) was not an easy task. Where, however, the focus on building of identity based on making an impact on sustainable regional development becomes part of the strategy, then the inclusiveness of the approach makes it possible to work with customers not only as users but as partners. When these partners are then supplied with 100 new products each year, the strategy is operationalised in tangible terms leading ultimately to staggering, quantifiable outcomes of 7.4 billion reals (or US$ 2.6 billion) in 2014 alone.

We note that Natura's strategic approach is to make an impact at different levels. Internally, the organisation remains focused on high yields. Externally, the attention is on working with the stakeholders and making products available to support a sustainable environment. The innovation process leads not only to the making of new products sourced from alternative suppliers in the community, but also to the creation of an organisational culture that is embedded in the community that Natura serves. Turning conventional wisdom on its head by replacing a fixation on growth to committing to an identity, by connecting cross-functional capabilities within the firm and outside in the community instead of simply pursuing the holy grail of world-class excellence in all aspects of business, by substituting constant organisation and reorganisation with leveraging cultural strengths, and by opting for future imagining instead of simply reacting to market changes, Natura's strategy itself was innovative. As the company demonstrates, it is not always in the commercialisation of new technology but often in the resetting of strategic direction that innovation can be secured.

Source: Adapted from Leinwand et al. (2016)

If innovation strategy can merge with business strategy to create one holistic enterprise strategy, then managers are more likely to offer innovation as a natural course of activities for the firm. The problem lies often with short-term demands for profitable returns associated with high risks not necessarily associated with innovation as a new idea introduced into practice to have a positive impact on the firm, the economy and society.

THE PROCESS OF MAKING AN IMPACT

Setting impact as an objective calls into question traditional shibboleths of innovation, namely the need to pump up profits, carry high levels of risk for high rates of return, accelerate dividend flows for shareholders and follow processes that foster such holy grails of corporate thought and management wisdom. As we have noted elsewhere, stereotypical models of innovation or strategic management do not necessarily work in all environments. More importantly, in a fast-changing global innovation landscape coupled with the style and collaborative behaviour of innovative firms, it is almost an imperative for managers these days to be adaptive and agile enough to consider alternative business models and different working practices and influences. This imperative has sharpened in our austere economic environment following the ineluctable recession that hit the world around 2008. In such an environment the received wisdom of high returns for high risk may not always hold. Proposing ideas about managing low risk for high return may not attract traditional management ridicule. Operating in environments where risk taking has to be factored in more tightly than before could mean being cognisant of possibilities for different returns. Notions about the yield value may need to be reframed together with the objectives of innovation. In putting forward such an argument we might need to move away from established notions of solutions to immediate problems and market advantage.

Sinfield and Solis (2016) suggest that what lies beyond solution perspectives (as in different types of innovation – radical, incremental, product and process), and indeed user perspectives which address a latent need or a problem, is the impact of innovation. It is only when we consider impact that we begin to comprehend the real drivers of innovation and its outcomes in terms of various forms of economic or social assessment (job creation, productivity gains and economic or social returns). The emphasis shifts from the investment or the technology to the process, helping us to understand how the innovation is being pursued, its context, its architecture and its instrumentation. Sinfield and Solis (2016) have developed an innovation impact model which is based on a proactive but less risky approach to realising high-impact innovation which they claim binds together 'lily pads' of capability-building investments, technical and conceptual advances, and market explorations into what we call *enabling innovations*. The model allows for an examination of impact along four dimensions:

1. *Reach* – Identification of the entire range of users and beneficiaries, from individuals to groups and social communities affected by the innovation.
2. *Significance* – The depth and range of benefits and advantages across a wide set of measures stretching from economics to the environment, health and culture, generated by the innovation.
3. *Paradigm change* – In common with strategic and radical innovation, the extent to which a specific innovation modifies directly or indirectly beliefs and views held in a particular domain of knowledge and practice.
4. *Longevity* – The extent of influence and the length of time over which an innovation is able to influence change, absorption and adoption in organisations and in society.

These four dimensions are operationalised through three key stages over time: the breakthrough period (major conceptual changes, inventions); the enabling window (the pursuit of a series of low-risk initiatives that allow current capabilities to be connected to end-user needs as early as possible); and the progressive innovation cascade (agglomerating capabilities). To illustrate these stages Sinfield and Solis (2016) refer to the following:

(a) The development of GPS, which provides the basis for a large number of applications including satellite navigation systems, Google Maps and wearable or handheld devices. These technologies have emerged because of breakthrough insights over a long period of time (over 50 years) based on a principle in physics called the Doppler effect and ways in which calculations were made to locate the Russian Sputnik satellite.

(b) The creation of mobile robotics by iRobot Corp., where its management ensured the matching of what it could achieve to application contexts of users to enable fairly rapid financial returns alongside the generation of cultural awareness and social acceptance of the product. iRobot has moved swiftly from space and military research to oil exploration, disaster management, pool cleaning, maritime applications, environmental monitoring and children's toys.

(c) Conceptual enablers such as crowdsourcing, which has spawned other conceptual innovations including crowdfunding, citizen science and the sharing economy, with each of them applying crowdsourcing techniques to solve problems, pool resources, curate collections and identify patterns of Big Data.

Readers would not be entirely remiss if they were to interpret Sinfield and Solis's ideas to be concerned primarily with major, strategic or radical innovations. Big breakthroughs take time to have an impact, and when they do they satisfy the high-risk takers. However, what these authors propose upends this notion of high risk and high returns by turning attention first to the cumulative nature of impact of different levels of insight and innovation, and then to the alignment of users with producers from the beginning to generate value through the innovation development process. By reframing the objectives of innovation and redefining impact holistically, they offer a lower-risk opportunity for enabling innovations. Firms adopting processes and practices based on 'lily pad' strategies are able to secure functional advantages of reduced cost, improved capabilities or better quality.

The 'enabling innovation' approach has a direct impact on how the innovation process is managed. It also has implications for how the process leads from the establishment of relatively new forms of innovation such as 'end-user', 'open' and 'platform innovation', to the constant modification of business models which are relevant for certain innovation and business outcomes, often leading to innovation in the business models themselves. Close alignment with contexts and customers can call for the use of 'frugal' and 'reverse' innovation processes where scarce resources and learning from unfamiliar environments can lead to productive outcomes.

PROCESS LEADING TO FORMS OF INNOVATION

Setting objectives is one thing firms need to do. However, as we have noted above, sticking to fixed objectives may not result in positive outcomes as circumstances change and ideas emerge from unexpected sources. Flexibility with demand might help to prevent being upstaged by either a technology that has different possibilities or from markets that emerge surprisingly. When low-cost airlines began to capture the imagination of airline companies, travellers and the tourist industry, many of the standard bearers of those industries, together with seasoned travellers, were caught napping. The disruptions in the industry affect both producers and users, and being able to anticipate these disruptions can help firms from losing competitive advantage. In a complex environment such as we have today, very few firms can acquire the full set of competencies to search for, select, implement and generate value. Networking and networked-based innovation (discussed in Chapter 8) can help to forge partnerships with other firms to manage the demands of disruptive information in a dispersed management platform where producers, intermediaries and end users become part of an open-sourced, open innovation management regime. The advent of platform technologies can augment this network-based process of managing innovation using smart technologies and processes. Where firms fail to harness these network-based forms of collaborative innovation, they fall behind. Delbridge (2003) and Delbridge and Barton (2002) refer to the motor sport industry and note that although the UK built most of the Formula One cars, its reluctance to collaborate for developing innovative products means that it does not capitalise on the internal capabilities as do, say, its Italian counterparts. Collaborating with end users in, for example, the luxury yacht industry should reveal the modern prevalence among yacht buyers to own floating palaces rather than boats with which to travel around the world (Cane, 2006).

CONCLUDING OBSERVATIONS

From what we have examined so far we note that the emergence and the use of different forms of innovation are a function of the process of innovation. While a firm may choose between product and process innovation types, or have a mix of the two as part of its product development portfolio, the forms are systemic models that will have a direct bearing on how those types will function in a business. Typically, the open innovation model will use networks and open source connectivity to support its product or process innovations.[1] 'Business model' innovation will look at ways in which all the components of a strategy implementation and value proposition model are reconfigured to meet new business objectives. The 'frugal innovation' model will examine ways in which constraints of scarcity of resources, institutions and other key elements in the innovation process in specific contexts will affect the making of new products or the provision of specific services. We discuss some of the most talked-about forms of innovation in the next chapter.

———— SELF-ASSESSMENT AND RESEARCH QUESTIONS ————

1. Distinguish between process innovation and the innovation process.

2. What constitutes the innovation process?

3. Consider the different stages of the innovation process and examine how they may apply to different types of firms.

4. How does the innovation process inform the business strategy of a firm?

5. How does the innovation process connect types of innovation to forms of innovation?

NOTE

1. Restating a point made previously, 'process innovation' is regarded as a type of innovation (see Chapter 8), while the innovation process refers to the set of functions, operations and use of resources and structures with which to implement an innovation strategy.

 ———— REFERENCES ————

Birkinshaw, J., Hamel, G. and Mol, M.J. (2008) 'Management innovation', *Academy of Management Review*, 33(4): 825–45.

Cane, A. (2006) 'Taking AIM to improve Britain's innovation performance', *The Edge: Economic and Social Research Council, UK*, Issue 21: 14–17.

CPI (2014) 'The innovation process', The Centre for Process Innovation, 3 May 2013; last updated 9 June 2014. Available at https://www.uk-cpi.com/news/the-innovation-process/ (last accessed 24 July 2016).

Delbridge, R. (2003) 'Knowledge, innovation and institutional change', *Work, Employment and Society*, 17(1): 187–96.

Delbridge, R. and Barton, H. (2002) 'Organizing for continuous improvement: structures and roles in automotive components plants', *International Journal of Operations & Production Management*, 22(6): 680–92.

Drucker, P.F. (1985a) 'The discipline of innovation', *Harvard Business Review*, May–June, 67–72.

Drucker, P.F. (1985b) 'Entrepreneurial strategies', *California Management Review*, 27(2): 9–25.

Jaruzelski, B. and Dehoff, K. (2010) 'The Global Innovation 1000: how the top innovators keep winning', *Strategy and Business*, 61(Winter Issue): 1–14.

Jaruzelski, B., Loehr, J. and Holman, R. (2011) 'The Global Innovation 1000: Why culture is key', *Strategy and Business*, 65(Winter Issue): 1–16.

Leinwand, P., Mainardi, C. and Kleiner, A. (2016) *Strategy that Works: How Winning Companies Close the Strategy-to-Executive Gap*. Boston, MA: Harvard Business Press.

Mol, M.J. and Birkinshaw, J. (2009) 'The sources of management innovation: when firms introduce new management practices', *Journal of Business Research*, 62(12): 1269–80.

Rothwell, R. (1992) 'Successful industrial innovation: critical success factors for the 1990s', *R&D Management*, 22(3): 221–39.

Sinfield, J.V. and Solis, F. (2016) 'Finding a lower-risk path to high impact innovations', *MIT Sloan Management Review*, 57(4): 79–89.

Tidd, J. and Bessant, J. (2013) *Managing Innovation Integrating Technological, Market and Organisational Change*, 5th edn. Chichester: Wiley.

FORMS OF INNOVATION

10

┌─ SCOPE AND OBJECTIVES ─┐

- Difference between forms and types.
- Form as strategic device.
- Open innovation and its characteristics, advantages and problems.
- Business model innovation.
- Frugal innovation and approaches to innovation in constrained circumstances.
- Frugality and thrift in different contexts.
- Reverse innovation.
- Design-centric innovation as form, function and strategic lever.

INTRODUCTION

In Chapters 8 and 9 we stated that we would like to distinguish between types and forms of innovation. This may sound like a semantic trope, but the readers' indulgence is solicited not least because we believe separating types from forms allows us to make an analytical distinction between what is given (types), in terms of our knowledge to date, and what emerges over time and through different interventions (forms). Types represent characteristics that explain the constituent elements of innovation. Different types have different characteristics. When these innovation types take shape in a specific context, for example within a specific organisation or in a particular geographical environment, or even as a result of the mix of two types of innovation, they begin to acquire forms that have an impact on the shape, structure and business model of a firm. Product and process or radical and incremental innovations can be regarded as types of innovation, as we noted in the previous chapter. However, when human or machine intervention enables intermixing of these types, they give shape to business activities. The way these activities are conducted and how resources are mobilised for market entry lead to the emergence of new innovations impacting on business models, the design of an organisational architecture and strategic approaches to the innovation activities in question. The conduct, administration and management of these activities constitute the innovation process.

Forms emerge as a consequence of the interplay of people, technologies and contexts. Forms can be imagined in terms of socio-political imperatives (underpinned by movements in the marketplace) as in the selection of specific strategic technologies over others that an organisation or a government intends to adopt. China's choice of solar and wind energies and the production of lithium batteries is a good example of strategic socio-political intervention as the country tries consciously both to discard its image as an environmental polluter and to harness the growth of new technologies as market leaders in innovation. IBM's decision to jettison the production of PCs was governed by a strategic choice for market leadership in the new era of Big Data and supercomputers. The Japanese company Softbank's acquisition of ARM Ltd in 2016 was perhaps motivated as much by the fall in the exchange value of the UK pound as it was by a far-sighted vision of the growth of the 'Internet of things'.

FORMS OF INNOVATION

It is impossible to do justice to all the different forms of innovation that constitute the systemic models used by businesses. However, a consideration of the more topical forms might help us to obtain insights into the innovation process that prevail today, namely 'open', 'business model', 'frugal', 'reverse' and 'design-centric' forms of innovation. Since there is a growing body of literature on each of these new forms, this section will only provide outlines of these models together with a set of references for further reading.

OPEN INNOVATION

The open innovation model is characterised by a dispersed distribution of resources, content, technologies and human capital obtained through networks of organisations. The network enables inflows and outflows of information (Chesbrough, 2003), technologies, knowledge and talent across borders and it therefore relies on connectivity, convergence of technologies, knowledge spillovers, and end-user involvement in the innovation process (von Hippel, 2005). The networked activities and the interlocking of firms create a flexible ecosystem of knowledge-based and knowledge-flowing organisations. The network also allows for the development of new, iterative business models (Chesbrough, 2006; 2008) centred around vertical disintegration, outsourcing, modularisation, niche technological expertise, global delivery platforms (Mitra and Natarajan, 2011) as well as access to resources, personalised and co-created experiences, and flexible, resilient business processes (Prahalad and Krishnan, 2008; Mitra, 2012).

The Prolific Linux Community

10,923 lines of code
= 300-page book, every day

Written by worldwide
open-sourced community
of people over 4 years
= 1,460 books

$10,800,000, 000
would be needed if conventional
software development
method was used to create Linux in
its entirety

Same team removes 5,547
lines of redundant code &
modifies 2,243

$50,000,000,000
– c size of
Linux economy
(inc. Linux related hardware,
consumer electronics & related
services

Open-source software
programming
supply chain-
2,700,000 lines
of code to Linux

C $ 0 – cost to start up
Linux

C 1 – person to start
Linux

5,000 developers + Large
Ecosystem

Bigger than GDP of
Costa Rica, Lebanon, Bolivia)

FIGURE 10.1   Open innovation: the Linux way

Source: Adapted from Tapscott and Williams (2010)

To obtain a simple understanding of the scale and depth of the open innovation model we need look no further than the organisational configuration of Linux. As Figure 10.1 shows, the organisation is made up of a worldwide community of individuals and businesses who operate voluntarily with Linux engineers to write and revise codes and who not only help to make considerable savings, but also help to generate significant value for the Linux economy.

WHY OPEN INNOVATION?

Open innovation works because it is difficult for any one firm to be the repository of the massive amounts of knowledge of technology and its multiple applications, changes in markets and customer behaviour across spatial borders, and the social and environmental factors affecting change. Much of this development is predicated upon the dependence of economic growth on specialisation and its concomitant diversification of the stock of knowledge from which opportunities for new technology development can grow (see Chapter 1). A geographical dimension emerges because the resources of knowledge, information, data and technology, and their diversification, no longer respect the hegemony of individual firms or local and national systems of innovation. Where there is specialisation and diversity firms disperse globally; firms seek complementarities in what we have come to describe as the knowledge economy (Smith, 2000). We can see that open innovation affects not only firms but also the geography of innovation. But how are these two levels of innovation affected by the open innovation model, and what can firms do to derive best value from such change?

In order to answer the questions above we need to pause briefly and try to understand the features and meaning of the open source configuration. Simply by being 'open' across industries and geographies, firms, by themselves and together with others, generate vast sources of data, endearingly referred to these days as Big Data. The vastness of such data means that it is generally out of control, and it is only by means of clever analytics and heavy doses of computing that we can begin to make sense of what we obtain. However, it is not just firms that produce data. Much of the data that is regarded as relevant is sourced from the interplay of technologies and the enabling role that the public sector, namely the government, plays in providing information to support their growth and development. So if 'open source' is the mechanism for data access, open data is the ingredient that is used to connect firms and their stakeholders vertically and horizontally, and open innovation is the model or form that makes use of open source and open data to create new products and services. People in open source environments within and outside a firm make use of social media. Technologies converge to make connectivity richer, firms rely on connected people and technologies to operate in networks of design and production, and the effect of this process is on all the players in society: the individual, the consumer and the citizen. Figure 10.2 encapsulates this explanation of the open configuration.

The 'Open' Configuration

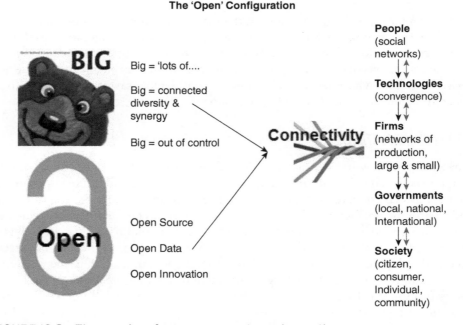

FIGURE 10.2   The meaning of open source and open innovation

OPEN INNOVATION AND THE BEHAVIOUR OF FIRMS

Firms involved in open innovation tend to intensify what is sometimes referred to as 'outside in' strategies for innovation (Ebersberger et al., 2011b). The term 'outside in' refers to processes of external technology commercialisation such as licensing out technology (as ARM Ltd does with its silicon chip technology for various handheld and mobile electronic devices), the sale of unused patents (Litchtenthaler and Ernst, 2007) or outsourcing (including externalised relationships created through offshore outsourcing or intra-firm trade which is based on offshore insourcing from affiliates).

Open innovation differs from traditional closed innovation in a number of ways. We have noted the involvement of multiple actors and the spread of the innovation process across firms and geographies, and the complexity of the process which mirrors the intricacies of innovation as firms try to obtain best resource value and optimal outcomes from their innovations. Table 10.1 shows the difference between closed and open innovation models and, as we can see, the objectives, environment,

TABLE 10.1 Differences between open and closed innovation

Innovation management approach, strategies and measures	Open innovation	Closed innovation
Core competency	Differentiation of core sets of skills and capabilities; link to external skill sets through collaboration; development of absorptive capacity	Internally focused, vertical integration of value chain from product design to development to service
Corporate culture and ethos	Open source; draw on capabilities and expertise widely	Keep closed to the firm and unerring faith in firm's tried and tested practices; 'not invented here' syndrome
Relationship with customers and the latter's function and roles	Collaborative and active co-designers, co-makers and co-producers	Passive end user; acceptance of what is given by producer with post hoc feedback
R&D	Internally focused, from design, development, market testing and market diffusion	Optimise use of own, shared and external assets
Intellectual property issues	Licensing, commercial development for monetising R&D; buy and sell approach	Own, protect and valorise
Evaluation metrics	Breakthrough business models; R&D ROI; economic and social bottom lines; network gain	Operationally and internally focused: cost reduction; reduction of time to market; increased revenue; increased market share

Source: Adapted from Forrester (2004)

methods, role of customers, metrics of measurement, ways in which intellectual property rights are secured and the nature of the R&D effort all vary substantially between these two forms.

Much of the difference is explained by the emphasis on externalisation as a means of generating creativity, design, production, process-level change and the effect and diffusion of innovation.

FROM CONNECTED FIRMS TO PRODUCTION NETWORKS OF OPEN INNOVATION

The real sophistication and complexity of open innovation models are found in global production networks (GPNs) such as those in the Pearl River Delta in China, where interconnected economic and non-economic actors are coordinated by a global lead firm, producing goods and services across multiple geographical locations for global markets (Coe and Yeung, 2015). For all firms involved in 'simple' or 'complex' open innovation activities, there is a greater need to enhance their 'absorptive capacity' and improve their integrative capabilities, together with the need to manage complex organisational structures that look both inside and outside the firm. Chesbrough (2006; 2007) argues that firms seek access to 'surplus markets of technology' either by way of purchasing them outright or by 'licensing in' their production. Indeed many firms do exactly that, but the real value of open innovation is derived from open innovation platforms in GPNs where it is not just the individual firm which obtains or appropriates economic value, but the wider network of interrelated firms which also accrue benefits because of their unique specialisation in labour or machine-intensive work. This is not to suggest that open innovation benefits are spread out evenly across all firms in different spaces, but rather that the mutuality of differentiated gains inherent in any networking arrangement appears to obtain in such an open innovation platform too.

THE PROCESS DIMENSION OF OPEN INNOVATION

In terms of functionality we can examine open innovation models using the standard components of the innovation process that we referred to earlier in the chapter, namely search, sourcing (for selection), collaboration (for selection and value generation) and externally supported sourcing and commercialisation (for implementation). Protection is another area of interest where patents are designed to create a market for knowledge (Geroski, 1995). Let us explore briefly four of these components: search, collaboration, external sourcing and protection.

SEARCH

Search in the open innovation model involves identification of resources external and novel to the firm and even sectors, thereby adding extra layers of uncertainty to the innovation process. A typical starting point could be the use of public registers of patents, academic publications and industry-focused market research. Beyond this formal level open innovation search routines will inevitably fall outside strong ties, with a greater reliance on weak ones emanating from information spillovers (Dahl and Pederson, 2004; Agarwal et al., 2006; 2008) from the community in which it is located. Firms are familiar with searching for information from the demand side among competitors, suppliers and consultants, as they constitute the normative behavioural pattern of any firm that scans the market for information. However, operating in the open innovation environment requires an openness of effort in searching for and retrieving external information (Fey and Birkinshaw, 2005), enabling firms potentially to manage the integration of a wide range of diverse but complementary sources of information. Knowing what and where to search, as between industrial sources and through more scientific channels, enables the firm to distinguish between complementary sources and those which are aimed at substituting existing ones. This distinction is particularly important for open innovation practitioners because of the multiple levels and types of stakeholder engagement, and choices that need to be made to ensure the best fit with the innovation process and the highest benefit from their use. Ebersberger et al. (2011a) show that industry-oriented search is highest among technology users, while science search, with its accent on R&D, is more likely to be size dependent. Larger firms tend to carry out more science-based search activities than SMEs.

COLLABORATION

The general literature on innovation refers to different forms of collaboration. So firms can collaborate with customers or suppliers and thereby 'extend their enterprises' (Dyer, 2000), connect with universities and R&D centres for acquiring new knowledge, form strategic alliances and partnerships with competitors and other firms to seek complementarities. The nature and scope of these linkages vary with the stages of the innovation process (Roper et al., 2008), and in some cases care has to be taken to avoid excessive reliance on strong ties of collaboration through the use of similar channels, thus precluding or impeding innovation (Danneels, 2003). Since collaboration can occur across spatial distances, it also has a geographical dimension. This form of collaboration becomes particularly important for firms located in low-agglomeration or isolated regions (Abubakar and Mitra, 2011). The impact of both diversity and geographical collaboration on management practices can be complicated, especially when there are pressures on people responsible for making effective use of these different forms of collaboration. The beneficial effects of collaboration tend to be pronounced in knowledge-intensive service sectors but not necessarily among high-tech manufacturers, generally the province of larger firms. Overall, smaller firms gain more from collaboration than their larger counterparts (Ebersberger et al., 2011a; 2011b).

EXTERNAL INNOVATION SOURCING

External sourcing occurs when large flows of technology resources occur internationally. These technologies are embodied in various products (components, machinery and patents) which are then used as inputs for innovation (Hauknes and Knell, 2009). Contract R&D is one form of external sourcing where innovative work is handed over to an external firm, but under predetermined contractual conditions and terms. This process involves actual technology transfer and is particularly useful when there is a need to obtain access to cutting-edge research, technologies and specific capabilities without incurring costs associated with the organisational change necessary for doing such work or being thwarted by internal rigidities (Leonard-Barton, 1992). Inevitably, outsourcing such work needs a process of readjustment as questions of integration of ideas or solutions provided by the external source may be difficult to achieve, and there may well be confidentiality and intellectual property issues which need early definition. The evidence of the benefits or disadvantages of knowledge sourcing is inconclusive. Sofka and Grimpe (2010) have found an inverted U-shape relationship between external innovation per employee and innovation outcomes or performance.

PROTECTION

Protection for innovation generally takes the form of patents. At least that is what the literature focuses attention on when making the link between R&D and innovation outcomes. If firms are better able to exploit their innovation investments that they wish to protect, then a firm can help to induce innovation. Beyond that, firms may also help promotion through disclosure and wider usage of inventions, facilitate commercialisation and make possible the systematic coordination of research among multiple actors. But it is unclear as to whether patent protection helps to appropriate profits out of innovation or whether there is a positive relationship between patents and R&D, particularly when so many innovations evolve from previous innovations. Since open innovation extends the scope of innovative activities of a firm outside its own boundaries, it is no longer appropriate to consider the firm to be the sole bastion of new product or service development. Patents enable the firm which is the knowledge producer in the main to protect its intellectual property (its knowledge assets) as this knowledge flows between firms and across borders.

Networked firms operating in open innovation platforms may include small, medium and large firms. Large and small firms are interlocked in their production networks across the value chain. Although large firms can be considered to be anchor firms in such networks, the size of firms is less important than the processes of networking and open innovation, and the outcomes resulting from these processes.

We referred above to the routine management process of search, collaboration, external outsourcing, protection and implementation that we expect to see in firms engaged in open innovation. There is, however, another level at which the open innovation model operates and that is the collective level. Here the focus is on what the mix of firms do as a collective, thus suggesting that without that collective endeavour open innovation does not obtain traction as a practising form of innovation. The key features of this collective process are dynamic socialisation and collective learning (Mitra, 2012).

DYNAMIC SOCIALISATION AND OPEN INNOVATION

The nature of connectivity among firms in global delivery platforms also involves a significant amount of dynamic socialisation at the organisation and individual levels. Producers, intermediaries and end users (von Hippel, 2005) create a social life of information and knowledge production (Seeley-Brown and Duguid, 2002). This social life is manifest in both the development and use of technologies, especially the Internet (Tuomi, 2008) and through the spillovers described above. The socialisation process reinforces the idea of business activity being embedded in society. More importantly it extends this notion of embedding by tying disparate social constructs established in different societies through networks of strong and weak ties across cultures and geographical domains. The socialisation process also serves to consolidate the strength of paradoxical ideas in innovation, business creation and growth. Social connectivity encourages collaboration among firms, including competitors. It can be argued that such collaboration simply allows the stronger (often larger) firm to dominate a network by virtue of the superior set of resources in its possession. Paradoxically, however, it is in the better value derived by smaller firms through open networking that we can measure the true effects of the socialisation of innovation. The greater the number of small firms involved in such networks, the higher their levels of participation, the larger the increase in the networked resource bank; and the wider the learning process, the stronger the gain that is derived from this socialisation process.

COLLECTIVE LEARNING AND OPEN INNOVATION

The connected, socialised, open innovation environment which affords a mix of different-sized and specialist firms enables the generation and acquisition of different forms of experiential learning about technologies, business processes, accessing resources and products and services. The open environment of learning is characterised by tacit forms, involving individuals (Polyani, 1966; Jones et al., 2007) and action learning 'on the job' by firms. Understanding the informal processes characterising learning in firms (Mitra, 2000) raises issues about the management process involved in capturing the different forms of learning, especially in global environments, and how that contributes to innovation. The learning agenda informs both the strategic and day-to-day practices of the innovative firm, which in turn leads to how firms manage the innovation process, together with their ability to adapt and be agile and ambidextrous – the three 'As' of innovative organisation that we discussed in Chapter 5 on the characteristics and features of innovative organisations. The confluence of the routines of open innovation which enable better internal management and effective externalisation, and the processes of dynamic socialisation and collective learning which engage many firms synergistically in an open innovation model, provides a framework for the open innovation process as exhibited in Figure 10.3.

The subject of open innovation has literally opened up exponentially to widespread use and enquiry. Consequently the subject of investigation is both vast and complex. Our purpose here is to identify some of its key strands and examine how

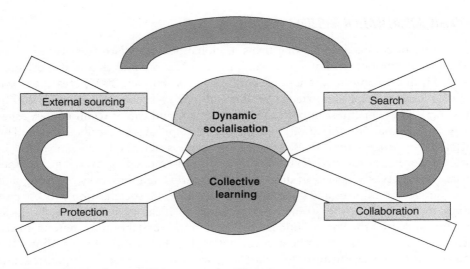

FIGURE 10.3   A framework for the process dimension of open innovation

open innovation has changed the direction of the innovation process in recent times, and how it either subsumes or works tangentially with business model innovation, designer-centric innovation, platform innovation, reverse innovation and even frugal forms of innovation. We move on to another of these forms – business model innovation.

BUSINESS MODEL INNOVATION

The combination of socialisation in the global open innovation environment with both individual and collective forms of learning leads to the generation of business models that are networked based in that they connect individual levels of expertise, often without transactional or pecuniary engagement. This is evident in the arena of Internet and computing technologies and software development (as in Skype, Linux or Apache), or in traditional industries using embedded software (as in Indian software firms working across different industry verticals). These processes help to establish different network-based business models, some of which are confined to specific network players, and others which are entirely open and organic. Brafman and Beckstrom (2006) use the metaphor of the 'starfish' to describe the type of mutating, network-centric, organisational model which is often leaderless and dependent on both trust and security. Here both organisational and individual expertise are leveraged, often freely to enhance products and services and where business models are developed as outcomes of such 'free' exchange.

Open, flexible business models help to realise the aggregate economic value of innovation in the market or multiple markets for different products and services by means of:

- access to resources – global access is more evident and critical than ownership because of the constantly changing nature of those resources and the use to which they can be put;
- co-creation with customers, distributors, suppliers and individuals outside the average business system as part of a process of socialisation;
- personalisation, where the end product or service is geared towards satisfying the individual customer experience; and
- convergence of technologies, talent, business models, even when each of these elements retains their individual character. (Prahalad and Krishnan, 2008)

But what is a business model and how do business models facilitate innovation? Can a business model be innovative? To answer these questions we need to take a brief look at what business models are and what they represent for any business.

WHAT DO BUSINESS MODELS REPRESENT?

It is perhaps tautologous to suggest that business models have been part of any business irrespective of their innovative capability. It has been integral to trading and economic activity since pre-classical times (Teece, 2010). The business model concept, however, became popular in the mid-1990s and some writers believe that the popularity may have been driven by the emergence of the Internet (Amit and Zott, 2001), rapid growth in emerging markets coupled with an interest in 'bottom of the pyramid' and frugal innovation ideas (Prahalad and Hart, 2002; Seelos and Mair, 2007; Thompson and MacMillan, 2010), and the growth of modern industries with their dependence on new technologies (Perkmann and Spicer, 2010). Business models have never been clearly defined and scholars have used different ways of explaining what they are. Typically, some researchers have referred to them as a statement (Stewart and Zhao, 2000), a description (Applegate, 2000; Weill and Vitale, 2001, 2002), a representation (Morris et al., 2005; Shafer et al., 2005), an architecture (Timmers, 1998; Dubosson-Torbay et al., 2002), a conceptual tool or model (Osterwalder, 2004; Osterwalder et al., 2005; George and Bock, 2009), a structural template (Amit and Zott, 2001), a method (Afuah and Tucci, 2001), a framework (Afuah, 2004), a pattern (Brousseau and Penard, 2007), and a set (Seelos and Mair, 2007). Zott et al. (2011) argue that the concept of the business model has been used to explain three phenomena: (1) e-business and the use of information technology in organisations; (2) strategic issues, such as value creation, competitive advantage and firm performance; and (3) innovation and technology management.

The acceleration of change and growth in ICT, the Internet and a drop in costs of communication and computing have made it possible to generate value through unusual forms of exchange and transaction architectures (Amit and Zott, 2001). Where this has been accompanied by the discovery of talent, expertise and resources outside the confines of a single firm and even across territorial borders, it has created the possibilities for designing new types of linkages with customers and suppliers (Brynjolfsson and Hitt, 2004) and connected organisational forms (Daft and Lewin, 1993; Mendelson, 2000; Dunbar and Starbuck, 2006). Flows of relationships and resources coupled with novel forms of value exchanges have led scholars to introduce schematics and tools for the design and analysis of Internet-based business initiatives (Zott and Amitt, 2002) or value maps to show the web of connectivities (Tapscott et al., 2001).

The core logic of a business model revolves around a firm's revenues and costs, its value proposition to the customer, and the mechanisms to capture value. As Zott et al. (2010) explain, business models tend to:

- focus on the how rather than the what, where and when of doing business;
- offer a holistic perspective rather than attending to functional aspects such as finance or marketing;
- have a sharper focus on value creation rather than value capture; and
- identify the role of partners and collaborators in the development of the business model for the focal firms.

It is this holistic approach emphasising value creation and external collaboration that distinguishes business models. It is also this approach that lends itself to the conceptualisation of business model innovation. Instead of continually trying to improve and innovate with products and processes, the interest in examining innovation across the board is what appears to attract business executives, as we noted in Chapters 5 and 6. This conceptualisation is different from Chesbrough's (2006) idea of using business models for technological innovation.

BUSINESS MODEL INNOVATION

Mitchell and Cole (2003) argue that firms can view the business model itself as a subject of innovation. In an 'open-sourced' environment the business model itself can become part of intellectual property (Rivette and Kline, 2000; Rappa, 2001).

Given the involvement of collaborators both upstream and downstream, firms with open innovation business models can trigger additional business model innovation in complementary markets (Gambardella and McGahan, 2010).

Scholars and practitioners appear to have arrived at a consensus that states that business model innovation is key to firm performance through the aegis of corporate transformation and renewal (e.g. Pohle and Chapman, 2006; Johnson et al., 2008; Demil and Lecocq, 2010; Sosna et al., 2010). Experimentation is deemed to be the norm in business model innovation (Hayashi, 2009). It would be short-sighted to ignore the need for a leadership agenda for the effective management of business model innovation centred around the agility of firms, dynamic decision-making structures, the overcoming of cognitive inabilities that can hamper cross-organisational relationships through outsourcing, joint project management and other channels that contend with novel ideas of mutual gain in the network of participating firms.

Despite all the fanfare of modern technologies, one way of understanding what business model innovation (BMI) does is to understand the concept at its simplest level. BMI demands 'neither new technologies nor the creation of brand-new markets:

It's about delivering existing products that are produced by existing technologies to existing markets. And because it often involves changes invisible to the outside world, it can bring advantages that are hard to copy' (Girotra and Nettesine, 2014). In many respects the advantages derive from unique ways of shaping the redirection of its business through BMI. BMI helps to consolidate the firm's inimitable resources, which according to the resource-based view of the firm (Wernerfelt, 1984; Barney, 1991; Teece et al., 1997; Kozlenkova et al., 2014) define the individual character of a business organisation.

Girotra and Nettesine (2014) stress several actions that firms should take to reap the best harvest from BMI. Their framework is presented and adapted in Vignette 10.1. We select three of the four actions that they present in their article. The fourth action point not referred to here is about providing and understanding the rationale for changes in decision making which is in part inherent in the actions taken.

VIGNETTE 10.1   A FRAMEWORK FOR THE PRACTICE OF BUSINESS MODEL INNOVATION

1. Selecting an optimal mix of products by focusing narrowly on offerings, searching for commonalities across products and creating a hedged portfolio.

NARROW FOCUS

The authors refer to a *Bloomberg* 2010 article on Diapers.com, a venture of Quidsi, an Internet start-up, and how Amazon allowed the firm to focus narrowly after its purchase of Quidsi. Diapers sell regularly at least for the first 2 years of a child's life. They are in constant demand, together with stable birth rates and the well-understood biological functions of babies, means that the firm can offset for the inconvenience of shipping them (bulky and costly) and their ready availability at most stores by focusing on the steady stream of revenue earned.

COMMONALITIES

Volkswagen's strategy to use common products across all its cars allows the car maker to share component parts and add new products across its portfolio. Amazon's sale of books, music, video games and now groceries relies on its well-honed logistics strategy. The focus on logistics also helps it to deal with quirky market-related problems, as in India where Amazon adds to its own distribution channels, local grocery stores who help to distribute their goods.

HEDGING

Chilean Lan Airlines (or LATAM Airlines) uses the same wide-body aircraft for cargo and passenger traffic for its international routes, especially between the Americas and Europe. Most international passenger flights on that route fly overnight, resulting in

(Continued)

(Continued)

many airlines simply holding their aircraft at other hours. Chilean LAN airlines makes use of those hours to ship cargo, thus hedging its products and services to mitigate any risk.

2. Choosing the Time for Decisions Carefully

POSTPONING DECISIONS

Postponing decisions to make the best use of services and seek high yields is often a matter of making the best decisions at the right time, a strategy which elides the attention of routine managers obsessed by fixed decisions made in times which suit the managers rather than the business. Using the semi-automated business research environment (SABRE) system, American Airlines is able to alter its prices by factoring in new information and not depend on fixing prices too early in an uncertain marketplace, thus setting the trend for dynamic pricing in the airline industry. As Uber riders know, the practice of 'surge pricing' and variable pricing according to the type of usage (sole or shared services) can help it reduce demand while increasing supply.

AMENDING THE ORDER OF DECISIONS

Amending the order of decisions can be productive for firms when they do not have the luxury of changing the time frame of their operations overall. This could mean turning on its head the new product development process. Instead of seeking investment first, firms such as 'Innocentive' and 'Hypios' rely on performance first and investment afterwards! Clients seeking solutions to problems are offered a website to present their R&D problems to a global freelance community of scientists, qualified engineers and product designers. The clients offer monetary rewards for the best solutions, which may range from the chemical synthesis of a specific molecule to the actual design of a new product.

SPLITTING KEY DECISIONS

Splitting key decisions prevents managers from embracing all aspects of complex decisions at any one point of time. This type of comprehensive decision making often holds in the preparation of business plans. However, in a start-up situation a lean approach would allow for a new venture to start with fairly unclear or a limited set of hypotheses for what opportunities might be available or what may work. Rather than working to a prepared business plan a start-up could gather information and resources at multiple stages and let the business model evolve through pivoting, before a final version can be validated. This method is close to the idea of effectuation of Sarasvathy (2001; 2009), who proposed that in situations of uncertainty goals may not be clearly known and that there is no assurance of an independent environment for an ultimate selection mechanism. With effectuation, entrepreneurs will determine goals according to the resources in their possession.

3. Identifying the Smart or Best Decision Maker

SHARING DECISION MAKING

The smartest decision makers are not always the managers of a firm. Evolved and shared decision making with committed employees and even with external partners can produce effective results. Walmart, for example, shifted some of the decision-making process about the stocking of its store shelves to Procter & Gamble, because the latter supplier had the right mix of information and incentives and optimal delivery and production schedules to maintain Walmart's stocks. Now Walmart uses this as a standard procedure with all its main suppliers.

PASSING RISK

Walmart's example also accommodates the idea of passing the risk to a third party. An even clearer example of such an approach can be found in Amazon's decision not to stock large volumes of books or music, but to engage with other wholesalers or publishers who ship products directly to customers sometimes using Amazon packaging. The wide distribution of risk makes it affordable for the sharing to be optimised in the business model of both Amazon and its partners.

SHARING AND PASSING ON GAINS

In sharing the gain from a decision-making and production process with partners, firms may be better able to retain their customers better and obtain higher yields. Firms making complex high-technology products often face the problem of passing on some of the gain to their customers who feel they do not necessarily benefit from the new product as much as the producer. 'Netafim', a drip irrigation technology firm, introduced a technology that adjusts water application according to the soil's water content, salinity and fertilisation, and to meteorological data. Farmers were promised increases in crop yields of above 300%. However, the reluctance of farmers to adopt such sophisticated technology meant that Netafim had to think of other ways of selling and diffusing the product. It did so by offering the farmers an integrated package that included system design and installation, all the required hardware, and periodic maintenance, all for free. Netafim earned its payback by negotiating a share of each farmer's increased crop yields. So while Netafim took on all the risks of the decision, the farmers simply had to choose between buying the product or not, with the possibility of earning more money with no risk if they made a positive selection.

Source: Adapted from Girotra and Nettesine (2014)

Our discussion about open innovation and BMI reflects the dynamics of the fast-changing environment of modern business activity. Part of this change process recognises the importance of contexts. One of the most disruptive elements about contexts is that it is no longer appropriate to expect linear models of innovation developing in any part of the world or in the adoption of innovation practices which are simply transferred from one environment to another.

FRUGAL INNOVATION

It is argued in common parlance that frugality begets opportunity. When resources are scarce then minds are concentrated to try and beat the scarcity trap through ingenious or innovative ways. Most businesses face scarcity of one kind or another, but not all managers have the necessary competencies for generating business models that help to overcome the deficit suffered, especially in the early years of a venture or during rapid growth under intensive competition, and in an environment of economic decline or recession. The 2007–8 recession and its obdurate hold on global economies since that time have made frugal innovation a very popular concept for consideration in both developed and developing countries.

The concept of frugality in business and its role as a source for innovation has evolved over time with links to other concepts such as bricolage. Many of the ideas germinate in the lives of people in either day-to-day conditions of hardship or under extreme conditions. The strength of people, the resourcefulness that they show and the ability to turn around situations under duress are key features of frugality in society from which business can learn a considerable amount. We will reflect on an extreme situation in the next vignette.

VIGNETTE 10.2   EXTREMETIES 8,000 FEET ABOVE SOUTH SUDAN

THE EMERGENCY SCENARIO

Early one morning in South Sudan, two British nurses of Médecins Sans Frontières (MSF; Doctors Without Borders) opened the door of their clinic to two patients with gunshot wounds. One of these people was a 10-year-old child and the other was his uncle, both shot during a cattle raid. They were hundreds of miles away from the nearest hospital and the only option available was to move them by land and by air to the capital, Juba. The nurses managed to stabilise the child and his uncle with the scant resources at their disposal, but halfway to Juba the boy started to suffocate in front of one of the nurses, Michael Sheki, because of the air pressure in the aircraft forcing his lungs to collapse. To save his life Michael had to insert a needle into his chest so that the trapped air could escape. But there was no chest X-ray or ultrasound equipment available. Michael had no experience of performing such a task in an aeroplane flying at an altitude of 8,000 feet (2,400 m).

Michael's reaction in this extreme environment of no real choice was to punch the needle into the child's chest. As he did so the air hissed out and the boy was saved for that moment. He continued to bleed, his blood pressure was alarmingly low, and it was difficult to get any tubes into his arm to give him fluids. What was necessary was to inject fluid directly into the marrowbone by way of a procedure called intraosseous infusion. In the UK this would be possible using a drill, the overall procedure taking about 10 seconds to accomplish. There in Leer in South Sudan they were in possession of only a child-size intraosseous needle. Michael and his fellow nurse, Chrissie McVeigh, took turns every half an hour to drill the infusion into the uncle, and fortunately, after some time, a sufficient volume of fluids was pumped into his veins to help him stabilise.

THE ENVIRONMENT OF RESOURCE CONSTRAINTS

The traumatic experience of both the child and his uncle, and indeed of the two nurses, though unexpected, is something that could be anticipated in that location. Michael had arrived in Leer to help with the re-establishment of the MSF hospital after it had been looted and destroyed in the summer of 2015. At that time they slept in tuluks (circular mud huts) without access to any electricity or running water. Snakes and scorpions roamed freely in the ruins of the hospital where the tuluks were situated. The eagles which nested in the trees would swoop down to steal their breakfast or dinner. In this environment a large number of people were being treated for gunshot wounds. If fighting broke out nearby the only recourse they had was the 'grab sacks' which would provide them with a supply of food and water for a couple of days if they have to find refuge in the bush.

Those people who emerged from the bush where they were hiding to seek healthcare were of course taking a big risk with their lives. Chrissie had established an outpatient clinic in the ravaged grounds of the old hospital. In another encounter a man and a woman came to the clinic with their very sick 21-year-old son who had been shot in the knee 4 months earlier. The parents had fled with the son when the town of Leer was attacked, sheltering in the bush and then finding a small island in a swamp where they continued to live. They rushed over to the makeshift clinic, walking through the night to the hospital when they heard that MSF was back, to try to salvage some peace of mind, determined to find healthcare for their son. They were given intravenous antibiotics and then referred to Juba.

Chrissie tells the story of the last day of her time in Leer, saying farewell to people when she saw a man with an extensive amputation of his right arm and shoulder who was stepping off the aeroplane on Leer's airstrip. It was the uncle of the boy who had arrived suddenly one morning at the MSF clinic. The boy, as Chrissie observed, was 'ticketyboo'. The 21-year-old son who was brought by his parents to the clinic also recovered.

Frugality had won the day for the people – the brave patients and the equally brave nurses.

Source: Médecins Sans Frontières (MSF) 'Without Borders' newsletter (n.d.), msf.org.uk/podcast (available through *New Internationalist*, August 2016)

What does this vignette tell us about frugal innovation? We note the extreme conditions of war and conflict in a very hostile environment, together with that of impending death and high trauma and the absence of adequate resources. MSF had returned to the spot to rebuild its hospital and continue its incomparable medical and humanitarian service. There was no proper technology to provide solutions to problems because the conditions did not or could not allow for its availability. The innovation centred around the motivation for not accepting the status quo (in this case not just a status quo that defines a form of survival, but death!), the mobilisation of whatever was at hand to address the urgency and immediacy of a life-threating situation, and then to find solutions for the problem at hand. There was no economic gain in the short run for anyone, except that the socially innovative act of saving lives with meagre resources could well have positive economic outcomes in the future.

An innovative business will want to gain from outcomes. This vignette will not offer any recipes for satisfying such a want. What it will recommend, however, to any enterprise is the vision, motivation, methods, alacrity of thought and action, and the art of making do with whatever is at hand to solve problems. Behind them all is the insatiable desire for the importance of meaning in life as opposed to any sense of resignation to a prescribed idea of inevitability, only because hope counts for so little when frugality is a bind.

DEFINITIONS AND APPLICATIONS OF FRUGAL INNOVATION

Most definitions and explanations of frugal innovation focus on the ability 'to do more with less'; that is, to create more business and social value while minimising the use of diminishing resources such as 'energy, capital and time' (Radjou and Prabhu, 2015). A good place to find its application is in developing countries where resources are always scarce, where poverty enforces people to find frugally innovative outcomes from the use of limited resources. In these economies scarcity is not limited simply to financial or technological resources (Sharma and Iyer, 2012), but also to weak or non-existent institutional settings (Mair and Marti, 2009) and an absence of other material resources and human capita, which in turn encourage the search for frugal solutions to significant economic and social problems (Baker and Nelson, 2005).

Pansera (2012) refers to case of Liter Bottles in the small town of Uberaba in the state of Minas Gerais in Brazil. Long and regular electric supply shortages were a problem for many people and especially Mr Alfredo Moser, because he was not willing to accept the deficit model status quo, but rather wanted to explore ways in which it would be possible to light up his house with solar light using plastic bottles hanging from the roof. It took nearly 10 years before the MyShelter Foundation remodelled this relatively simple eco-friendly innovation as a smart solution to a major energy supply problem and began to install them in the slums of Manila in the Philippines for only 1 dollar each. Thousands of slums from around the country were provided with solar-based electricity brought to them by the very low-cost 15,000 'Liter Bottles' by September 2011.

Another well-known story is that of Mitticool. We present this story in Vignette 10.3.

VIGNETTE 10.3   THE 'MITTICOOL' EXPERIENCE

THE BACKGROUND AND THE PROBLEM

In 2001, an earthquake in the Indian state of Gujarat ruined hundreds of thousands of lives. Survivors lost most of their possessions. Mansukhlal Raghavjibhai Prajapati, an ordinary and modest clay craftsman in rural India who grew up in a family of traditional clay manufacturers, spent a good deal of time in the disaster zone in Gujarat as a relief worker. He observed that many families were without fresh food and water and that they had no means of storage of limited supplies. While reading a local newspaper, Mansukhbhai's attention was drawn to a picture of a smashed clay pot. The image of the clay pot together with his notes on the problem local villagers faced made him wonder what he could do with clay to offer a solution to the problem of preserving basic food and health products for farmers. To help to try and meet this need, he designed a cheap clay refrigerator – the 'Mitticool' refrigerator – that does not require electricity to keep food fresh, in a tiny village near Rajkot in rural Gujarat, for the rural population (Mahadevan, n.d.).

A 'fridge' can be considered to be out of bounds of many people in India, where much of the population falls below the poverty line despite India's recent economic surge as measured by GDP. If a fridge is purchased then it does consume a lot of electricity. It is believed that often as much as one-fifth of a household's annual electricity shifts heat from the interior of a fridge to the exterior, so that the inside is cooled to a temperature below the ambient temperature.

THE TECHNOLOGY AND THE SOLUTION

The idea of the 'Mitticool' is based on an earthenware food preservation system drawn from ancient times – the age-old principle of 'Surahi', or cooling through evaporation (Mahadevan, n.d.). It relies on harnessing water and its ability to remove heat through evaporation. Inspired by antecedents, Mansukhbhai developed the idea of an affordable fridge that works without electricity based on this principle of evaporation. The water that drips down the side of an upper chamber evaporates, thus taking the heat away from the inside, leaving the chambers with porous clay surfaces cool. So as the water evaporates from the porous clay surface, it cools the interior, enabling people to store fruit, vegetables, milk and other perishable food items.

Weighing 20 kg and with a capacity for 20 litres of water, 5 kg of vegetables and fruit and 5 litres of milk or any liquid material (Mahadevan, n.d.), the refrigerator can keep vegetables fresh for 4 to 5 days. It can also keep milk and buttermilk fresh for 24 hours. It is also claimed that the original taste of the food is kept intact. The inside temperature of the refrigerator can fall to a level approximately 8°C lower than the outside temperature. A tap on the front of the unit doubles up as a water cooler. The only major complaint that Mansukhbhai has had to deal with was the magnet on the fridge door giving way (Mahadevan, n.d.)!

(Continued)

(Continued)

The refrigerator is ideal for dry climates where evaporative cooling works effectively and where it operates as a major and innovative replacement for expensive electricity-driven refrigerators. This aspect limits its use to such climates, but with the increasing prospect of warmer climates and parched earth, the refrigerator could have universal applications as a low-cost and eco-friendly way to extend the shelf life of farm produce.

THE ECONOMIC AND SOCIAL GAIN

Costs are kept low because the refrigerator requires no maintenance other than basic cleaning. It reduces electricity bills, thus helping many rural families to save money over time. Reduced costs also help to keep down the price of the fridge, which at $50 has enjoyed rapid success across India and elsewhere, especially in tropical countries. Monthly sales of around 50 refrigerators, 500 clay water filters, 500 pressure cookers and 1,000 frying pans a month (Mahadevan, n.d.) have generated quite a lot of attention for this unique innovation and its innovator. Energised by the success of the product, Mansukhbhai has managed to scale its production successfully. He has diversified his product portfolio by making a variety of clay products such as non-stick frying pans, clay pots and water filters. Today he employs a large number of people in his own community and serves consumers in India and abroad. A few years ago *Forbes* magazine named him among the most influential grassroots Indian entrepreneurs (Radjou et al., 2012).

THE NEXT COOL STAGE

Mansukhbhai has orders from all over the world and has been a recipient of many awards. He has received ISO certification and his frying pans have been approved as having a food-grade quality coating. His future plans include starting a factory with the aid of the National Innovation Foundation at IIM Ahmedabad and making a Mitticool house!

Sources: Mahadevan (n.d.); ecoideaz; Pansera (2012); Permaculture Research Institute (2013)

The 'Mitticool' story is about frugal innovation which works with natural constants that are built into the design of the product. It is a graphic illustration of how highly industrialised and sophisticated technology products simply do not work in specific environments because that industrial mindset can overlook simple solutions to acute problems. It also exposes the fallacy of ranking regions and countries based on criteria that emphasise technological superiority rather than the necessary service provided and the purpose of the innovation.

FRUGAL AND JUGAAD

Low-cost, frugal innovation niches are diffused across different developing countries which all have their own approach to offering low-cost innovative solutions to problems.

In India, the colloquial term 'Jugaad' refers to a creative idea or a quick workaround to get through commercial, logistic or legal issues (Radjou et al., 2012). Jugaad innovation enables the transformation of, for example, waste into a useful product. Western tourists much enthused by the emotions wrought in films such as *Slum Dog Millionaire* recount heart-warming stories from their visits to the Dharavi slums of Mumbai in India! It is argued that the creative and clever ideas of slum dwellers contribute to the development of many small enterprises in India (Brem and Wolfram, 2014).

Radjou et al. (2012) define Jugaad innovation as a kind of 'innovative fix' stemming from clever and smart ideas for an improvised solution to a problem. Such a statement romanticises the basic idea of doing 'more with less', but there is a view which looks at Jugaad from the perspective of art, culture, mentality, and not just as a process or result (Bubel et al., 2015). Counting the pluses and minuses of Jugaad we find that while Jugaad-led enterprises use improvised approaches to solving problems to satisfy needs quickly at low cost, the activity involved in such improvisation tends to lack discipline and a systematic approach (Lacy, 2011; Brem and Wolfram, 2014). Prahalad and Mashelkar (2010) find in Jugaad the reality of radical innovation that involves the search for alternative solutions and improvisations, which not only 'make do' and overcome the lack of resources, but also find seemingly insoluble problems. The authors stress, however, that this term can be associated with the poor quality of solutions being used. Proposed innovative and radical solutions for problems are mainly based on simple assumptions, aimed at the provision of uncomplicated products at low costs that give large benefits. These products are offered to the poorest people, locating Jugaad innovation in poverty and often manifest in the rush to produce quick and easy solutions, leading to the making of makeshift or low-quality products.

Terms with fairly similar meanings are used in Brazil (*gambiarra*), China (*zizhu chuangxin*) and certain parts of Africa (*jua kali*) (Radjou et al., 2012). Those innovations share some very basic features (Tiwari and Herstatt, 2011). They must be (1) robust to deal with infrastructure shortcomings such as voltage fluctuations, (2) fault resistant to cope with unsophisticated or even illiterate users, and (3) affordable for larger sections of the society.

The association of Jugaad or frugal innovation with development, and very often poverty, can generate rather stereotypical ideas of the value and the limitation of its deployment in varying environments. Quick, easy solutions based on making do with whatever is available is what one can apparently expect when people are starved of resources. In the process ingenuity is also confined to what is possible given not only limited resources, but also constrained human capital, especially formal human capital. If limited resources meant a simple redesigning of solutions to suit limited resources and capacities and the finding of immediate or temporary solution to problems, then its purchase or value as a concept of innovation, especially technological innovation, would be more or less insignificant. But as Zeschky et al. (2014) suggest, the concept of frugal innovation itself is not necessarily limited to redesigned solutions, but rather to the use of the scarce resources available in a given environment to produce originally designed products and services. These products are characterised by new product architecture, with new features and applications.

According to Gupta (2009; 2010a; 2010b; 2012), frugal innovation is like a new management philosophy which integrates market-specific needs, especially those at the bottom of the pyramid, starting where it matters most in that market and then working in reverse to find appropriate solutions that may be profoundly different from solutions available previously for the needs of upmarket segments. It is this transformation in the design, use and value to the specific market that defines the process of frugal innovation. Frugality in innovation is not concerned with the use of cheap technological and human resources, but with the reconstruction, reorganisation, modernisation and enhancement of products and processes in a way that avoids unnecessary costs (Woolridge, 2010; Zeschky et al., 2014).

FRUGALITY IN DEVELOPED AND DEVELOPING ECONOMIES

According to Govindarajan and Trimble (2012), there are five gaps that separate developing and developed economies.

- performance gap;
- infrastructure gap;
- sustainability gap;
- regulatory gap;
- preferences gap.

It is assumed that the quality of products is a function of the level of income in a country or a region. So the low level of income in a poor country could mean acceptance of a decrease in the quality of offered products in exchange for a lower price. The accepted performance-to-price ratio can be accounted for by the decrease in technological features by 50% and a 15% decrease in price. The performance gap as measured by the quality of products and services is, therefore, dependent upon income in a country or a region. A relatively low level of infrastructure can affect investment plans, leading to what is referred to as the 'infrastructure gap', as is sometimes the case in emerging markets. Here, however, one can derive a unique innovation advantage for the country or the region because the construction of infrastructure does not always have to be the same as those in other countries which provide existing solutions in developed economies but have limited relevance to developing ones.

The lack of environmental protection can generate a 'sustainability gap', but this is not necessarily confined to emerging economies. China and the USA are close, environment-polluting bedfellows! However, a focus on investment that can support technology and environmentally-friendly solutions can attract investment for innovative solutions to the problem, especially in developing countries, as China has demonstrated with its concentration on wind and solar energies. Advanced regulatory systems and institutions are the hallmark of stable developed economies, but it is uncertain whether any economy can maintain a permanently stable economic environment. While strong regulatory conditions and institutions provide for the effective deployment of market rules – safeguards for customers and sellers, consumers and employees, they may also result in rigid systems which can have a negative effect on the innovation process. Hence, the regulatory gap can apply both ways for both developed and developing economies. Finally, it is all about people and their social, cultural and moral diversity as a group of customers and citizens. This diversity can encourage innovation and increase absorptive capacity for innovative change, but also hinder the innovation process. The impact of this variety of outcomes shapes and results in the 'preferences gap'.

The five gaps referred to above are reflected in the innovativeness of products and services produced in different countries and regions. They can be used to measure innovation performance but their use to rank countries and regions in terms of their innovative capabilities may be limited, not least because of the mixed effects of some of these gaps which can create unexpected outcomes. This suggests that similar types and forms of innovation can occur in varied environments, but with the necessary differentiation resulting from the resource pool available in those environments. The gaps referred to may not necessarily distinguish innovation in developed and developing economies in terms of a technological or a skills hierarchy. Superior technology in a prosperous economy may not generate appropriate innovations because of the rigidity of institutions or regulatory burdens. Recessionary conditions may prompt changes in an approach to innovation, resulting in the adoption of frugal approaches borrowed from other countries. Higher levels of environmental awareness could foster leaner and more locally-oriented innovations. Growing income inequality in developed economies may usher in an era of thrift, a far cry from the bonanza years of the recent past. These are some of the underlying reasons which also help to explain why frugal innovation has emerged as a new route to finding creative solutions to business problems. Coupled with technological advances designed to disrupt standard business models, we note the emergence of different business practices in what is sometimes referred to as the sharing economy.

Plastyc, a start-up, aims to put the power of a bank in our mobile phones by providing affordable 24-hour links to Federal Deposit Insurance Corporation (FDIC)-insured virtual bank accounts that can be accessed from a mobile device or from an Internet-enabled computer in our homes or in an office. Radjou and Prabhu (2015) explain that the consumers cannot go overdrawn and incur no late fees, while the low-fee, no-frills online banking services has attracted nearly 70 million 'underbanked or unbanked' Americans who are not in a position to pay extortionate bank charges. A very different example is found in the work of the Italian artist and designer who, drawing on constructivist principles, transforms materials such as wire, bamboo and fragments of electric components into unusually witty, useful and elegant objects. The cardboard cathedral in Christchurch, New Zealand, showing how inexpensive materials can help to construct affordable housing in natural disaster areas, was the work of the Japanese architect, Shigeru Ban:

> The cardboard cathedral is a symbol of moving on. So while a fully intact stone cathedral still remains on the city council's letter head and the top image in a Google search, there are signs of a city doing just that. When visitors to

Christchurch get a tourist map, for example, the cover of it features a newer vision – a cathedral made of cardboard … The cathedral has elements of wood, steel and poly-carbonate and is built to 130% of the current earthquake stand-ard. It is designed to last for 50 years – it was never meant to be permanent. Barrie says it also shows how such structures can be a model of what is possible in post-disaster environments. 'It was one of the first things that Christchurch could point to and say "we are rebuilding".' (Andrew Barrie, professor of archi-tecture at Auckland University, quoted in the *Guardian*, 17 September 2014)

COST-DRIVEN PRODUCERS OR COST-SAVING USERS?

By the measures adopted by Plastyc, frugality is not necessarily a cost-driven form of innovation. It is rather a process that induces cost savings among users. The switch to aluminium cars by the likes of BMW and Jaguar is testimony to frugality in manufac-turing emanating from an interest in lighter cars and lower fuel consumption. This does not make the car cheaper in the short run, but it appeals to a different form of social consciousness among those who can afford it. Digitisation in technology has also created opportunities for the disruption of business models and supply chains as manufacturers attach sensors to car tyres and refrigerators to collect data on the quality of driving, the use of tyres, and enabling the busy man or woman in the home to remember when to replace milk.

We need, however, to be careful about the use of the concept of 'frugality' in dif-ferent contexts. In poorer economies frugality may well be a necessity because the starting point could be that of comprehensive scarcity – money, materials, skills base (measured in formal terms), access to new knowledge (if we can assume an artificial hierarchy of knowledge), and an often forgotten resource of time (given the preoc-cupation with survival) and cognitive range. The objective of innovation in such a context is often that of delivering on survival. As the Mitticool story shows, it was critically necessary to respond to a major disaster in a productive way that earned sur-vival first and improvement in conditions second. The fact that a degree of ingenuity in and among the individual's network makes it possible to develop a longer-term benefit based on the specific model of a new kind of refrigerator is a function of the necessity that generated it. Questions of sustainability, cost-consciousness and social benefits are all products of ingenious actions, discoveries and inventions. They are also built into the innovation process in the sourcing of materials, the use of limited infrastructure, and critically time and money. There is no other alternative that users and producers have in those environments.

In a developed economy context the starting point is that of abundance, tem-pered sometimes by economic downturns or mismanagement, and its social and ecological ramifications. In these circumstances, an approach to frugality in inno-vation is predicated upon the need for better resource management and improved governance, not an overwhelmingly constrained environment. The continuing advances in technology make it possible to depend on additional resources which are generally not available in developing economies. There is, therefore, a greater possibility for introducing a range of social, environmental and other objectives as *ex ante* considerations for innovation.

In both types of economies referred to above, we find increasingly a greater push towards the socialisation of both innovation and entrepreneurship. This entails, first, a greater sense of networking among the public, private and social (third-sector) actors, a form of social invention to describe new forms of social relationships (Coleman, 1970). It also reflects the increased user–producer relationships that we referred to earlier, and finally the growing realisation of not only the role of government in creating new services for the public good, but the active involvement of citizens in the creation, design and financing of innovation projects.

REVERSE INNOVATION

One of the consequences of a greater focus on frugality (albeit for different reasons in varied economies) is a reversal in the traditional flow of innovations from rich countries to poor countries. This reversal marks a conceptual turnaround of our understanding of innovation based on the simple idea of making ultra-affordable products and providing services dependent on clever processes and smart business models. This is increasingly evident in the availability of cheaper cars, washing machines, the drilling of oil and open heart surgery. Good examples include Chinese medical device firms such as Mindray and Wandong, whose ultrasound and X-ray machines are offered at bargain prices to the American consumer. Mahindra Truck and Bus Division from India has introduced highly sophisticated but affordable tractors for new farmers in the land of seemingly invincible John Deere tractors, the USA. Other outstanding examples include wireless banking by Safaricom from Kenya, which does more business in just that one African country than Western Union does in the global marketplace; open heart surgeries by the Narayana Hrudalaya Clinic in India at one-tenth of the price offered by the likes of the Mayo or Cleveland Clinics in the USA; and deep-sea oil drilling by Petrobas in Brazil (Ramamu, 2013).

The reverse direction of the innovation process, as exemplified above and as explained by Immelt et al. (2009), involves the development of ideas and products or services in emerging markets, and then introducing them in developed countries. A central feature of this form of innovation is the greater emphasis on quality and not the price of the product or service, thus allowing for altered propositions (Hossain, 2013). These elements are captured in Trimble's (2012) definition of reverse innovation, which states that a reverse innovation is first adopted in the developing world and offered to customers wherever they might be. The actual geography of the creator, ideas generator, innovator or innovating firm is less important than that of the customer. What is also occurring in reverse is the role of the developing economies in that they not only consume but also produce technological solutions and innovative products or provide innovative services. This has particular implications for entrepreneurship development as there is a rising trend in the demand for high-quality goods and services being available at an affordable price (Hang and Garnsey, 2011). It is not surprising therefore to see multinational companies such as Nestlé and Unilever introducing single-use varieties of their products in a ravaged western world economy such as Greece.

What we can discern in this new form of innovation is the role of design in creating innovative products and services based on knowledge, observation and learning from different environments, coupled with the idea of making design critical to the innovation process.

DESIGN-CENTRED INNOVATION

Received public wisdom associates design with style, good looks, user-friendliness and perhaps quality too. Good design is also associated with tangible products and their special feel-good factor when a customer chooses between similar products on sale. A well-designed product attracts and delights the customer, but it is not artifice or complexity that makes a product stand out from others. We refer to its elegance, to its shape, to the way it feels when we hold it in our hands or admire it in a particular setting. In fact it is often simplicity and clarity that create the special value that makes us commend a product for its good design. In such simplicity lies its sophistication, because a beautifully designed product grows in value and meaning over generations of varied users and beyond its purely utilitarian value. Consider an old Chinese ceramic vase, the source of pronounced imitation by the potters of Delft in the Netherlands. Consider too Aztec-influenced shawls or the miniature-painting-engraved jewellery boxes of Rajasthan in India, and the Chinese music box.

The uniqueness of design lies in its universal application across a wide range of products and in services too. Think of the Rolls-Royce car, the Concorde aircraft, the Rolex watch, the iPhone, and then think too of the simple IKEA desk, the V&A or the Oxfam Christmas catalogues, the Ermenogildo Zegna suit, birthday cards and many more, simple, day-to-day products that make us select specific goods over others. Think too of the organisation of services in restaurants or retail outlets and the ambience created by well-designed outlets which makes us return to these establishments for our next, sometimes irrational, purchase. The difference that buyers of such products experience accounts for the innovation, and the innovation is design inspired.

Design-inspired innovation is a function of creativity of a

> higher order, whether the products are professional tools, machinery for production, consumer goods, or services. It is in essence a synthesis of technology and users' experiences – boundaries that we observe blurring. Increasingly, products succeed because they have associated software and services that enhance their value. In the end, what the user remembers is a delightful experience with the entire package, and not whether that experience was provided or enabled by any particular aspect of the design. (Utterback et al., 2010)

This comprehensive quote identifies key factors that explain design-inspired innovation. It is of a higher order, because design permeates all aspects of a product or a service due to the synthesis of technology and the experience of the users. No organisation producing goods can achieve excellence without this synthesis. The delight is obtained in the totality of the product and its use, not through the discovery of any one component of the product. Utterback et al. refer to the combination of 'excellence and elegance' which need not be the province only of products that are available in advanced economies. Part of the significance of design-inspired innovation is that the wide variety of needs of people, increasingly expressed in terms of basic or meaningful products, simplicity, economy of means and low impact, can be met through this combination of excellence and elegance. Utterback et al. refer to the development of the disposable injection pen for providing insulin for diabetics, a simple emergency shelter and effective food packaging, which help to provide better experience.

FORM AND FUNCTION

One way of looking at design-inspired innovation is by comparing 'reliability' with 'validity'. Martin (2006) suggests that, while most businesses have well-developed capabilities for innovation which earn benefits for the business, fewer firms consider the value that a customer obtains beyond the utility or price of a product. He argues that it this 'validity perspective' which is enshrined in design thinking. Design thinking is in itself different from design function, as much as form is different from function. The combination of the two enables design to be incorporated as part of a strategy for a design-oriented firm which best manages the synthesis between the technology embedded in a product and the user experience.

Design thinking, or human-centred design or integrative thinking, requires a systematic approach that optimises the benefits to the firm with the value to the customer (Sato, 2009). Many businesses are likely to focus on the 'reliability dimension' when they offer gadgets that offer 'point solutions to a minor need' or over-featured products that aim to satisfy multiple customer needs. Such behaviour can be linked to non-systematic approaches to innovation, ending up in perhaps an excessive attention to firm-specific resources, an outcome typical of 'first to market'-led strategies adopted by highly competitive firms.

Sato (2009) argues that design thinking needs to be supported by 'design research', which is different from traditional market research. While the latter tends to focus on potential customers, design research searches for insights about customers and their real-life circumstances that may be associated with a potential offering. Ethnographic methods and social mapping techniques can help to reveal the less functional and the more emotional or cultural needs of customers because they help to study the products in contexts of use.

Being heuristic in approach rather than formulaic (Martin, 2006), design thinking utilises multidisciplinary co-development with different actors, an iterative development process that can often involve people outside production departments, such as marketers, financiers, engineers and, increasingly, users, especially in open source environments. Multidisciplinarity can scupper innovations, not least because of inadequacies in management processes that fail to deal with different points of view and

TABLE 10.2 A version of the HP design strategy frame

	Strategic and operational business objectives	Optimal or best innovation and accompanying business models	Design planning	Applied design
Design to innovate (market and customer)	Market share	Customer-centred approaches to business modelling Developing customer-based ecosystems Differentiated and winning new product categories Star or iconic products for measured release (customers will wait for them)	Integrating design research data with business model strategies and new products compelling to customers Brand definition	Enhanced design research to continually improve business models aligned to customers
Design to differentiate (customer and product/service focus)	Revenues	Designed features-based or value-added products attracting higher revenue Simplified but consistent customer experience of products	Use of existing technology assets to integrate design research data to generate more value	Iterative prototyping to address customer needs by using research design data
Design to simplify (product, internal process and customer focus)	Margins Savings	Systematic design practice Elements of reusable design	Developing plans to apply reusable elements across different HP products and services to improve value Reinforcement of brand	Leveraging reusable design elements and generating new design assets to increase customer value

Sources: Adapted from Lucente et al. (2008); Sato (2009)

derive synergistic value from varied approaches to solutions to problems. What makes it worse for managers, is that designers in particular are motivated by the exciting prospects of turning concepts into compelling products and profitable outcomes. Cost reduction does not form part of any design equation among such creative people. Much of what companies strive for when innovating is the possibility of lowering cost through better processing techniques, the use of new, alternative materials and other techniques that enable innovation. To help solve this conundrum Sato (2009) refers to the need for design planning and applied design as key components of design thinking. While design planning facilitates conceptualisation, applied design over-laps conceptualisation, development and production. Sato refers to the example of designers at Hewlett Packard (HP) who had been working on a project to help reduce the cost of products. By developing three design dimensions – design to simplify, design to differentiate and design to innovate – HP was able to address clear business objectives, identify the best types of innovation, adopt design planning and introduce applied design to secure savings, improve margins and revenues, and acquire greater market share. Table 10.2 is an adaptation of HP's design strategy where, in return for increased investment and dependence on design, the firm acquires a sustained competitive advantage in a wide range of products, from its hardware, software and services at different stages of maturity of the product categories.

Inherent in this approach is the integration of technology (resources), language (communication) and needs (values) – the three types of knowledge about opportuni-ties that enable the organisation of technology and other resources (new and reusable elements), products and services and the needs of the customers (Verganti, 2003).

Judging by what we have discussed so far, design-centric innovation is an all-encompassing multidisciplinary activity which needs careful husbandry and management. So care has to be taken in not 'overegging the design pudding' by not allowing function to override form. Design as *function* can lead to obsessive change in minor aspects such as expensive changes of logos (did either Gap or British Airways derive much value in terms of customer satisfaction or revenue from the changes they made to their logos?) or predictive SMS text writing. Design as *form*, and especially as a form of innovation, implies holistic, strategic management that stretches beyond tangential or revamped aesthetics and style. This is because good design that helps to differentiate 'great' products and services from their 'great' counterparts has more to do with problem solving and the realisation of competitive advantage, as evinced in Apple's grand sway over many competitors in disparate markets where there were not even established players (music through iPods and iTunes), not to forget their ever-bulging financial muscle, aided and abetted in part by friendly corporate tax-haven partners. So how can effective management enable productive design-centric innovation?

MANAGING DESIGN TO MANAGE INNOVATION

Various writers have identified key characteristics and steps that are common to forms that make design-inspired products or provide design-driven services that combine excellence with elegance, reliability with validity and technology with user experience, and create flexible business models that help firms to secure competitive advantage. These characteristics can be found in the formulation of certain actions that underpin strategies and specific steps that involve the coordination of people and resources. Let us begin with the actions.

UNDERSTANDING DESIGN

We could think of design as a system made of several subsystems and their interfaces that shows how these subsystems connect with each other using components within each of them. The superior value of good design is in the adequate synthesis of the components in each subsystem and the combination of the subsystems, in creating what is sometimes referred to as product or service architecture, and critically in the improvement of all parts. The focus on the whole system prevents sub-optimisation. Also of importance is the control of each part in such a way that each of the parts is not optimised individually because that may undermine the performance of the whole system. A good example of system optimisation can be found in the success of the British Olympic team, which did not rely on winning all pre-Olympics events to become the second-ranked team in the medals table for the 2016 Olympics. Rather specific sports generating their own excellence helped to create a carefully crafted sports system.

The improvement may not include the introduction of any new technology, yet it may alter the performance of a product significantly. Utterback et al. (2010) refer to the example of combined electrical generation systems for energy conservation. These systems bring together gas and steam turbine generators so that the high outlet temperature of the former can generate steam from the latter. The synergy resulting from this combination is a doubling of the efficiencies of the steam and gas units operating separately. Similarly, the surplus power of an engine in a hybrid car is used to charge the battery, so that if a thrust of energy is required, the engine, the generator and the battery can be combined to help to turn the electric motor.

DEVELOPING ARCHITECTURE AND DESIGNING MODULARITY

By making a reference to product architecture, consideration is being given to a configuration which brings together all the subsystems. A map is another metaphor that Utterback et al. (2010) offer. So a product architecture or map defines the design in that key elements of the architecture, as in the Sony Walkman's reading head, tape drives, controls and earphones, feature in all products with variations as required for different products. The variations are made possible through modularity. A small stock of colours, pigments and ingredients helps to make a variety of meals in restaurants, while the LEGO block is a good example of how prefabricated buildings use sectional modularity (Utterback et al., 2010).

TRANSPARENCY IN INTERFACES

Apart from Apple products, we find that customers are generally happy when they find that their product does not restrict them to a single supplier or the use of specific software. Opening up the supply chain to modular interfaces becomes a key part of supply chain management, allowing customers to have a wide choice of applications. This process does, however, expose firms to competition but also allows for a faster pace of technological growth. Apple's case is unique, and its sophisticated marketing and popularity among its devoted users might suggest that Apple bucks the trend by sticking to proprietary design; but we also know that Apple iPhones have a lower market share than Samsung Android phones, and that older Apple products such as the Apple Macintosh did not manage to beat the PC in attracting customer interest.

The corollary to transparency in design is open innovation, which we discussed in detail earlier.

SYNTHESIS AND INTEGRATION IN DESIGN MANAGEMENT

Openness in the approach to design management, the modularity in product design architecture, together with the involvement of multiple players, require a significant amount of complexity management. This complexity can be traced to the uses of tacit and explicit forms of knowledge, discussed in the chapters on innovative organisations, different forms of communication implicit in the two forms of knowledge and their users, frequent transfers of such knowledge among actors and networks within and outside the organisation, and data management including effective analysis and visualisation. A systematic step-by-step approach is an inevitable necessity in the management of the actions entailed for design-centric innovation.

COORDINATION, RESPONSIBILITY AND MYTHOLOGY

The actions referred to above do not have purchase unless design is accepted as a form and a strategy, and this means close and productive rapport between the chief executive of the firm, its designers and the rest of the operations of the organisation. As Steve Jobs had demonstrated in his relationship with Jony Ive, Fast Company's designer of the decade, at Apple, and as Tim Cook continues to do after taking up the mantle, or as the Google designer Jon Wiley noted, the lead responsibility and the connected management style (despite all that has been revealed about Job's authoritarianism) of the CEO are central to the design-led success of these leading firms. Observers note similar chemistry between Angela Ahrendts, CEO of Burberry, and Christopher Bailey, the company's Chief Creative Officer; the 'doodling bond' between Nike's CEO, Mark Parker, and his Vice-President of Design, John Hopke; and the 'unabashed support' that Indra Nooyi, PepsiCo's CEO, provides for Mauro Porcini, her Chief Design Officer (Safian, 2013). Connected endeavour entails conversation and collaboration which help to sort out specific applications of design for different companies and their varied projects.

Leadership and coordinated team work can also help to safeguard design strategy against the onslaughts of quarterly earnings reports. Failure and flops do occur, as Apple learnt when its Cube product did not make it to market. But Apple executives also learnt a good deal about materials, curved plastics and touch switches, leading eventually to the iPod and the iPad, as Jon Rubenstein of Apple explained to Safian (2013). Tolerating failure is of course central to most entrepreneurial activity, as is recognition of the absence of any overriding model for design-driven solutions. Obviating for the need to control costs without question was part of the plan to include the Genius Bar in Apple Stores at a time when fraught discussions about financial penalties were taking place in the firm. Its inclusion may have led Apple to boast its highest sales per square foot of any retailer. Beyond the desire to improve if not perfect well-designed products, it is the determination to run a well-designed company that fuels managers to integrate product design with the realities of finance and marketing. A well-designed product or service does not equal a well-designed business (Safian, 2013) unless the various functions are integrated into an effective form.

Design has entered the imagination and spurred on people, organisations and whole environments to devise strategies and choreograph activities which blend design with organisational routines both to delight the customer and ensure a healthy bottom line for the business. Design literacy is no longer confined to Milanese shop-keepers or shoppers. The average shopper can identify a Michael Graves tea kettle, a Dyson vacuum cleaner or a NAIM hi-fi system and revel in the new iPhone. Better informed and leading academic institutions have introduced high-profile design management programmes of study and research due to philanthropic gestures by the likes of Hasso Plattner, whose gift of $35 million helped to establish the d.school in the middle of Stanford University's campus (Tishler, 2013). Hosts of the Olympic Games from Beijing in 2008 to London in 2012 and Rio de Janeiro in 2016 have vied with each other to produce lasting visual spectacles of the games that located the perennial values of the games in both the richness of the local environment and its universal import:

> From the High Line to the Olympics, from crowdfunding to logomania, from infographics to molecular gastronomy, design has entered every facet of our lives and every corner of the economy. (Tishler, 2013)

Design-centric innovation reinforces the case for business managers to look beyond their business competitors and networks to the wider canvas of people and society using the open-sourced technological tools to borrow and integrate ideas, styles and methods that are generally not available in the ordinary world of commerce and industry. Table 10.3 provides a snapshot of how design-led innovation has gener-ated a raft of projects that have drawn the attention of customers, redefined business activity and created opportunities for others to take up.

Despite the evidence of design's benefits to both the maker and the user, for growth and for social value creation, it has not been easy to persuade decision makers in the political, educational and business sectors to foster creativity at all levels of education and their application in industry. John Mathers, CEO of the Design Council in the UK, recollects one of his corporate clients referring to the absence of design education in higher education as the 'missing semester' (Mather, 2015). Perhaps the efforts of the Design Council, its work on the Design Academy and other initiatives could be replicated at all levels, and especially in business, to secure the future of both design and innovation.

TABLE 10.3 Exemplars of design-centric innovation

(1) The Beijing headquarters of China's state television (CCTV) *Modernity in tradition in innovation*	(2) Grant Achatz's Chicago restaurant *Imagination for innovation*	(3) P&G's Herbal Essences *Rebooting and reuse for innovation*	(4) One Lap per Child Project, the BioLite Campstove *Social innovation*
The massive jigsaw of steel and glass construction is almost a definition of 21st-century China and the passion for Gonzo architecture. Designed by Ole Scheeren and Rem Koolhas, it is understood to be symptomatic of the east's hunger for change and reinvention, embedding the design in an historical context. Note the use of local architectural style and the use of western architects suggesting an openness to new combinations which lies at the heart of innovation.	The opening of the restaurant helped to popularise a new and radical cooking style referred to as molecular gastronomy. Achatz waxes eloquent about the use of green almonds which are spicy, sweet, acidic and salty, which together form the essential foundation of taste. The method of 'salsification' is representative of the roots of a tree overturned in a storm. Roe and pickled mustard seeds create the impression of mushrooms growing on the roots, an example of 'one visually strong natural form evoking another'. Lamb is cooked with sauce that was inspired by Picasso so that diners can feel something when they eat the dish. Holding leaves upright when serving them instead of placing them on a plate helps to generate a sense of life in them.	Procter & Gamble (P&G) decided to bring together 10 members of staff to work on rebooting its moribund Herbal Essences hair care brand. It gave these key staff 10 weeks to focus exclusively on this rebooting exercise with the design strategy being led by Claudia Kotchka, the then VP of design for P&G. In the end, the relaunch aimed at the young consumer proved to be very successful. A key element of the rebooting work was the way in which different specialists were brought together and directed to act outside their professional boxes. For example, the finance lead was expected to go out, talk to people, ideate and prototype alongside the engineer. Design was seen as a critical function with a design leader on every business unit.	This project attempted to make the Internet available to every child on earth at a cost of $100 for a new XO-1 laptop. This objective fitted in nicely with many designers' belief that their power to design effectively and beautifully could generate massive social change. It was understood that although the product was aimed at the market in developing economies, users would emerge worldwide. Unfortunately, when it was first delivered in 2007 it became apparent that a number of mistakes had been made. The product cost twice as much and did not meet its distribution goals. From this failure, however, designers learnt new lessons. The One Laptop has regrouped with Walmart on a new tablet. Other examples of design-focused initiatives show the breadth and depth of socially useful innovations. The New York School of Visual Arts offers a Design for Social Innovation MFA; and the producers of BioLite CampStove are developing products together with co-producers and users groups from India and Ghana.

(Continued)

TABLE 10.3 (Continued)

(5) Stockholm Design Lab and IKEA *Simple packaging for innovation*	(6) Bioinformatics and science *Data visualisation design for innovation*	(7) The fast chair *Frugality in design thinking*	(8) Embrace and the international doctor *Design for developmental innovation*
Stockholm Design Lab has an ongoing relationship with IKEA which is over 20 years old. It creates packaging for its non-furniture items and in 2005 was approached to redesign the food line with a conscious desire to promote the Swedishness of the brand. This meant simplicity, humour, directness and smartness, all combined together, while removing clutter and merely decorative aspects. A focus on Swedishness also meant dealing with the pedagogical problem of understanding what a Swedish name meant to global customers. This was overcome with pictures on the label that show the purpose of the product. The packaging was kept very simple because the private-label brand is placed in stores where there is no competition at all. Take the example of the marinated herring. The pull tab was redesigned to resemble the head and eye of a fish, thus informing the consumer what is inside the packaging. The private food label of IKEA, which was introduced in 2006, has a portfolio of 150 products with the same approach to simple packaging described above.	The problem with science is not the science itself but the rather confusing, opaque and unintelligible way it is communicated. Yet as Newton remarked, science is meant to experiment and communicate what is found. Fortunately, science is appreciative of design and design is supposed to embrace science. A *British Medical Journal* article reported that when doctors were asked to rate two kinds of visuals after looking at four of them, their choice of an icon graphic was not liked by anyone else even though their choice was dependent on the accuracy of the information conveyed. The icon graphic did not communicate pleasure and user-friendliness as much as the simple bar graph and the pie chart did. Relying on visualisations that may look good or precise does not necessarily mean communicating effectively. For example, 'Hairball' visualisations of networks raise questions about whether people are being fooled into thinking they know something. Similarly, the problem with Big Data is that the output from any analysis or number-crunching exercise can be as complex as the input itself! While computers may be good at processing the data, what design can do is to help people express the meaning of the data.	Making a chair in 3 minutes and 12 seconds may not be an art known to many. But Brad Sewell, an entrepreneur trained as an auto engineer with no pretensions for furniture design, took up the challenge of cramming a full four-cushion sofa into two FedEx packaging boxes. His start-up firm, Campaign, began with a team of engineers with varied backgrounds from kayak building to consumer gadgets. Settling on California-milled steel instead of fibre board as the best possible material by both weight and price, the team fastened the skeleton of the couch with a wingnut with folding flanges. This allowed for extra torque with hand-tightening. Their mothers were the first product testers. As a YouTube video shows, most users can put together a modern Campaign couch without the aid of any tools and with only a bit of elbow grease (with IKEA sofas you need both!). The first three pieces – a chair, a love seat and the sofa – were available from June 2016 at prices ranging from $495 for the chair, to $745 for the love seat and $1,000 for the sofa.	Jane Chen is a social entrepreneur who found that one of the biggest problems facing premature babies was keeping them warm while trying to regulate their body temperature. In India, for example, shortages in electricity meant that incubators could not be used and sometimes people did not know how to use them. Chen came up with the idea of the Embrace Warmer after meeting a woman with a premature baby in South India who was asked to travel for 4 hours to a hospital because of the lack of electricity in her village. The baby died because the woman did not have the money to travel. Resembling a sleeping bag for a baby, Embrace uses a wax-like substance which on melting retains the same temperature for 8-hour periods. More than 200,000 babies have been helped in 14 countries. Leeda Rashid, a doctor in Afghanistan, used 75 to 80 of the warmers (with over 10,000 uses in the past 3 years) in four of the largest public sector hospitals through her non-profit organisation. She now plans to start deploying these warmers in public ambulances to enable take-up in rural settings. New product lines including sleeping bags, blankets and swaddles, have been launched under the brand name Little Lotus for healthy babies in the US market.

Sources: Cases (1)–(4): Fast Company (2013); Cases (5) and (6): *Bloomberg* (2013); and Cases (7) and (8): *Bloomberg* (2016)

CONCLUDING OBSERVATIONS

This chapter has explored different forms of innovation, distinguishing forms from types of innovation and enabling an understanding of how firms using different types of innovation manage the innovation process which creates different forms of innovation. The innovation process makes use of these forms of innovation to implement different business strategies enabling innovation. While the world is awash with different forms of innovation, we focused on specific forms which have made a direct and strong impact on businesses across the world. Our consideration of these forms of innovation has been predicated upon the belief that these forms have universal application and that they are not limited by technological advances made in developed economies only. Thus open innovation's dependence on networks and openness to multiple producers, intermediaries and users is not circumscribed by advanced new technologies. It is rather a form that can be adopted by an approach to innovation which acknowledges the socialisation of the innovation process that can be shaped contextually through interactions among people.

Business model innovation complements the open innovation form with its emphasis on the organisational aspects of innovation and the strategic value that lies in linking revenue streams to customer alignment and the goals of an organisation. We note that frugal forms of innovation have applications globally, although their meaning and purpose can vary dramatically between developed and developing economies. The universality of the value of innovation, coupled with open innovation forms, allows businesses to adopt reverse innovation strategies and modify their business models, often with an insightful approach to design thinking and design-centric innovation. Design-centric innovation helps to marry the aesthetics of innovation with the functional advancement that it helps to achieve in products and services. Much of this is enabled by open innovation practices as innovators and business managers learn to adopt and use ideas from a variety of commercial and non-economic sources. These then are the forms of innovation. Having established what they are, we need to evaluate them, and one of the ways in which we can do this is to measure their qualitative and quantitative worth. We attempt to explain in the next chapter what measuring innovation means and how forms can use effective methods of measuring the real value of innovation.

 SELF-ASSESSMENT AND RESEARCH QUESTIONS

1. What constitutes 'forms' and what do we mean by 'types' of innovation?

2. Open innovation embraces multiple ideas of openness across communities, technologies, organi-sational arrangements, and so on. What management principles can be best used to optimise the value of open innovation for both producers and users?

3. How does business model innovation contribute to effective innovation management practice?

4. Discuss the critical features of designer-centric innovation and how it can help to develop business strategy.

5. What forms of innovation are best suited to businesses in developed and developing economies?

 REFERENCES

Abubakar, Y.A. and Mitra, J. (2011) 'Sources of small firm innovation in regions: comparing high and low agglomeration regions', Paper submitted to the International Council of Small Business Conference, Stockholm, 15–18 June.

Afuah, A. (2004) *Business Models: A Strategic Management Approach*. New York: Irwin/McGraw-Hill.

Afuah, A. and Tucci, C.L. (2001) *Internet Business Models and Strategies: Text and Cases*. New York: McGraw-Hill.

Agarwal, A., Cockburn, I. and McHale, J. (2006) 'Gone but not forgotten: knowledge flows, labour mobility, and enduring social relationships', *Journal of Economic Geography*, 6(5): 571–91.

Agrawal, A., Kapur, D. and McHale, J. (2008) 'How do spatial and social proximity influence knowledge flows? Evidence from patent data', *Journal of Urban Economics*, 64(2): 258–69.

Amit, R. and Zott, C. (2001) 'Value creation in e-business', *Strategic Management Journal*, 22: 493–520.

Amit, R. and Zott, C. (2012) 'Creating value through business model innovation', *MIT Sloan Management Review*, 53(3): 41–9.

Applegate, L.M. (2000) 'E-business models: making sense of the internet business landscape', in G. Dickson and G. DeSanctis (eds), *Information Technology and the Future Enterprise: New Models for Managers*. Englewood Cliffs, NJ: Prentice Hall. pp. 49–101.

Baker, T. and Nelson, R.E. (2005) 'Creating something from nothing: resource construction through entrepreneurial bricolage', *Administrative Science Quarterly*, 50(3): 329–66.

Barney, J.B. (1991) 'Firm resources and sustained competitive advantage', *Journal of Management*, 17(1): 99–120.

Bloomberg (2013) 'The design issue', *Bloomberg Businessweek*, 28 January–3 February, Special Double Issue: 57 and 60.

Bloomberg (2016) 'The design issue', *Bloomberg Businessweek*, 11–24 April, Special Double Issue: 54 and 74.

Brafman, O. and Beckstrom, R.A. (2006) *The Starfish and the Spider: The Unstoppable Power of Leaderless Organizations*. London: Penguin.

Brem, A. and Wolfram, P. (2014) 'Research and development from the bottom up – introduction of terminologies for new product development in emerging markets', *Journal of Innovation and Entrepreneurship*, 3(9): 1–22. Available at: www.innovation-entrepreneurship.com/content/3/1/9 (last accessed 21 March 2016).

Brousseau, E. and Penard, T. (2007) 'The economics of digital business models: a framework for analyzing the economics of platforms', *Review of Network Economics*, 6(2): 81–114.

Brynjolfsson, E. and Hitt, L. (2004) 'Intangible assets and the economic impact of computers', in W. Dutton, B. Kahin, R. O'Callaghan and A. Wyckoff (eds), *Transforming Enterprise*. Boston, MA: MIT Press. pp. 27–48.

Bubel, D., Ostraszewska, Z., Turek, T. and Tylec, A. (2015) 'Innovation in Developing Countries – a New Approach'. International Conference on European Integration – Realities and Perspectives (EIRP) Conference Proceedings, Vol. 10.

Chesbrough, H.W. (2003) *Open Innovation: The New Imperative for Creating and Profiting from Technology*. Boston, MA: Harvard Business School Press.

Chesbrough, H.W. (2006) *Open Innovation: The New Imperative for Creating and Profiting from Technology*. Boston, MA: Harvard Business Press.

Chesbrough, H.W. (2007) 'Business model innovation: it's not just about technology anymore', *Strategy and Leadership*, 35: 12–17.

Chesbrough, H.W. (2008) 'Introduction', *California Management Review,* 50(3): 6–11.

Chesbrough, H.W. (2010) 'Business model innovation: opportunities and barriers', *Long Range Planning*, 43: 354–63.

Coe, N.M. and Yeung, H.W.-C. (2015) *Global Production Networks: Theorising Economic Development in an Interconnected World*. Oxford: Oxford University Press.

Coleman, J.S. (1970) 'Social inventions', *Social Forces*, 49(2): 163–73.

Daft, R.L. and Lewin, A.Y. (1993) 'Where are the theories for the "new" organizational forms? An editorial essay', *Organization Science*, 4(4): i–vi.

Danneels, E. (2003) 'The dynamic of product innovation and firm competencies', *Strategic Management Journal*, 23: 1095–121.

Demil, B. and Lecocq, X. (2010) 'Business model evolution: in search of dynamic consistency', *Long Range Planning*, 43: 227–46.

Dubosson-Torbay, M., Osterwalder, A. and Pigneur, Y. (2002) 'E-business model design, classification, and measurements', *Thunderbird International Business Review*, 44(1): 5–23.

Dunbar, R.L. and Starbuck, W.H. (2006) 'Learning to design organizations and learning from designing them', *Organization Science*, 17(2): 171–8.

Dyer, J.H. (2000) *Collaborative Advantage: Winning Through Extended Enterprise Supplier Networks*. New York: Oxford University Press.

Ebersberger, B., Herstad, S.J., Iversen, E., Kirner, E. and Som, O. (2011a) 'Analysis of innovation drivers and barriers in support of better policies', Report, Economic and Market Intelligence on Innovation. Oslo: European Commission: Enterprise and Industry.

Ebersberger, B., Herstad, S.J., Iversen, E., Som, O. and Kirner, E. (2011b) 'Open innovation in Europe', *Findings of the WP 3 Inno Grips Project*, Preliminary Draft (5 January).

Fast Company (2013) 'Timeline: a decade in design, 2004–2013', *Fast Company, The Annual Innovation by Design Issue*, October: 36, 42, 48 and 52.

Fey, C.F. and Birkinshaw, J. (2005) 'External sources of knowledge, governance mode and R&D performance', *Journal of Management*, 31(4): 579–621.

Gambardella, A. and McGahan, A.M. (2010) 'Business model innovation: general purpose technologies and their implications for industry structure', *Long Range Planning*, 43: 262–71.

George, G. and Bock, A.J. (2009) *Inventing entrepreneurs: Technology innovators and their entrepreneurial journey*. Upper Saddle river, NJ: Pearson Prentice Hall.

Geroski, P.A. (1995) 'What do we know about entry?', *International Journal of Industrial Organization*, 13(4): 421–40.

Girotra, K and Netessine, S. (2014) 'Four paths to business model innovation', *Harvard Business Review*, 92(7): 96–103.

Govindarajan, V. and Trimble, C. (2012) *Reverse Innovation: Create Far from Home, Win Everywhere*. Boston, MA: Harvard Business Review Press.

Guardian (2014) 'How temporary "cardboard cathedral" rose from the ruins to become most recognised building in Christchurch'. Available at: www.theguardian.com/cities/2014/sep/17/temporary-cardboard-cathedral-ruins-christchurch-new-zealand-earthquake (last accessed 10 October 2016).

Gupta, A. (2009) 'Seduce the scientist', *Farming Matters*, December: 17.

Gupta, A. (2010a) 'Grass green innovations for inclusive, sustainable development', in A. Lopez-Claros (ed.), *The Innovation for Development Report*. Basingstoke: Palgrave Macmillan. pp. 137–46.

Gupta, A. (2010b) 'Empathetic innovations: connections across boundaries', in R. Mashelkar (ed.), *Timeless Inspirator – Reliving Gandhi*. Pune: Sakal Papers.

Gupta, A. (2012) 'Innovations for the poor by the poor', *International Journal of Technological Learning, Innovation and Development*, 5(1–2): 28–39.

Hang, C.C. and Garnsey, E.W. (2011) 'Opportunities and resources for disruptive technological innovation', Centre for Technology Management, Working Paper No. 2011/03 [online]. Available at: http://ssrn.com/abstract=1923036 (last accessed 20 July 2016).

Hauknes, J. and Knell, M. (2009) 'Embodied knowledge and sectoral linkages: an input-output approach to the interaction of high and low tech industries', *Research Policy*, 38(3): 459–69.

Hayashi, A.M. (2009) 'Do you have a plan "B"?', *MIT Sloan Management Review*, 51(1): 10–11.

Hossain, M. (2013) 'Adopting open innovation to stimulate frugal innovation and reverse innovation', [online]. Available at: http://papers.ssrn.com/sol3/papers.cfm?abstract_id=2197782 (last accessed 20 July 2016).

Immelt, J., Govindarajan, V. and Trimble, C. (2009) 'How GE is disrupting itself', *Harvard Business Review*, 87(10): 56–65.

Johnson, M.W., Christensen, C.C. and Kagermann, H. (2008) 'Reinventing your business model', *Harvard Business Review*, 86(12): 50–9.

Jones, B., Failla, A. and Miller, B. (2007) 'Tacit knowledge in rapidly evolving organisational environments', *International Journal of Technology and Human Interaction*, 3(1): 49.

Kozlenkova, I.V., Samaha, S. and Palmatier, R.W. (2014) 'Resource-based theory in marketing', *Journal of the Academy of Marketing Science*, 42(1): 1–21.

Lacy, S. (2011) *Brilliant, Crazy, Cocky (How the Top 1% of Entrepreneurs Profit from Global Chaos)*. Hoboken, NJ: Wiley.

Leinwand, P. and Mainardi, C. (2016) 'Creating strategy that works', *Strategy + Business*, Spring: 43–51.

Leonard-Barton, D. (1992) 'Core capabilities and core rigidities: a paradox in new product development', *Strategic Management Journal*, 13: 111–25.

Litchtenthaler, U. and Ernst, H. (2007) 'External technology commercialisation I: large firms', *R&D Management*, 37(5): 383–97.

Lucente, S., Mrazek, D., Sato, S., Menter, A., Wai, C. and Wakid, D. (2008) 'The holy grail of design measurement', in *International Design Management Institute Education Conference*, Cergy-Pointoise, France, April.

Mahadevan, D. (n.d.) 'Mitticool: affordable refrigeration'. Available at: www.ecoideaz.com/innovative-green-ideas/mitticool-refrigerator (last accessed 1 August 2016).

Mair, J. and Marti, I. (2009) 'Entrepreneurship in and around institutional voids: a case study from Bangladesh', *Journal of Business Venturing*, 24(5): 419–35.

Martin, R. (2006) 'Tough love', *Fast Company*, 129: 54–7.

Médecins Sans Frontières (MSF – Doctors Without Borders) 'Without Borders' Newsletter (n.d.). Available at: msf.org.uk/podcast.

Mendelson, H. (2000) 'Organizational architecture and success in the information technology industry', *Management Science*, 46(4): 513–29.

Mitra, J. (2000) 'Making connections: innovation and collective learning in small businesses', *Education+Training,* 42(4/5): 228–37.

Mitra, J. (2012) *Entrepreneurship, Innovation and Regional Development: An Introduction.* Abingdon: Routledge

Mitra, J. and Natarajan, G. (2011) 'Technology, Entrepreneurship and the Indian Software Industry', in S.A. Mian (ed.), *Science and Technology-Based Regional Development*, Cheltenham: Edward Elgar.

Morris, M., Schindehutte, M. and Allen, J. (2005) 'The entrepreneur's business model: toward a unified perspective', *Journal of Business Research*, 58(6): 726–35.

Osterwalder, A., Pigneur, Y. and Tucci, C.L. (2005) 'Clarifying business models: origins, present and future of the concept', *Communications of the Association for Information Science (CAIS)*, 16: 1–25.

Pansera, M. (2012) 'Frugality, grassroots and inclusiveness: new challenges for mainstream innovation theories', *Proceedings of the GLOBELICS International Conference on Innovation and Development: Opportunities and Challenges in Globalisation*, Hangzhou, China, 9–11 November.

Perkmann, M and Spicer, A. (2010) 'What are business models? Developing a theory of performative presentation', in N. Phillips, G. Sewell and D. Griffiths (eds), *Technology and Organization: Essays in Honour of Joan Woodward*. Bingley: Emerald. pp. 265–75.

Permaculture Research Institute (2013) 'Energy systems, processing and food preservation'. Available at: http://permaculturenews.org/2013/01/15/mitticool-clay-refrigerator (last accessed 20 July 2016).

Pohle, G. and Chapman, M. (2006) 'IBM's global CEO report 2006: business model innovation matters', *Strategy & Leadership*, 34(5): 34–40.

Polanyi M. (1966) *The Tacit Dimension*. New York: Doubleday.

Prahalad, C.K. and Hart, S (2002) 'The fortune at the bottom of the pyramid', *Strategy + Business*, 26: 2–14.

Prahalad, C.K.and Krishnan, M.S. (2008) *The New Age of Innovation: Driving Co-created Value through Global Networks*. NewYork: McGraw-Hill.

Prahalad, C.K. and Mashelkar, R.A. (2010) 'Innovation's holy grail', *Harvard Business Review*, 88(7/8): 132–41.

Radjou, N. (2004) 'Innovation Networks', Forrester Big Idea, Forrester, June 17. Available at: http://www.urenio.org/el/wp-content/uploads/2015/10/Radjou-N.-2004.-Innovation-Networks.-Forester-Research..pdf (last accessed 15 July 2016).

Rajdou, N. and Prabhu, J. (2015) *Frugal Innovation: How to Do More with Less*. London: *The Economist* and Profile Books.

Radjou, N., Prabhu, J. and Ahuja, S. (2012) *Jugaad Innovation: Think Frugal, Be Flexible, Generate Breakthrough Growth.* San Francisco, CA: Jossey-Bass.

Ramamu, R. (2013) 'Trickle-up innovation', World in 2013, *Wired*, 34–5.

Rappa, M. (2001) 'Managing the digital enterprise – business models on the Web'. Available at: http://ecommerce.ncsu.edu/business_models.html (last accessed 20 March 2016).

Rivette, K. and Kline, D. (2000) *Rembrandts in the Attic: Unlocking the Hidden Value of Patents*. Boston, MA: Harvard Business School Press.

Roper, S., Du, J. and Love, J.H. (2008) 'Modelling the innovation value chain', *Research Policy*, 37(6–7): 961–77.

Safian, R. (2013) '10 lessons for design driven success', in Fast Company, *10th Annual Innovation by Design Issue*, October: 26–34.

Sarasvathy, S.D. (2001) 'What makes entrepreneurs entrepreneurial?'. Available at: www.effectuation. org/sites/default/files/documents/what-makes-entrepreneurs-entrepreneurial-sarasvathy.pdf (last accessed 2 April 2016).

Sarasvathy, S.D. (2009) *Effectuation: Elements of Entrepreneurial Expertise*. Northampton, MA: Edward Elgar.

Sato, S. (2009) 'Beyond good: great innovations through design', *Journal of Business Strategy*, 30(2/3): 40–9.

Seeley Brown, J. and Duguid, P. (2002) *The Social Life of Information*. Boston, MA: Harvard Business Press.

Seelos, C. and Mair, J. (2007) 'Profitable business models and market creation in the context of deep poverty: a strategic view', *Academy of Management Perspectives*, 21: 49–63.

Shafer, S.M., Smith, H.J. and Linder, J.C. (2005) 'The power of business models', *Business Horizons*, 48(3):199–207.

Sharma, A. and Iyer, G.R. (2012) 'Resource-constrained product development: implications for green marketing and green supply chains', *Industrial Marketing Management,* 41(4): 599–608.

Smith, K. (2000) 'What is the knowledge economy? Knowledge intensity and distributed knowledge bases', Discussion Paper Series no. 2002–6, INTECH, United Nations University, Maastricht.

Sofka, W. and Grimpe, C. (2010) 'Specialised research and innovation performance – evidence across Europe', *R&D Management*, 40(3): 310–23.

Sosna, M., Trevinyo-Rodríguez, R.N and Velamuri, S.R. (2010) 'Business model innovation through trial-and-error learning: the Naturhouse case', *Long Range Planning*, 43: 383–407.

Stewart, D.W. and Zhao, Q. (2000) 'Internet marketing, business models, and public policy', *Journal of Public Policy & Marketing*, 19(2): 287–96.

Tapscott, D. (2001) 'Rethinking strategy in a networked world (or why Michael Porter is wrong about the Internet)', *Strategy + Business*, 26(3): 34–41.

Tapscott, D.A. and Williams, A.D. (2010) *MacroWikinomics: Rebooting Business and the World*. London: Atlantic Books.

Teece, D., Pisano, G. and Shuen, A. (1997) 'Dynamic capabilities and strategic management', *Strategic Management Journal*, 18(7): 509–33.

Teece, D.J. (2010) 'Business models, business strategy and innovation', *Long Range Planning*, 43:172–94.

Thompson, J.D. and MacMillan, I.C. (2010) 'Business models: creating new markets and societal wealth', *Long Range Planning*, 43: 291–307.

Timmers, P. (1998) 'Business models for electronic markets', *Electronic Markets*, 8(2): 3–8.

Tishler, L. (2013) 'A decade in design, 2004–2013', in Fast Company, *10th Annual Innovation by Design Issue*, October: 26–34.

Tiwari, R. and Herstatt, C. (2011) 'Lead market factors for global innovation: emerging evidence from India', Hamburg University of Technology Working Paper, No. 61.

Trimble, C. (2012) 'Reverse innovation and the emerging-market growth imperative', *Ivey Business Journal,* 76(2): 19–21.

Utterback, J., Vedin, B.-A., Alvarez, E., Ekman, S., Sanderson, S.W., Tether, B. and Verganti, R. (2010) *Design-Inspired Innovation*. Singapore: World-Scientific.

Verganti, R. (2003) 'Design as brokering of languages: the role of designers in the innovation strategy of Italian firms', *Design Management Journal*, 13(4): 34–42.

von Hippel, E. (2005) *Democratising Innovation*. Cambridge, MA: MIT Press.

Weill, P. and Vitale, M.R. (2001) *Place to Space: Migrating to eBusiness Models*. Boston, MA: Harvard Business School Press.

Weill, P. and Vitale, M. (2002) 'What IT infrastructure capabilities are needed to implement e-business models?', *MIS Quarterly*, 1(1): 17.

Wernerfelt, B. (1984) 'A resource-based view of the firm', *Strategic Management Journal*, 5: 171–80.

Woolridge, A. (2010) 'The world turned upside down', A Special Report on Innovation in Emerging Markets, *The Economist*. Available at: www.economist.com/node/15879369 (last accessed 21 March 2015).

Zeschky, M.B., Winterhalter, S. and Gassmann, O. (2014) 'From cost to frugal and reverse innovation: mapping the field and implications for global competitiveness', *Research-Technology Management*, 57(4): 20–7.

Zott, C. and Amit, R. (2002) *Measuring the performance implications of business model design: evidence from emerging growth public firms*. Fontainebleau: Insead.

Zott, C., Amit, R. and Massa, L. (2010) 'The business model: theoretical roots, recent developments, and future research', *IESE Business School, University of Navarra*, 3: 1–43.

Zott, C., Amit, R. and Massa, L. (2011) 'The business model: recent developments and future research', *Journal of Management*, 37(4): 1019–42.

MEASURING INNOVATION

11

┌─── **SCOPE AND OBJECTIVES** ───┐

- Generating and evaluating the innovation outcome and the innovation process.
- The innovation metrics.
- Input, process and output measures.
- Contexts.
- Measuring objective outcomes.

INTRODUCTION

We can identify innovation in terms of types, forms, capabilities, organisational strategies and the wider environment in which it occurs. But we also need to understand how best we can evaluate its outcomes. In other words, we need to measure innovation. It is almost tautologous to suggest that accelerated competition at the organisational or indeed the national level demands that we have appropriate tools and methods with which to weigh up what we generate and also to improve innovative capability, partly with the objective of assessing performance and growth of businesses and economies, but also to examine how problems can be solved through innovation.

Along with the popularity of innovation and the recognition of its significance to industry, societies and nations, it has become important to measure and evaluate it in terms of the inputs that enable its gestation, the processes that convert the resource inputs into functional activity, and the outputs that emerge as products and services from the processes. How else would firms compete with each other and how can governments know what innovation works better or more effectively? Standard measurement metrics have used particular indicators covering inputs of innovation such as R&D spending, or human capital investment, on intermediary inputs such as patents filed and licences granted, and final outputs such as the number of new products made or new services offered by a firm (often self-evaluated). The first two sets are probably the most well-known among researchers, practitioners and policy makers, while results of final outputs have often been obtained by conducting interview-based innovation assessments and the allocation of rankings drawn from self-assessments made by industry practitioners.

There are those who argue that innovation's essential intangibility (as a process or an outcome) is difficult if not impossible to measure. Indeed, there are various limitations to the standard measures used. Their uses have been called into question because they may offer a narrow understanding of innovation. For example, the innovation process has a gestation period from identification to implementation through to diffusion and adaptation, and conventional metrics seldom take the time factor into account.

The absence of appropriate and relevant data is also a perennial challenge, especially when comparisons are made between different firms in various sectors over a period of time. Many have argued that measuring inputs or even intermediary outputs does not necessarily help to obtain any serious evaluation of innovation because not all R&D or patenting activity leads to a final, marketable product. Often the measurement of success in innovation performance is not connected to the overall business performance of the firm, making the so-called innovation success questionable as to its purpose. There is considerable confusion between the brand, other superficial marketing effects and personal drivers, especially when self-assessment of innovation takes place (Schramm, 2008). The success of the firm depends on the support of both the shareholders and the stakeholders together with the capability and capacity of its management to introduce and manage such innovative ideas and practices. This includes its quality of handling the business that includes its people and internal resources and the client base itself. Each business has different techniques and methods for managing such important issues.

However, as Smith (2005) argues, the overall characteristics of innovation and especially the critical dimensions – inputs, process and outputs – are not beyond measurement. These dimensions could be accounted for as follows:

Input measures: These include specific metrics that measure particular variables related to the essential preconditions or the basis of innovation. These inputs for innovation can be accounted for in terms of resources invested and dedicated to the innovation process as in:

- *money* – the amount of capital or retained earnings invested in clearly identified innovation programmes;
- *talent* – the proportion of time employees are trained and organised for innovative activities; and
- *time* – time spent by managers on leading innovative projects as opposed to routine operations.

Process measures: These measures cover metrics that consider specific variables that contribute to the flow of ideas, operations and techniques enabling the innovation process. Typical examples include:

- *time flows* – the length or average time taken from ideation to commercialisation;
- *cycles* – the frequency and duration of ideas and actual revenue earnings.

Output measures: The output metrics count or grade the results of innovation and help to evaluate the outcomes. Typical examples include:

- *returns on investment* – returns on capital invested for innovation;
- *portfolio growth* – numbers of actual innovation products or breakthroughs in new markets; and
- *social impact* – the outcome of innovation evaluated in terms of contribution to reductions in carbon emission, environmental degradation and alleviation of poverty.

THE SCOPE AND BOUNDARIES OF INPUT, PROCESS AND OUTPUT MEASURES

The basic set of metrics referred to above provides an elementary framework for capturing and evaluating what enables the innovation process to occur in the first place (input measures), how the process evolves (process measures), and what emerges at the end of the process in terms of outputs and outcomes (output measures). This chapter attempts to answer such questions on measuring and evaluating innovation.

Since the 1950s, measuring R&D inputs has been the mainstay of much research activity on innovation and technological change. These measures were used to make comparisons at the inter-industry or inter-firm level. The problem, however, with this measure is that it is concerned only with the resources used to producing the output, often within formal R&D units but not the innovative activity and what that represents. Formal R&D activity represents only half the truth about innovation inputs and the true passage of technical change. As Mansfield (1985; Mansfield and Romeo, 1980) notes, imitation and technology transfer are also legitimate forms of innovative activity.

By way of contrast to R&D, which is an input measure, patents have come to be regarded as an intermediate measure of innovative output. Patents, as Acs and Audretsch (2005) argue, may reflect new technical knowledge but we do not obtain any indication of the productive economic value of such knowledge. Not all patents are converted to successful innovations, and it is only those which manage a smooth transition to the marketplace as viable products that can be regarded as innovations. So a patent is more closely associated with an invention rather than an innovation. The other important issue about patents and innovation is that not all innovative outputs carry patents with them. Where products have very short shelf lives (as in the case of software products), many regard patenting as a wasteful and expensive exercise. It is the cost of patents and their resulting value which vary across industries, and it may not be useful to make comparisons between either products or enterprises across all industries.

If both R&D (as an input measure) and patents (as an intermediate measure) do not provide robust measures of innovative output, we are probably left with direct measures of actual outputs as the best solution to the problem of measurement. Acs and Audretsch refer to the pioneering work of Gellman Research Associates (1982) and their identification of 500 major new products and processes that were found in the market over the 20-year period 1953–73 in the USA, UK, Japan, West Germany, France and Canada. Another data source was compiled by the well-known Science and Policy Research Unit (SPU) at the University of Sussex in the UK, which identified 4,378 innovations over a period of 15 years. The reference here is to technical innovations that were commercialised successfully during that time period as reported by experts in different industries. Later, the Futures Group, working on behalf of the US Small Business Administration's Data Base, also compiled data on 8,074 innovations that were introduced in the US market in 1982. This database consisted of innovations by four-digit standard industrial classification (SIC) industries, and were used by Acs and Audretsch (1990) to find that small firms introduced 2.38 more innovations per employee than larger firms. This statistic is in the same league as that found by Gellman, namely that small firms generated 2.45 times more innovations per employee.

While the three measures referred to above all help to achieve rather distinct results, there is one problem that is common to all of them. None of them distinguish the different types of innovation, as in product, process and even organisational innovation. Various other measures have been tested to assess the value of techno-logical activities for different constituencies of interest. One such traditional measure is the data on national receipts and payments for patents and know-how licences. But such a measure does not help us to measure the main channels through which technology is transferred.

Neither do they indicate the currency of financial flows because of time lags in licensing agreements. Exports of high- and medium-technology products are another measure, but here the emphasis on R&D intensity means that the technological importance of production or information-intensive products are undervalued. The reliance on high-technology products as the key measure of performance tends to ignore the function of medium-technology products such as machinery and bulk chemicals. Surveys of technical experts and technometrics have also been used to measure technological activity. While expert opinion can be useful, self-interest can scupper objectivity. Technometrics measures the different dimensions of technological performance of products or production processes. However, weighting the various dimensions of performance cannot be easy, while correlating cost with performance is a difficult proposition in most circumstances.

Attempts have been made to offer specific market value solutions to the measure of innovative activity. FitzRoy and Kraft (1990), for example, measured the innovative activity of 57 German firms as the proportion of sales consisting of products introduced in the past 5 years, while Schulenburg and Wagner (1991; and Wagner and Schulenburg, 1992) came up with the measure of the proportion of shipments of those products that were brought to the market and are still in the early stage or market entry phase. Bringing innovation measurement closer to the market lends a degree of authenticity to such measures and helps to overcome the problems posed by the three important measures discussed above.

Measuring technological change and innovation where it matters, in the market, brings us closer to the reality of the innovation process and the complex set of factors that needs to be studied to understand the organisation of innovation. We attempt to capture and understand the techniques, purpose, contexts and variations of different measures of innovation in this chapter.

THE WHAT AND HOW OF MEASURING INNOVATION

What can be measured helps managers to differentiate between the economic and social values of innovative and other products and services. Measurement allow for the evaluation of their innovative capability in terms of the skills and managerial know-how that is invested in making those innovations happen. Policy makers at the regional or national level are also able to determine how best to promote innovation by using appropriate measures that account for the effectiveness of policies and instruments used by government to develop nation- or region-wide strategies to support innovative firms. A good example of the latter is the EU's Community Innovation Survey (CIS), now used widely by researchers and decision makers to evaluate the quantum and quality of innovation in member states of the EU.

We can understand what measurement means in the field of metrology, that is, an operation that allows for the determination of the value of a specific variable linking the act of measurement to the social practice of the measurement technique. This means using mathematical tools together with knowledge of the institutions, and social behaviour and practice within a community of interest (Vuola and Hameri, 2006; Rejeb et al., 2008).

LARGE SURVEYS

Measuring innovation in organisations has often involved large-scale surveys, and various approaches have been developed over time. Armbruster et al. (2008) point to four different approaches. The first approach examines innovation at a high level of aggregation, either at the level of multiple countries as in the CIS of the EU, or of those which gather detailed information about the many different concepts that help to explain innovation in and by organisations. The latter model includes the following examples:

- NUTEK (National Board for Industrial and Technical Development) of Sweden, which is focused on human resources and flexible organisations.
- DISCO (Danish Innovation System in a Comparative Perspective), which explores and measures the flexibility of firms to react to turbulent environments by developing new products and new technological processes 'based on integrative organisational forms and a culture oriented towards renewal and learning' (Lund, 1998, cited in Armbruster et al., 2008).

- EPOC (direct Employee Participation in Organisational Change), promoted by the European Foundation for the Improvement of Living and Working Conditions, and a project that was directly aimed at investigating direct employee participation in organisational change.
- INNFORM – a French national survey (Enquête sur les) which tried to identify the changes that had taken place between the years 1994 and 1997 in specific aspects of the organisation of work, such as a firm's functional structure and devices, especially to manage task and work time-sharing, relations with other firms, etc., and the use of information technologies (hardware, structure, function, software applications and data transfer).

METHODS AND USAGE

A second approach involves the measurement of use or change in methods to under-stand better the change process resulting from the adoption of innovation. Surveys classify firms into adopters and non-adopters of specific concepts or enquire about changes over a given period of time.

EXTENT AND TYPE OF USE

The extent and type of use constitute a third approach which in turn allows for a nuanced approach that attempts to measure effects on employees affected by changes due to adoption, thus enabling the monitoring of intra-firm diffusion.

LABELS, FEATURES, CONCEPTS AND PRACTICES

Finally, a fourth approach looks at labels and features for new organisational concepts and practices that emerge from the adoption of innovation, such as team work or continuous improvement. Alternatively, a quasi-constructivist variation of this approach also allows for the questioning of the existence and use value of some of these organisational innovation concepts, with the resulting analysis relying less on the judgement or understanding of a respondent, but more on the existence of the label or concept (Ambruster et al., 2008).

THE EVOLUTION OF INNOVATION METRICS

The well-acknowledged complexity of innovation has inevitably spawned a number of approaches and measures. This development has not, however, eased the difficulties associated with the measurement of complex, non-linear, multidimensional and unpredictable nature of innovative activity. If understanding the innovation process is difficult then grasping and using an adequate set of metrics is even more challenging. Nevertheless, the metric adventurers have sought to find a holy grail over the ages.

Milbergs and Vonortas (2004) suggest that innovation metrics have evolved through four generations: the first generation reflected a linear conception of innovation with a particular focus on the importance of inputs such as R&D investment; the second generation shifted the focus to intermediate outputs of science and technology activities; while the third generation found a richer set of innovation indicators and indexes based on surveys and integration of publicly available data; and finally, the fourth generation metrics emerging in the knowledge-based networked economy appear to be ad hoc, combining tangible and intangible measures and whole systems alongside traditional inputs and outputs, and are the subject of measurement. Table 11.1 shows the evolutionary development of innovation metrics.

So in this chapter we examine some key concepts and indicators used to measure innovation at mainly the micro (organisational) level. The study of macro-level (country or regional level) indicators and measures is made possible by a large volume of literature, but its contents and substance are outside the scope of this book. Given, however, the connections we can make between what happens at the level of an organisation and what influences the wider environment brings to bear on innovative organisations, it is worth looking briefly at some of the key concepts and theoretical arguments underpinning our appreciation of measures of innovation.

TABLE 11.1 The evolution of innovation metrics

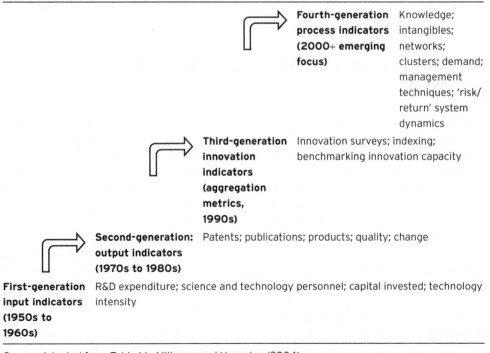

	Fourth-generation process indicators (2000+ emerging focus)	Knowledge; intangibles; networks; clusters; demand; management techniques; 'risk/return' system dynamics
	Third-generation innovation indicators (aggregation metrics, 1990s)	Innovation surveys; indexing; benchmarking innovation capacity
	Second-generation: output indicators (1970s to 1980s)	Patents; publications; products; quality; change
First-generation input indicators (1950s to 1960s)	R&D expenditure; science and technology personnel; capital invested; technology intensity	

Source: Adapted from Table 1 in Milbergs and Vonortas (2004)

SOME USEFUL THEORETICAL AND UNDERLYING CONCEPTS AND PRINCIPLES: MEASURING INNOVATION AT THE ORGANISATIONAL AND WIDER ECONOMIC OR GEOGRAPHICAL LEVELS

WHAT CAN WE MEASURE?

Three key factors make the task of measuring innovation problematic:

- what is being measured (the object);
- the meaning of the concept of measurement (its scope and value); and
- the application or feasibility of the different types of measurement (methods and frameworks).

It follows that these three factors may not be identified clearly when we attempt to measure innovation, and it, therefore makes sense to separate what can be measured from what cannot (Smith, 2005). Innovation implies novelty or newness understood in terms of the qualitative difference that is seen in a product, a service offering or indeed the process by which it is made or provided. Learning how to effect such change may lead to tangible outcomes, as in the efficiency of heating systems in a building with reduced energy consumption or improved manufacturing processes involving the use of nanotechnology. Readers will recognise that these two examples are those that are associated with incremental innovation based on technical ingenuity. But novelty stretches to radical or strategic innovations too.

MEASURING TECHNOLOGY AND HUMAN CAPITAL FOR INNOVATION

One reason why technical measurement comparisons do not work across different products and services, and especially in different contexts, is because the novelty value lies not only in the technical factors, but also in the skills that are deployed (human capital) and even the organisational arrangements that are made to enable the innovation process to work successfully. The organisational arrangements leading to the success of an innovation depend on the ability to identify, seize and implement opportunities. The overall capacity for innovation is correlated to a set of competencies, knowledge, tools and financial resources which are then used to evaluate both the innovation and its effect on the business and a comparison of this capacity with rival firms (Rejeb et al., 2008). The skills, expertise and capacity of people, or an organisation's human capital, can provide for distinctive competitive advantage for firms (Hewitt Dundas, 2006), and human capital is therefore an essential part of innovation (OECD, 2011). Firms that are capable of identifying and evaluating the competitive advantage, their employees' innovative capabilities and transferable competencies are those with well-defined strategies.

One way of examining the importance of human capital is to understand that specific human capital (in the form of particular types of education and experience including managerial, commercial and technical experience) allowed for positive contributions to firms' performance and survival (Ganotakis, 2012). How the manager makes decisions, allocates resources, sets priorities, controls costs and spending, and filters ideas (Herrmann et al., 2006; Leiva et al., 2011) underscores the importance of the role that managers play in the innovation process of firms. Some studies have looked critically at tangible internal and external conditions and the attitudes towards innovation of the individual manager. Some, such as Coronado et al. (2008) for example, find a positive value of employees' qualifications and firm size in terms of their attitude to innovation. McGuirk and Jordan (2012) find that diversity in an organisation in terms of nationality and educational attainment in the workforce relates positively to firms' probability to engage specifically in product innovation. However, empirical research on such tangible and intangible factors remains limited, especially when differences in the size of firms are considered (McGuirk et al., 2015). These authors argue that education alone is not necessarily a sufficient factor in securing competitive advantage through innovation training; the intangible attitudes and the characteristics and willingness of people to accept change in the working environment and derive job satisfaction or well-being are equally important.

Education and training have had a long history of being good proxies for measuring human capital (Romer, 1990; Cohen and Soto, 2007). Add to that industry experience and learning (Santarelli and Tran, 2013) coupled with specific measures by age, gender, parental background and education (Ganotakis, 2012) and we enter the complexity and challenge of the effort required in measuring human capital for innovation. Teixeira and Tavares-Lehmann (2014) have distinguished between specific human capital, by which they mean top-skilled workers, and general human capital, as referring to educated workers. Firms which make use of the results of such measurements and invest in human capital tend to improve the performance of employees (Bosma et al., 2004) and generate greater productivity (Ucbasaran et al., 2008). However, as stated above, it is not entirely clear that education is consistently beneficial for innovation. A study of firms in Germany found that there was no positive correlation between highly skilled employees and the firms' ability to innovate (Schneider et al., 2010).

What is worth mentioning is the emergence of the view that subjective characteristics of the individual are also of importance to innovation. The relationship between innovation and subjective well-being is examined (Dolan and Metcalfe, 2012) as part of the resource-based view of the firm and the differences in the performance of firms are sometimes attributed to the variations in the resources of those firms. Here, some writers have argued that intangible resources are more likely than tangible resources to produce a competitive advantage (Hitt et al., 2001: 14). Shipton et al. (2006) also noted that if there was job satisfaction employees were more likely to support innovation and not resist the burden of change. Job satisfaction as a predictor of innovation is also part of Zhou and George's (2001) research that examined conditions under which employee job dissatisfaction could lead to creativity.

OTHER FACTORS AFFECTING MEASUREMENT

Measuring innovation at the organisational level is an internal firm-specific and firm-comparison process. We could find differences in ways in which measurement is carried out from marketing, accounting or operational perspectives. We may also take on board various ways in which customers and consumers behave, such behaviour having an impact on what innovations to pursue and when and what to abandon.

Another important point to consider is the broader field of measurement of innovation at the geographical and national levels, where measurements often connect innovation at the aggregate level to particular outcomes such as growth or productivity at specific spatial levels, with R&D and patent indicators often forming the basis of a linear form of measurement that follows a sequential process of R&D, patenting, ideation, development and commercialisation, a model that has thankfully been jettisoned in modern practice. The modern conceptual foundations for measurement at this level can be traced back to the work of Rosenberg (1976; 1982), who challenged the primacy of R&D as the starting point in the innovation process and who also incorporated diffusion as part of the process. Rosenberg's ideas influenced the well-regarded Oslo Manual of the OECD (1992; 1997). Rosenberg, together with Kline, identified three key dimensions of innovation: that the innovation process is interactive with many feedback loops; that because it is interactive the invention and discovery of new principles do not determine how innovation occurs; and that the interactive process inevitably engenders learning from multiple sources and inputs.

Measuring innovation using sensible and reliable indicators allows for various inputs to be considered, from R&D to design and experimentation, and for a proper acknowledgement of both radical and incremental innovations being of significant value. In many ways this rich format makes it possible to explore the challenging new developments in the innovation process through crowdsourcing, networked-based and open innovation models. But our purpose in this book is to examine the underlying concepts of measuring innovation at the organisational level, and that is where we take stock of the objectives, ideas, indicators and measures that have evolved over time.

ORGANISATIONAL INNOVATION METRICS

Building on the theoretical points made by Rosenberg and others, it is useful to obtain some insights from industry to understand how firm-specific innovation can be measured. Despite the difficulties of measuring and interpreting performance related to innovation, firms tend to use specific key performance indicators (KPIs) to help manage innovation. These KPIs may not be sufficiently robust (A.D. Little, 2012) because of the difficulty in obtaining and organising relevant data, particularly for benchmarking exercises, and also due to the problem of differentiating between cause and effect. As the A.D. Little survey asks:

> if your average time to market is 14 months, should it go down because your execution is simply too slow compared to competitors', or should it go up since you are only considering incremental low-return innovations? (2012)

Even where sufficient information is obtained in-house, interpretations tend to vary between the different users of innovation. Typically, an R&D manager may find it difficult to persuade a purchasing counterpart that the business should work on collaborative innovation with its suppliers, given the latter's objective of meeting annual targets. Making the business case is often a very difficult proposition, even when improvements are demonstrated, because it is not easy to disentangle the innovation aspects of any improvement from general organisational efficiency or external market factors linked to those improvements. Add to that the problem of the modern competitive environment being markedly different from the industrial and economic environment in which the traditional innovation metrics were created.

Typically, large Fortune 1000 businesses which do attempt to measure innovation tend to use the following metrics:

- Annual R&D budget as a percentage of annual sales.
- Number of patents filed in the past year.
- Total R&D headcount or budget as a percentage of sales.
- Number of active projects.
- Number of ideas submitted by employees.
- Percentage of sales from products introduced in the past X year(s) (the 3M target of 35% of revenues from products introduced in the past 4 years).
- Time afforded for each employee to experiment with new opportunities (based on the classic 3M model of 10% of employee time for experimentation).

In a networked, open and disruptive innovation scenario for competitive firms these measures, despite their general usefulness, can be called into question. The sourcing of ideas, collaborative R&D work, the fuzzy boundaries between design services and manufacturing, and networks of production make it difficult to apply the metrics stated above indiscriminately.

Then there is the question routinely avoided by consultants, researchers and textbooks on innovation management, namely the one on measuring innovation in small firms. Many of these small firms do not pursue traditional R&D activities.

DEVELOPING A STRUCTURE FOR INNOVATION

Measurement implies the availability of a structure. Therefore, for the creation and use of metrics in a way that ensures that all key areas are measured, innovation needs to be structured and be seen to be systemic, so that performance measurements can be linked to particular frameworks for innovation at the organisational level.

The two tables that follow provide descriptions of the various metrics suggested by four different authors. Note that while Table 11.2 accounts for specific, quantifiable measures across the organisational spectrum, Table 11.3 seeks to enable a conceptual appreciation of the different metrics which are organised in theoretical categories.

TABLE 11.2 Input, process and output measures

Davila et al. (2006)	Goffin and Mitchell (2005)
Input measures	**Input measures**
Financial:	*Commitment and focus on innovation:*
• Per cent of revenues invested in product R&D	• Time dedicated to innovation
• Per cent of revenues invested in process R&D	• Budget percentage allocated to innovation efforts
• Per cent of revenues invested in technology acquisition	• Performance-based compensation links to innovation success of ideas passing through selection and execution processes
• Per cent of projects delayed or cancelled due to lack of funding	• Investment in training
Customer perspective:	*Balanced innovation of networks inside and outside organisation:*
• Per cent mix of projects by their strategic drivers (e.g. meeting customer needs; reactions to competition; technology-driven; based on internal ideas; etc.)	• Level of innovation integration across business units and functions and outside of organisation
• Resources	• Mix of innovation sources
• Per cent of total employees involved in innovation projects	• Percentage of innovation projects outsourced
• Per cent of personnel trained in creativity and problem-solving techniques	• Number of strategic alliances
• Per cent of personnel who have worked in two or more functions	• Number of experienced innovation team members
• Number of ideas per source (e.g. ideas from employees, ideas from customers)	• Assessment of supplier capabilities
• Number of ideas generated per year for development into new products, services and processes	*Coherent and aligned innovation:*
• Number of ideas considered per year for new products, services and processes	• Number, cost, price and perception of new products strategy offered from innovation projects
• Efficiency of links to external organisations	• Number, cost, price and perception of new services offered from innovation projects
• Per cent of projects delayed or cancelled because of lack of human resources	• Perception of brand
	• Profitability of innovation operations
	• Objectives for innovation efforts clearly communicated to senior managers and employees
	• Competitive position within industry
	• Number, complexity and size of competitors, customers, partners and suppliers

Davila et al. (2006)	Goffin and Mitchell (2005)

Goffin and Mitchell (2005)

Appropriate management infrastructure

- Percentage of performance measures and rewards aligned for effective innovation implementation and linked to innovation activities
- Quality of IT infrastructure
- Quality of information for innovation
- Market and technology research resources
- Amount and quality of customer data acquired related to innovation
- Dollars of resources available for innovation
- Free time allowances for R&D employees
- Geographic diversity of production and sales
- Level of empowerment to strategic business unit (SBU) and functional managers
- Cross-functional initiatives

Process measures

Portfolio:

- Percentage of innovation efforts devoted to radical, semi-radical and incremental innovation
- Portfolio balances over time, returns, risk and technologies
- Alignment between innovation strategy and resource allocation

Execution:

- Product platform effectiveness
- Reduction in new product/process development time/cost
- Within-target sales/profits
- Projected within-time, budget, product performance targets
- R&D productivity
- Number of new patents granted each year
- Number of gateway returns
- Rate and quality of experimentation
- Cost, development time, delivery time, quantity and price of products and services offered

Davila et al. (2006)

Process measures

Financial:

- Average project costs
- Costs of/savings through outsourcing

Process efficiency:

- Average break-even time; average time to market; hours worked per project
- Average time for a specific task (e.g. initial design)
- Per cent time spent on project-related tasks
- Per cent time spent on non-project tasks (administrative and support) tasks
- Number of patents received/number commercialised
- Per cent mix of product/process/service/business process innovation projects
- Per cent usage of appropriate tools and techniques (e.g. advanced market research projects; computer-aided design; computer-integrated manufacturing, and so on)

(Continued)

TABLE 11.2 (Continued)

Davila et al. (2006)	Goffin and Mitchell (2005)
• Per cent of projects that entered development and were ultimately considered commercial successes • Per cent of projects killed too late (i.e. after significant expenditure) • Per cent of employees actively contributing to innovation ***Learning:*** • Per cent of projects where post-project reviews are conducted • Number of improvements to innovation processes ***Specific service measures:*** • Customer throughput time • Complaints: number and type • Staff satisfaction • Efficiency of innovations in products and service augmentations • Cost per customer • Profit per customer • Retention rates **Output measures** ***Financial:*** • Per cent of sales revenues from new products/enhancements • Per cent of sales revenues from new services • Per cent of cost savings/revenues from process innovation • Quality improvements from process innovation • Return on innovation investment • Profitability of the new product programme • Earnings from patent licensing ***Customer perspective:*** • Innovation rate (number of new products compared with total number of product in the portfolio) • Number of new products compared with competitors • Number of new services compared with competitors • Number of enhancements to service augmentations	**Output measures** ***Financial:*** • Long-term corporate profitability: stock price • Projected residual income • Short-term corporate profitability: residual income growth • Sales growth • Return on equity • Percentage of sales from new products

Davila et al. (2006)

- Number of process innovations (number of innovations per year compared with the total number of major processes used in operations)
- Per cent mix of first to market, a fast follower, and me-too projects
- Market share growth due to new products/enhancements
- Market share growth due to new services
- Strike rate (ratio of orders to enquiries or quotations)
- Per cent of orders delivered on time
- Customer satisfaction indices

Goffin and Mitchell (2005)

Outcomes

Customer acquisition:

- New customers gained through innovation
- Number of customers through existing products/services who buy new products/services
- Number of new customers of new products/services who go on to buy existing products/services
- Market share

Customer loyalty:

- Frequency of repeat customers
- Average annual sales per customer
- Customer satisfaction with innovation activities
- Percentage of customer attrition
- Ratio of new visitors to repeat visitors

Value capture:

- Margin of product and services offered to customers
- Average of prices paid by customers
- Number of new product and service lines introduced
- Profitability of innovation operations
- Revenues generated through innovation efforts (total revenue, innovation revenue, revenue per innovation customer)
- Customer profitability

Source: Adapted from Kallman (2009)

TABLE 11.3 A nuanced conceptual approach to input, process and output measures for innovation

Conceptual/theoretical underpinning Muller et al. (2005)	Conceptual/theoretical underpinning Regnell et al. (2008)
Resource view	**Innovation identification**
Inputs (capital, talent, time):	**Internal collection:**
• Percentage of capital that is invested in innovation activities such as submitting and reviewing ideas for new products and services and developing ideas through an innovation pipeline	• Number of ideas coming from different sources
	• Number of patents that have been analysed in existing portfolio of patents
	• Time between cooperation activities and the patent department in the company
• Number of entrepreneurs in the company, i.e. individuals who have previously started a business, either within the company or before joining the company	**External collection:**
	• Number of and time between collection activities that focus on specific external stakeholders (users, customers, competitors, owners, etc.)
	• Number of visited events (conferences, courses, fairs, etc.)
• Percentage of workforce time that is currently dedicated to innovation projects	• Amount of researching of other companies (potential threats, suppliers, mergers, etc.)
	• Number of developed patents or prototypes that build upon existing portfolio of patents
Output (return on investment):	**Internal generation:**
• Number of new products, services and businesses launched in the past year	• Number and time between activities for presentations on a team's work
	• Number of activities for systematic generation of ideas
• Percentage of revenue from products or services introduced in the past 3 years	• Change over time of number of suggestions to the team (e.g. examination of whether or not the number of suggestions rise after a presentation)
	External generation:
• Share of wealth, i.e. the change in the company's market value during the past year divided by the change in the total industry's market value during the same period	• Number of observation studies conducted by users
	• Number of projects based on ideas from external stakeholders
	• Number of customer meeting about future needs
	Reversion:
	• Number of suggestions from people who previously have had their suggestions rejected (it is important that people continue to come up with suggestions even though their previous suggestions have not been turned into projects)
	• Time between suggestions and reversion on the suggestion
	• Number of hours set aside to reversion

Conceptual/theoretical underpinning Muller et al. (2005)	Conceptual/theoretical underpinning Regnell et al. (2008)
Capabilities view	**Project selection**
Inputs (preconditions):	**Timing:**
• Percentage of employees for whom innovation is a key performance goal	• Appreciated time to implementation of the results of a project
	• Number of short-term projects compared with long-term projects
• Percentage of employees who have received training in innovation, e.g. instruction in estimating market potential of an idea	• Appreciated lead time for the results of the project to be received by internal stakeholders
	Risk:
• Number of innovation tools and methodologies available to employees	• Subjective valuation of risk of project (applicability, technical uncertainty)
	• Number of parallel examinations of alternatives (by uncertainties concerning future choice of technique)
Output (renewal):	• Number of projects that turn out to be non-value adding (some risk must be taken in connection with innovation, which means that not all projects will not be successful)
• Number of new competencies (i.e. distinctive skills and knowledge domains that spawn innovation) measures as a simple count among a threshold proportion of employees	**Size:**
	• Appreciated access to resources per project
	• Allocation of project sizes in the project portfolio
• Number of strategic options (i.e. newly created opportunities to significantly advance an existing business)	• Change over time of number of suggestions to the team (e.g. examination of whether or not the number of suggestions rises after a presentation)
	Internal stakeholders:
• Number of new markets entered in past year	• Allocation of projects between different types of internal stakeholder
	• Number of projects that challenge current business models
	• Number of projects that focus on stepwise improvements of existing product attributes (if only these types of projects are implemented, the level of innovation is probably too low)
	External stakeholders:
	• Number of projects based on radical future scenarios
	• Number of projects with user relevance
	• Number of projects with customer relevance
	Return on investment:
	• Appreciated return on investment per project
	• Alternative costs if a project is not implemented (analysis of worst case scenario)
	• Number of directions of decisions from management, about what innovation projects should be prioritised

(Continued)

TABLE 11.3 (Continued)

Conceptual/ theoretical underpinning Muller et al. (2005)	Conceptual/ theoretical underpinning Regnell et al. (2008)
Leadership view	**Innovation projects and ways of working**

• Percentage of executives' time spent on strategic innovation rather than day-to-day operations	***Process:***
	• Subjective valuation of the efficiency of the way of working
• Percentage of managers with training in the concepts and tools of innovation	• Amount of time laid down on actual value-creating work, compared with for example administration
	• Subjective evaluation of how well the method of evaluating the innovation results actually works
• Number of times during the past 5, 10, and 20 years in which senior management has redefined the company's core business	• Number of projects that change status from innovation projects directly to product development projects
	• Remaining investment costs until the product is finished
	• Amount of the innovation teams' development ground that can be reused directly in product development
	Climate:
	• Amount of coherent non-booked time in the calendar of each employee
	• Amount of time suited for working with own ideas
	• Time between delivery deadlines for each employee
	• Subjective evaluations of the opportunities for open, constructive debates
	• Subjective evaluations of the lack of personal conflicts and other negative factors (too much pressure, fear of being unsuccessful, etc.)
	Incentive:
	• Economical compensation for reaching personal and team goals
	• Economical compensation for reporting of patents and new inventions
	• Number of acknowledgements and distinctions for individuals and teams
	Competency:
	• Allocation based on the employees' backgrounds, level of experience, age, gender, etc.
	• Number of different areas of knowledge in the team
	• Evaluation of how well the team covers strategic competences
	• Prevalence of rotations between position
	• Number of projects that each individual carries out, respectively has been responsible for

		Conceptual/theoretical underpinning Muller et al. (2005)		Conceptual/theoretical underpinning Regnell et al. (2008)

Organisation:

- Resources per project (man-hours, procurement budget, etc.)
- Total number of projects per year
- Average time to realisation of projects
- Amount of the budget that is allocated to sub-suppliers

Improvements of the innovation process:

- Number of improvement suggestions on the way of working coming from the team
- Number of improvement suggestions on the way of working, based on reversion from the environment, on the results of the team
- Number of implemented process changes (changes in the ways of working)
- Subjective evaluations of how many improvement suggestions that have actually affected the ways of working
- Number of process changes that are evaluated as giving clear improvements
- Subjective evaluations of the value of implemented process changes

Process

- Number of ideas submitted by employees in the past 3, 6 and 12 months
- Ratio of successful ideas to ideas submitted
- Number of ongoing experiments and ventures
- Average time from idea submission to commercial launch

Effects and influence

Product attributes:

- Number of product attributes affected by the work of the team
- Number of other projects affected by the work of the team
- Number of objects in the change process of the product development which are based on the results from the work of the team
- Number of end users that are affected by the product attributes that the work of the team has affected
- Number of results from the innovation project's team that are accepted by the product planning department, or other internal stakeholders that manage the product development
- Subjective evaluations of the degree of the team's influence on the launched product that are positive compared with neutral or negative influence

Interaction:

- Number of people in the network of the team
- Number of stakeholders covered by the network of the team
- Number of resources dedicated to internal marketing

(Continued)

TABLE 11.3 (Continued)

Conceptual/ theoretical underpinning Muller et al. (2005)	Conceptual/ theoretical underpinning Regnell et al. (2008)
	• Number of people attending presentations by the team
	• Number of other employees that are aware of the work of the team
	• Number of cooperations with people in the organisation compared with external people
	• Resources suited for preparations for passing on the idea, or integration and interaction with surroundings
	• Resources dedicated to activities for internal marketing
	Trust:
	• Number of invitations for presentations, meetings, courses, etc.
	• The receiver's subjective evaluation of the quality of the team work
	• Number of accesses to documents and reports conducted by the team
	• Results from surveys regarding the presentations from the team, among the participants of the presentations
	• The surrounding subjective evaluations of the teams' trustworthiness and competencies within strategic technical areas
	Patent:
	• Number of patent suggestions, patent applications, granted patents, etc. (number per person and year, etc.)
	• Resources spent on patent suggestions and reporting of new inventions
	• The teams' share of the company's allocation of patent bonuses
	• The teams' share of the company's database of reported new inventions
	Practice and standards:
	• Number of organisations that conduct industry standards and practice where the team standard is participating (actively contributing or passively following)
	• Number of occasions where the work of the team is affected by practice and standards
	• Share of standards that have really affected vs the total share of standards that desirably would have been affecting
	• The ability to affect practice and standards compared with competitors
	• Resources spent on affecting practice and standards

Davila et al. (2006) use balanced-scorecard theories to establish their model of innovation management. In doing so they are paying due regard to a range of measures that stretch beyond standard financial measures and take into account other critical issues such as process efficiency, customer perspectives and learning. The rationale for this approach appears to be based on the notion that effective measures are dependent on the appropriateness of the innovation model, which in turn feeds off from an organisation's innovation strategy. While there is a common processual element in managing and measuring innovation, not all the metrics will apply equally to all types of organisations. Goffin and Mitchell (2005) use the Pentathlon Framework, which uses the traditional idea-development funnel and introduces human resource management to innovation strategy. A comprehensive and holistic approach relies on managers to look continually for ways in which they can stimulate creativity by facilitating the flow and exchange of ideas, information and knowledge in an organisation. Larger firms are expected to manage several projects at the same time, and critical management requires prioritisation of projects, activities and resources in as optimal a manner as possible. Ideas are best implemented through good project management with clearly identified deliverables. Consequently, numerous techniques such as project definition, task analysis, resource allocation and monitoring of progress are essential components of effective and commendable project management. Where human resource management plays a key part in Goffin and Mitchell's model is in the creation of environments conducive to innovation, the creation of innovation teams, people motivation and performance management (Kallman, 2009) (see the discussion on people and innovation in Chapter 7).

It is understood that most of the metrics stated above have been derived by the authors from a variety of teaching, consulting and other practices (Kallman, 2009). Definitions and appropriate explanations or distinctions between the different models may be missing, as indeed is any clear guidance on specific levels of measurement, but what we do find is the need to address the complex case of innovation measurement in as comprehensive a fashion as possible. In other words, there are many aspects of innovation, from inputs to outputs to processes, and from ways of working to effects and influences. They all represent ways in which we can understand better the organisation and management of innovation (Kallman, 2009).

In Muller et al. (2005) we find a theoretical and a structural approach to innovation management. Rather than identify a variety of metrics only, they attempt to provide an organisational backdrop to the metrics in terms of the allocation of resources at tactical and strategic levels and the capability and competencies of the organisation to manage the innovation process. Processes cover both functions and structures such as incubators, venture funding and incentives.

A distinctive innovation management framework, referred to as MINT (Main Inspiration for Innovative Team), was created by Regnell et al. (2008) as part of a group of 26 Swedish researchers. The focus here is on the sourcing of innovation in a firm with four categories of measurement:

1. *Innovation identification* – internal or external and passive and active sourcing of ideas, development and encouragement of internally or externally-sourced initial ideas.

2. *Project selection* – selection of ideas based on clearly identified criteria mediated by the need to maintain a balanced portfolio of projects in terms of size and estimation of value generation, timing and value-based priorities.
3. *Innovation projects and ways of working* – the importance of the 'innovative team' and the way it implements ideas; the necessary incentives that the team needs and the enumeration of competencies required for this purpose.
4. *Effects and influence* – transfer of ideas by the 'innovative team' to the 'development team' and various forms of interaction with the whole organisation, the inculcation of trust and review of previous practice.

Measurement, as we can conclude from the above discussion, is as complex an exercise as innovation itself. However, we can draw down some key interlinked principles for measuring innovation which can help forms to devise suitable strategies and instruments for innovation governance. In addition to the above discussion, the development of the set of principles below is also influenced by interventions in practice and policy, in particular the observations made by Schramm (2008) and Muller (2014; see also Muller et al., 2005).

PRINCIPLE 1: CULTURE, CAPABILITIES, STRATEGY AND LEADERSHIP

i. There is a need to create an organisational culture that embeds and drives strategic innovation.
ii. It is crucial to develop an imperative for nurturing and supporting critical capabilities (including talent and well-being) of employees that correspond with the evolving competitive business scenarios. Organisational capability metrics take into account infrastructure and the process of innovation. Capability measures help to ensure that initiatives are geared towards continuity of purpose through replicable and sustainable approaches to invention, reinvention, adjustment, implementation and diffusion.
iii. It is necessary to evaluate innovation activities to compute both return on investment (ROI) and appropriate feedback for critical learning, improvement and renewing.
iv. An important reckoning comes in the form of driving profitable but sustainable growth – measuring innovation based on bottom-line outcomes which do not simply consider ROI, but variations of returns that include social returns and capability returns. Procter & Gamble, for example, uses an organisational capability input metric focused on 'the percentage of external sourcing of ideas and technology' as a way to drive its Connect and Develop strategy for open innovation. In 2000, 10% of the company's R&D was outsourced; today, 50% of all ideas and technology come from the outside.

v. Improved data on innovation should permit industry- and sector-specific analysis, recognising that innovation manifests itself differently in different parts of the economy. In particular, international comparisons would help explain why different countries are experiencing different economic growth rates. When compared with different national policy mixes, it may be possible to achieve a better understanding of the impact that public policies have on growth and innovation.

vi. Typical tactics for diffusing innovation culture could embrace communication and storytelling, training and development, innovation jams and social networks.

PRINCIPLE 2: CREATING A 'FAMILY OF METRICS'

In measuring the complexity of innovation a key objective should be to find solutions that create simplicity from such complexity. Some of that simplicity is afforded by the synergies from complementary success factors, and therefore nesting these factors by way of creating a family of metrics can help to obtain a clear direction for innovation management in a firm and establish a well-rounded portfolio of measures:

i. The measures need to reflect strategic objectives that are understood by all parts of a business so that each part can contribute to the family and gain from the connections with the other parts to support the collective innovation objectives of the firm.

ii. Both input and output metrics help to establish measures that drive resource allocation and capability building, as well as ROI. While input measures stand for the optimal contributions made to the innovation process, output metrics represent the desired outcome results for the metric category.

iii. ROI metrics address two measures: resource investments and financial returns. ROI metrics enable fiscal discipline and help to justify and recognise the economic value of strategic initiatives, programmes and the overall investment in innovation.

iv. Leadership metrics can be measured in terms of both inputs and outputs. They address the behaviours that senior managers and leaders must exhibit to support a culture of innovation within the organisation, including the development of capabilities. Leadership metrics help to justify and recognise the social and cultural value of the overall investment in innovation.

v. Measurement is an iterative process that does not have a finite start and finish date as in a project. Learning, enhancement, augmentation and improvement are to be obtained from each stage of the process There is a need to recalibrate strategies and metrics on a regular basis. Since not all measures of innovation are strictly quantifiable, adopting qualitative approaches to measurement could actually improve quantification later. Typically, a degree of experimentation, for example in measuring qualitatively the benefits of networking and collaboration, might generate spillover effects that affect market share or product portfolio enhancement.

vi. Since the business entity does not operate in isolation, it is important to identify better ways to continually quantify innovation in the marketplace. A key institutional factor impinging on innovation is the impact of legislation and regulations, such as tax relief on R&D, and education and training policies, which can have a direct and explicit impact on innovation, while other policies such as those on immigration and the restricted movement of talent across borders could have a negative effect. Both effects should be measured.

vii. Innovation measures should allow for analysis at the firm, industry, regional, country and international levels, especially when businesses are operating across borders or are part of a networked global community of firms.

PRINCIPLE 3: DATA COLLECTION

Collecting relevant data for innovation is critical for all firms that need to work out nuanced methods and practices and use up-to-date technologies for data at all stages and across all aspects of the innovation process:

i. Data collection needs to be appropriate to the firm's activities and neither determined by theory nor based on a universal 'one-size-fits-all' approach.

ii. Given variations in the size of firms and the resources available to them, the cost and time burden for collecting data should be minimised, bearing in mind that data has to be relevant, that it can be used effectively and that it can be interpreted and analysed.

iii. Trade-offs between expected costs and potential benefits should be considered, especially because of resource and regulatory issues.

iv. Where feasible, the introduction of new measures should not be at the expense of carrying out 'back-testing' and being applied to historical data, so that the interpretation and analysis of the relationship between innovation and productivity, inputs and outputs, and other connections can be compatible over time.

MEASURING OBJECTIVE OUTCOMES

Part of what measurement is about at its simplest is the evaluation of objective outputs and outcomes. McKinsey, the management consultant firm, has proposed an alternative way to measure innovation which 'focuses on objective outcomes, is based upon publicly available data, takes a broad look at innovation, and assesses the power of good ideas over time' (Berwig et al., 2009). Vignette 11.1 showcases McKinsey's approach to measuring objective outcomes.

VIGNETTE 11.1   MEASURING THE OBJECTIVE OUTCOMES OF INNOVATION

The starting point is McKinsey's proprietary granularity of growth database, which includes revenue streams from more than 750 firms across 16 sectors. McKinsey believes that the analysis could be applied to any business that can provide a sufficient level of granular data ('sufficiency' here is not explained). It can also go beyond the level of the firm by examining data across business sectors and segments, or geographical space. Data can then be dissected by considering all of these variables and identifying revenue growth attributable to innovation.

There are several steps that taken together constitute the McKinsey approach and its innovation performance score.

STEP 1

The first step in the process is to define innovation. McKinsey does so by defining innovation to cover all 'novel activity with impact on company', including product, process and business model innovation. Therefore, any new approach that creates economic value for a firm is regarded as innovation in McKinsey's index. This also means that the index includes both disruptive and incremental innovations since both forms have an impact on growth performance. McKinsey also assumes that competitors can initiate or replicate an innovation over a prolonged period of time if the markets operate fairly and that there are other negative institutional filters (monopolistic or oligopolistic markets, unfair regulatory stipulations) impeding this replication process. Under these circumstances the innovation advantage may not be sustained indefinitely: 'Therefore, if a company is continually outperforming in its segment over time, there is a good chance that the company is continually leading the pack on new products/processes/models.' Finally, superior innovative strategy is not equated with good business strategy, which may lead a firm to buy out an innovative business. The buying-out process is disregarded in McKinsey's scheme of innovation measurement.

STEP 2

The second step is to evaluate the market creation power of a particular segment in terms of being 'new' to the world or market entry as in being new to the firm. This is accomplished by identifying revenues generated by new segments (resulting from new initiatives or from acquisitions of new firms with different product portfolios). Account is also taken of revenues accruing from acquisitions that lead to new products and activities, even when they are not regarded as a new segment by the firm.

STEP 3

As a third step, the revenue growth of the firm is then compared with the overall market and 'attribute any out-performance to the business's ability to innovate'. The assumption that is made here is that if the firm consistently outgrows the market over a significant period of time (say, 5 to 7 years), it must be introducing new products, processes or business models that allow it to perform better than its competitors.

(Continued)

(Continued)

Comparisons can be made for different firms along these lines. Short-term effects of techniques such as marketing or sales campaigns are controlled and/or eliminated.

The resulting analysis establishes an innovation performance score (IPS). IPS is expressed as a percentage, which shows the compound annual growth rate for a specified period attributable to innovation. McKinsey points to top innovators in the television industry, such as LG, Samsung and Sharp, which generated scores significantly above other well-known brand names: 'LG generated a score of 13.7 percent from 1999 to 2007, because of early and significant investments in liquid crystal display (LCD) panels, an aggressive culture, and flexibility in adapting to evolving trends'.

McKinsey's focus on consumer packaged goods, pharmaceuticals and consumer electronics shows major differences in scores among industries. Beer and drug firms tend to score lower than TV and telephone makers. The other big finding is that of business model innovation, which tended to generate larger gains than product or process innovation. This is partly because innovation on business models is a direct function of the uniqueness of a firm (objectives, strategies, people, combination of resources, markets), and also because it is difficult to imitate. IPS also appears to be a reliable indicator of a company's stock market performance. Results showed a relatively strong correlation (with $R^2 \sim 0.3$) between a company's IPS and its total return to shareholders (TRS): 'This correlation is stronger than it is for other growth-related metrics – a result that suggests that innovation performance measured in IPS is strongly correlated with overall company performance.'

Innovation capability yields a surplus that is higher than growth, and this excess benefit is dependent on playing in the right market and growing faster than one's peers in any industry.

Using IPS, McKinsey found that:

1. Strong innovators do consistently well by outperforming the markets that they are already in and not by entering or creating new segments.
2. Top innovators continue to outperform their peers even in inclement economic conditions because of their capacity and agile capabilities for innovation, which in turn make it simpler for them to deal with crises and other challenges of lean economic times.
3. Strong innovating firms demonstrate the power of business model innovation, which appears to have far higher impact than product or process innovations.
4. The lower the rate of innovation in firms, the greater the possibility of problematic economic performance by those organisations. It was also noted that the firms with the highest IPS do not always reap the highest rewards in terms of TRS.

While McKinsey's IPS does indeed offer a new approach to measuring innovation, questions remain, as various commentators have suggested directly to the consulting company. For example, real and significant profits emanating from any innovation tend to appear quite late in its cycle, when it has been diffused by way of adoption by the firm's largest number of customers and the majority of the investment for product development and marketing has already been made. There is, therefore, an inevitable lag of a few years after the initial innovation is made in any profits- or revenues-based measurement of innovation.

McKinsey continues its search for the holy grail of appropriate indicators, and one of the interesting set of conclusions that it has drawn in recent times is that there are eight key principles, or 'eight essentials', that enable measurable innovation performance. In other words, the IPS model can be seen to work most effectively when these eight essentials are in place in any substantial, high-performing business. McKinsey drew these conclusions from its survey results from over 2,500 executives based on its research and database covering a wide range of industry sectors. The key to the analysis of the survey is the holistic approach that is taken to evaluate a firm 'from the inside out, focusing down on the critical mindsets, processes, skillsets and decision-making routines needed to make innovation happen'.

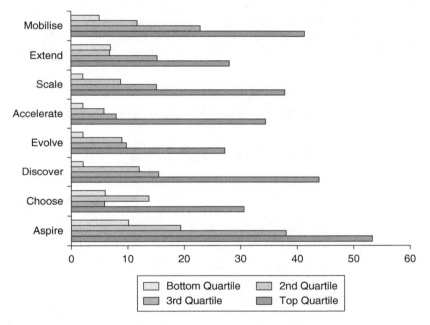

FIGURE 11.1 The eight essentials and how high-performing firms in the McKinsey database follow them (percentage of respondents per performance quartile; *N* = 623)

Notes:

1. Performance defined as a weighted index of measures for organic growth and innovation performance (per cent of growth from new products or services developed in-house; per cent of sales from new products and self-assessment of innovation performance).

2. Respondents who answered 'yes to some degree', 'no' or 'don't know/not applicable' to questions on any of the items are not shown in the figure above.

(Continued)

(Continued)

Performance quartiles help to categorise firms in terms of their respective performance and enable comparison with their counterparts in their industry and across the entire data set. A comparison of the top quartile group of innovators with the less well-performing firms was made to obtain an understanding of differences in practice.

Figure 11.1 shows the eight essentials, the verbs – aspire, choose, discover, evolve, accelerate, scale, extend and mobilise – that indicate a pattern of activities necessary to achieve successful innovation outcomes. What the chart shows is that an aspiration for innovation is probably the most important essential, particularly for the top quartile of firms, with discovery and mobilisation of resources being the second and third most important factors for the same group of firms. The data also reveals the difference between the high-end innovation performers and the bottom quartile of firms. In all cases, there are stark differences between the use of the eight essentials: 45% (for 'aspire'), 42% (for 'evolve'), 37% (for 'scale') and 36% (for 'mobilise').

Figure 11.2 shows the combined effect of all the essentials and how different types of innovators demonstrate a capability of managing the very difficult task

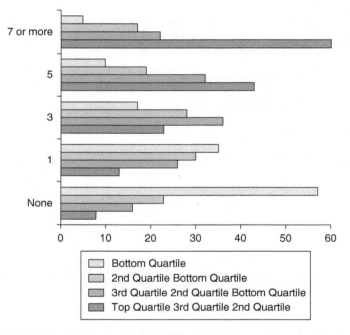

FIGURE 11.2 Combined effect of mastering multiple essentials (percentage of group falling within each percentage quartile; *N* = 2,463)

Note: Number of essentials mastered ('agree' or 'strongly agree' with all benchmark practice questions per essential).

Source of data: Adapted from McKinsey quarterly panel survey, 'Innovation at Scale', November 2012

of making the links work effectively, thereby providing for a genuinely strategic approach to innovation. As we would expect, the bottom quartile consists of the largest percentage of firms with no ability to combine any of the essentials, while the top quartile includes firms with almost the exact opposite set of combinatory capabilities. Elsewhere in the book we have referred to innovative firms having that special combinatory capability which allows them to fuse differences in varied ingredients, functions, talents and resources to generate Schumpeterian innovation excellence. Once again the top quartile of firms is able to register a much higher level of performance, with the highest number of combinations (seven) of the essentials.

Sources: Adapted from Berwig et al. (2009); de Jong, et al. (2013)

AT THE END (OR IS IT AT THE BEGINNING?) WHAT DOES THE CUSTOMER THINK?

However sophisticated the measures and whatever the levels of satisfaction over the types and levels of innovation achieved within an organisation, measurement cannot be complete if the customers' response to the innovation is given insufficient consideration. General firm performance outcomes do not always tell the whole story about customer reactions, and for any one firm it is difficult to sustain successful innovation outcomes consistently. The fall in the popularity of iPhones in the last 12 months (since 2015) or the drop in sales of Jaguar cars in China bears testimony to the fact of customers not accepting a permanent innovation revolution in any one firm. At a more mundane level, observing, noting and computing customer behaviour and reactions are critical so that later fallout can be avoided or mitigated. Societies benefit when new products and services are accepted and adopted by customers, paving the way for wider usage and the further development of those products and services.

Social scientists have produced a range of relevant measures of acceptance of innovation and technology. Consumer behaviour and marketing-oriented journals, such as the *Journal of the Academy of Marketing Science*, the *Journal of Marketing*, the *Journal of Marketing Research*, the *Journal of Consumer Research* and the *Journal of Retailing* have all published critical articles on various measurement scales for technology and innovation acceptance. Bruner (2014) selected 30 scales used in scholarly research and organised them in terms of five fields that cover the description, background and usefulness of the measures:

(a) Scale name – assignment of a descriptive title to the scale which can take into account multiple issues.
(b) Scale description – to enable assessment of the theoretical construct plus the number of items, points on a rating scale and a response format (such as a Likert or semantic differential).

(c) Scale origin – citing of at least one usage, although in many cases a scale's origin and development may not be known because the users may not have identified them.

(d) Scale reliability – internal consistency using Cronbach's alpha or construct reliability or even temporary stability (test–retest correlation), with higher numbers having better reliability fit. Test scores less than 0.7 or 0.6 are disregarded.

(e) Scale validity – some evidence drawn from various types of validity.

Table 11.4 provides a summary of the five fields against 10 of the 30 items selected by Bruner (2014) and chosen randomly for the purpose of illustration measuring innovation and technology acceptance.

The other 20 scales include items such as 'Change Seeking', 'Compatibility of Product Usage Outcomes', 'Compatibility of the Product', 'Ease of Use (General)', 'Ease of Use of the Product', 'Gadget Loving', 'Innovativeness Importance of the Consumer (Product Specific)', 'Innovativeness Importance to the Consumer (Technological)', 'Innovativeness of the Consumer (Product Trial)', 'Innovativeness of the Consumer (Technological)', 'Innovativeness of the Consumer (Usage)', 'Involvement with Technology', 'Novelty (General)', 'Pace of Technological Innovativeness', 'Relative Advantage of the Product', 'Technological Anxiety', 'Technology Usage Discomfort', 'Technology Usage Motivation (Intrinsic)', 'Usefulness (General)', 'Usefulness of the Product', 'Visibility of the New Product's Usage'. What we do find from this exercise undertaken by Bruner (2014) is the level of complexity that one has to mine in order to try to obtain as complete an evaluation process as possible from a specific perspective. In taking the measurement out of the black box of the organisation to the consumer, we obtain a nuanced understanding of behavioural issues affecting the usage of novel products and services, with the actual measurement attempting to quantify qualitative responses to the acceptance of these products and services. Readers interested in further details of this highly interesting aspect of innovation measurement are directed towards the work of Bruner and the several authors identified in the table.

CONCLUDING OBSERVATIONS

This chapter has covered a wide array of approaches and methods for measuring innovation. It has looked at perspectives of the firms, the managers and workers involved in the innovation process, and crucially the beneficiary of the innovation process – the customer and end user. In doing so the importance of a firm's strategy and innovation focus has been emphasised along with the need to adopt a holistic approach to the measurement activity. Such an approach provides a definition of the measurement process and a purpose for doing so ultimately for the benefit of the innovative organisation. Numerous accounts referred to in the chapter point to the dearth of adequate measurement tools and, critically, the absence of any clear strategy for innovation, let alone its measurement. Measurement is, therefore, a handmaiden to strategy.

TABLE 11.4 Measuring innovation and technology acceptance: the five fields of the scales of measurement

Scale name	Scale description	Scale origin	Scale reliability	Scale validity
Adoption intention	4-item, 7-point Likert scale used to measure inclination to buy new product. Urgency of adoption is suggested	Fisher (1993): to measure student's intention to buy a fictional new product idea: cordless headphones	Cronbach's alpha of 0.93 (Fisher, 1993; Fisher and Price, 1992)	Not addressed specifically. Fisher and Price (1992) stated that the variance extracted for the scale was 0.79
Attitude towards the innovation	11-item, 7-point scale measures attitude of consumer to a specific product – referred to as the 'attractiveness of innovation' (Boyd and Mason, 1999)	Boyd and Mason (1999): specific items developed based on by Rogers' (1962) innovation characteristics + focus group feedback	Alpha score of 0.91 (Boyd and Mason, 1999)	No mention of scale validity but exploratory factor analysis suggested that items were unidimensional
Attitude towards the product (high-tech)	Semantic differential scale to measure person's general evaluation of a high-tech product or service	Roehm and Sternthal (2001): use of bipolar adjectives with limited previous usage	Three versions of the scale used in four experiments (Roehm and Sternthal, 2001). Two different 10-item versions had alphas of 0.93 and 0.90. Other studies with higher numbers of items had alphas of 0.90 and 0.93	No examination of scale validity but factor analysis showed scale was unidimensional
Behavioural control	How much a person feels they are in control of an object or a process; measured with 4- or 7-point Likert-type items or use of self-service technology (SST)	Collier and Sherrell (2010) based on key words and concepts from measures used by Dabholkar (1996), Zhu (2002), Yen and Gwinner (2003)	Alpha score of 0.901 (Collier and Sherrell, 2010)	Collier and Sherrell (2010) used Confirmatory Factor Analysis to show that measurement fitted data. Also found support for convergent and discriminant validities. Average Variance Extracted scale was 0.74
Behavioural intention (general)	Semantic differentials measuring expressed inclination of people to engage in a specified behaviour (as in the purchase of a technology product)	Fishbein and Ajzen (1975); Ajzen and Fishbein (1980). One of the first uses of the multi-item scale in a consumer context was related to the purchase of a new diet suppressant (Oliver and Bearden, 1985; Ko et al., 2005)	Four-item version had construct reliability of 0.87 (Oliver and Bearden, 1985). Alphas reported for the 3-item version are 0.91 (Bruner and Kumar, 2000) and 0.89 (Ko et al., 2005)	Not addressed in any of the studies referred to here. Use of CFA by Oliver and Bearden (1985) showed that the variance extracted for behavioural intention was 0.67. Mackenzie and Spreng (1992) provided a correlation matrix between items in the behavioural intention scale with inter-correlation cores ranging between 0.47 and 0.88

(Continued)

TABLE 11.4 (Continued)

Scale name	Scale description	Scale origin	Scale reliability	Scale validity
Communication of product usage	Three 5-point Likert items measuring degree to which a consumer understands a product and communicating them to others	Van Ittersum and Feinberg (2010) relied on published and validated scales referring to the scale as 'perceived observability' based on construct by Rogers (2003)	Alpha scores were 0.71, 0.64 and 0.83 (Van Ittersum and Feinberg, 2010)	Not addressed
Innovation complexity	Three 7-point items used to measure degree of challenge to learning to use a new product as perceived by a consumer	Wood and Moreau (2006)	Alpha scores of 0.90 at two points in time (Wood and Moreau, 2006)	None available
Emergent nature	Measured in 8- and 7-point Likert scale: ability to imagine how new product concepts could be developed to become more useful and relevant to consumers	Hoffman et al.'s (2010) construct was a mix of personality traits and processing abilities	Alpha score of 0.93 (Hoffman et al. (2010)	
Innovative ability of the company	Three 7-point Likert-type items: measures a person's belief that a business company is competent enough to create original and interesting products	Schreier et al. (2012); four studies	Alpha score of 0.92 (Schreier et al., 2012)	Not discussed. In third study authors used two scales measuring innovative ability. Both measures were highly correlated
Lead user (domain specific)	Five, 7-point Likert-type items: measures a person's interest in plus generation and promotion of new and different ways to satisfy needs within a specific domain (as in product category)	Hoffman et al. (2010) validated the scale along with 'emergent nature' scale drawing upon work by Morrison et al. (2000)	Alpha score was 0.93 (Hoffman et al., 2010)	Survey instrument of first study used 8 items to measure lead user status. This was then reduced to 5 items. Further examination showed the scale's unidimensionality and discriminant validity

The fact that measurement is a complex process, not least because of the complexity of the innovation process, suggests that it is not only the inputs, processes and outputs that need to be evaluated, but also the motivation for and the approach to innovation, the means by which innovation outcomes are achieved, and how the end user accepts the innovation products and services.

Studies point to various 'essentials' and models for measuring innovation, reflecting the demands of a particular place, time and context for innovation. The core essentials of what is being measured (the object), the meaning of the concept of measurement (its scope and value) and the application or feasibility of the different types of measurement (methods and frameworks) remain the same over time. It is the purpose and the realisation of value that can change according to different environments. For example, how you measure the use of solar technology innovation to overcome energy problems would inevitably be different from how you measure the social impact of an apps-based innovation that improves our ability to hail taxi services. What we do know is that we need to measure the results that flow from both and all the other innovations that sweep across the world.

 SELF-ASSESSMENT AND RESEARCH QUESTIONS

1. Why is measuring innovation important for business managers, researchers and policy makers?

2. Examine the different measures of innovation and their application to different types of firms.

3. Discuss how effective measurement policies can help to shape productive business strategies.

4. What are some of the key principles that could guide managers and policy makers to help develop appropriate metrics for innovation?

5. How do culture and the environment influence the adoption and use of innovation metrics?

REFERENCES

Acs, Z.J. and Audrestsch, D.B. (eds) (1990) *Innovation and Small Firms*. Cambridge, MA: MIT Press.

Acs, Z.J. and Audretsch, D.B. (2005) 'Entrepreneurship, innovation, and technological change', *Foundations and Trends in Entrepreneurship*, 1(4): 149–95.

A.D. Little (2012) 'Innovation: measuring it to manage it', M. Kolk, P. Kyte, F. van Oene and J. Jacobs. Available at: http://www.adlittle.com/downloads/tx_adlprism/Prism_01-12_Innovation.pdf (last accessed 2 February 2017).

Ajzen, I. and Fishbein, M. (1980) *Understanding Attitudes and Predicting Social Behaviour.* Englewood Cliffs, NJ: Prentice Hall.

Armbruster, H., Bikfalvi, A., Kinkel, S. and Lay, G. (2008) 'Organizational innovation: the challenge of measuring non-technical innovation in large-scale surveys', *Technovation*, 28: 644–57.

Berwig, J.O., Marston, N., Pukkinen, L. and Stein, L. (2009) 'Innovation: What's your score?', *What Matters*, McKinsey Digital, September: 4. Available at: http://innovbfa.viabloga.com/files/McKinseyQuaterly___Innovation___what_is_your_score___sept_2009.pdf (last accessed 26 April 2016).

Bosma, N., van Praag, M., Thurik, R. and deWit, G. (2004) 'The value of human and social capital investment for the business performance of start-ups', *Small Business Economics*, 23: 227–36.

Boyd, T.C. and Mason, C.H. (1999) 'The link between attractiveness of "extrabrand" attributes and the adoption of innovations', *Journal of the Academy of Marketing Science*, 27(3): 306–19.

Bruner II, G.C. (2014) *Measuring Innovation and Technology Acceptance*. Fort Worth, TX: GCBII Productions.

Bruner, G.C. and Kumar, A. (2000) 'Web commercials and advertising hierarchy-of-effects', *Journal of Advertising Research*, 40(1–2): 35–42.

Cohen, D. and Soto, M. (2007) 'Growth and human capital: good data, good results', *Journal of Economic Growth*, 12: 51–76.

Collier, J.E. and Sherrell, D.L. (2010) 'Examining the influence of control and convenience in a self-service setting', *Journal of the Academy of Marketing Science*, 38(4): 490–509.

Coronado, D., Acosta, M. and Fernandez, A. (2008) 'Attitudes to innovation in peripheral economic regions', *Research Policy*, 37: 1009–21.

Dabholkar, P.A. (1996) 'Consumer evaluations of new technology-based service options: an investigation of alternative models of service quality', *International Journal of Research in Marketing*, 13(1): 29–51.

Davila, T., Epstein, M.J. and Shelton, R. (2006) *Making Innovation Work: How to Manage it, Measure it, and Profit from it.* Upper Saddle River, NJ: Pearson Prentice Hall.

Dolan, P. and Metcalfe, R. (2012) 'The relationship between innovation and subjective wellbeing', *Research Policy*, 41: 1489–98.

Fishbein, M. and Ajzen, I. (1975) *Belief, Attitude, Intention and Behavior: An Introduction to Theory and Research.* Reading, MA: Addison-Wesley.

Fisher, R. and Price, L.J. (1992) 'An investigation into the social context of early adoption behaviour', *Journal of Consumer Research*, 19(December): 477–86.

Fisher, R.J. (1993) 'Social desirability bias and the validity of indirect questioning', *Journal of Consumer Research*, 20(September): 303–15.

Fitzroy, F.R. and Kraft, K. (1990) 'Innovation, rent-sharing and the organization of labour in the federal republic of Germany', *Small Business Economics,* 2(2): 95–103.

Ganotakis, P. (2012) 'Founders' human capital and the performance of UK new technology based firms', *Small Business Economics*, 39: 495–515.

Gellman Research Associates (1982) *The relationship between industrial concentration, firm size and technological innovation.* Glastonbury, CT: US Small Business Administration, Futures Group.

Goffin, K. and Mitchell, R. (2005) *Innovation Management: Strategy and Implementation Using the Pentathlon Framework.* Basingstoke: Palgrave Macmillan.

Herrmann, A., Tomczak, T. and Befurt, R. (2006) 'Determinants of radical product innovations', *European Journal of Innovation Management*, 9: 20–43.

Hewitt-Dundas, N. (2006) 'Resource and capability constraints to innovation in small and large plants', *Small Business Economics*, 26(3): 257–77.

Hitt, M.A., Ireland, R.D., Camp, S.M. and Sexton, D.L. (2001) 'Strategic entrepreneurship: Entrepreneurial strategies for wealth creation', *Strategic Management Journal*, 22(6–7): 479–91.

Hoffman, D.L., Kopalle, P.K. and Novak, T.P. (2010) 'The "right" consumers for better concepts: identifying consumers high in emergent nature to develop new product concepts', *Journal of Marketing Research*, 47(5): 854–65.

Kallman, K. (2009) 'Innovation metrics – keys to increase competitiveness', Masters thesis, Stockholm School of Economics.

Ko, H., Cho, C.H. and Roberts, M.S. (2005) 'Internet uses and gratifications: a structural equation model of interactive advertising', *Journal of Advertising*, 34(2): 57–70.

Leiva, P.I., Culbertson, S.S. and Pritchard, R.D. (2011) 'An empirical test of an innovation implementation model', *Psychologist-Manager Journal*, 14: 265–281.

Mackenzie, S.B. and Spreng, R.A. (1992) 'How does motivation moderate the impact of central and peripheral processing on brand attitudes and intentions?', *Journal of Consumer Research*, 18 (March): 519–29.

Mansfield, E. (1985) 'How rapidly does new industrial technology leak out?', *The Journal of Industrial Economics*, 34(2): 217–23.

Mansfield, E. and Romeo, A. (1980) 'Technology transfer to overseas subsidiaries by US-based firms', *The Quarterly Journal of Economics*,95(4) : 737–50.

McGuirk, H. and Jordan, D. (2012) 'Local labour market diversity and business innovation: evidence from Irish manufacturing businesses', *European Planning Studies*, 20: 1945–60.

McGuirk, H., Lenihan, H. and Hart, M. (2015) 'Measuring the impact of innovative human capital on small firms' propensity to innovate', *Research Policy*, 44(4): 965–76.

McKinsey (2013) *Strategy: The Eight Essentials of Innovation Performance*, by M. de Jong, N. Marston, E. Roth and P. van Biljon, December.

Milbergs, E. and Vonortas, N. (2004) 'Innovation metrics: Measurement to insight'. Washington, DC: George Washington University for the National Innovation Initiative 21st Century Working Group.

Morrison, P.D., Roberts, J.H. and von Hippel, E. (2000) 'Determinants of user innovation sharing in a local market', *Management Science*, 46(12): 1513–27.

Muller, A., Välikangas, L. and Merlyn, P. (2005) 'Metrics for innovation: guidelines for developing a customized suite of innovation metrics', *Strategy & Leadership*, 33(1): 37–45.

OECD (1992; 1997 – revised) *Innovation Manual: Proposed Guidelines for Collecting and Interpreting Innovation Data* (Oslo Manual). Paris: OECD Directorate for Science, Technology and Industry.

OECD (2011) *Skills for Innovation and Research*. Paris: OECD Publishing. Available at: www.oecd-ilibrary.org/science-and-technology/skills-for-innovation-and-research_9789264097490-en (last accessed 20 April 2016).

Oliver, R.L. and Bearden, W.O. (1985) 'Crossover effects in the theory of reasoned action: a moderating influence attempt', *Journal of Consumer Research*, 12(December): 324–40.

Regnell, B., Ritzén, S., Höst, M., Larsson, T., Nilsson, F. and Sundin, E. (2008) 'Innovationsförmåga – mätning av innovationsförmåga i team', [Innovation Capacities – Measuring Innovation Capability in Teams]. Product Innovation Engineering Program, Lund Universitet.

Rejeb, H.B., Morel-Guimaraes, L., Boly, V. and Assie-Lou, N. (2008) 'Measuring innovation best practices: improvement of an innovation index integrating threshold and synergy effects', *Technovation*, 28: 838–54.

Roehm, M.L. and Sternthal, B. (2001) 'The moderating effect of knowledge and resources on the persuasive impact of analogies', *Journal of Consumer Research*, 28(September): 257–72.

Rogers, E. (2003) *Diffusion of Innovations*. New York: Free Press.

Rogers, E.M. (1962) *The Diffusion of Innovation*. New York: Free Press.

Romer, P.M. (1990) 'Endogenous technological change', *Journal of Political Economy*, 98: S71–102.

Rosenberg, N. (1976) *Perspectives on Technology*. Cambridge: Cambridge University Press.

Rosenberg, N. (1982) *Inside the Black Box: Technology and Economics*. Cambridge: Cambridge University Press.

Santarelli, E. and Tran, H.T. (2013) 'The interplay of human and social capital in shaping entrepreneurial performance: the case of Vietnam', *Small Business Economics*, 40(2): 435–58.

Schneider, L., Gunther, J. and Brandenbury, B. (2010) 'Innovation and skills from a sectoral perspective: a linked employer–employee analysis', *Economics of Innovation and New Technology*, 19: 185–202.

Schramm, C. (2008) *Tracking the State of Innovation in the American Economy*, a Report to the Secretary of Commerce by The Advisory Committee on Measuring Innovation in the 21st Century Economy, January.

Schreier, M., Fuchs, C. and Dahl, D.W. (2012) 'The innovation effect of user design: exploring consumers' innovation perceptions of firms selling products designed by users', *Journal of Marketing*, 76(5): 18–32.

Schulenburg, J.M.G. and Wagner, J. (1991) 'Advertising, innovation and market structure: A comparison of the United States of America and the Federal Republic of Germany', in Z.J. Acs and D.B. Audretsch (eds), *Innovation and Technological Change: An International Comparison*. Ann Arbor, MI: University of Michigan Press. pp. 160–82.

Shipton, H., West, M.A., Parkes, C.L., Dawson, J.F. and Patterson, M.G. (2006) 'When promoting positive feelings pays', *European Journal of Work and Organizational Psychology*, 15: 404–30.

Smith, K. (2005) 'Measuring innovation', in J. Fagerberg, D. Mowery and R. Nelson (eds), *The Oxford Handbook of Innovation*. Oxford: Oxford University Press. pp. 148–77.

Teixeira, A.A.C. and Tavares-Lehmann, A.T. (2014) 'Human capital intensity in technology-based firms located in Portugal: Does foreign ownership matter?', *Research Policy*, 43: 737–48.

Ucbasaran, D., Westhead, P. and Wright, M. (2008) 'Opportunity identification and pursuit: does an entrepreneur's human capital matter?', *Small Business Economics*, 30: 153–73.

Van Ittersum, K. and Feinberg, F.M. (2010) 'Cumulative timed intent: a new predictive tool for technology adoption', *Journal of Marketing Research*, 47(5): 808–22.

Vuola, O. and Hameri, A.P. (2006) 'Mutually benefiting joint innovation process between industry and big-science', *Technovation*, 26(1): 3–12.

Wagner, J. and Schulenburg, J.M.G. (1992) 'Unobservable industry characteristics and the innovation-concentration-advertising-maze: Evidence from an econometric study using panel data for manufacturing industries in the FRG, 1979–1986', *Small Business Economics*, 4(4): 315–26.

Wood, S.L. and Moreau, C.P. (2006) 'From fear to loathing? How emotion influences the evaluation and early use of innovations', *Journal of Marketing*, 70(3): 44–57.

Yen, H.J.R. and Gwinner, K.P. (2003) 'Internet retail customer loyalty: the mediating role of relational benefits', *International Journal of Service Industry Management*, 14(5): 483–500.

Zhou, J. and George, J.M. (2001) 'When job dissatisfaction leads to creativity: encouraging the expression of voice', *Academy of Management Journal*, 44: 682–96.

Zhu, Z. (2002) 'Fix it or leave it: antecedents and consequences of perceived control in technology-based self-service failure encounters', Doctoral dissertation, University of Illinois at Chicago.

EPILOGUE

I will try to keep this concluding section as brief as possible, and in doing so I will try and resist the temptation of directing or corralling the reader to observe and study only what I might value as important. In any case, drawing conclusions on innovation can be rather fatuous. Innovation is cumulative, restorative, disruptive, tangential and above all inconclusive. As many writers have noted, we may not necessarily find innovation as something which evolves incrementally and progressively in a linear fashion, but rather as being in part dependent on what went before and what amounts to paradigmatic change. Further, the concluding observations here are about wrapping up the contents of the book by noting their flow, their limitations and where future endeavour may lead us to write on the subject.

We started this book with a reference to Robert Gordon, and also in the first chapter about the nature of technical change and its effect on innovative people, organisations and the environment. Gordon's (2012) paper asked questions about the basic economic assumption held ever since the 1950s when Solow made his seminal contribution: that economic growth will be a persistent phenomenon because it is a continuous and incremental process. But if there was no growth before 1750, what is the guarantee that we may not slip into stasis again? There is every sign across the globe of a persistent slowing down of developed and, sadly, emerging economies despite the large-scale advances made in the technology sphere.

Gordon further argued that the rapid progress made over the past 250 years, in the era of the Anthropocene, may well be a unique episode in human history. If we add to that the effects of moving out of the Holocene epoch marked by regular shifts in and out of the ice ages, and the entry into a human-made epoch, we find (or as Paul Scrutzen, the acclaimed atmospheric chemist, notes) 'trawlers scraping the floor of seas to their dams impounding sediment by the gigaton, from their stripping of forests to their irrigation of farms, from their mile-deep mines to their melting of glaciers, humans were bringing about an age of planetary change' (*The Economist*, 2011). Somewhere along the line such change has generated innovation to offer possibilities for both new creation and the destruction of our habitat. So on the one hand we have had growth in per capita real GDP in the frontier country since 1300, the UK until 1906 and the USA afterwards, but on the other we find that with it we have also opened up many possibilities for irreversible environmental change. Growth in this frontier gradually accelerated after 1750, reached a peak in the middle of the twentieth century, and has been slowing down since. In the meantime new ecological arrangements yield more trees on farms than in forests and a 'planetary system homogenised through domestication' (*The Economist*, 2011). There is a strange, almost ineffable duality of scope and purpose in the drive for innovation in that the benefits that we witness can be obscured by the implications in aggregate terms for the planet on which they occur.

It is this duality of innovation which we are left with at the end of any consideration of innovation as a process, as a construct and as a phenomenon which is inevitable. Ecologically we may be relying on our creative intelligence and our imagination to remake the earth 'dam by dam, mine by mine, farm by farm and city by city' (*The Economist*, 2011). Add to that the vision of Kurzweil and the power of artificial intelligence for deep reasoning and to carry out human functions with or without human intervention. We can visualise the prospect of driverless cars, remote surgeries, robot friends for the elderly, and a plethora of activities that could displace agricultural, service, sector and sophisticated analytical jobs through a combination of advanced robotics and artificial intelligence (Ford, 2015). We have the possibility of making change occur which could elide our own expectations of a productive and worthwhile future.

Then there is also the possibility of not being swept away by the hyperbole of radical changes, not least because of the fact that they tend to be few and far between. Brynjolfsson and McAfee (2014) argue that most innovations are a recombination of things that exist already. The writers refer to Kary Mullis, the 1993 Nobel Prize-winning chemist, who recombined well-understood techniques in biochemistry to create a new one. The digital world is also seen as a new combination of mind and machines made possible by networked devices running and using a wide range of software on what are referred to as platforms.

Other questions remain. Gordon (2016) refers to building on previous references by Deaton (2013); Picketty (2013; 2015) and others write about six headwinds – demography, education, inequality, globalisation, energy/environment, and the overhang of consumer and government debt – that could affect our ability to generate innovation and long-term growth to half or less of the 1.9% annual rate experienced between 1860 and 2007. The multiplier effect on those at the bottom 99% of the income distribution pyramid could fall below 0.5% per year for decades to come.

Much will depend on how organisations manage the process where they can foster innovation through people inside and outside the firm, within loose networks of open innovation platforms. Much will also depend on the policies of governments. Innovation's new world order is changing rapidly, as we discussed earlier.

Much will also depend on shattering some of the myths of innovation at the manageable levels of education, observation and practice. It could be prudent not to believe in the 'epiphany' moment, to consider the various directions of technological change and innovation throughout history, to be obscured either by organisational entropy or by a cultural obfuscation of the art of the possible. The lone and persistent innovator is probably less productive than a team of varied, multicultural players, and it is possible that many innovations lead to inequality sometimes directly and on other occasions as a by-product of its use (Berkun, 2007).

This book has not been able to consider all the developments, the various permutations and the implications of innovation in thought and practice. Some readers will be left a bit bereft perhaps, and to them I can only offer an apology but with the hope of tackling a wider range of issues for research and learning in the future. There is more that the student needs to understand about an overwhelming focus on technology-based innovation and the inequalities that it can leave in its wake. Identifying why innovation matters and how innovation occurs everywhere could be seen as being more useful for practitioners and policy makers than as a ranking system derived from algorithmic ingenuity, by ideological imperatives or even by a neutral stand that tries to make a point about the importance of benchmarking or the pursuit of a technological holy grail. Gender studies have begun to unravel theoretical conservatism in more ways than one, and there is more to be understood with the rise of women in science, engineering and management positions and the realisation of the team contribution made by women in technological development, as recent discoveries about women in computing have shown. Will race and class be given wider consideration as we find that many contributions of black or poor people go well beyond the excitement of Jugaad?

Just a few final words on innovation and economic growth in the digital era, this time with reference to a visionary politician from an analogue past! Innovation in the digital era and the information revolution is not only transforming areas as varied as medicine, transportation and energy, but also challenging the nature of power and political leadership. Whereas many a civilian technology and innovation in the past grew out of investment in the military, much of what a nation needs will depend on the creativity of its people and its organisations. Vision might be more important than just experience, not least because 'People are trained to live in the past. But we need a society based on imagination, of memories'. These are the words of Shimon Peres, who was the Prime Minister of Israel in the mid-1990s and then President of the country for 7 years from 2007 to 2014 (Thornhill, 2016). He went on to say in two conversations at the Ambrosetti forum, which brings together people from business, policy and academia: 'All the experts are experts on what was. There is no expert on what will be.' At the age of 93 and with his faith in the young across the Middle East and Africa, Mr Peres launched the Israeli Innovation Centre in Jaffa, both to showcase Israel's achievements and to promote collaboration and innovation across all communities. In his vision for innovation for economic growth and interdependency, and peace in the region, Shimon Peres reflected on what we all know to be essential for innovation to flourish but perhaps refrain from committing to ourselves: an overarching and an integrated technological, economic, social and political vision for new value creation.

So I will sign off in an Eliotesque mood, reimagining his refrain about all things ending only to have a beginning. In incompleteness lies the virtue of innovation in that it makes possible the prospect of something different emerging in the future. I hope the reader will join me in those new endeavours.

REFERENCES

Berkun, S. (2007) *The Myths of Innovation*. Sebastopol, CA: O'Reilly.

Brynjolfsson, E. and McAfee, A. (2014) *The Second Machine Age: Work Progress, and Prosperity in a Time of Brilliant Technologies*. New York: W.W. Norton.

Deaton, A. (2013) *The Great Escape: Health, Wealth, and the Origins of Inequality*. Princeton, NJ: Princeton University Press.

Ford, M. (2015) *The Rise of the Robots: Technology and the Threat of a Jobless Future*. New York: Basic Books.

Gordon, R.J. (2012) 'Is US economic growth over? Faltering innovation confronts the six headwinds', NBER Working Paper No. 18315. Available at: www.nber.org/papers/w18315 (last accessed 20 August 2016).

Gordon, R.J. (2016) *The Rise and Fall of American Growth: The US Standard of Living since the Civil War*. Princeton, NJ: Princeton University Press.

Picketty, T. (2013) *Capital in the Twenty-First Century*. Cambridge, MA: Harvard University Press.

Picketty, T. (2015) *The Economics of Inequality*. Cambridge, MA: Harvard University Press.

The Economist (2011) 'A man-made world', The Briefing, *The Economist*, 399(8735): 81–3.

Thornhill, J. (2016) 'The digital idealist's path to peace in the Middle East', *Financial Times*, 13 September.

INDEX